The Sporting Scots
of Nineteenth-Century
Canada

Also by Gerald Redmond

*Sporting Heritage: A Guide to Halls of Fame,
Special Collections and Museums in the United
States and Canada* (co-author with Guy M. Lewis)

The Caledonian Games in Nineteenth-Century America

The Sporting Scots of Nineteenth-Century Canada

Gerald Redmond

Rutherford ● Madison ● Teaneck
Fairleigh Dickinson University Press

London and Toronto: Associated University Presses

© 1982 by Associated University Presses, Inc.

Associated University Presses, Inc.
4 Cornwall Drive
East Brunswick, N.J. 08816

Associated University Presses Ltd
69 Fleet Street
London EC4Y 1EU, England

Associated University Presses
Toronto M5E 1A7, Canada

Library of Congress Cataloging in Publication Data

Redmond, Gerald, 1934-
    The sporting Scots of nineteenth-century Canada.

    Bibliography: p.
    Includes index.
    1. Sports—Canada—History—19th century. 2. Scots—
Canada—Recreation—History—19th century. I. Title.
GV585.R4   796'.0971   80-67124
ISBN 0-8386-3069-3   AACR2

Printed in the United States of America

for P. A. S.

The panorama of world sport in the middle of the twentieth century shows game and sports from many different countries of origin. . . . Nevertheless, the majority of sports in current practice, and the very great majority of the more popular, were exported from Britain. They were taken abroad as soon as they were sufficiently refined and well organized to stand the journey and as soon as ambassadors, official and unofficial, colonial administrators, missionaries, merchants, soldiers, sailors and settlers took a mind to playing games in their new homes, whether these homes were temporary or permanent. The Scots in exile showed a particularly strong inclination to form Caledonian Societies and to play golf.

Peter C. McIntosh (1963)

It was this hard ethic, so forcefully expressed by Stephen, that explains the dominance of the Scot in pioneer Canada. . . . The Irish outnumbered them, as did the English; but the Scots ran the country. Though they formed only one-fifteenth of the population they controlled the fur trade, the great banking and financial houses, the major educational institutions and, to a considerable degree, the government. The CPR was built to a large extent by Irish navvies and Irish contractors; but it was the Scots who held the top jobs. Almost every member of the original CPR Syndicate was a self-made Scot.

Pierre Berton (1970)

Contents

A beautiful example of Scottish tradition in Canada: fifteen-year-old Lynn Sinclair performs at the Fergus Highland Games in 1966.

Preface

I am indebted to many people for their assistance throughout the preparation of this publication. I am grateful to Dr. M. L. Howell, now of the University of Ottawa, for initial guidance; and then especially to Dr. P. L. Lindsay of the University of Alberta for later advice and constant encouragement. The consideration and interest of my other colleagues at the University of Alberta, Dr. R. G. Glassford, Dr. H. J. McLachlin and Dr. R. S. Patterson, is also appreciated. External assistance was given by Dr. J. Dewar, now of the University of Saskatchewan, who also provided material on the history of the Highland Games in Canada. Similar material was also kindly supplied to me by R. Lund of Queen's University; and by Dr. B. Mutimer and Dr. A. A. Mackenzie of St. Francis Xavier University. Special thanks must go to Judge Hugh J. MacPherson of Antigonish, who trusted me with some valuable old Scottish papers in his possession, from which I derived benefit in my research. Of the many archivists and librarians in various institutions across the country who gave so willingly of their services, I must thank in particular Tom Nesmith, Archivist at the Public Archives of Canada in Ottawa; and Tom West, curator of Canada's Sports Hall of Fame in Toronto. Both provided me with useful source material, and their expertise was invaluable. Much of the travelling and research in Canada was conducted while I was the recipient of a scholarship from the Province of Alberta, and I am naturally grateful for this award. Lynn Sinclair kindly donated the Highland Dancing photograph.

Outside of Canada, my thanks are due once more to David Webster, author of two books on the Scottish Highland Games, for his hospitality at Irvine, and for sharing with me his personal collection of memorabilia as well as his knowledge of Scottish sports history. The courtesy extended to me in Glasgow, especially by G. B. Wright, Director of the Scottish School of Physical Education at Jordanhill College, and several of his colleagues, was very much appreciated, also. D. M. Torbet, Chief Librarian at Dundee Public Library, was helpful, too. Professor A. McDonald of Queen's University, Belfast, generously supplied information on the history of shinty.

The first manuscript was typed by my wife, Madge; and the revised version by Mrs. Hilda Harris. Their conscientious cheerfulness as they efficiently accomplished this unexciting task, among many others demanding their attention, impressed me greatly. To them both I extend my most sincere thanks.

*The Sporting Scots
of Nineteenth-Century
Canada*

1
Introduction

Many of the countries of the Empire were colonised from Britain, and during the whole of the 19th century and earlier, thousands of families settled in Canada, Australia, New Zealand, South and East Africa. Those settlers took with them the skill of their trade, the religion of their ancestors and the recreation of their leisure time. . . . Games, like curling, bowls and golf, were introduced to most of those countries, by the early settlers and when, towards the end of the 19th Century, national associations for the major games such as soccer, cricket and rugby were formed, visiting teams from Britain toured the Colonies and helped to strengthen and popularize these games.

David McNair (1975)

THE British influence in Canadian history has been an undisputed fact, especially since the fall of Quebec in 1759, and the Treaty of Paris in 1763, when France ceded to Britain all North American possessions (except the fishing stations of Miquelon and St. Pierre). The British Parliament passed the British North America Act in 1867, when the Dominion of Canada was formed by confederation of New Brunswick, Nova Scotia, Ontario, and Quebec. Subsequent entries into Confederation were Manitoba (1870), British Columbia (1871), Prince Edward Island (1873), Alberta and Saskatchewan (1905), and Newfoundland (1949). As Canada progressed from *Colony to Nation*,[1] participating in two World Wars in the process, the cultural, economic, political and social relationships with the United Kingdom inevitably altered. The British legacy which remains in

Canada is perhaps exemplified best by the retention of the monarchy, and membership in the Commonwealth.

As with the histories of most countries, the social aspects of the links between Britain and Canada have not been stressed to the same extent as the economic or political factors. In recent years, however, historical accounts of a social nature which particularly pertain to sport in Canada, have appeared more frequently.

This increase has been largely due to the inauguration of the graduate program in the Department of Physical Education at the University of Alberta, in Edmonton, with a specialization in the History of Sport. As a result of this initiative, many beneficial studies of Canadian sport—at both M.A. and Ph.D. level—have been completed.[2] These complement studies in the same area at other Canadian universities; as well as a number of works in general Canadian sport history by such authors as Bull; Cosentino and Leyshon; Cochrane, Hoffman, and Kincaid; Davidson; Dunbar; Howell and Howell; Roxborough; and Wise and Fisher.[3]

In the Epilogue of his comprehensive history of Canadian sport from 1807 to 1867, Lindsay stated in 1969:

> The present study should be viewed in relation to its place in a hierarchy of studies concerning the history of sport in Canada, which is developing at the University of Alberta. The first stage, of which this dissertation is an example, is designed to show the growth of the various sporting activities, while pointing out the influences which have been instrumental in bringing about that growth. The next level of studies is designed to investigate, in greater detail, these influences, such as technological change, urbanization, British Colonialism, the rise of professionalism, etcetera.[4]

Since then, part of this recommendation has been answered by such subsequent studies as those of Cosentino, Jobling, and Lansley;[5] and a number of further studies that build on the foundation provided by these authors are being undertaken at present. The work offered here on the Scots and sport in nineteenth-century Canada can obviously be placed under Lindsay's "British Colonialism" label.

This term has been synonymous to many historians with

"English Colonialism," although the full title of "Great Britain" refers to England, Northern Ireland, Scotland, and Wales. The total population may be correctly referred to as "British," but within the separate countries, people have retained aspects of their distinct cultures, even their own language. The Cornish dialect survives in southwest England, as does Gaelic in Northern Ireland and Scotland, and of course the Welsh language in Wales. However, the fact that England is the largest and most heavily populated of the four countries, in all of which English is the most common language, and has the seat of central government in London, no doubt contributes to the common interchangeable use of the terms "British" and "English."

Such usage has appeared in a Canadian sports history, where it is stated:

> The English settlers were composed of the British soldiers, United Empire Loyalists, Scotch and Irish immigrants—all of whom settled alongside the French Colonists without much attempt to alter the economic or social organization of the country.[6]

The Scotch and Irish immigrants might condescend to be termed "British" settlers, as second-best to "Scottish" or "Irish," but hardly as "English" settlers, especially those who spoke only Gaelic. And there were plenty of distinctly Irish and Scottish people among the British soldiers and United Empire Loyalists. Apart from a technical inaccuracy which might offend ethnic feelings, the more important danger is to attribute to English origins those influences which were characteristic and cultural to other parts of the British Isles. As far as the history of sport in Canada is concerned, the English influence is undeniable. Bearing in mind the long tradition of sport in England, allied with other reasons stated, this is understandable. Yet there has also been in the history of Canadian sport a definite, significant and unique Scottish influence. This influence has not been surpassed by the English influence, and it has greatly contributed to the total British sporting tradition in the Dominion.

In fact, the contribution of the Scots to Canadian life in general has been phenomenal. The geography of Canada alone bears testimony to this fact, as mountains, rivers, towns, cities, and provinces, from coast to coast, bear Scottish names. Often the same name appears in several parts of the country. Some of these names are tributes to the Scottish businessmen, educators, engineers, explorers, fur traders, pioneers, and politicians who left their mark on the continent.[7] Much has been written of Canada within the British Empire, but in a book entitled *Scottish Empire*, Gibb has even maintained that:

> The great names in the early history of Canada are, in the main, the names of Frenchmen; in her later history they are the names of Scotsmen. . . . To follow out the story of Canada from the middle of the eighteenth century is to pursue a record mainly of Scottish achievement.[8]

The Scottish achievement of which the author wrote is possibly without parallel in colonial history. Rarely can an ethnic minority immigrant group have so dominated events in its adopted country as did the Scots in Canada, particularly in the nineteenth century. In his popularly acclaimed work of Canadian history, Berton has indicated this fact, when seeking to explain "the dominance of the Scot in pioneer Canada":

> The Irish outnumbered them, as did the English; but the Scots ran the country. Though they formed only one-fifteenth of the population they controlled the fur trade, the great banking and financial houses, the major educational institutions and, to a considerable degree, the government. The CPR was built to a large extent by Irish navvies and Irish contractors; but it was the Scots who held the top jobs. Almost every member of the original CPR Syndicate was a self-made Scot.[9]

This Scottish dominance has been established by the many other authors of works devoted solely to this elevated position of the Scots in Canadian history.[10] Most of these writers were Scots themselves, or of Scottish descent, from whom such panegyrics might be expected. But other historians as well, less prone to a charge of bias, have confirmed their judgment regarding the special status of the Scots. Apart from its obvious effect on other aspects of life in Canada, this status had far-reaching implications for the origins and development of sport during the nineteenth century.

This is not surprising, either, since within the acknowledged British sporting heritage, Scotland has had a long tradition of sport in her own right. As in England, sport has been customary there for centuries. Joseph Strutt's *The Sports and Pastimes of the People of England*, first published in 1801, has long been regarded as a classic work. Less well known, but indicative of a separate sporting identity, is the later work published in 1891, and modelled on Strutt's book, by Robert Scott Fittis, entitled *Sports and Pastimes of Scotland*.[11] In fact, although their actual origins remain obscure, certain sports have been acknowledged as "Scottish" throughout the world, such as curling and golf. It was in Scotland that these sports were gradually refined and codified, and the governing bodies of the Royal Caledonian Curling Club and the Royal and Ancient Golf Club of St. Andrews emerged in the first half of the nineteenth century. The Highland Games and shinty also survived in Scotland for centuries, and were popular in the nineteenth century. Indigenous varieties of football have existed since medieval times in Scotland, too; although the two forms of association football (soccer) and rugby football were codified in England during the nineteenth century. Cricket was also put into systematic form in England, where it has been played since at least the seventeenth century, and the Marylebone Cricket Club in London became the arbiter of the sport. But cricket has been played in Scotland, also, since at least the eighteenth century, and was included in Fittis's *Sports and Pastimes of Scotland*. Since their inception, soccer and rugby have enjoyed a greater popularity than cricket in Scotland, however, and Scottish teams in these sports have had considerable success in national and international competition. Other sports such as lawn bowls and quoits enjoyed a traditional popularity in Scotland, as well as in other parts of the British Isles. In short, the people of Scotland have exhibited their ingenuity, enthusiasm, and prowess, in many sports, for a considerable time, and have greatly contributed to the sporting reputation and tradition associated with the term ''British.'' The emigration of Scots from their homeland, ensured that these talents were not confined to Scotland.

The economic, political and social changes in Scotland during the eighteenth and nineteenth centuries—from the Act of Union, through the Highland Clearances, to the Industrial Revolution—resulted in a consistent and massive emigration of Scots to many parts of the world, including the North American continent. This regular emigration, allied with their widespread distribution and patterns of group settlement, together with the Scottish propensity for hard work and acquaintance with hardship, enabled the Scots to survive and prosper. Indeed, their successful general influence in pioneer Canada has already been noted, and has also been described as ''disproportionately large in comparison to their numbers.''[12] The same can be said of their contribution to sport in Canada during the nineteenth century.

It was natural that people with such an ancient and distinct sporting tradition should pursue their sports in the New World, which the Scots did to a significant degree. They formed the first organized sports club in British North America, the Montreal Curling Club, in 1807. Subsequently many other curling clubs were formed by the pioneering Scots, aided by the favorable geography and climate of Canada, until the sport was nationwide before the end of the nineteenth century. Other factors such as the provision of indoor curling rinks, the democratic character of the game, affiliation with the Royal Caledonian Curling Club in Scotland, viceregal patronage, and the increase of local, provincial and international competition (versus the United States), all featured in its growth. In fact, by the time of the first tour of the Dominion by a visiting Scottish curling team in 1902–3, the previous ethnic sport of a minority group had become a national sport for all the inhabitants of Canada. In the twentieth century, the number of curling clubs in the Dominion, their membership and facilities, and the standard of play, exceeded even those in Scotland itself, or anywhere in the world.

Scots also founded the first permanent golf club in the Western Hemisphere, again at Montreal, in 1873. Like curling, this sport became very popular in Canada, as indeed it did in other countries, due to the efforts, enthusiasm and perseverance of Scottish protagonists. Both curling and golf were popular sports for women during the late nineteenth century, in which women gained a large part of their sporting emancipation.

Outside of Scotland, the Highland Games also enjoyed their greatest popularity on the North American continent during the nineteenth century. They were usually referred to as ''Caledonian Games,'' being sponsored mainly by Caledonian Clubs, and were promoted in small townships as well as in large cities. Thousands of people attended the Games to enjoy the athletic contests, as well as the parades, music, and dancing. In fact, so popular were these Scottish Games in both Canada and the United States, that International Caledonian Games were begun in 1867, and a North American United Caledonian Association was formed in 1870. As the ruling body for Caledonian Games in both countries, it was the first such international sports association on the continent. The Caledonian Games were a major and significant influence on the subsequent development of amateur track and field athletics in both countries, also, a fact noted by many sports historians. This development actually represented a counter-attraction to the Caledonian Games, and led to a decline in their popularity in the late nineteenth century, particularly in the United States. Caledonian Games have survived better in Canada, owing to its Scottish heritage. Excluding Scotland, there are more Highland Gatherings in the Dominion today than anywhere else.

Quoits and tug-of-war were two sports which were often featured at Caledonian Games, and Scots were the greatest exponents of both in nineteenth-century Canada. One Scottish tug-of-war team from the small township of Zorra in Ontario, even won a world championship in 1893. The ancient Highland game of shinty was also very popular among Scots throughout the Dominion in the nineteenth century, and is frequently referred to as a forerunner of ice hockey. Scots naturally participated in the British sports of cricket, soccer, and rugby, and were active in varying degrees in the introduction and promotion of these sports. But Scots were not absolutely parochial in their sporting attitudes or actions, and they also took part in the indigenous Canadian sports, such as lacrosse, ice hockey, and snowshoeing. Nor were they averse to participating in the American sport of baseball. Scottish influence on sport in Canada in the nineteenth century also extended from predominance in checkers (draughts) to the founding of the Canadian Alpine Club.

It has already been mentioned that the Scots controlled the major educational institutions in Canada in the nineteenth century. In fact, all the leading nineteenth-century universities, with scarcely one exception, were founded by Scots. These were certainly established for educational purposes, but when the cult of athleticism in the English public schools of the nineteenth century spread to Canada, the concomitant rise of student sport was accommodated within the Scottish institutions, especially McGill University, Queen's College, and the University of Toronto. Scots belonging to such institutions were naturally among others directly involved in the increase of collegiate and intercollegiate sport.

Of course, the advent of ''muscular Christianity'' was but one of many influences which affected sport in nineteenth-century Canada, and one that was a part of the more general British influence. This in turn was related to the factor of consistent immigration, with the accompanying influx of traditional games, since most new settlers before the twentieth century were of British stock. Another major influence was the effect of technological changes on the development of sport, and particularly industrialization and urbanization. There were obviously strong influences upon Canada from the trends of sport in the United States. Nationalism was also soon evident in sport, reflected in the promotion of indigenous games, and the feelings expressed upon the success of Canadian individuals and/or teams in any sport against foreign opposition.

No book has appeared to date which has been devoted solely to the contribution of the Scots to sport in nineteenth-century Canada. Obviously, any Scottish influence may be included under the more comprehensive label of ''British influence.'' But this hardly does justice to a people who have left their mark in distinct and peculiar fashion, besides contributing to more general influences. As stated, many authors have recognized the phenomenal influence of the Scots in other aspects of Canadian life in the nineteenth century; but none has devoted himself to detailing their similar accomplishments regarding sport. However, the inescapable nature of their contributions to sport in nineteenth century Canada has meant that the Scots are inevitably mentioned in most general Canadian sports histories, mostly in connection with curling. In fact, although literature devoted to a total Scottish contribution is practically nonexistent, the same cannot be said for curling. There are at least three main books which pertain to the origins and development of this sport in the Dominion. The most comprehensive and useful of these works is the Rev. John Kerr, *Curling in Canada and the United States* (Edinburgh: Geo. A. Morton, 1904), 787 pp. Although only 56 of these pages are devoted to the United States, the author does not discuss any developments further west than Winnipeg in Canada. A detailed study of a hundred years' curling in Ontario is provided by John A. Stevenson, *Curling in Ontario, 1846–1946* (Toronto: Ontario Curling Association, 1950). Part one and part two of W. A. Creelman, *Curling, Past and Present* (Toronto: McClelland & Stewart, 1950), 256 pp., are devoted to Scottish Origins and Curling in North America respectively. While a definitive history of curling in Canada has yet to be written, the works of these three authors are useful for the student of the nineteenth century. *A History of Golf in Canada* by L. V. Kavanagh, was published in 1973; but to date no history of Canadian Caledonian Games has appeared to accompany these studies of curling and golf.

The nearest approach in any published work on the Scots and sport in nineteenth-century Canada is a brief chapter of only 13 pages entitled "By Way of Scotland," in Henry Roxborough, *One Hundred–Not Out* (Toronto: The Ryerson Press, 1966), 252 pp. Apart from its brevity, its usefulness is limited by the lack of bibliography, documentation, or index, a comment applicable to other works by the same author. However, this writer agrees with the sentiments expressed in the chapter, particularly the concluding sentence:

Thus, in athletics as well as curling, golfing, quoiting and tugging, Canadian sportsmen during the nineteenth-century were greatly indebted to those sons of Scotland who participated in and sponsored a great variety of games.[13]

The influence of the Scots was indeed a major and significant factor in the development of sport in nineteenth-century Canada, and especially so in the sports mentioned by Roxborough. It was also an important element in the progress of other traditional British sports, such as cricket, soccer, and rugby football. Indigenous Canadian sports, such as ice hockey, lacrosse and snowshoeing, were also partly assisted and promoted to varying degrees in their early years, by an enthusiastic Scottish presence. So, too, were other sports as dissimilar as checkers (draughts), lawn-bowls, and mountaineering. The initial establishment by the Scots of the major educational institutions in nineteenth-century Canada, such as McGill University, Queen's College, and the University of Toronto, provided the base for Canadian collegiate and intercollegiate sport. The proximity of the United States, where Scots also pioneered sports, enabled regular international competition to take place, especially in curling, the Caledonian Games, and golf. The emancipation of women through sport in the nineteenth century was assisted in part by their participation in curling and golf, also. The recognized impact of the military garrisons on the development of sport in nineteenth-century Canada was also partly due to the activities of soldiers in Scottish regiments, as well as of English soldiers.

A study of the contribution of the Scots to sport in nineteenth-century Canada complies with suggestions made by historians of previous studies in Canadian sports history. An eminent Scottish historian, Professor Gordon Donaldson of Edinburgh University, has also noted:

But the story of the Scots overseas is no less a contribution to the history of the United States, the British Dominions and many other parts of the world. The subject is a vast one, which presents an almost inexhaustible field for investigation, and many specialized studies ought to be undertaken.[14]

Like the Scots overseas, the history of sport itself is also ''an inexhaustible field for investigation.'' This specialized study of
emigrant Scots and nineteenth-century sport, in the largest of
those ''British Dominions,'' is obviously but one of the many
''which ought to be undertaken.''

Notes

1. Arthur R. M. Lower, *Colony to Nation: A History of Canada* (Toronto: Longmans, Green & Co., 1959).

2. A complete list of these can be obtained from the author upon request.

3. *To Know Ourselves: The Report of the Commission on Canadian Studies*, vol. 1 (Association of Universities and Colleges in Canada, 1975), p. 221; William Perkins Bull, *From Rattlesnake Hunt to Hockey: The History of Sports in Canada and of the Sportsmen of Peel, 1798 to 1934* (Toronto: George J. McLeod, 1934); Frank Cosentino and Glynn Leyshon, *Olympic Gold: Canadian Winners of the Summer Games* (Toronto: Holt, Rinehart and Winston of Canada, 1975); Jean Cochrane, Abby Hoffman, and Pat Kincaid, *Women in Canadian Life: Sports* (Toronto: Fitzhenry and Whiteside, 1977); Stewart A. Davidson, ''A History of Sports and Games in Eastern Canada prior to World War I'' (Ed.D. diss., Teachers' College, Columbia University, 1951); Nancy J. Dunbar, *Images of Sport in Early Canada* (Montreal: McGill-Queen's University Press, 1976); Nancy Howell and Maxwell L. Howell, *Sports and Games in Canadian Life: 1700 to the Present* (Toronto: Macmillan of Canada, 1969); Henry Roxborough, *Great Days in Canadian Sport* (Toronto: Ryerson Press, 1957); also, *One Hundred—Not Out: The Story of Nineteenth-Century Canadian Sport* (Toronto: Ryerson Press, 1966). (Other titles by Henry Roxborough include *Canada at the Olympics*, *Olympic Hero*, and *The Stanley Cup Story*.); S. F. Wise and Douglas Fisher, *Canada's Sporting Heroes: Their Lives and Times* (Don Mills, Ontario: General Publishing Co., 1974).

4. Peter Leslie Lindsay, ''A History of Sport in Canada, 1807–1867'' (Ph.D. diss., University of Alberta, 1969), p. 398.

5. Frank Cosentino, ''A History of the Concept of Professionalism in Canadian Sport'' (Ph.D. diss., University of Alberta, 1973); Ian F. Jobling, ''Sport in Nineteenth Century Canada: The Effects of Technological Changes on its Development'' (Ph.D. diss., University of Alberta, 1970); Keith L. Lansley, ''The Amateur Athletic Union of Canada and Changing Concepts of Amateurism'' (Ph.D. diss., University of Alberta, 1971).

6. Davidson, ''History of Sports and Games,'' p. 24.

7. Gordon Donaldson, *The Scots Overseas* (London: Robert Hale, 1966), pp. 57–81, 129–51.

8. Andrew Dewar Gibb, *Scottish Empire* (London: Alexander Maclehose & Co., 1937), p. 31.

9. Pierre Berton, *The National Dream: The Great Railway, 1871–1881* (Toronto: McClelland and Stewart, 1970), p. 319.

10. George Bryce, *The Scotsman in Canada*, vol. 2 (Toronto: Musson Book Company, n.d.); Wilfred Campbell, *The Scotsman in Canada*, vol. 1 (Toronto: Musson Book Company, n.d.); Charles W. Dunn, *Highland Settler: A Portrait of the Scottish Gael in Nova Scotia* (Toronto: University of Toronto Press, 1968); John Murray Gibbon, *Scots in*

Canada (Toronto: Musson Book Company, 1911); J. M. Le Moine, *The Scot in New France* (Montreal: Dawson Brothers, 1811); and James A. Roy, *The Scot and Canada* (Toronto: McClelland and Stewart, 1947); W. Stanford Reid, ed., *The Scottish Tradition in Canada* (Toronto: McClelland and Stewart, 1976). See also: W. J. Rattray, *The Scot in British North America*, 4 vols. (Toronto: Maclean and Co., 1880).

11. Robert Scott Fittis, *Sports and Pastimes of Scotland* (Paisley: Alexander Gardner, 1891).

12. *Encyclopedia Canadiana*, 10 vols. (Toronto: Grolier of Canada, 1968), 9: 249.

13. Henry Roxborough, *One Hundred—Not Out: The Story of Nineteenth-Century Canadian Sport* (Toronto: Ryerson Press, 1966), p. 111.

14. Donaldson, *Scots Overseas*, preface.

2
The Traditional Sports
of Scotland

While the Scots are traditionally thrifty they have also been very generous in many of their contributions. This has been especially evident in the sports world, where some of the most exciting games have been gifts from Scottish sportsmen. Included in these "boons to mankind" have been golf, quoits, tug-of-war, the Caledonian Games and particularly curling.

Henry Roxborough (1966)

THE land now known as Scotland has an ancient history, not unlike that of other Western European countries. No evidence has been found of a paleolithic presence, but mesolithic people were there until superseded by neolithic immigrants. Bronze Age Beaker Folk then seem to have fused with their culture, until the country was invaded by the Celts. This largely Celtic population was in turn subjected to the formative experience of Rome over five centuries, and also received a strong infusion of Germanic and Scandinavian blood. Romans referred to the country as "Caledonia," but it was the Scots who came as colonists from Ireland in the fifth and sixth centuries A.D. who gave their name to the whole country.

These Scots, together with the Angles, Britons, and Picts, eventually united into a single nation under a dynasty which ruled Scotland for over two hundred years, although this union took centuries to accomplish. This feudal kingdom subsequently survived with difficulty the consistent attempts of English monarchs to annex it. Relations with England varied from opposition, which led to a closer alliance between Scotland and France, and cooperation, which was reinforced by diplomatic marriages. When Elizabeth of England died childless in 1603, James VI of Scotland adopted the title "King of Great Britain," but could not unite the two countries, each of which retained its own church, institutions, and laws. The ensuing difficulties of succeeding monarchs who could not be responsible to two separate parliaments, which might pursue completely different policies, were alleviated by the Treaty of Union in 1707. Under the terms of settlement, each country kept its own church and laws, but the separate parliaments ended and the parliament of Great Britain emerged. Under this fusion of common monarch and parliament, the two countries have merged into a British or Commonwealth experience, while each retained its own nationality.[1]

British sport has reflected this experience in its unity and diversity, and has been an essential element in the culture of Britain for centuries. Many writers have paid tribute to a British sporting tradition.[2] Although often attributed to an Anglo-Saxon or English heritage, sport also flourished in those parts of the British Isles inhabited mainly by people of Celtic descent. In Scotland, particularly, people participated in a unique manner, and certain sports have been acknowledged as "Scottish" throughout the world. These sports eventually appeared in other parts of Britain. Similarly, other sports chiefly associated with England also became common north of the border, many of them from an early date.

Ironically, two sports most associated with Scotland, curling and golf, may have originated in other parts of Europe. And the Scottish Highland Games may well have derived from Ireland. Even the English sport of cricket is now thought to have its origins in France. But from the sixteenth century onwards, these sports were developed in England and Scotland to an extent not realized elsewhere, and became customary in British life. Other sports were also pursued, being codified mainly in the nineteenth century, and all served to establish further the British tradition in sport. The sporting activity within Scotland itself during these centuries was a consistent and significant factor in the creation of that tradition.

The Highland Games were the earliest form of athletic endeavor to be later acknowledged as thoroughly Scottish, with a pedigree dating back to Celtic times. Yet they were apparently not the first sporting festival of this nature within the British Isles, for the Tailtin or Tailteann Games in Ireland preceded similar pastimes in Scotland. These Irish Games are said to have originated at Telltown, County Meath, as early as 1829 B.C., and survived until late in the twelfth century A.D. They consisted of running, jumping, wrestling, fencing, sham battles, chariot racing, the gaelbolga, or feat of throwing the dart, and the roth-cleas, or wheel-feat. Although the ''roth-cleas'' was a chariot wheel, it has been claimed by one author that hammer-throwing derived from this event.[3]

No valid connection has yet been established between Tailtin Games and Highland Games beyond that of a distinct possibility. The Highland Games were responsible for the later formalization and popularity of throwing the hammer as an event within organized competition.[4] As stated earlier, Scotland was named after a race of Gaelic-speaking people who had established themselves in Ireland and later raided the Roman province of Britain in the fourth century. By the sixth century, they settled in the Southern Hebrides and on the mainland. These Scots may have brought athletic customs with them, for the Highland Games have an undoubted Gaelic heritage and were established in Scotland before the demise of the Irish Tailtin Games in A.D.1168 or 1198.

In a book entitled *The Scotish [sic] Gael*, a Fellow of the Society of Antiquaries of Scotland has written of

> Celtic manners, as preserved among the Highlanders, being an historical and descriptive account of the Inhabitants, Antiquities and National Peculiarities of Scotland; more particularly of the Northern, or Gaelic parts of the country, where the singular habits of aboriginal Celts are most tenaciously retained.

Among the most tenaciously retained manners of "aboriginal Celts" in Scotland were sporting customs similar to the Tailtin Games, i.e., "a sort of tournament," wrestling, fencing, running, and throwing a heavy sledgehammer. The clach-neart was a putting-stone, customarily laid by a chieftain's house for visitors to try their strength. The gael ruith "was sedulously practised," and has been claimed as the forerunner to the hop, step and jump event.[5]

The most famous Highland festival is the Braemar Gathering, traditionally traced back to King Malcolm Canmore in the eleventh century. A hill race on the Braes of Mar at this time has been quoted as the first example of royal interest and patronage in Scottish athletic prowess.[6] Such activities subsequently survived amongst the Clans until the Disarming Act of 1747, after the Jacobite Rebellions in the early eighteenth century threatened their existence.[7] But the repeal of the Act in 1782, together with the formation of Highland Societies, ensured their survival. In 1800, a Provident Society was formed in the Braemar district which later became the Braemar Royal Highland Society.[8]

The St. Fillans Highland Society was formed in 1819 by Lord Gwydir, mainly for the people of his Drummond Castle estate. As well as "the usual manly feats of strength," there were contests for playing the bagpipes and recitals of Gaelic poetry, and boat races (probably on Loch Earn), bagpipes, dirks, suits of tartans and "snuff mulls" were given as prizes for successful competitors.[9] Prizes pertaining to Highland dress and culture became traditional in succeeding Games, and there were many to compete for them, for "By the 1820's there were Highland Gatherings, on almost identical lines to those of today, extensively organized throughout the country."[10] Money prizes, too, soon became characteristic of Scottish Games. When the Braemar Royal Highland Society held its games on 23 August 1832, the events were: "putting the stone, throwing the hammer, tossing the caber, running and length of service," and five pounds was given in prizes for the five events. More events were featured in these Games five years later, when the program consisted of throwing a 12-lb. and 16-lb. hammer, putting the 21-lb. stone, hop, step and leap, 250 yards race, 100 yards sack race, wheelbarrow race, rifle-shooting, and wrestling. There were money prizes for all these events, and the winner of the wrestling gained'' £3 and a collection of 35s. as well.''[11] In later years it became customary for competent athletes to make a tour of various Games for financial reward, not only in their native Scotland, but in other countries also where their countrymen had fostered Highland Games.[12]

Highland Games in Scotland received the benefits of royal patronage ten years after the above program, when Prince Albert visited the Braemar Gathering in 1847. The following year he was accompanied by Queen Victoria, who seemed suitably impressed by the feats of the ''stalwart Celts.'' The popularity and prestige of Highland Games were increased by the subsequent and consistent visits of royalty.[13]

Although historically associated with the Highlands, the Games appeared quite early in other parts of Scotland, as well as south of the border with England. The Innerleithen Border Games of 10 August 1835 had featured a standing and running hop, step and leap, putting a 16-lb. and 22-lb. ball, and throwing a 15-lb. hammer. The Galashiels Games six years later also included the first two events, as well as a running leap and the hitch and kick. Lowlander Scots and Borderers often disputed the asserted athletic superiority of the Highlanders. The Games were naturally featured in the two largest cities in Scotland, Edinburgh the capital, and Glasgow. ''Vaulting with the pole'' was one of the events at the Edinburgh Games in July 1850.[14] In 1867, the *Illustrated London News* published a large illustration of Highland Sports at the Meeting of the Celtic Society on College Green, Glasgow.[15] Five years later, the same journal published a report and illustration of the second Crystal Palace Highland Gathering in London, England. This was not the first time that Scottish Games were featured in the English capital, however, for the organizers were ''reviving the custom that was annually practised in the grounds of Holland House, Kensington, within the memory of elderly Londoners.''[16] Highland Games were indeed part of the Scottish Fete held at Lord Holland's Park in 1850.[17]

But similar athletic pursuits had of course been popular in England long before the Scots brought their Highland Games to

London. There are medieval references to running, jumping, and throwing pastimes, as well as examples of Royal patronage there, also.[18] Most of these occurred at rural sports during local festivals. Perhaps the most famous such celebration, and the one most similar to a Highland Gathering, was the Cotswold Games meeting.[19] These local English festivals declined through the advent of organized track and field athletics and for other reasons in the nineteenth century.[20] Carl Diem, the German sports historian, has maintained that track and field developments in England were greatly influenced from Scotland.[21] Whether or not this is true, a Scottish Highland Gathering remained distinctive despite comparable athletic activities elsewhere. The cultural elements of Gaelic readings, bagpipe music, and Highland costume and dancing, made it unique. And the Highland Games not only survived intact but indeed flourished to the present day. The answer mainly lies in the determination to restore Highland culture as fully as possible when time had sufficiently eroded the bitter aftermath of Culloden and the Highland Clearances.[22] Highland Games were essential in this restoration of a large part of Scottish dignity and served to help redress the balance.

Apart from Braemar, the best known Gatherings were at Aboyne, Ballater, Banff, Cowal, Inverness, Lonach, Luss, Oban, and Tobermory, although they were also featured in other places. (Aboyne was the birthplace of "the immortal Donald Dinnie," the most famous Scottish athlete of all.) By the end of the nineteenth century, there was hardly a district in Scotland where Highland Games had not taken place.[23] With the bagpipes and the tartans, they have since become an indispensable element in Scotland's culture, perhaps the most traditional of all Scottish sports.

Athletic sports, Highland dancing and music formed the major part of a Highland Games program, but other events were often included for amusement and variety. Boat races, sack races, wheelbarrow races and rifle shooting have already been mentioned; in addition, there were other "out-of-the-ordinary-items" such as archery contests, bicycle races, horse races, and greased pig chases.[24] This willingness on the part of the Scots to consistently allow new items alongside traditional events helped to maintain the appeal of the Games. While adhering closely to tradition, they were never completely parochial or inflexible. This policy was seen to greater effect when Highland Games appeared in other countries. There the essential Scottish characteristics were rigorously maintained, while activities indigenous to the new environment were included as well. However, one of the "novelty items" sometimes included at home and abroad was a traditional game of similar Gaelic heritage and possibly of even more ancient origin. This was the game of shinty.

Shinty is an English derivation from the Gaelic "sinteag," meaning a "bound" or a "skip." First references to the game are found in some of the oldest manuscripts in the ancient Gaelic language of Ireland, and it is associated with many important legends, that of Cuchulainn in particular. Whether or not other Gaelic athletic pastimes were transmitted to Scotland, it has been categorically stated that "Shinty came over from Ireland along with the Scots or Gaels in the fifth century." It became commonplace in the Scottish Highlands, being known as "camanachd." The "caman" was the curved stick or club used to strike the leather-covered ball.[25]

References to the game are found in Scottish Gaelic literature and in "the Sassenach language." A sport known as "Irish Gamayne," taken to be shinty, was a pastime of King James IV. "Club-ball," also assumed to be shinty (perhaps wrongly), was mentioned in 1769 as being common to the people of Moray.[26] Mclain, famous Scottish author of the nineteenth century, provided a generous description of the game:

> This exhilarating amusement is very popular among the Highlanders; two opposing parties endeavour, by means of the Caman or club, to drive a ball to a certain spot on either side, and the distance is sometimes so great that a whole day's exertion is required to play out the game. A vigorous runner, it is obvious, has a great advantage, but agility is not the only requisite; great skill in preventing the ball being driven to the desired goal is necessary, and many awkward blows and falls take place during the contest. Different parishes frequently turn out to try their abilities at this exciting game, and no better exercise could be enjoyed in a winter day. When there is a

numerous meeting the field has much the appearance of a battle scene; there are banners flying, bagpipes playing, and a keen
melee around the ball. Young and old, rich and poor, join in
this athletic sport, and though it is usually engaged in con
amore, prizes are frequently contended for.[27]

The most well-known illustration of shinty appeared in the
Penny Magazine in 1835, together with a description similar to
the above, and the additional information that it was customary
"in the winter season," when "large parties assemble during the
Christmas holidays." In 1836, Londoners in England were apparently entertained by Gaelic songs in praise of "the shinnie,"
as well as a friendly match with "exiled Gaels" taking part. Five
years later, the Society of True Highlanders also organized
another match there, near Islington, before which "half the glens
of Lochaber had been ransacked for shinty clubs."[28]
Shinty games were not always friendly in Scotland, where hard
knocks were given and taken, and where Clan feuds could add to
the tension. One memorable inter-Clan match was between the
Campbells and Macleans, about the beginning of the nineteenth
century, at Calgary Sands in Mull. By the end of the century
however, such inter-Clan games were rare, since many district
Shinty Clubs were formed. A national governing body, the
Camanachd Association, did much to ensure the game's survival
through a Cup Competition.[29] Described as an "intermediate between hurling and hockey," shinty is another ancient, traditional
Scottish sport:

> Wi' bonnet blue, wi' kilt and plaid
>   of ilka clannish hue arrayed;
> Up! muster in the greensome shade,
>   To fight this day at shinty,

> *Chorus*

> Then drain the quaich, fill again,
>   Loudly blow the martial strain;
> An' welcome gie wi' might and main,
>   To gude auld Hielan' shinty.[30]

Etc.

Although no one has adequately claimed a Gaelic heritage for the two other sports most commonly described as Scottish, i.e., curling and golf, both have a tradition in Scotland which spans centuries. Curling is often called "Scotland's ain game," and golf as "Scotland's gift to the world."[31] The origins of both games have been the subject of considerable enquiry and debate,[32] and to date no theory has been plausibly substantiated to the satisfaction of all expert opinion. If it can only be said that one or both games may have originated in Scotland, it is beyond doubt that they were subsequently developed and codified there. Scots transformed both games into organized sports in their own country and others. References to both are found in Scottish literature, from acts of Parliament to poetic fiction, from the fifteenth century onwards. Artifacts and relics of both have been located from an early date in Scotland. In fact, once past the query of origin, the Scottish contributions in curling and golf are unsurpassed, and both qualify as traditional Scottish sports.

The *Encyclopaedia Britannica* states:

> Curling, like golf, is especially associated with Scotland. But the earliest representation of it is a winter scene by the Flemish painter Pieter Bruegel (c. 1525–69), in which a band of hunters with their dogs look down upon two expanses of ice. On the farther one are skaters; on the nearer are pairs of curlers with brooms and stones with handles. The Grand Caledonian Curling Club was founded at Edinburgh in 1838 "to unite curlers throughout the world into one Brotherhood of the Rink."[33]

The winter scene referred to above is entitled: "The Hunters in the Snow," painted in 1565. Actually, another Bruegel painting of the same year, entitled "Winter Landscape with Skaters and a Bird-Trap," also clearly depicts some curlers on the ice.[34] But if these were the earliest representations of curling, the earliest artifacts of the game were discovered in Scotland, dated before 1565.

The most prolific author on the history of curling, the late John Kerr, has described three distinct types of stones, by which he traced the progress of the game:

(a) the Kuting-Stone, Kutty-Stone, or Piltycock, or Loofie.
(b) the Rough Block (with handle).
(c) the Polished or Circular Stone.

These were approximately dated: (a) from 1500 to 1650, (b) 1650 to 1800, and (c) from 1800 onwards. One kuting-stone in a Scottish museum bears the date ''1511,'' and another there ''has the appearance of being older and more primitive, and may have been originally a water-worn boulder taken from the bed of some stream.'' The term ''channel-stones'' refers to stones from river channels; and those used for the ''putting the stone'' event at Highland Games came from river beds, also.[35] Another river curling-stone found near Dunblane bears the date ''1551.'' Other sixteenth- and seventeenth-century stones have been discovered in various parts of Scotland.[36]

These earliest stones had no handle but a niche for the player's finger or thumb, and were probably intended to be thrown part of the way. They were much lighter than later types, weighing from 5 lbs. to 25 lbs. Because of this, early curling has been described as ''a kind of quoiting on ice.''[37] Quoits probably had its origin in England or Scotland in the late fifteenth century.[38] Quoits were flat rings of iron weighing from 10 lbs. upwards, with a hole of at least 4 inches diameter, which were thrown at a pin in the ground about 18 yards away. Players aimed the quoit to land over the pin, usually exposed only an inch above the ground, or as near to it as possible.[39] The early form of curling was often described as ''coiting, kuting, or quoiting.'' Curlers were described as ''quoiters'' and stones as ''curling or quoiting stones.'' As curling developed, however, the similarities lessened and the analogy became less frequent. James Hogg, the ''Ettrick Shepherd,'' was adamant about the two games in one of his poems:

> I've played at quoiting in my day,
>   And maybe I may do't again,
> But still unto myself I'd say,
>   This is no the channel-stane.[40]

From the time that heavier curling stones were used and despatched entirely along the ice, the ''loofies'' were superseded by stones with handles. These were of all sizes, shapes, and weights, and numerous examples exist. Three historians of curling have provided many illustrations of these, with vivid descriptions. Many stones have been given interesting names such as "The Soo," "The Baron," "The Fluke," "The Egg," "The Girdle," "The Grey Hen," "The Provost," "The Saut Backet" (the Salt Bucket), and so on.[41]

The insertion of handles represented an improvement, but the greatest advance in curling came with gradual adoption of the circular, polished stone. This Scottish innovation has not been precisely attributed or dated, but in Kerr's words, "was not the inventor of the circular stone the true originator of curling?"[42] The present accepted techniques of the game certainly derived from the use of a symmetrical stone, "beautifully rounded, brilliantly polished and supplied with a suitable handle."[43]

Scottish enthusiasts soon formed themselves into curling clubs and more than forty of these existed in the eighteenth century, in Angus, Ayr, Dumbarton, Dumfries, Fife, Lanark, Linlithgow, Midlothian, Perth, Renfrew, Roxburgh, and Stirling.[44] With the possible exception of the northern parts of Angus, Dumbarton, and Perth, these are all Lowland or Border counties. Unlike the Highland Games and shinty, curling did not have a Highland heritage. It has been maintained, in fact, that the game "was hardly known" in the Highlands in the mid-eighteenth century.[45] This was borne out by the subsequent increase in clubs. Before the halfway mark had been reached in the nineteenth century there were nearly two hundred curling clubs in existence. All these were in the counties previously mentioned, together with the other Lowland areas of Bute, Clackmannan, Kinross, Kirkcudbright, Peebles, Selkirk, Wigton, and the remaining Border county of Berwick. The capital city of Edinburgh had eighteen clubs before 1839. Also, in 1834, the first move was made towards a national organization for curling, entitled the "Amateur Curling Club of Scotland," but this too élite and exclusive attempt not surprisingly failed. But four years later, as a result of advertisements in the *North British Advertiser* calling for meetings at the Waterloo Hotel in Edinburgh, interested parties eventually formed the "Grand Caledonian Curling Club" on 25 July 1838. Thirty-six clubs were originally represented from various districts of Scotland. The constitution of the club was framed on 15 November 1838.[46]

As with the Braemar Highland Gathering, royal patronage was given to curling as a result of a visit by the Queen and Prince Consort to Scotland. In 1842, they were entertained by the Earl of Mansfield at the Palace of Scone, who at that time was President of the Grand Club. Subsequently, Her Majesty allowed the club to assume the title of ''The Royal Grand Caledonian Curling Club'' in a letter dated 12 August 1843. The superfluous adjective ''Grand'' was soon omitted and it became the Royal Caledonian Curling Club.[47] This club became the parent body of curling throughout the world in the nineteenth century, and clubs in other countries affiliated to it.[48] When Albert died, the Prince of Wales consented to become patron of the Royal Club on 21 July 1862, and his active support helped the game's progress.[49] By the end of the century, there were nearly six hundred curling clubs in Scotland.[50]

First references to curling in Scotland appeared in the literature and in some personal diaries of the seventeenth century, beginning in 1638. Although the most famous Scottish literary figures of the next century, Robert Burns and Sir Walter Scott, only referred to the game briefly, the increasing mention of it by others attested to its growing popularity. Curling literature and paintings became commonplace in the nineteenth century and reflected its greater prosperity.[51] The game had comfortably survived the early wars with England and the reprisals after the Jacobite Rebellions. Although it was very definitely Scottish and never common in England,[52] it was a Lowland winter pastime and unaffected by the Disarming Acts leveled at Highland mores. (At the battle of Culloden, in fact, many Lowlander Scots had fought with the Duke of Cumberland's army against the ''rebel Scots'' of Bonnie Prince Charles.) Curling, therefore, suffered no interruption in its progress towards the Victorian era and its development as a traditional Scottish sport.

Neither did the other Lowland pastime of golf, possibly because it was not unknown in England, too, long before the Act of Union; and probably because it was one of the most popular activities in eastern Scotland. Also, it had survived royal displeasure in the fifteenth century, only to be accorded much royal favor and patronage in subsequent years. Many references were made to this game in early Scottish literature. Golf, as indicated, was later referred to as "Scotland's gift to the world."[53] This was because the present game of golf derived from its Scottish origins.

In medieval times, archery was a popular activity and both English and Scottish governments promoted it as essential to the defense of the realm, particularly during the period of the Hundred Years' War (1338–1453). Consequently, when the populace spent too much time on other amusements, the Parliaments issued edicts against them. In 1349, Edward III of England attempted to prohibit other sports in favor of archery. James I of Scotland, in 1424, passed a statute to have archers trained from twelve years of age, and targets set up by every parish kirk. He even wrote a satiric poem, entitled "Christ's Kirk on the Green," ridiculing his subjects' inept shooting with the bow.[54] James II indicated his similar annoyance in a Scottish Act of Parliament of 21 May 1457, and provided the first reference to golf in recorded form:

> decreeted and ordained that wapinschawing is be holden by the Lordis and Baronis spirituale and temporale, faure Times in the zeir, and that the Fute-ball and golfe be utterly cryit downe and nocht usit.[55]

Another caution was necessary in an act of 1471, and again in an act of 1491.[56] But none of these acts proved effective against people who "were passionately fond of football and golf."[57] In fact, it was during the reign of James IV (1473–1513) that the last-named act was passed, yet this king himself "developed into an avid golfer."[58]

The activities of the monarchs and nobility naturally attracted most attention of early chroniclers and later historians. Accounts of their social life often provided early references to, and information about, various sports. Golf was no exception, since it was patronized by royalty and the nobility from an early date.

The conversion of James IV into an "avid golfer" began at least as early as 1503, when the Royal Accounts revealed a sum spent "for the King to play at the golf with the Earl of Bothwell."[59] James V of Scotland (1512–42) played golf on private links at Gosford in East Lothian. His daughter, Mary, Queen of Scots (1542–87), also played golf at St. Andrews, and one of her husbands was a "prominent golfer."[60] Her son, James VI of Scotland, later James I of England (1566–1625), also played the game at Blackheath Common in London.[61]

James's reign began in 1603, and resulted in "the introduction of certain Scottish games into the country."[62] A society of golfers was formed at Blackheath in 1608.[63] A decade later James set the royal seal of approval on an anti-Puritan reaction which had gained force during preceding years with his famous Declaration of Sports, or Book of Sports as it became known. The declaration, issued at Greenwich on 24 May 1618, argued that the prohibition of sports on Sunday bred discontent, hindered the conversion of Catholics, and deprived common people of lawful and beneficial recreation. This led to a revival of many pastimes, although the question of sport on the Sabbath was never absolutely resolved, and this Scottish king undoubtedly influenced the sporting habits of his English subjects.[64] The Declaration of Sports did not apply officially to Scotland, but ". . . it was probably not without influence there."[65] As far as golf was concerned, however, it did not escape its Scottish associations. Indeed, the game, like the king's accent, probably served to remind the English of the "foreign" presence on their throne. It remained the sport of royal exiles and of the nobility during the Elizabethan and Stuart periods.[66]

James's son, Henry, was reported as playing "at Goff, a play not unlike Pale maille," indicating the similarity of two popular games.[67] Other indications of royal participation during the Stuart period denoted Scottish influence, also. Charles I (1600–49) is reputed to have broken off a match at Leith in 1642 when news came of the Irish Rebellion.[68] He also played golf later at Newcastle during its occupation by the Scots army. His two sons followed their father's pastime, Charles II at Scone, and James II regularly on the Leith Links.[69] It has been claimed that there was, in fact, only one specifically English reference to golf in the Stuart period, when boys of Westminster School damaged local fields by playing games, including golf, in 1658.[70] A publication entitled "Westminster Drollery" (London, 1671) also mentioned "goff" and football.[71]

The acts of Parliament in the fifteenth century provide the first mention of golf in recorded form, and a similar act provides the first printed reference to golf in the next century, in 1566. But it was not until almost two hundred years later that the first book devoted entirely to golf appeared, although several works published in the interim period contain references to the game.[72] The importance of archery in warfare diminished in the seventeenth century with the increasing use of firearms, and the previous prohibitions against golf and other sports in acts of Parliament ceased. However, local edicts against "Sabbath-breakers" endured for a time in Scotland.[73] Through pressure from the clergy, the Town Council of Edinburgh passed resolutions in 1592 and 1593 forbidding play at golf during sermons on Sunday. Two early martyrs of the game, John Henrie and Pat Togie, were prosecuted for offending in this manner on the links of Leith. This edict was also enforced in other parts of Scotland in the next century, and offenders were made to make public amends by sitting in the Seat of Repentance at the local church.[74]

The diary entries of a young Edinburgh medical student in 1687 and 1688 contained entries which "might properly be called the very first recorded golf instructions"; and the earliest mention of golf in the daily press, in 1724 described a match at Edinburgh.[75] The capital city of Scotland was, in fact, the main center of early golfing activity. The Royal Burgess Golfing Society of Edinburgh claims to have been founded in 1735.[76] The Company of Gentleman Golfers, now the Honourable Company of Edinburgh Golfers, was formed in 1744 by a group that played over the five holes of the Links of Leith.[77] The *Scots Magazine* of April 1744 contained an account of the Edinburgh Town Council ordering its treasurer to have made a silver club, valued at £15, to be played for annually, at the request of the Gentleman Golfers. It was first played for in April 1745 and won by an Edinburgh surgeon, John Rattray. The earliest known rules of golf are the thirteen recorded in the first minute book of these Edinburgh golfers.[78]

The president of the Edinburgh Club was the famous Duncan Forbes, Lord President of the Court of Session, and apparently a good golfer.[79] This pioneering sporting activity took place against the background of the Forty-Five Jacobite Rebellion, and it was Forbes who used his powerful influence to prevent many clans rallying to Prince Charles's standard. Generally, the Lowlands were hostile to the Jacobite cause; nevertheless, Prince Charles secured the support of a hesitant Edinburgh on 17 September 1745, and remained there for several weeks.[80] Possibly his mission was too urgent for him to dally on the Link of Leith, but the prince is credited with having introduced golf into Italy a few years earlier, when Lord Elcho found him playing in the Borghese gardens. As Hutchinson has observed: "Would that he and Forbes could have met on the links!" before the battle of Culloden in 1746.[81]

The first edition of the first book entirely devoted to golf was published in Edinburgh in 1743,[82] the second edition in Leith twenty years later, and the third edition again in Edinburgh in 1793. Significantly, this later work was dedicated "To all the Lovers of Goff in Europe, Asia, Africa and America." Five years later, in 1797, golf was mentioned for the first time in the third edition of the *Encyclopaedia Britannica*, and before the turn of the century it had also been featured in various British books on sports. But if there were golf lovers all over the world by the end of the eighteenth century, the game retained its traditional Scottish aspect in England for some time afterwards. Golf was one of the amusements mentioned in verses published in Manchester in 1833 and relating to merchants of that city, many of whom were Scots.[83] When Donald Walker's *Games and Sports* was published in London in 1837, the author stated: "In the northern parts of this country, golf is much practised." He went on to provide a clue later in the chapter which may explain part of the widespread popularity of the game: "This amusement is healthful but not laborious, as there is time for conversation between every stroke."[84]

Although the capital city had been the focal point of early golf in Scotland, the traditional home of golf was destined to be located in the small seaside town of St. Andrews, situated across the Firth of Forth in the district of Fife. The Society of St. Andrews had been formed ten years after the Edinburgh Gentleman Golfers by a group of twenty-two golf enthusiasts. The links they used had been consecrated to golf two years earlier. Their rules were almost identical with those of the Gentleman Golfers and probably copied from them. As in Edinburgh, the game thrived in St. Andrews through the activities of this Club. Eminent persons, including professors from the town's famous university, were donors of the St. Andrews Silver Club and participants in the golf club's activities. The members were also remarkably good golfers considering the crudeness of their implements and the condition of the links, as their scores attested.[85]

Until almost halfway through the nineteenth century, golf had been played for centuries with a leather covered ball stuffed with feathers, the ''feathery.''[86] This was seldom exactly round and practically useless in wet weather, but nevertheless could be driven up to about 175 yards.[87] Most ball makers, essential in every golfing community, could only produce about four or five good balls a day, sold at up to five shillings apiece.[88] Bobson, of St. Andrews, was a celebrated ball maker whose praises were lavishly sung in *The Goff*.[89] In the mid-nineteenth century, Douglas Gourlay at Leith, and his son at Musselburgh, were among renowned ball makers. Their principal competitor was another St. Andrews man, Allan Robertson, son of a noted player, who apparently made 2,456 featheries in 1844.[90]

In 1848, a Scottish reverend, Dr. Robert Paterson, invented a ball made of gutta percha. The ''gutty'' was ''smoothly solid, and more durable'' and, an important point, was also less expensive.[91] Significantly, the next major technical development in the manufacture of golf balls occurred on the other side of the Atlantic Ocean, in 1899,[92] by which time the game of golf had been firmly established in countries outside of Scotland.

The earliest known golf club maker was William Mayne of Edinburgh, appointed by royal warrant of James VI in 1603. This same enthusiastic monarch gave James Melville a monopoly of ball making fifteen years later.[93] A notebook from Mayne's period lists payments for the repair of ''play clubis,'' ''bonker clubis,'' and an ''iron club.'' These rudimentary clubs had wooden shafts, usually made from ash. Club making advanced in the last century of the feather ball era with the advent of noted craftsmen, such as Simon Cossar of Leith and James Wilson of St. Andrews. By the first half of the nineteenth century clubs had been divided into the four categories of drivers, spoons, irons, and putters, and the techniques of the modern game of golf became apparent.[94] After the introduction of the harder and less fragile gutta percha ball in 1848, significant changes were necessary in the manufacture of clubs, and players now required a greater number of different types as the game became more sophisticated. The average set of eight clubs could be selected from some thirteen varieties, including: woods—cleek, midiron, lofting-iron, mashie, niblick, and iron putter.[95]

These technical developments, allied with the increase in club formation and membership, new competitions, and progress towards generally accepted rules of the game, ensured the position of golf as one of the most popular of all traditional Scottish sports. The tradition was most firmly established by 1834, when King William IV approved the addition of the prefix ''Royal and Ancient'' to the Golf Club of St. Andrews. This was several years before the Grand Caledonian Curling Club was permitted the use of the word ''royal,'' and in similar fashion to its curling counterpart, the Royal and Ancient Golf Club of St. Andrews eventually became the governing body of the game in Scotland and around the world. Its clubhouse, erected in 1840, remains as the symbolic ancestral home of golf.[96]

Although golf had been popular with ''Commoners and Kings'' for centuries, it was probably not the most popular game in Scotland. It required expensive equipment and considerable leisure time to indulge in this pastime, therefore it was not the most usual game for the crowd or the common man. Large numbers of the poorer classes needed to expend their energy on activity without too much organization or paraphernalia. For centuries, variations of what is now described as ''football'' provided this need in the British Isles.

As with other sports mentioned, the ancient origins of football are also hypothetical and obscure, but the British contribution is undeniable. The recorded history of football is generally supposed to date back to the twelfth or thirteenth century in England and the fifteenth century in Scotland. Early royal edicts were first issued against football before they were decreed against golf and other sports for similar reasons. And likewise, although not to the same extent, these were followed by examples of royal patronage and even participation. Unlike curling and golf, football cannot be associated solely with any one country or part of the British Isles. Certainly, most major developments occurred in England, and the English contribution to the organization and codification of this sport is unsurpassed. But it was really a general British pastime, popular for centuries in Ireland, Scotland, and Wales, also.[97] For this reason, it may be included among the traditional sports of Scotland.

One reason for the early edicts against football was that it, too, tended to detract from the vital practice of archery. There was another good reason as well. Football as played then was both a public nuisance and highly dangerous to all involved. In fact, it was the cause of considerable conflict between authority, from the monarch to local mayors and aldermen, and a mass of players, until the nineteenth century. Before then the existing techniques of communication and social control proved inadequate to suppress football, which continued widespread according to custom, which was stronger than the law.[98]

The game was first banned in London by English King Edward II at his departure for Scotland, which culminated in his defeat at Bannockburn. Nicholas de Farndone, Lord Mayor of London, on 13 April 1314 proclaimed in the King's name:

> Forasmuch as there is great noise in the city caused by hustling over large footballs in the fields of the public from which many evils might arise which God forbid: we command and forbid on behalf of the King, on pain of imprisonment, such game to be used in the city in future.[99]

This provided an authentic description of the mass football which remained in force for more than five hundred years. Exception was particularly taken to the "hustling," the great melee and forerunner of the scrimmage, and not without cause, since injury or death often resulted from its violence. One of the first acts of Edward III after gaining power was to issue another edict against football in 1331. Seven years later the outbreak of the war led to a succession of edicts by many English monarchs, prohibiting football and other sports. The end of the Hundred Years' War in 1453 did not bring respite to football players for long. Edward IV soon found himself involved in antifootball legislation, as did his successors. But there is no evidence that the game suffered in popularity in England, and it survived the Elizabethan period and the attacks of the Puritans until its apogee in the nineteenth century.[100]

It survived in similar fashion in Scotland, also. Like curling and golf,

> it was confined to the Lowlands or to those regions inhabited by Scots of non-Gaelic origin. The Highlanders never apparently had any interest in the game, and have none to this day, which is curious, seeing that football in various forms seems indigenous to the other Celtic regions, Wales, Brittany, Cornwall, and Ireland, and may even be in origin a Celtic game.

Celtic game or not, every Scottish king in the fifteenth century banned it. The first parliament of James I, held at Perth on 26 May 1424, decreed "that na man play at the futeball," under the penalty of a 4d fine. Other prohibitions were made by James II in 1457 against football, golf, and other sports. Yet the latter seems to have played or patronized the game, since an entry in the accounts of the Lord High Treasurer for Scotland in 1497 reads "Item. The 22nd day of April, given to James Dog to buy football for the King . . . 2s." James V may have taken part in the famous Jedburgh game on Fastern's E'en.[101]

Fastern's E'en was actually Shrove Tuesday, and festival times were commonly used for football games, such as Ash Wednesday, Candlemas, Easter, Christmas, and New Year's Day. Other dates such as the "12th March" or "Monday after St. Ive's Feast, which is the Sunday before Candlemas Day" were also used. The rules, if there were any at all, were minimal and varied from place to place. So, too, did the age and number of contestants. There were games for children, boys only, and young and old, and ladies were known to participate in some games. The Jedburgh game was played between the "Uppies" and "Doonies." An "Uppie" was born above the Market Place, and a "Doonie" below it. The Town Clock was the determining line at Hawick in the "Eastenders versus Westenders" affair. "Married against Single" games took place, as well as intertown contests. Football games were played through streets and across fields, and the distances between scoring places varied from about 200 yards to 3 miles. Most scores were called a "goal" or a "hail." Leather balls of varying sizes, stuffed with hay, were most common and frequently "gaily beribboned."[102]

It has been suggested that football came naturally to the Scots, "who were even wilder and more high-spirited than their English contemporaries," and that street football in Scotland, even the Sabbath variety, was not prosecuted so vigorously or so early by authorities there as in England. Shrove Tuesday football in Glasgow was even encouraged by the municipal authorities in the sixteenth century, and the first recorded prosecution for playing football in the streets dates from 1682, when players at Banff were fined 40s.[103] But it was down near the border with England that Scottish footballers revealed their wildest high spirits.

In fact, "one very interesting aspect of Scottish football" from about 1600 was its association with border raids and violence. A football game often preceded a foray into England where the authorities learned to keep an eye on football players. The game was played elsewhere in eastern Scotland, in Perth and Midlothian, for example, and even to the far north in the Orkney Islands,[104] but it was most popular in the border counties, especially Roxburgh. There it survived all attempts to suppress it. The Town Council at Jedburgh in 1704 decided that, "since sometimes both old and young men lost their lives" at the annual game on Fastern's E'en, they should "discharge the game now and all time coming." However, their efforts were in vain and the game continued. A similar attempt at Duns in Berwick, in 1724, to avoid the customary "effusion of blood among the inhabitants" also failed.[105] When Frank N. Punchard published his *Survivals of Folk Football* two hundred years later, he listed nine Scottish games (eight of them in Roxburgh) and seven English games. Wild the Scottish versions of football may have been, but at least none of them suffered his indictment that "the play at Atherstone does not justify the term 'game,' " or that "in the games of Wednesday (1892) and Tuesday (1907) the ball was kicked to pieces" at Ashbourne.[106]

Of course, this author was writing of the few surviving relics of Folk Football in the twentieth century. It was in the first half of the nineteenth century that

> a complete transformation took place. On the one hand, with the rise of the modern public school, the schoolboy game emerged from its isolation, carried its influence to the universities and thence affected the whole of English football, so that in a sense it would be true to say that the entire structure of the modern game is built on a foundation laid by public schoolboys of the early Victorian period. Meanwhile the old festival game, still traditional in many towns, was coming more and more into collision with the forces of law and order . . . and was at last suppressed, except in those few places where in a disciplined form it is allowed to survive today [*sic*] as an interesting relic.[107]

On the playing fields of these English Public Schools, the traditional forms of violent football were refined during the cult of athleticism. Games were organized with accepted rules and permeated by ideas of sportsmanship, team spirit, and "gentlemanly conduct."[108] Two forms of football, association and rugby, arose out of controversy between two rival groups of Old Boys. Both types survived and flourished as separate games. Until such distinctions became clear, there were many kinds of football which included the characteristics of both rugby and soccer to a greater or lesser extent.[109]

Rugby football derived its name from Rugby School in Warwickshire, immortalized by its famous headmaster, Dr. Arnold, and the novel *Tom Brown's Schooldays*, when sixteen-year-old William Webb Ellis is said to have broken the unwritten conventions in 1823 by running forward with the ball in his hands.[110]

Although this probably never happened,[111] the rules codified at Rugby in 1846 facilitated the export of the game to other public schools and universities, many of whom adopted the Rugby way of playing football. This export happily coincided with a time of great expansion of such institutions, when the rise of a new and well-to-do middle class demanded more public school education on Rugby lines.[112]

Rugby football was introduced to the boys of Edinburgh Academy in 1851,[113] attained immediate popularity, and spread to other Scottish public schools. There the students "took to it even more readily than English boys," and there "inter-school matches started earlier than [in] England." Schools which have since become famous for their rugby prowess in Scotland, such as Merchiston, Fettes, and Loretto, competed in friendly matches by the 1860s. It has also been maintained that "the present neat way of tackling was first practised, characteristically enough, in the Scottish public schools."[114] At a meeting held on 26 January 1871 at the Pall Mall Restaurant, Charing Cross, in London, several English football clubs formed an organized body known as the Rugby Union. Two months later, Scotland defeated England in the first international rugby game played under the new Rugby Union rules. England gained revenge and its first international victory the following year when Scotland lost a twenty-a-side game at Kennington Oval, London. After six seasons the teams were altered to the present fifteen a side. Since their first encounters, England and Scotland have continued their rivalry in the game traditional to both countries.[115]

Association football came into being because a handful of the oldest and proudest schools, notably Charterhouse, Eton, Harrow, and Westminster, "resisted the Rugby influence, and preferred to retain the traditional forms of the game which they had been developing on their own account perhaps for centuries." This "dribbling" game, like rugby, also spread from the schools to the universities. A number of Old Boys joined together to form a "soccer" club at Sheffield in 1857, and clubs were also formed in Hallam and Blackheath in the same year. Other early dribbling clubs were Crystal Palace (1861), Nottingham County (1862), Barnes (1863), Civil Service (1863), and Stoke City (1863). The latter club was started by Old Carthusians apprenticed at the North Staffordshire Railway works.[116]

It was in 1863 that representatives of eleven London clubs and and schools met on 26 October to settle the need for general codification of football rules. By 8 December that year, the faction favoring rules more akin to the Rugby-type game had withdrawn, and the Football Association had been formed. Described as "at first a feeble and puny organization," it held on to become the governing body of soccer through the British Isles.[117]

Soccer developments in the remainder of the nineteenth century were affected by many influences, some of them from Scotland. The famous Queen's Park club in Glasgow was formed in 1867, and dominated the Scottish Challenge Cup Competition (begun seven years later) for the rest of the century, appearing in the final twelve times and winning the Cup on no fewer than ten occasions before 1900.[118] An English Challenge Cup Competition had begun in 1872 and Queen's Park entered. But having drawn its game with the Wanderers 0-0, the club was unable to remain in London for the replay and retired. However, this Scottish club contributed one guinea (21s) towards the purchase of the Cup, although its income for the year was only £6. Wanderers won five of the first seven English Finals between 1872 and 1878, and one of their best players was the Hon. Arthur Kinnaird. This amazing amateur played in nine Cup Finals between 1873 and 1883, represented Scotland, and was president of the Football Association for thirty-three years.[119]

As with rugby, the first international match in soccer was also between England and Scotland, played at Partick in Glasgow, in the year following the first international rugby game. The Queen's Park club represented Scotland while the England team was selected from nine leading clubs. The game ended in a 0-0 draw, which was not a bad result for Scottish supporters, considering that there were about a hundred clubs south of the border at this time compared with only ten clubs playing association football rules in Scotland. This match led to the formation of the Scottish Football Association in 1873, and in turn to those of Wales (1876) and Ireland (1880). An international series was begun in 1883 and has been dominated by England and Scotland. In the nineteenth century, the Scots just took the honors, winning the series outright on eight occasions between 1883 and 1900, and sharing first place with England twice.[120]

The origin of the English Football League in 1888 was actually the idea of a Scotsman, William McGregor. At that time he was living in Birmingham and associated with the famous Aston Villa Football Club. Organized soccer was then conducted in a rather haphazard manner, and arranged matches often had to be cancelled for a variety of reasons. It was not a satisfactory state of affairs for clubs which had wage bills and other expenses to meet. McGregor conceived the idea of a league system and on 2 March 1888, he wrote to five of the leading clubs suggesting regular home-and-away fixtures. With strong backing from an influential sporting paper, the *Athletic News*, eventually twelve clubs constituted the League: Accrington, Aston Villa, Blackburn Rovers, Bolton Wanderers, Burnley, Derby County, Everton, Notts County, Preston North End, Stoke, West Bromwich Albion, and Wolverhampton Wanderers. All have survived in the league today except Accrington. A Second Division was added in 1892, and the First Division of the League increased to sixteen clubs. A Scottish Football League had been formed in the previous year. These leagues had an immediate stabilizing effect on the game and were mainly responsible for "the phenomenal increase in the number of spectators at the matches of important clubs during the eighties and nineties."[121]

The first international soccer match between England and Scotland, as stated, was played at Partick in Scotland. The actual venue was the ground of the West of Scotland Cricket Club. Cricket has often been described as the most English of games. Again, its real origin is debatable,[122] but the game was developed in England from the seventeenth century onwards. It arose in the southeastern part, especially in Kent where it had a distinguished history, before spreading to other English counties and later to Ireland, Scotland, and Wales. Like other sports, the game enjoyed the patronage of royalty and the nobility, but became associated with rural villages in particular, where all social classes participated in the game.[123] Although cricket and England are synonymous and inseparable in an historical context, the game has also been played in Scotland for over two hundred years.

Cricket appeared in Scotland shortly after the battle of Culloden when the military played the game at Perth. But the first recorded game in Scotland took place in 1785 on the estate of the Earl of Cathcart, as depicted on a glass goblet presented by Sir Ronald Campbell to Haddington C.C., on which is inscribed: "First Cricket Match in Scotland." The first known century in Scotland was scored in 1789, when a Colonel Lennox of Aberdeen made 136 runs.[124] In 1812, the cavalry stationed at Perth Barracks played cricket on the North Inch nearby, and also ". . . at that time the boys of a public school formed themselves into a club, and pursued the game on the same ground." The game was also played on Glasgow Green a few years later, and a cricket club instituted at Greenock in 1823. The Perth Cricket Club was formed in 1827, and not surprisingly the "Fair City" has been described as the birthplace of cricket in Scotland. The capital city of Edinburgh had a cricket club, the Grange C.C., five years later.[125]

The increase coincided with the rise of other sports already noted, with one important difference. Cricket was an English import of recent origin when compared with the other more traditional sports. As such, it had no particular cultural associations with either Highlands or Lowlands except at various ports in the Highlands for many years after Culloden. County cricket clubs existed in Dumfries by 1855 and in Stirling soon afterwards.[126] They were also formed in Aberdeen and West Lothian in 1867, Peebles in 1870, Banff in 1872, and Kincardine and Nairn in 1874. A county cricket club was formed for Moray by 1875, in which year Roxburgh had one also.

Other events attested the prevalence of cricket in Scotland around this time. In 1871, Percival King's *Scottish Cricketer's Annual* was first issued, and in 1879 a Scottish Cricket Union was formed. This union lasted only four years and was dissolved in 1883 (not to be reformed until 1908). The end of the *Scottish Cricketer's Annual* came in 1888, after sixteen issues. But between the demise of the union and the *Annual*, at least two Scottish cricketers left their individual marks. In 1884, W. F. Holms made 303 runs at a match in Scotland, then the Scottish record. The following year, J. S. Carrick made 419 runs for the West of Scotland Cricket Club against Priory Park in Chichester, "a fresh individual record'' of the time.[127] Obviously, at least some of the cricket in Scotland was of a high standard.

As already noted, the royal family's sojourns in Scotland, especially at Balmoral, were frequently enlivened by sporting occasions. Cricket was also offered for royal entertainment. In 1881, when the Scottish Cricket Union existed, a cricket match took place between the two royal residences of Balmoral and Abergeldie before several members of the royal family, including Her Majesty the Queen. Several days later a tug-of-war between the same teams took place. Illustrations and accounts of both events, as well as deer stalking and grouse shooting, were featured in the *Illustrated London News* under the caption (and by permission) ''The Royal Family in the Highlands.''[128]

The peak of cricket's popularity in Scotland during the nineteenth century was probably reached during the short reign of the Scottish Cricket Union, in fact. Most of the county clubs referred to, that were formed in Scotland then, do not exist today. Cricket never attained any mass popularity in Scotland comparable to that of curling, football, or golf. An encyclopedia writer observed, *circa* 1835, ''It is a curious fact that for one reason or other it has never taken the same hold on the people of Scotland and Ireland as it has on those of England.''[129] The cricketing activity in Scotland before 1900 never approached in volume, intensity, or importance, the developments of the game in England, or even some other countries, during the same period. England was the cradle of cricket, birthplace of most early famous players, county games and championships, Gentlemen versus Players matches, and even a whole code of conduct and way of life based upon this one game. The rules of cricket were formulated and codified there, and the Marylebone Cricket Club of London eventually became the arbiter of cricket everywhere.[130] Its position in this sport became more preeminent than that of the Royal Caledonian Curling Club or the Royal and Ancient Golf Club of St. Andrews, even without the ''Royal'' prefix. Nevertheless, the game of cricket has survived in its inferior state in Scotland for over two centuries and should be included with other sporting habits there.

Cricket was of course the summer game, just as curling was

necessarily the winter sport. Another winter pastime which was enjoyed in both England and Scotland was ice skating. On 1 December 1662, Samuel Pepys noted in his diary:

> To my Lord Sandwich's, to Mr. Moore and then over the Parke where first in my life, it being a great frost, did see people sliding with their skeetes, which is a very pretty art.[131]

Two weeks later, Pepys also accompanied the future James II to a frozen pond to watch him skate. From then on skating increased in popularity, especially in the English Fen Country. Dutch exponents of the art were particularly admired.

Being situated in the northernmost part of the British Isles, Scots were accustomed to enduring the most rigorous winters. The rise of curling could not have taken place without consistent and plentiful ice upon which to participate. It is therefore not surprising that skating was practiced in Scotland also from an early date. In fact, a unique Scottish contribution was made to the new sport:

> Absolute control of certain difficulties of balance had yet to be obtained and so long as skating continued to be an amusing and fashionable pastime it would remain undeveloped until some kind of organising element was introduced.

> Such an important step was made in Scotland sometime during the second half of the eighteenth century when the Edinburgh Skating Club, the first ice club in the world, began its activities.

The exact date for the founding of the Edinburgh Skating Club is usually given as 1642, but it was probably formed sometime between 1683 and 1742. The club played an active and important part in the development of skating, and candidates for membership were required to pass stringent skating tests before admission:

> The contribution of the Edinburgh Skating Club so early in the real story of figure-skating cannot be over-estimated. It was

the first organising body that disciplined and guided skating into
the right channels and popularized its practice among a wider
circle. It may be claimed that through it the tradition of British
influence on this new sport was to play such an important role
up to modern times.[132]

In time, more skating clubs came into existence in Scotland,
which has even been described as "the home of the skating
sport."[133]

It was the home of many sports, and the Scottish contribution
to the tradition of British influence referred to in skating could
also be substantiated elsewhere. Apart from the sports already
mentioned, Britain also had a long tradition in field sports. Hunting after many kinds of fowl and game was pursued by nobility
and peasants alike for centuries, as well as fishing. Horse racing,
too, was common, but particularly identified with the nobility.
Strutt included hunting, hawking and horse racing in his Book 1
under the heading "Rural Exercises Practised by Persons of
Rank."[134] Many of these sports were pursued in Scotland. Its deer
forests, grouse moors, and salmon rivers enjoyed a reputation second to none for the sport they offered to devotees.[135] Horse racing
was a sport of some antiquity in Scotland, and like many others,
benefited from extensive patronage by royalty. In fact, the impact
of one Scottish monarch on "the Sport of Kings" was immense.
It has been claimed that "the modern system of horse-racing may
be said to date from the reign of James I," during whose reign
public race meetings were first instituted.[136]

Brailsford is more specific:

> The most permanent contribution of James I to English na-
> tional life was, after the production of the Authorized Verson
> of the Bible, the establishment of Newmarket as the centre of
> English horse racing.[137]

Two other Scottish individuals also left their mark on other
British sports, one of them achieving fame at Newmarket. In the
seventeenth century, professional runners and walkers performed
their "pedestrian feats" at fairs or as private messengers for the
nobility. These footmen often competed against each other, often

backed heavily by their patrons for large prize monies and witnessed by excited crowds with many wagers on the result. The distances for challenge races were as varied as some of the fancy names adopted by these popular pedestrians, among whom were actually members of the upper class by the eighteenth century:[138]

> One of the most notable was Captain Barclay Allardice who was a Scottish landowner drawing as much as £3,000 a year from his estates. By 1808 he had a number of athletic feats to his credit and in that year he accepted a wager to go on foot one thousand miles in one thousand successive hours at the rate of one mile in each and every hour for a wager of one thousand guineas. He began his walk on 1st June, 1809, on Newmarket Heath without previous specific training. He completed this extraordinary performance on 12th July more than two stone, i.e., 28 pounds lighter in weight but still in good fettle so that five days later he was able to join the military expedition to Walcheren as aide-de-camp to the Marquis of Huntly.[139]

Allardice's pedestrian career actually began in 1796 when he walked six miles in an hour for a wager of 100 guineas, but the event of 1809 was his greatest feat and he was "the first pedestrian to make a national impact." The momentum of all his feats "carried pedestrianism into the 1820s," after which there came a recession in the sport's popularity until its brief "Golden Era" in the 1880s.[140] Pedestrianism declined in the twentieth century with the popularity of rugby, soccer, and track and field, but still survives today in Britain, especially the famous Powderhall sprint in Edinburgh.[141] Many famous "peds" ran in Britain but none superseded Allardice in importance. After his greatest feat, "the first book on track and field was written by Walter Tom, *Pedestrianism, or an Account of the Performance of Celebrated Pedestrians During the Last and Present Century with a Full Narrative of Captain Barclay's Public and Private Matches, and an Essay on Training* (Aberdeen, 1813)." Diem maintains that Allardice "was far above the professional athletes of his time" and greatly influenced subsequent training methods and interest in athletics.[142]

Before Allardice's performances were surpassed in later years, another Scot had obtained fame in another sport. On 9 July 1865, John McGregor set out alone ''on a 1,000 mile voyage which was to have far wider repercussions than the paddler, visionary that he was, could ever have imagined.'' In his clinker-built craft, the ''Rob Roy,'' this advocate of muscular Christianity voyaged on many of the most famous rivers of Europe, shooting rapids where necessary, and sending regular accounts of his travels back to the *Record* newspaper. On his return in October he was famous and ''called upon to lecture and attend all manner of functions.'' In January 1866, his book, *1,000 Miles In The Rob Roy Canoe*, was published and became an immediate best-seller. Later in the same year the Canoe Club (later to become the Royal Canoe Club) was formed as a result of this publicity, and ''a steady stream of canoeists began to explore the waterways of Europe.'' McGregor himself, the outstanding pioneer of this sport in Britain, made later voyages in the Baltic and on the Jordan.[143]

Within the total British sporting tradition the Scots revealed themselves as an innovative and sports-loving people in their own right. When Joseph Strutt first published his comprehensive *The Sports and Pastimes of the People of England* in 1801, it was small wonder that a Scottish author felt compelled later to produce a *Sports and Pastimes of Scotland*, stating modestly in the preface:

> Its sole object is to set forth a sort of history, somewhat after (though confessedly a long way behind) the model of Strutt's *Sports and Pastimes of the People of England*: ''only this and nothing more.''

> The compilation has been the pleasing labour of years. Portions have previously appeared in print here and there; but these have been much amplified with new matter; and, so far as I am aware, the book, as it now stands, is the only one dealing with the generality of Scottish sports on the same lines. I trust it will be found both interesting and useful, as illustrative of varied phases of the habits, manners, and customs of bygone generations of Scotsmen of all ranks and classes.[144]

Scotland's people also soon acquired a reputation as "wanderers far from their own land, and settlers in other lands."[145] A variety of causes combined to effect a massive emigration of Scots over the past three centuries to many parts of the world. One result of this was that Scottish sports appeared in other countries, beginning in the eighteenth century. Scotsmen themselves were the natural pioneers in this process. They also naturally contributed to the export and assimilation of other British sports. In common with other immigrants, they also participated in sports and pastimes indigenous to their new environment.

Notes

1. J. D. Mackie, *A History of Scotland* (Harmondsworth, Middlesex: Penguin Books, 1969), pp. 7–249.

2. See, for example, H. A. Harris, *Sport in Britain: Its Origins and Development* (London: Stanley Paul, 1975); Joseph Strutt, *The Sports and Pastimes of the People of England* (London: Thomas Tegg, 1838); and Norman Wymer, *Sport in England: A History of Two Thousand Years of Games and Pastimes* (London: George G. Harrop and Co., 1949).

3. Malcolm W. Ford, "Hammer-Throwing," *Outing*, September 1892, pp. 448–50. See also Roberto L. Quercetani, *A World History of Track and Field Athletics, 1864–1964* (London: Oxford University Press, 1964), p. xv; and Melvyn Watman, *History of British Athletics* (London: Robert Hale, 1968), p. 1.

4. Ford, "Hammer-Throwing." Charles Donaldson, *Men of Muscle and the Highland Games of Scotland, with Brief Biographies of the Leading Athletes of the Last Fifty Years, with Portraits* (1901), p. 2, states: "Throwing a stone may have been practised in other lands than Scotland and Ireland, but tossing the caber and throwing the hammer are certainly of home manufacture. . . . Throwing the hammer originated in the use of an ordinary blacksmith's fore hammer, and it is probable that the smiths themselves, or some young Highlanders waiting until their horses were shod, and just to pass the time, took the smith's hammer outside and tried who could throw it farthest. This, or something like it, was the beginning of hammer-throwing."

5. James Logan, *The Scotish* [sic] *Gael*, 5th American ed. (Hartford: S. Andrews and Son, 1851), frontspiece, and p. 442.

6. David Webster, *Scottish Highland Games* (Glasgow and London: Collins, 1959). For references to Highland Games in the fourteenth and sixteenth centuries, see Carl Diem, *Weltgeschichte des Sports und der Leibeserziehung* (Stuttgart: J. G. Cotta'schen Buchhandlung Nachf., 1960), pp. 685–86; and Wyness Fenton, *Royal Valley: The Story of the Aberdeenshire Dee* (Aberdeen: Alex P. Reid and Sons, 1968), pp. 281–82.

7. *The Scottish Annual and Book of the Braemar Gathering* (Arbroath: Herald Press, 1968), p. 120, states: "The Disarming Act of 1747 sealed the doom of every Highland meeting, the Braemar Gathering among many others."

8. Sir Iain Colquhoun and Hugh Machell, *Highland Gatherings* (London: Heath Cranton, 1927), pp. 61–66.

9. *Encyclopaedia Canadiana*, 10 vols. (Toronto: Grolier of Canada, 1968), 9: 124.

10. David Webster, *Scottish Highland Games* (Edinburgh: Reprographia, 1973), p. 11.

11. Colquhoun and Machell, *Highland Gatherings*, pp. 86–87, 142.

12. Webster, *Highland Games* (1959 and 1973), passim. See also Donaldson, *Men of Muscle*, passim. This is not readily available, although there is a copy in the British Museum, London. For a list of titles of books pertaining to Scottish Highland Games, many of which are rare, see Peter Lovesey and Tom McNab, *The Guide to British Track and Field Literature, 1275-1968* (London: Athletics Arena, 1969).

13. *Scottish Annual*, p. 107; Webster, *Highland Games* (1973), pp. 15–16; the royal family also witnessed Highland Games by Loch Laggan in 1847; see the account and illustrations in *The Illustrated London News*, 4 September 1847. Her Majesty the Queen also distributed the prizes.

14. *Scottish American Journal*, 21 November 1868, p. 2.

15. *Illustrated London News*, 10 August 1867, p. 160.

16. *Illustrated London News*, 3 August 1872, p. 108.

17. *Scottish-American Journal*, 21 November 1868, p. 2.

18. Especially King Henry VIII; see Watman, *British Athletics*, pp. 15–16; Ford, "Hammer-Throwing," pp. 448–49; and Webster, *Highland Games* (1959), p. 45.

19. Dennis Brailsford, *Sport and Society: Elizabeth to Anne* (London: Routledge and Kegan Paul, 1969), pp. 103–4, 107–8, 111–14, 135, 206–7, 211, 240, 252; J. K. Ruhl, *Die "Olympischen Spiele" Robert Dovers* (Heidelberg: Carl Winter Universitäts Verlag, 1978).

20. Brian T. Mutimer, "Arnold and Organized Games in the English Public Schools of the Nineteenth Century" (Ph.D. diss., University of Alberta, Edmonton, 1971), pp. 51–57; Montague Shearman, *Athletics and Football* (London: Longmans, Green and Co., 1889), p. 26.

21. Diem, *Weltgeschichte*, pp. 685–86.

22. See the two works by John Prebble: *Culloden* (Harmondsworth, Middlesex: Penguin Books, 1961), and *The Highland Clearances* (Harmondsworth, Middlesex: Penguin Books, 1963).

23. Colquhoun and Machell, *Highland Gatherings*, pp. 90–104, 173–86; Webster, *Highland Games* (1959, and 1973), passim. See also W. L. Inglis, *A History of the Cowal Gathering* (Dunoon: Dunoon Observer, 1957).

24. Webster, *Highland Games* (1959), p. 87.

25. Alexander Macdonald, "Shinty: Historical and Traditional." *Gaelic Society of Inverness* 30 (1924): 27–32.

26. Ibid., p. 36. Macdonald's assumption is difficult to reconcile with other descriptions of "club-ball," and possibly his enthusiasm for Scottish shinty overwhelmed his usual meticulous scholarship on this point. Strutt, *Sports and Pastimes*, pp. 173–74, gives a description of club-ball which is unlike any descriptions of Highland shinty, and goes on to state on page 175: "From the club-ball, I doubt not, that pleasant and manly exercise, distinguished in modern times by the name of cricket." Christina Hole, *English Sports and Pastimes* (London: B. T. Batsford, 1949), p. 59, states that cricket probably originated from club-ball and stoolball. The people of Moray may have been playing club-ball, or a form of shinty which was wrongly described as club-ball.

27. As quoted in Macdonald, "Shinty," p. 37.

28. Ibid., p. 43.

29. Ibid., p. 51–56.

30. Ibid., p. 54; *Encyclopaedia of Sports, Games and Pastimes* (London: Fleetway

House, n.d.), p. 548. Judging from its contents, this was probably published in 1935.

31. The most obvious example from a well-known authority is John Kerr, *History of Curling* (Edinburgh: David Douglas, 1890), with the subtitle of "Scotland's Ain Game." See Joseph S. F. Murdoch, *The Library of Golf, 1743-1966* (Detroit, Mich.: Gale Research Co., 1968). This is a bibliography of golf books, indexed alphabetically, chronologically and by subject matter, which provides the most comprehensive reference to the Scottish influence on golf.

32. For curling, see Kerr, *History of Curling*, pp. 3-25; Robert Scott Fittis, *Sports and Pastimes of Scotland* (Paisley: Alexander Gardner, 1891), pp. 189-99; John A. Stevenson, *Curling in Ontario, 1846-1946* (Toronto: Ontario Curling Association, 1950), pp. 1-6; and Gerald William Bowie, "The History and Trends of Curling" (M.S. thesis, Washington State University, 1962), pp. 1-59. For golf, see Will Grimsley, *Golf: Its History, People and Events* (Englewood Cliffs, N.J.: Prentice-Hall, 1966), pp. 3-5; and Horace G. Hutchinson, *Golf* (London: Longmans, Green and Co., 1898).

33. *Encyclopaedia Britannica* (1968), s.v. "golf."

34. Marguerite Kay, *Bruegel* (London: Hamlyn Publishing Group, 1969), p. 34.

35. Kerr, *History of Curling*, pp. 27-58. See Diem, *Weltgeschichte*, pp. 685-86; and Webster, *Highland Games* (1973), p. 61.

36. Kerr, *History of Curling*, pp. 29-37.

37. Ibid., pp. 27-28.

38. *Encyclopedia of Sports*, p. 483. See also Hole, *English Sports*, pp. 36-37; and Strutt, *Sports and Pastimes*, pp. 141-42.

39. *Encyclopedia of Sports*, p. 483. See also Donald Walker, *Games and Sports* (London: Thomas Hurst, 1837), pp. 176-77.

40. As quoted in Kerr, *History of Curling*, pp. 28-29.

41. W. A. Creelman, *Curling Past and Present* (Toronto: McClelland and Stewart, 1950), pp. 67-83; Kerr, *History of Curling*, pp. 36-52; Stevenson, *Curling in Ontario*, passim.

42. Kerr, *History of Curling*, p. 53.

43. Stevenson, *Curling in Ontario*, p. 20.

44. Kerr, *History of Curling*, p. 115.

45. Stevenson, *Curling in Ontario*, p. 23.

46. Kerr, *History of Curling*, pp. 172-75, 229-38.

47. Ibid., pp. 242-43. See also chapter 7, entitled "The Royal Caledonian Curling Club," in Robin Welsh, *Beginner's Guide to Curling* (London: Pelham Books, 1969), pp. 46-54.

48. *Encyclopaedia Britannica* (1968), s.v. "curling."

49. Kerr, *History of Curling*, pp. 243-44.

50. John K. Munro, "Curling in Canada," *Canadian* 18 (1902): 527.

51. Creelman, *Curling Past*; Kerr, *History of Curling*; Stevenson, *Curling in Ontario*; and Welsh, *Guide to Curling*, are all liberally endowed with examples of curling literature. The most famous of all curling paintings, "The Curlers," by Sir George Harvey, P.R.S.A., is in the National Gallery of Scotland at Edinburgh. The original oil painting of the first Grand Match of the Royal Club at Penicuik House, High Pond, on 15 January 1847, is owned by Sir John Clerk, Bart., of Penicuik House. The "Grand Match at Linlithgow Loch" (1848), by Charles Lees, R.S.A., is owned by the Royal Club and hangs in Perth Ice Rink.

52. Walker, *Games and Sports*, p. 244, states flatly: "This is one of the games of Scotland." Pennant, in his Tour of Scotland, thus describes it; 'of all the sports of these parts, that of curling is a favorite, and one unknown in England.'" Macdonald,

"Shinty," pp. 36–37, quotes from "Pennant's Tour in Scotland" (1769); and Kerr, *History of Curling*, pp. 55–56, has the same quote from Pennant as Walker, but gives the source as Pennant, *A Tour in Scotland and Voyage to the Hebrides*, 2nd edition (1772), part 1, page 93. Fittis, *Sports and Pastimes*, pp. 195–96, explains that Pennant visited Scotland in 1769 and in 1772.

53. Murdoch, *Library of Golf*, p. 304.

54. Fittis, *Sports of Scotland*, pp. 129–30. But although "Lowland Scots never took kindly to the bow," apparently Highlanders adapted it and were skillful archers.

55. *Acts of the Parliament of Scotland* (1424–1567), 11 (1814), 48 a and b (M). For photograph of the Articles of Parliament showing the page on which this quote appears, see Grimsley, *Golf History*, p. 7.

56. *Acts*, 100, chap. 6 (M); *Acts*, 11, 226 b, chap. 13 (M).

57. Fittis, *Sports of Scotland*, p. 129.

58. *Encyclopaedia Britannica* (1968), s.v. "golf."

59. Hutchinson, *Golf*, p. 14.

60. Grimsley, *Golf History*, pp. 7–8; R. Bruce Forbes, "Golf: The Royal and Ancient Game," *IAC Merit News* 17 (July 1965): 2; O. Paul Moncton, *Pastimes in Times Past* (London: West Strand Publishing Co., 1913), p. 151.

61. *Encyclopaedia Britannica* (1968), s.v. "golf."

62. Brailsford, *Sport and Society*, p. 108.

63. *Encyclopaedia Britannica* (1968), s.v. "golf."

64. Brailsford, *Sport and Society*, pp. 102–12.

65. Morris Marples, *A History of Football* (London: Secker and Warburg, 1954), p. 60.

66. Brailsford, *Sport and Society*, pp. 109–10.

67. Ibid., p. 71. To this Prince of Wales was also attributed the first witticism recorded on a golf course. This concerns an anecdote in the Harleian MSS as quoted in Brailsford, *Sport and Society*, p. 71: when playing golf on one occasion, he was about to drive off when he was warned that his tutor was standing in the way and that he might hit him, "wherewith the Prince, drawing back his hand, said: 'Had I done so I had but paid my debts.' " Grimsley, *Golf History*, p. 8; and Moncton, *Pastimes*, p. 152, among others, recite the same story.

68. Hutchinson, *Golf*, p. 16.

69. Brailsford, *Sport and Society*, p. 109; Grimsley, *Golf History*, p. 8.

70. Brailsford, *Sport and Society*, p. 109.

71. Hutchinson, *Golf*, p. 17.

72. Murdoch, *Library of Golf*, pp. 9–10.

73. The inside cover of Grimsley, *Golf*, features a double-page reproduction, in color, of a painting by J. C. Dollman in 1896, entitled: "The Sabbath Breakers," which shows two golfers being discovered by two disapproving clergy.

74. Hutchinson, *Golf*, pp. 13–15.

75. Murdoch, *Library of Golf*, p. 11.

76. Hutchinson, *Golf*, p. 26.

77. *Encyclopaedia Britannica* (1968), s.v. "golf."

78. *Scots Magazine* 6 (April 1744); *Encyclopaedia Britannica* (1968), s.v. "golf."

79. Fittis, *Sports of Scotland*, p. 154, states: "The President was so ardent a golfer that he was known sometimes to take a turn of the Links of Leith in the dead of winter, when they were sheeted with snow and ice." Hutchinson, *Golf*, p. 19, describes him as "a good golfer, and very hard drinking."

80. Mackie, *History of Scotland*, p. 273.

81. Hutchinson, *Golf*, p. 19.

82. This was *The Goff: An Heroi-Comical Poem in Three Cantos* (Edinburgh: J. Cochran and Co., 1743).

83. Murdoch, *Library of Golf*, pp. 12–15.

84. Walker, *Games and Sports*, p. 178, 183.

85. *Encyclopaedia Britannica* (1968), s.v. "golf"; Hutchinson, *Golf*, pp. 24–26.

86. Some of these featheries can be seen today in many golf museums around the world. They were laboriously hand-made in tedious fashion by compressing boiled goose feathers inside a leather cover which had been softened with alum.

87. Carl T. Felker, "Golf: From First Feather Ball to Modern Solids," *The Sporting Goods Dealer*, May 1969, p. 99.

88. Hutchinson, *Golf*, pp. 14–16.

89. *The Goff: An Heroi-Comical Poem in Three Cantos* (Edinburgh: J. Cochran and Co., 1743).

90. *Encyclopaedia Britannica* (1968), s.v. "golf."

91. Felker, "First Feather Ball," p. 99. Understandably perhaps, the diligent Robertson was bitterly opposed to the new type of ball. It is said that when he came across "Old Tom" Morris using a gutta percha ball in 1852, an argument ensued after which Morris left St. Andrews, not to return until after Robertson's death six years later.

92. Ibid., p. 100. See also John Stuart Martin, *The Curious History of the Golf Ball: Mankind's Most Fascinating Sphere* (New York: Horizon Press, 1968).

93. Hutchinson, *Golf*, p. 14.

94. *Encyclopaedia Britannica* (1968), s.v. "golf."

95. Grimsley, *Golf History*, p. 21.

96. Ibid., pp. 27–28. Also: "The Marylebone Cricket Club and the Royal and Ancient Golf Club at St. Andrews were not set up to govern or organize their respective sports, but, because of the prestige of their members, they were called in to settle disputes or to draw up agreements on rules or etiquette and gradually assumed control," P. C. McIntosh, *Sport in Society* (London: C. A. Watts and Co., 1963), p. 59. For a comprehensive "history of the first two hundred years of the Royal and Ancient Golf Club of St. Andrews," see J. B. Salmond, *The Story of the R. and A.* (London: Macmillan and Co., 1956).

97. Marples, *History of Football*. See also: Montague Shearman, *Athletics and Football* (London: Longman's, Green and Co., 1894).

98. E. G. Dunning, "Football in its Early Stages," *History Today*, December 1963, pp. 838–39. See also: Eric Dunning and Kenneth Sheard, *Barbarians, Gentlemen and Players: A Sociological Study of The Development of Rugby Football* (Oxford: Martin Robertson and Co., 1979), pp. 21–45.

99. As quoted in Marples, *History of Football*, p. 24.

100. Ibid., pp. 25–197.

101. Ibid., pp. 38–39.

102. Frank N. Punchard, *Survivals of Folk Football* (Birmingham, 1928).

103. Marples, *History of Football*, pp. 60–61.

104. Ibid., p. 61, 85. Also, Fittis, *Sports of Scotland*, pp. 144–49, has an interesting chapter on Scottish football in which he states: "Football was the chief pastime on the Border, where it often occasioned broil and bloodshed amongst its moss-trooping patrons," and goes on to give examles. A photograph of "The ba' game at Kirkwall, Orkney" is in Marples, *History of Football*, pp. 52–53.

105. Marples, *History of Football*, pp. 83–84.

106. Punchard, *Folk Football*, p. 3, 12.

107. Marples, *History of Football*, p. 97.

108. Peter C. McIntosh, *Physical Education in England Since 1800* (London: G. Bell and Sons, 1968), pp. 15–76. Several references could now be given, but McIntosh is a major authority on athleticism in English Public Schools during the nineteenth century. See also: McIntosh, *Sport in Society*, pp. 57–79.

109. Marples, *History of Football*, pp. 136–63.

110. Ibid., pp. 136–37.

111. Dunning and Sheard, *Barbarians, Gentlemen and Players*, pp. 60–62. See also: J. L. Manning, "Who Took the Ball in His Arms?," *Observer*, 12 April 1970.

112. Marples, *History of Football*, pp. 138–39.

113. Ibid, p. 139. However, Rev. F. Marshall, ed., *Football: The Rugby Union Game* (London: Cassell and Co., n.d.), p. 51, states: "So far as I know, Rugby football was introduced into Scotland in 1855 by a small knot of men connected with the Edinburgh Academy." The book was probably published in 1895.

114. Ibid., p. 156. See also the chapter by H. H. Almond, entitled "Rugby Football in Scotish Schools" in Marshall, *Football*, pp. 51–66.

115. Ross McWhirter, "A Century of Rugby," *World Sports,* September 1970, pp. 11–16.

116. Marples, *History of Football*, pp. 139–46.

117. Ibid., pp. 148–50.

118. Dennis Signy, *A Pictorial History of Soccer* (London: Paul Hamlyn, 1969), p. 17; Frank G. Menke, *The Encyclopedia of Sports* (New York: A. S. Barnes and Co., 1953), pp. 798–99.

119. Signy, *History of Soccer*, pp. 18–20. The author relates the story of Kinnaird's mother, who said to the President of the F.A., "I'm afraid one of these days Arthur will come home with a broken leg." The President replied, "Never fear, dear madam, it will not be his own!"

120. Ibid., p. 23; Menke, *Encyclopedia of Sports*, p. 797.

121. Marples, *History of Football*, pp. 186–87; Signy, *History of Soccer*, pp. 34–35.

122. Many historians have discussed the origins of cricket. Rowland Bowen, *Cricket: A History of its Growth and Development Around the World* (London: Eyre and Spottiswoode, 1970), probably surpasses any other account available including the question of origin in chapter 1, entitled "Prehistory" (pp. 27–36). See also the chapter entitled "Beginnings" in Erick Parker, *The History of Cricket* (London: Seeley Service and Co., n.d.), pp. 17–22; and H. S. Altham, *A History of Cricket: From the Beginnings to the First World War*. 5th ed. (London: George Allen and Unwin, 1962).

123. Bowen, *Cricket*, pp. 37–137; Parker, *History of Cricket*, pp. 23–210.

124. Bowen, *Cricket*, passim.

125. Fittis, *Sports of Scotland*, p. 212. The North Inch was evidently a favorite place for sport near Perth; the same author gives examples of golf being played there, also (p. 152). It is interesting to note that while Parker, *History of Cricket*, devotes no space to cricket in Scotland, Fittis gives over the last chapter of his *Sports and Pastimes of Scotland* to the game (pp. 209–12). One of the distinguishing features of Bowen, *Cricket*, is the brief but valuable information he provides about the development of cricket in Scotland.

126. Bowen, *Cricket*, p. 276. See also: Alfred O'Neil, *Annals of Brechin Cricket, 1849–1927* (Brechin: Black and Johnston, 1927).

127. Ibid., pp. 282–92.

128. *Illustrated London News*, 1 October 1881, p. 324; and 29 October 1881, pp. 430–33.

129. *Encyclopedia of Sports*, p. 182.

130. Bowen, *Cricket*, passim; Parker, *History of Cricket*, passim.

131. As quoted in Nigel Brown, *Ice-Skating: A History* (London: Nicholas Kaye, 1959), p. 33.

132. Brown, *Ice-Skating*, pp. 37–39.

133. Menke, *Encyclopedia of Sports*, p. 606. The author also gives the founding date of the Edinburgh Skating Club as 1642 (p. 607).

134. Strutt, *Sports and Pastimes*, p. vi.

135. Fittis, *Sports of Scotland*, pp. 50–105. The author has chapters entitled "The Deer Forest and the Grouse Moor" (3, pp. 50–70); "Fox-Hunting" (4, pp. 71–80); "The Salmon River" (5, pp. 81–105). Trevelyan offers a vivid picture of this aspect of Scottish life at the time of Union (1707): "And all over Scotland hares, grouse, blackgame and partridges were pursued with dogs, hawks and snares, and less often with the long gun. But the red deer, once common, were already withdrawing into the Highland glens. The extraordinary abundance of salmon and trout afforded not only good sport, but a cheap food for the people. In some parts the gentry despised salmon as a dish that cloyed, and farm-hands struck if they were fed upon it every day." G. M. Trevelyan, *English Social History* (London: Longmans, Green and Co., 1955), p. 424.

136. Fittis, *Sports of Scotland*, pp. 106–25.

137. Brailsford, *Sport and Society*, p. 210.

138. Ibid., p. 211; Diem, *Weltgeschichte*, pp. 681–83. Some of the fancy names may be of interest: Hepper called himself "Lightfoot," Winterbottom was "Young Sparrow," other pedestrians' names were Swallow, Young Volcano, Flea, Wind, North Star, Antelope, Stag, Newcastle Phenomenon, Wonder, Flying Shuttle, Wild Merrylegs, Crowcatcher, The Gateshead Clipper, The Blue Streak, etc. One of the most famous in the 1860s, of course, was "Deerfoot," i.e., Louis Bennett, who claimed to be a full-blooded Seneca Indian and ran in Red Indian regalia. See the chapter entitled "Deerfoot" In Peter Lovesey, *The Kings of Distance* (London: Eyre and Spottiswoode, 1968), pp. 15–40.

139. McIntosh, *Sport in Society*, pp. 60–61.

140. Tom McNab, "The Life and Sudden Death of Pedestrianism," *Sport and Recreation*, July 1966, p. 27. See also: J. I. Lupton and J. M. K. Lupton, *The Pedestrian's Record* (London: W. H. Allen and Co., 1890).

141. D. A. Jamieson, *Powderhall and Pedestrianism* (Edinburgh: W. and A. K. Johnston, 1943).

142. Diem, *Weltgeschichte*, pp. 682–84.

143. Brian Skilling, "The Remarkable Voyage of John MacGregor," *Sport and Recreation*, July 1966, pp. 52–54.

144. Fittis, *Sports of Scotland*, preface.

145. Gordon Donaldson, *The Scots Overseas* (London: Robert Hale, 1966), p. 23.

3
Scottish Emigration and Settlement in Canada

> *Mass emigration is not an act of adventurous courage, the joyous rejection of security for the challenge of the unknown. It is the choice of what is hoped will be a lesser evil, and as such it is a cry of protest which later generations stifle into a statistic.*
>
> John Prebble (1975)

THE beginnings of Scottish expansion go back several centuries, before emigration and colonization in the modern sense were realized, as Scottish churchmen and scholars, craftsmen and traders, and their famous soldiers, traveled all over the European continent. England was obviously one abode of many Scots, and France was particularly favored by others as Scotland's ally in wars with the English. But even in Poland in the early seventeenth century, the number of Scots was estimated at no less than 30,000.[1] What proved to be "the first successful Scottish colony of any magnitude, and indeed the most successful Scottish colony of all time," however, was only a few miles across the sea from the southwest corner of Scotland. This was Ulster, Northern Ireland, where there were 40,000 to 50,000 Scots by the middle of the seventeenth century and twice that number by 1691.[2]

Not all of these Ulster Scots remained there until that time. Even before the seventeenth century ended many of them had made a second migration to the New World, joining thousands of their countrymen who had crossed a much bigger sea to settle on the North American continent.[3] Scots had appeared in Newfoundland as early as 1620, but were preceded by other nationalities. In the next year, however, Sir William Alexander received a grant from King James designated "Nova Scotia in America," and New Scotland was to join New England, New France, and the New Netherlands.[4]

Actually, its name was somewhat premature and the intention did not prosper.[5] But the name Nova Scotia endured on the east coast, where a later emigration of Scots ensured its permanence and validity. Early in the nineteenth century a Scottish explorer named a "New Caledonia" on the west coast of what became British North America in 1763.[6] By the end of the nineteenth century there were Scottish names of every description in many regions of Canada, which a writer later referred to as the most fundamental part of a "Scottish Empire."[7]

His judgment, credible in view of the record of Scottish achievement in Canada, has been largely shared by several other authors.[8] It was made possible by consistent emigration and widespread settlement over three centuries. There were many reasons for this movement—economic, political, social, religious—relating to events both in Scotland and Canada. The Scottish character and customs of early settlers were well suited to survival in a pioneering environment. In fact, an outstanding number of them prospered, so that a confident Scottish welcome could be extended to the large numbers of their countrymen who came to Canada after them.

Until after 1900, the country was mainly inhabited by British, French, and the native Indian population. Of the British stock, the Welsh were always the minority group, and the Scottish were outnumbered by the English and Irish.[9] All were an integral part of Britain and its Empire and the majority were loyal to the monarchy. Indeed, the Nova Scotia venture had illustrated that Scotland could not pursue an independent foreign policy or maintain a colony without English diplomatic support.[10] Yet in Canada, the Scots were able to retain their distinct culture to a remarkable extent within the British framework, and to exercise an influence out of proportion to their number, as Pierre Berton has succinctly indicated.[11] Small wonder, then, that Scottish associations and clubs of every kind covered all parts of the Dominion before the twentieth century, especially since the first had been formed as early as 1768 in Halifax, Nova Scotia.[12] In fact, probably nowhere outside of the United Kingdom could a Scot have felt more at home than in nineteenth-century Canada.

One of the major reasons for the appearance of the Scots on the North American continent at all, of course, was dissatisfaction with their own homeland. This did not apply so much to the seventeenth century, when the fact was that more Scots emigrated by compulsion rather than of their own free will, being transported as criminals or political offenders. But in the eighteenth century "A New Order in the Highlands" caused a greater Scottish exodus, both compulsory and voluntary.[13]

The old order was the clan system, with the chief, who owned the land; his intermediary the tacksman (usually a relative), who managed his affairs; and the clansmen who were his tenants. This dependence of lesser men on greater men gave cohesion to Highland society, long after it had disappeared elsewhere. Clans were indeed "ready-made fighting units," and some clans rallied to the cause of the House of Stuart in the Jacobite Risings of 1715 and 1745 on behalf of the Old Pretender, James II's son, and the Young Pretender, his grandson.[14] Compulsory and voluntary emigration on a large scale from the Highlands followed their final defeat at Culloden in 1746, but Jacobitism was not the sole cause:

> The Jacobite risings, just because they are one of the episodes in Scottish history of which everyone has heard, are too readily regarded as the explanation of changes which in truth had other causes, and in particular the reasons for individuals and groups of people leaving the Highlands or leaving Scotland, are too often assigned to the aftermath of Jacobitism. This persistent error extends across the Atlantic.[15]

The Scottish nation as a whole did not support the Jacobite cause, which was not even a Highland movement in the sense that all the Highlanders supported it. Prince Charles's support came from a relatively small area, and there were only about 5,000 men in his army at Culloden at a time when the population of the Highlands was around 30,000 people. A great many Scots, Highland and Lowland, fought in the government army, which was not an "English" Army.[16] And it was not a military defeat which transformed Highland society—a transformation which began before the Forty-Five Rebellion.

From 1725, General Wade was responsible for the administration in the Highlands, becoming famous for his road making there.[17] But he also recruited for service members of the Clans which had been loyal to the government, and in 1739 ten companies of these were formed into the Black Watch Regiment.[18] This was the first of many regiments of Scottish Highlanders that later gained fame in many of Britain's wars; regiments which also had significant roles to play in the pattern of Scottish emigration and settlement. Around this time, too, the tacksman came to be seen as an unnecessary middleman, and the process of eliminating him from the structure of estate management seems to have begun in Argyll in the 1730s, and to have continued in various areas for a half-century. Before the Forty-Five, also, came the introduction of industries to provide peaceful occupations, such as lead mining and iron smelting, and the manufacture of linen was expanded. Agricultural innovations included the introduction of the potato. Also, in the thirty years between the two rebellions, the Presbyterian church gained in influence at the expense of areas which were Episcopalian and Roman Catholic.[19]

After 1746, all these changes ''were accelerated and intensified.'' The traditional clan structure was overthrown in Scotland by the government commissioners who administered the estates previously owned by chiefs loyal to Prince Charles, which had been annexed to the Crown. These commissioners made many alterations to Highland landholding and agriculture and further expanded the linen industry and road system. A major development was the advent of sheep raising in the Highlands, where previously the tenants had concentrated on cattle. The Industrial Revolution, with its vast concentration of population in new towns, had increased the demand for mutton as food, and wool was a prized commodity also. From the 1760s onwards, Lowland sheep-farmers began to stock the hills, for the simple motive of profit, and the values of the estates increased accordingly. This led to vast social changes, for the advance of sheep inevitably involved the retreat of men.[20] Many of the men involved retreated to the colonies,[21] especially across the Atlantic, and particularly (after 1783) to Canada. Here the Highlanders found the largest and most enduring refuge for their way of life, where for a time the clan system lingered on longer than in its native land. The bitterness of their dispossession and indignity of their plight is summed up in the brief quotation on the title-page of John Prebble's classic work, *The Highland Clearances*:

> Since you have preferred sheep to men,
> let sheep defend you![22]

In arable farming, too, there was a changeover to the crofting system, and as population increased, the crofts tended to become subdivided into increasingly smaller units. Although a small croft could sustain life by growing potatoes in a good year, it could not keep cattle, which previous tenants had sold to acquire their only cash for rents and so on. Another innovation was the kelp industry, which provided employment along a large part of the west coast of Scotland and the islands.[23]

These were the forces, then, that changed Scotland in the eighteenth century, many of which contributed to the loss of her sons and daughters overseas. Before 1783 the exodus was almost inevitably to the British colonies in America which were to form the United States, since there were as yet no other British possessions of any consequence. Most of Nova Scotia had indeed been ceded to Britain by France in 1713, but it was not until the 1760s, after the French had been dispossessed, that Scots began to multiply there.[24] Cape Breton Island and Prince Edward Island finally passed into British hands at the Treaty of Paris in 1763, along with the rest of New France (except Louisiana).

A party of Scottish settlers from the Highlands and Dumfries arrived in Prince Edward Island in 1767, to be joined by two more parties three years later. A band of a hundred Scottish

emigrants went to Nova Scotia in 1770. Twice this number arrived there from South Uist in 1772.[25] In this year also, John
MacDonald, the laird of Glenaladale, sold his estate in Scotland
and brought out 250 followers with him to Prince Edward
Island.[26]

> One migration shows the relation between Highlanders and
> Lowland entrepreneurs, for a Greenock merchant who had
> shares in a company which had been allotted 200,000 acres in
> Pictou County, Nova Scotia, offered a free passage, land and a
> year's provisions to Scottish Highlanders.[27]

Few canny Scots in distress at home would refuse such an offer,
and in 1773 some 180 Highlanders came out in the *Hector*.[28]
The vast majority of these early Scots tended to emigrate and con-
gregate in groups of the same religious faith, and from the same
areas of the homeland. They and their descendants

> filled in the lands on the Gulf coast. Other Highlanders, some
> Presbyterian, but many of them Roman Catholic, worked their
> way up into the fastnesses of Cape Breton. That island was to
> become another Scotland, whose very speech was Gaelic, as in
> many districts it remains. In this way, the eastern third of
> Nova Scotia including Cape Breton became veritably New
> Scotland.[29]

But in the eighteenth century this future veritable New
Scotland was not only being gradually filled with Scots from the
homeland overseas; they also came overland, from the American
Colonies and from Quebec, because of two developments which
greatly helped to foster settlement in Canada. Scottish Regiments
which had fought in the Seven Years War were disbanded when
the war ended, and many of the soldiers remained to settle in
Canada, thus forming a nucleus which in turn attracted others.
Secondly, the Scots in the United States who had not supported
the revolutionary party in the American war of Independence
found there was no longer a place for them there after 1783, and
with other United Empire Loyalists, removed to British North
America.

It has been claimed, in fact, that "the forerunners of the great emigration, apart from independent fur-traders, were the soldiers of the Fraser Highlanders, who after being disbanded in 1763 settled with their families in Canada."[30] The Fraser Highlanders, or 78th Regiment, saw its first service at Louisburg, where the Black Watch, or 42nd Regiment, also fought. The 77th Montgomeries were also shipped out with the Frasers and were sent on to attack Fort Duquesne. The Fraser Highlanders played a major part in the capture of Quebec by General Wolfe in 1759–60, wearing their full Highland dress. It was a Franco-Scot, Major de Ramezay, who handed the keys of the citadel of Quebec to Scottish General James Murray, who later earned the respect of French Canadians by his considerate treatment as Governor.[31] After the peace of 1763, many disbanded soldiers of the Frasers, Black Watch, and Montgomeries accepted offers of grants of land to settle in the newly conquered country, forming "a Scottish nucleus in Montreal, Quebec, and elsewhere. They attracted others."[32] This was a politic move, since from their settlements in years to come Canada was able to raise regiments of volunteers "whose loyalty and valour proved her salvation in her hour of need."[33] After 1783 the migrations northwards of the Loyalists provided more of such people. But before the Loyalists' presence was felt, Scottish explorers and merchants connected with the fur trade were establishing themselves in Canada and extending the white man's influence, largely French and Scottish, westward. As Lower has described it:

> In the fur trade, as later in lumbering and other activities, the Scotch and French, as masters and men, formed an irresistible combination.[34]

With the acquisition of British North America, "the enterprising Scot naturally coveted the still more profitable fur trade, some taste of which he had already known in Albany." It was more profitable than the American tobacco trade which was already in the hands of the so-called Virginia merchants of Glasgow. Alexander Henry, a native of the Scottish colony in New Jersey, actually accompanied General Amherst during his advance on

Montreal and saw the possibilities of this fur trade. He went to
Michilimackinac, a main trading centre for the West, in 1761
and joined forces with Jean Baptiste Cadotte of Sault Ste. Marie.
In 1765 he obtained a license for the trade of Lake Superior and,
with M. Cadotte and the brothers Frobisher, formed an alliance
which was the nucleus of the famous North-West Company. He
later navigated the Saskatchewan River into the Hudson's Bay
Company territory of Rupert's Land, and helped to pioneer the
development of the St. Lawrence fur-trading route to the North-
west. The story of his adventures and travels was published in
1807.[35]

Henry was typical of many early Scots who began to acquire
control of the fur trade in Canada. To prevent wasteful competition, most of the traders came to agreements and formed the joint
stock company known as the North-West Company in 1779,
which was reconstructed in 1783 with Simon McTavish and the
Frobisher brothers in control. During this organization period,
" . . . several of the retired officers of the 42nd and 78th joined
it. This service suited the adventurous spirit of the Gael, not less
than the Army or Navy."[36] McTavish had been engaged in the
fur trade at Albany, but moved to Montreal when the Quebec
Act of 1774 annexed fur-trading Indian territory. James McGill
was also one of the original partners in the North-West Company.
He had originally emigrated to Virginia but came north in 1774,
with his brothers John and Andrew, to engage in the fur trade.

Another group of Scots fur-traders was absorbed in 1787,
namely, Gregory, McLeod & Company, to whose firm
belonged Alexander Mackenzie, his cousin Roderick Mackenzie, James Finlay . . . and William McGillivray, nephew of
Simon McTavish himself.[37]

When his firm joined forces with the North-West Company,
"perhaps the most effective commercial organization that had
arisen in the New World,"[38] Alexander Mackenzie was trans-
ferred to Fort Chipewyan on Lake Athabasca. It was during his
tour of duty here that he made his two historic voyages to the
Arctic Sea and to the Pacific Ocean, and the Mackenzie River was

named after him.[39] (A later Scottish explorer, Simon Fraser, born in NewYork of Scottish parents, gave his name to another river from the Rockies to the Sea.[40] By the end of the century, the North-West Company "had an annual turnover of 120,000, employing 50 clerks, 71 interpreters and clerks, 1,120 canoemen, and 35 guides."[41]

Despite its efficiency, however, the North-West Company was not the first or the largest fur-trading company on the continent to employ Scots. The Hudson's Bay Company was at first an English company, which acquired its Scottish complexion later. Its main interest was the fur trade and it held rights over "all countries which lie within the entrance of Hudson's Straits, in whatever latitude they may be, so far as not possessed by other Christian States." In this vast area the company established fortified trading posts, usually on navigable rivers, stretching from the Labrador coast to the Pacific. The men it employed at first represented the only white population of that extensive domain.[42] Again, many of them were Scots, consisting "very largely of Orcadians, who were recruited when the Company's ships touched at the Orkneys before beginning their transatlantic voyages."[43] The North-West Company was formed as a rival to this older company, and the fierce competition between them was carried on until they merged in 1821.[44]

The attainment of independence by the thirteen colonies that became the United States meant that emigrants who wanted to live in British territory had to go elsewhere. This fact diverted much of Scottish emigration to Canada, and resulted in the influx of the United Empire Loyalists. Many were compelled to leave the United States before the war was over, and "by the spring of 1783 they were pouring over the frontier in their thousands." It has been estimated that no fewer than fifty thousand left their old homes during this migration.[45]

Some went abroad, but most of the Loyalists had to be accommodated within North America. Some settled in the part of Quebec which became Lower Canada in 1791, but this was predominantly French, and most settled elsewhere. The British Government also allocated free allotments of land in Nova Scotia to Loyalists. Such were the numbers that moved north from New

England, that in 1784 New Brunswick became a separate province. Upper Canada became a separate province, also, seven years later, where Loyalists had settled in the expanse of land along the northern shores of Lake Ontario. Among these new settlers were many Scots, and their arrival further consolidated the Scottish base in North America.[46]

Again, many of these were discharged soldiers, this time from regiments which had been active during the American War of Independence. After their discharge in 1783, the King's Royal Regiment of New York, which largely consisted of Catholic Highlanders from Glengarry in Scotland, migrated north to Upper Canada and founded Glengarry County.[47] This has been described as "the first distinctively Scottish settlement . . . in Ontario."[48] It became even more so when they were later joined by disbanded soldiers of the Royal Highland Emigrant Regiment, some five hundred Highlanders from Knoydent in 1786, and by more disbanded soldiers of the Glengarry Fencibles in 1803.[49] Many other Scots helped to fill up neighboring areas, including Lowland Presbyterians from Johnson's Regiment, and later the counties known as Dundas and Stormont were formed.[50] Demobilized men from Scottish regiments settled in parts of New Brunswick and Nova Scotia in 1783 and 1784. Other Loyalists, including Scots, sailed direct to Halifax in the spring and fall of 1783.[51]

These scattered Scots were to act as magnets for many of their countrymen still in Scotland. Their letters home (of which many still survive) often praised life in their new environment, and encouraged relatives and friends to join them. This provided the casual "pull" of emigration, which for some time diverted Scottish immigrants away from the United States and to British North America. And conditions and events in Scotland in the next century provided a dramatic "push."[52]

The changes which wrought the new order in the Highlands in the eighteenth century continued to have their effect after 1800. In fact, in common with the rest of Britain, the whole of Scotland underwent drastic changes in the nineteenth century, by the end of which its population had increased threefold to 4.5 million. There was above all a great economic expansion brought about by industrialization. The growth of railways corresponded with the advent and success of the heavy industries: coal, iron, ship-building, and engineering. The cotton industry expanded until superseded by Scotland's now famous jute and woolen industries. Goods were being specially manufactured for the colonists overseas, such as wrought iron work, leather goods, pottery and crystal, rope, hats, and furniture. In short, "the general pattern of Scottish industry in the nineteenth century, therefore, is one of progress and prosperity and of great opportunities for Scotsmen of capacity." There were agricultural changes, too, which made use of the new technology to increase efficiency.[53]

Yet the increase of collieries, factories, furnaces, and shipyards accentuated the ugly side of such progress. Overcrowding in the industrial centers of Scotland created slums to match those of industrial towns in England. Industries were prone to booms and slumps, and during the phases of depression," either generally or in particular industries, some men's minds naturally turned towards emigration."[54] Also, many of the agricultural changes led to a surplus of manpower in the countryside and consequent migration, particularly the notorious "Highland Clearances."[55] There were natural disasters, too, such as the failure of the potato crop in 1845 and again in 1882, which led to famine and emigration. In fact, emigration became a business in the nineteenth century which involved individuals, churches, companies, governments, and trade unions. The outcome of it all was that many more "Scotsmen of capacity" arrived to settle in Canada and take advantage of the "great opportunities" there.[56]

Emigration from the Highlands tended for many years to reflect the communal, close-knit character of Highland society. In the eighteenth century many tacksmen brought out their clans, and acted as their leaders in the New World.[57] Sometimes a chief came across the ocean, like Macnab of Kinnell in 1822, who arranged the acquisition of 5,000 acres in the County of Renfrew, on the Ottawa River. In 1824, he established a settlement of his own clansmen in McNab township and "lorded it over them very much as a tyrannical chief in Scotland might have done."[58] Sometimes their leaders were clergymen, like Angus MacEachern who led his people from North Uist to Prince Edward Island in 1790, and later became bishop of Prince Edward Island; or Alexander Macdonell, who brought settlers to Glengarry County in 1803, and later became bishop of Kingston, and first Catholic bishop of Upper Canada. The year before, no fewer than eight hundred Roman Catholics from Barra settled at Antigonish with their priests.[59]

Thomas Douglas, eighth Earl of Selkirk (1771–1820), provided another type of leadership. Although a Lowlander, he developed a concern for destitute Highlanders and a desire to assist their emigration and settlement in British North America. In 1803, he took about eight hundred of them from Skye, the Uists, and the mainland of Ross, Argyll, and Inverness. They landed at Orwell Bay in Prince Edward Island, and with Selkirk's leadership allied to their own pioneering efforts, the colony prospered. In the next year, Selkirk established another settlement by Lake St. Clair, which he named Baldoon after his estate in Scotland.[60] But he was really interested in a colony much further west, "at the western extremity of Canada, upon the waters which fell into Lake Winnipeg."[61] He bought shares in the Hudson's Bay Company in 1808, and three years later acquired from the company, for a nominal payment, no less than 166,000 square miles of land, and proposed a settlement on the Red River. By 1815, many shiploads of Scots, mostly evicted Highlanders, had settled there. But this vast tract lay right across the route to the fur country of the West, and the North-West Company objected strongly. For the next few years, life was unpleasant and dangerous for the Red River settlers, many of whom moved elsewhere after bloodshed and coercion. After legal battles, this famous dispute in Canadian history, which set Scot against Scot, was not settled until after Selkirk's death, when both companies merged under the name of the Hudson's Bay Company in 1821.[62]

A distinguished Canadian historian, A. R. M. Lower, has found this year of 1821 significant:

The men who were the bearers of the commercial state were mostly "old country" in origin: a few of English descent, most of Scottish. There was an occasional American, such as

Horatio Gates, the prominent merchant of the 1820's and 1830's. By 1821 a good many must have been native-born, but few of them, native-born or not, would have considered themselves "Canadians," a term of opprobrium which was reserved for the French. They were still Englishmen and Scotsmen overseas—colonials—and their living as a kind of garrison in a semi-hostile sea of 'natives' accentuated their colonial psychology.[63]

This was true in 1821, and it was to remain true for most of the nineteenth century, and for many good reasons.[64] (In fact, a national Canadian identity was to prove an elusive concept even in the twentieth century.)[65] Scottish emigration had not yet reached its peak. There were still thousands of immigrants from that "old country" yet to arrive, and many Scots had yet to join some of their predecessors in obtaining for themselves an indelible place in the history of their "new country." Throughout the nineteenth century there were Scottish cultural and social activities across the continent, which served to retain the traditions of the homeland and provide a sense of kinship and identity in the vast pioneering environment.

Even before 1821, however, Lower's "semi-hostile sea of 'natives' " was becoming less hostile in certain areas, and being transformed in neighborhoods inhabited more and more by their own kind. After 1815, the British government was anxious to foster the development of British North America. It was a time of economic difficulty at home and unemployment following the Napoleonic Wars; and after the War with the United States (1812–14), Britain wanted to protect the Canadian frontier. Accordingly, once more, regiments were disbanded and the soldiers with their families settled along the frontier, including men from the Royal Scots and the Royal Scots Fusiliers. The British government also granted free passages, 100 acres of land, foot rations, and agricultural implements to "industrious families" prepared to emigrate to Upper Canada. In 1815, about 250 people sailed from Greenock on these terms, and their settlements became the enduring community of Perth, southwest of Ottawa. Many others followed under the same scheme. In 1818, a group of 300 Scots settled in the Rice Lake district of Upper Canada. Distressed weavers from Scotland were also settled in Dalhousie, Lanark, and Ramsay, all in Upper Canada, in 1820. During this period, Scottish settlement also continued in New Brunswick, Nova Scotia, Cape Breton, and Prince Edward Island, such as the "New Glasgow" founded by weavers in Nova Scotia in 1819.[66]

Some Highlanders were settled on land granted to Colonel Talbot, a member of the lieutenant-governor's staff, in 1803, on the north side of Lake Erie. They were joined by others in later years, who provided the names of Campbeltown, Cowal, Crinan, and Iona, all in Elgin County, Ontario. Talbot apparently did not like Highlanders (one of them once threw him out of a window),[67] but they were available as a result of the clearances. But the community endured despite his malice, retaining its Scottish character and enabling one of its descendants, a most distinguished Harvard economist, to produce a pertinent and personal "memoir of the clansmen in Canada."[68] Also in Upper Canada was a Scot, William Dickson, who emigrated there in 1792 and practiced as a lawyer. He bought a block of nearly 100,000 acres there in 1816, and by the end of the following year there were thirty-eight families settled, mainly Scots from New York State. Dickson had been born in Dumfries, Scotland, which name was given to the area. But regarding emigration, "the greatest single impact made on Upper Canada was an effort which owed a great deal to the Scottish novelist, John Galt."[69] This came a few years later, and Dickson was also involved.

Also by 1821, there were many Scottish associations and societies in British North America, formed to commemorate Scottish patriotism. Membership was limited to "Scotsmen or descendants of Scotsmen who wish to become members."[70] The oldest such institution, already referred to, was the North British Society, or Scots Club, of Halifax, Nova Scotia, instituted on 26 March 1768, by "the natives of Scotland and those descended from Scots parentage in the Town of Halifax":[71]

> As is well known the Scottish element predominated in Halifax from the period of its settlement down to a recent date, giving to the community most of its leading men, and main-

taining the good fellowship and charitable disposition which generally characterize that element.

The objects which our founders had in view appear to have been the assistance of Scottish emigrants landing in the Colony, and the establishment of a medium of communication with kindred societies in the neighbouring Province . . . as well as the maintenance of a friendly feeling among the Scotchmen resident in the community, and those who visited the country for the purpose of trade.[72]

Although preceded by many counterparts in the United States,[73] this was the first of many such Scottish Societies which spread across Canada throughout the nineteenth century, such as Highland Societies, St. Andrew's Societies, the Sons of Scotland, Caledonian Clubs, the Royal Order of Scottish Clans, and numerous individual clan associations. In fact, no other ethnic immigrant group could match the Scots in the number, variety, and membership of their cultural societies. Besides the assistance of newly arrived Scottish immigrants, they also cultivated Scottish literature and customs, and consistently observed the unique celebrations of Scotland, e.g., Burns night, St. Andrew's Day, and Hogmanay (New Year's Eve). In particular, they were the foremost agencies for the appearance and sponsorship of Scottish sports in the New World, and the maintenance of their country's social traditions.[74] The St. Andrew's Society of St. John, New Brunswick, was founded there on 8 March 1798.[75] The very active Reverend Father Macdonell of Glengarry, whose other endeavors have been mentioned, also organized a Highland Society there in 1819, which held many successful gatherings before ". . . it was allowed to lapse" and was "resuscitated in 1843."[76] Around the time of its revival, there began a great expansion of Scottish societies, particularly at first in the Upper Canada region, but later following Western settlement across Canada.[77]

Scots in Canada during the nineteenth century also had their own books, newspapers, and periodicals to make them feel more at home.[78] The first Gaelic book known to have been written and published in the New World was printed at Pictou, Nova Scotia, in 1836, and entitled *Companach an Oganaich, no An Com-hairliche Taitneach* (The Youth's Companion; or, The Friendly Counsellor). The author was MacGillivray, a six-foot-five Highlander from a talented family. In 1840, there was a Gaelic newspaper by the name of *Cuairtear na Coille* (The Forest Traveller) in Ontario, and another named *Am Fear-Teagaisg* (The Teacher) in 1850.[79] The fiery Scot George Brown first issued a Presbyterian weekly there when he emigrated to Canada after living briefly in New York. But on 5 March 1844 he published the first issue of the *Toronto Globe* as a weekly Liberal paper, which became a daily one in 1853. Brown became a famous leader in the Reform (Liberal) party, which many Scots supported, and the *Globe* became known as *"the Scotchman's Bible."*[80] Probably the most appealing publication of all to Scots in North America, however, was the *Scottish-American Journal*. This circulated in Canada and the United States and reported current Scottish events of both countries, as well as Scotland.[81] A Gaelic magazine was published by John Boyd of Antigonish in 1851, and in the next year he brought out a weekly newspaper, *The Casket*. This innovation still had editorials, songs, and stories written in Gaelic, but the news section was written in English. Boyd admitted that the Gaelic language was yielding to English rapidly at this time, as Scottish youngsters in Antigonish County "had acquired English and no longer took any great interest in the language of their parents."[82] Another Scot, Angus Nicholson, edited an English paper in Toronto, Ontario, which carried occasional Gaelic columns, *Albannach Chanada: The Canada Scotsman*. In 1871, he brought out the first issue of *An Gaidheal* (The Gael), devoted entirely to material of interest to Highlanders, which obtained subscribers in New Brunswick, Nova Scotia, Ontario, Prince Edward Island, and Quebec (as well as in Illinois, Michigan, and North Carolina in the United States).[83] Highlanders undoubtedly lost the Gaelic through generations of settlement in Canada, but it never completely disappeared. The market for *An Gaidheal* from 1871, four years after Confederation, is an indication of why the Gaelic language has survived today in the Maritime Provinces. During the nineteenth century, whether in English or Gaelic, there was material enough in print to preserve a Scottish character in Canada and complement the efforts of the Scottish societies.

The ''garrison'' of Lower's Scottish colonials of 1821, in fact, in a ''semi-hostile sea,'' was destined to become far more homely. Events in Britain and Canada afterwards ensured a constant supply of eligible members for Scottish societies and prospective readers of Scottish news. Emigration, continued as government policy, supported by official propaganda, organized by an increasing number of emigration societies, became a source of revenue for shipping companies and others, and was now a process that could never be reversed.

The ''push'' for emigrants from Britain became stronger as the nineteenth century progressed, allied with a more established and confident ''pull'' from Canada. Various writers in the Old Country recommended emigration as a solution to many problems. The Under-Secretary for War and Colonies even advocated, in his writings between 1823 and 1830, ''the removal of paupers to Canada on the ground that this would in the long run cost less than maintaining them at home.''[84] This deplorable policy, bitterly resented in Cape Breton and elsewhere,[85] did not long continue. But many other companies set up to organize emigration were active, such as the North American Colonial Committee (1840), the British American Association for Emigration and Colonization (1841, with predominantly Scottish membership), the Highlands and Islands Emigration Society (1852), and even such Scottish denominational ones as the Protestant Emigration Society of Glasgow (1840), the Glasgow Protestant Canadian Emigration Society (1841), and the Glasgow Wesleyan Emigration Society (1841). Some trade unions even organized emigration of their members to relieve unemployment at home, among them the Scottish Typographical Union in 1858.[86]

Emigration was indeed a thriving business, especially for the shipping companies catering for the increasing numbers of emigrants. They often ''found it profitable to send a smooth-tongued salesman among the Highlanders to gather up human cargo.''[87] Aided by more published propaganda, many of these agents profited from the misery of their own countrymen. One of the most notorious was Archibald McNiven in Islay, who claimed to have transported twelve thousand Highlanders between 1821 and 1832 to Cape Breton, Nova Scotia, Prince Edward Island, and Upper Canada.[88] Conditions for emigrants on the early sailing ships were extremely bad, and the voyages from British ports to North America could take anywhere from three weeks to three months. At the end of their journey their troubles were not always over, either, for "major immigration centres like New York, Quebec and Montreal were infested with adventurers and rogues of all kinds waiting to prey on the new arrivals."[89] But voyage conditions improved when steamships began to ply the Atlantic; by the 1870s most transatlantic emigrants were travelling by them, and a ten-day crossing was common.[90] Also, the Scottish societies in Canada often eased the arrival of their countrymen as a part of their duties:

> In 1873, on May 10th, the steamer *Castalia*, of the Anchor Line, arrived at St. John with 565 emigrants from the east of Scotland. They were to be settled on the upper waters of the river St. John, and were known as the Kincardineshire Colony. The society gave these immigrants a warm welcome and a good send-off up the river to Fredericton.[91]

The provincial governments in Canada, and later the Dominion Government, also played their parts in wooing the emigrant.[92] The "pull" was characterized by the offer of free or cheap land, by a system of assisted passages, by bonuses and commissions to agents and settlers, by colonization companies, and other means.[93] The first-mentioned offer greatly appealed to Highland Scots, who became distinguished by their "land-hunger."[94] One famous Scottish entrepreneur helped to satisfy his countrymen in this respect on a large scale, similar to the previous efforts of Lord Selkirk.

John Galt, a native of Greenock in Scotland, was the founder and first superintendent of the Canada Company in Upper Canada, 1824 (chartered in 1826). He was also later involved in the British American Land Company (chartered in 1834) in Lower Canada. Among his associates were Dr. William Dunlop and William Dickson, already mentioned, who gave the name

"Galt" to the chief place in his Dumfries settlement. From their efforts came the colonization of a vast area—over a million acres—lying between Lake Huron on the northwest and Lakes Erie and Ontario on the south.[95] A social potpourri of Scots, Irish, English, Welsh, Belgian, and German were eventually settled there; and the towns of Dundas, Galt, Goderich, Guelph, and Hamilton developed in this settlement. There are many other place-names in Ontario which reveal the Scottish origins of early settlers, among them Arnprior, Arran, Athol, Carrick, Crawford, Douglas, Dunrobin, Dunvegan, Elderslie, Glencoe, Greenock, Haliburton, Paisley, and Renfrew. Both Orkney and Shetland are also commemorated in the province, and in Lanark County are rivers named the Clyde and the Tay. On the shores of Lake Huron there are three villages called Annan, Johnstone, and Leith.[96]

The name "Douglas" in Ontario also appears in five other Canadian provinces, but the strongest individual connection is in British Columbia, after another famous Scot in Canadian history, Sir James Douglas.[97] He distinguished himself as a young man in the fur trade in New Caledonia, and later became first governor of Vancouver Island in 1851, and of British Columbia when it became a colony in 1858. In that year, approximately twenty thousand people landed at Victoria "on their way to the gold diggings."[98] Douglas was the force behind the construction of roads into the interior, to provide food for the miners and to maintain order, which also encouraged settlement and the mining industry. He also encouraged Scottish settlers, many of whom also prospered on the west coast. By 1865 it was said of Vancouver:

> The Scotch, who are numerous in this city, are represented by a St. Andrew Society, established for affording relief to their needy countrymen, and the annual dinner connected with that institution is the most popular celebration of the sort in Vancouver.[99]

British Columbia, in fact, was destined to become the Canadian province which, after the maritime provinces, had the highest percentage of Scots in its population. The province entered Confederation in 1871, the year in which the first Dominion census was taken, showing Canada to have a population exceeding 3.5 million. In 1840, it had only been 1.5 million.[100] By Confederation in 1867 the Scots were particularly well dispersed across the Dominion, from Cape Breton Island in the east to Vancouver Island in the west.

As we have seen, many individuals among these Scottish colonists attained distinction in all parts of their adopted country; too many, in fact, to mention them all.[101] Apart from the fur trade and the military, Scots also "shared vigorously in the politics of Canada's formative years."[102] And any impression that the Scots were one big, united and happy ethnic family group in Canada must be dispelled. This was not the case, any more than it had been in Scotland itself. The commercial interests of the Scots-dominated trading companies had sometimes conflicted, and Scots had fought on both sides in some military campaigns in the New World. So, too, in politics and religion there were differences between Scots which set them against each other. This was especially true in Upper Canada, later Ontario, a province which happened "to attract a number of fiery Scots who did much to enliven its history."[103] But often there was cooperation and compromise between certain fiery Scots, which played a significant part in Canadian history, also.

In 1820, two Scots landed in Canada who were to play very different parts in Canadian history, John A. Macdonald and William Lyon Mackenzie.[104] Four years after his arrival, Mackenzie established the *Colonial Advocate* as the organ of the Reform Party, and led the English-speaking attacks against the oligarchy in Upper Canada, the Family Compact. He became Mayor of Toronto in 1835 (the name given to the former town of York in 1834), and led the Rebellion of 1837. This failed and Mackenzie fled to the United States. Yet this, in turn, paradoxically led to the Durham Report and the granting of responsible government. Its establishment was also

> due largely to the Scot, Lord Elgin, who served as Governor-General during a critical seven years notable for the tact and diplomacy with which he conciliated French and English, Scots and Irish, Tories and Reformers.[105]

Scottish tact and diplomacy were not always evident around this time. Robert Gourlay was another Scottish radical like Mackenzie, even though they had their differences, but both saved most of their wrath for their fellow countryman John Strachan. Gourlay once referred to him as "that lying little fool of a renegade Presbyterian" and Mackenzie called him "a diminutive, paltry, insignificant Scotch turn-coat parish schoolmaster,"[106] mainly because of Strachan's allegiance to the conservative position and alliance with the Family Compact. Another fellow Scot, John Galt, had actually tried first to obtain "crown and clergy reserves" land for his Upper Canada Settlement already mentioned, but was successfully opposed in this by Strachan.[107]

Whatever else he may have been, Strachan was hardly insignificant. Originally a native of Aberdeen, he came to Kingston at the age of twenty-one, in 1799. After teaching privately for a while, he then decided to take orders in the Episcopal Church, even though his mother was Presbyterian. He was ordained a deacon in 1805, a priest in 1806, and later became the bishop of Toronto, nicknamed "The fighting Bishop."[108] Strachan was first president of the Canadian Board of Education, in 1823, the founder of many schools and universities, and has been described as "Canada's greatest educationalist of the first half of the nineteenth century."[109] In fact, the efforts of Strachan and other Scots stirred a Scottish author to claim an educational reason, among others, for regarding Canada as a "New Scotland":

> In all grades of our educational development from the University to the common school, the personality and influence of the Scotsman have been prominent. It is a significant fact in our intellectual history, and one remarkable in the history of any young country, that all our leading Universities, with scarcely one exception, and our other higher institutions of learning, have been from the first established and controlled by Scotsmen. This fact, more than any other, shows to how great an extent Canada has been a New Scotland in character and ideal.[110]

These institutions were either independent, or, reflecting the diversity from "renegade Presbyterian" to Roman Catholic, were variously connected with different churches in Canada.[111]

Strachan was involved in solely religious disputes, also. The first Presbyterian ministers to arrive in Upper Canada direct from Scotland had been secessionists from the Church of Scotland, whose ministers did not arrive in any numbers until the later 1820s. There was hostility between the two, and the Church of Scotland had few in its congregations. Its claims for equality with the Church of England, therefore, were opposed by Strachan; and by Charles Stewart, the Anglican bishop of Quebec, another Scot. (Strachan had good relationships with yet another Scottish bishop already mentioned, Macdonell, the Roman Catholic bishop of Upper Canada.)[112] When the disruption occurred in Scotland in 1843,[113] many congregations in Canada also went over to the Free Church. However, here the schism ended in 1875, when the eleven separate Presbyterian Churches in Canada united to form one self-governing national church—the Presbyterian Church in Canada—an achievement which S. D. Clark refers to as ''spectacular,'' although he goes on to point out that ''the period from 1850 to 1885 was one characterized by a growing national consciousness within all the churches in Canada.''[114]

It was during this period, also, that Confederation in 1867 provided Canada with its greatest sense of national consciousness. The first prime minister of the new Dominion of Canada was John A. Macdonald, probably the most famous figure in Canadian history, certainly the one who dominated the nineteenth century.[115] A flattering but not altogether inaccurate summary of this remarkable Scot's career is given in the dedication of one of the many books devoted to him:

> This is the story of how Sir John A. Macdonald conciliated Nova Scotia, acquired the North-West Territories, created the province of Manitoba, induced British Columbia and Prince Edward Island to enter Confederation, and built a nation which extended from sea to sea.[116]

Obviously, he had a lot of help, but nevertheless his contribution was indeed remarkable. No man did more to bring about Confederation, or make it work, and retain Canada's links with Britain. Yet he was very Scottish, and had apparently little regard for Englishmen.[117] And when Lord Sydenham came to Kingston in 1841 to open the first Parliament of the United Canadas, Macdonald represented the St. Andrew's Society and was dressed in a kilt.[118] Most of his closest associates were also Scots, as were some of his most vociferous opponents. George Brown was the leader of the left-wing Clear Grits who opposed the Liberal-Conservative Coalition with some success, but when it became clear that no administration could sustain a majority in both Canada East and Canada West, he suggested a federation of party leaders, which eventually paved the way towards Confederation.

Macdonald was prime minister from 1867 to 1873, and from 1878 to 1891. In the interim period, Canada had another Scottish prime minister in the person of the Liberal Alexander Mackenzie.[119] It was during their tenure that the CPR railway was built, a project about which Macdonald himself said: "Until this great work is completed, our Dominion is little more than a 'geographical expression.' "[120] Once again, many Scots were greatly involved in this most significant feature of Canadian history.[121]

It was completed, and at a place in British Columbia specially named "Craigellachie." The American vice-president and general manager of the CPR, William Cornelius Van Horne, had a private but valid reason to call it thus, after a Scottish poem which began: "Not until Craigellachie shall move from his firm base."[122] The famous last spike was driven home by Donald A. Smith (later Lord Strathcona), perhaps John A. Macdonald's main Scottish rival for the center stage in Canadian history.[123] The camera's record of this incident has been described as "The Great Canadian Photograph."[124] It was the climax to four and a half years' effort by some thirty thousand sweating laborers—"French and English, Scots and Irish, Italians and Slavs, Swedes and Yankee, Canadians and Chinese"[125]—nationalities due to become all "Canadians" in the future, in a country united from the Atlantic to the Pacific.

All had played their part. Yet there had been a Scottish theme from first to last, from Nova Scotia in 1621, through to Craigellachie (in what used to be New Caledonia) in 1885. The CPR created many new towns in the West, and some new Scottish names, such as Banff and Calgary (Gaelic for "clear running water"), appeared to take their place with all the others previously mentioned. Its metal cars travelled on steel rails alongside the rivers in which the fur traders had paddled their canoes. Scots had been prominent in this transition, as noted when Donald A. Smith was about to drive the last spike:

> The old fur trader represented much more than the CPR. His presence recalled that long line of Highlanders—the Mackenzies and McTavishes, Stuarts and McGillivrays, Frasers, Finlaysons, McLeods and McLaughlins—who had first penetrated these mountains and set the transcontinental pattern of communication that the railway would continue.[126]

But perhaps the Scottish element in Canadian life has been captured best of all, and for all time, in the five verses of the *Canadian Boat Song*. The author is not known, although the poem is usually credited to either John Galt, the Scottish novelist who founded the Canada Company in Upper Canada, or his friend, David Macbeth Moir, the Musselburgh doctor.[127] The most exquisite and often-quoted verse runs:

> From the lone shieling of the misty island
> Mountains divide us, and a waste of seas;
> Yet still the blood is strong, the heart is Highland,
> And we in dreams behold the Hebrides.

> *Chorus*:

> Fair these broad meads—these heavy woods are grand,
> But we are exiles from our fathers' land.[128]

Whether written by a Highland or a Lowland Scot, as James Roy has stated in *The Scot and Canada*, "These few words express much of the sorrow and suffering on which Canada has been built."[129]

What was the explanation of "the dominance of the Scot in pioneer Canada"? Why was it that "Scots and their descendants played an important role in the development of Canada"? By the year 1871, there were 550,00 people of Scottish origin in

Canada, including native Canadians of Scottish male descent, forming only 15.8 percent of the total population. Theirs was patently not the only important role, but it was uncommonly effective, as C. W. Dunn has tactfully pointed out in the *Encyclopedia Canadiana*:

> That is not to say that their contribution was remarkable just because they were Scots, or that people of other origins in like circumstances would have failed to make a somewhat similar contribution. But it is probably true to say that their contribution has been disproportionately large in comparison to their numbers.[130]

The reason for the "disproportionately large" contribution and the outstanding place of the Scots in Canadian history is found in the Scottish character, the pioneering environment, and the pattern of settlement.

Much has been written of the Scottish character, and much of it by Scots themselves. A Scotsman "has been unable to conceal the fact that he has a 'gude conceit' of himself'' at home and abroad.[131] A great many humorous stories are told about his alleged meanness—again, largely by Scots themselves. Many would say that Scots are not mean, only very careful. The Scottish adjective "canny" reflects this care and may be equated with showing prudence and demonstrating shrewdness. Yet generosity is another trait demonstrated far and frequently by Scotsmen. They have been pictured as a nation of "grave—livers Calvinistic curmudgeons, Pharisees and Palistines, Presbyterians and Prohibitionists, Malvolios,"[132] noted for being dour, reticent, and taciturn. Sobriety has been everywhere associated with the Scot; and so has his native whisky. The Scottish climate is said to have much to do with its distinctive taste, and one Scot gives it as a reason for its consumption by his countrymen:

> Indeed it is likely that our long dark winters have given us a hearty propensity for the compensations of good cheer. We often say that every Scot is a Calvinist so far as his conscience is concerned, that he cannot enjoy himself without feeling the "agenbite of inwit," the kick-back of remorse. But many a

normal hangover has been mistaken for a Calvinistic conscience.[133]

Writers throughout history have grappled with the complexities and contradictions of the Scottish character. As an analytical Albert Mackie has observed:

> Our nature, however, is full of contradictions. Life north of the Tartan Curtain can be as sober as Sabbath blacks and the next moment as gay as a swinging kilt. Our solemnity is a device to keep in check our talent for whooping it up. . . . It is said of a Scot, when he is happy, either through an acquisition of wealth or of health, or through the sheer euphoria which comes of imbibing the national beverage, that ''he wadna ca' the king his cousin.''[134]

The phrase ''acquisition of wealth'' is significant. The outstanding proclivity exhibited by Scotsmen in all the countries in which they have settled is an acquisitive nature, not only for wealth or health, but for land, education and, status. Allied with this acquisitiveness has been another well-attested trait, the Scotsman's propensity for hard work. The two tendencies have formed a devastating combination, in conjunction with a traditionally puritanical upbringing and moral way of life, beautifully summed up in a ''Prayer attributed to a Scot'':

> O Lord, we do not ask you to give us wealth,
> but show us where it is.[135]

Once shown that way, whether in the fur trade or banking or any form of business, politics, or professional life, the Scot pursued his objective with a single-minded tenacity of purpose and absolute devotion to its accomplishment, in unequaled fashion. He expected no favors once he had been granted an equal opportunity.

This talent for rising up through their own efforts and sacrifice has been demonstrated by many Scots in Canada and other countries. John A. Macdonald was the son of an evicted Sutherland crofter, who was brought to Canada at the age of five and left school at the age of fifteen. He studied while he worked, and was admitted to the Bar at the age of twenty-one. Then came his meteoric rise in politics, and in 1884, on the fortieth anniversary of his entrance into parliamentary life, the award of a G.C.B. In the following year he saw the completion of the CPR, with which he had been so involved. At his death in 1891, he was assured of an immortal place in Canadian history, one that could not have been foreseen from his humble origins.[136] Donald A. Smith was a low-paid clerk with the Hudson's Bay Company in 1838, promoted to be a chief factor in 1862, and head of the Company's Montreal department in 1868. He went on to become a member of the federal parliament for several years, and in 1897 was created a baron, as Lord Strathcona and Mount Royal. His acquisition of company shares over the years, and business acumen and enterprise in the new railways, enabled him to become one of the richest men in Canada—a nation which has benefited considerably from his many philanthropic endowments.[137] Alexander Mackenzie, prime minister from 1873 to 1878, was a former stonemason; and his namesake who achieved distinction of a different sort, William Lyon Mackenzie, was the son of poor parents.[138] Sir Hugh Allan was a penniless, half-educated Scottish boy who amassed a great fortune through his Montreal Steamship Company, popularly called the Allan Line.[139] There are many other instances in Canadian history of Scots of lowly beginnings who applied themselves successfully in many fields, of which the above are famous examples. George Stephen was another, a former draper's assistant who became president of the Bank of Montreal, and president of the CPR, before being created Lord Mountstephen.[140] When he was presented with the freedom of the city of Aberdeen, Stephen commented:

> Any success I may have had in life is due in great measure to the somewhat spartan training I received during my Aberdeen apprenticeship, in which I entered as a boy of 15. . . . It was impressed upon me from my earliest years by one of the best mothers that ever lived that I must aim at being a thorough master of the work by which I had to get my living; and to be that I must concentrate my whole energies on my work, whatever that might be, to the exclusion of every other thing. I soon discovered that if I ever accomplished anything in life it

would be by pursuing my object with a persistent determination to attain it.[141]

Work, indeed, was the real religion of the majority of Scots. Since hard work is inevitable in a pioneering environment, which also held out the promise of abundant future opportunities, the Scots thrived. To quote again from Berton in his so apt judgment:

> It was this hard ethic, so forcefully expressed by Stephen, that explains the dominance of the Scot in pioneer Canada. . . . For the Scots it was work, save and study; study, save and work. . . . [They were] living embodiments of the popular copy book maxims of the time . . . Waste not, want not . . . Satan finds more mischief still for idle hands to do . . . God helps those that help themselves . . . A penny saved is a penny earned . . . Remember that time is money . . . Early to bed, early to rise . . . Keep your nose to the grindstone . . . See a pin and pick it up.[142]

The Scots had also been inured to hardship in their own country. Poverty and a harsh climate were no strangers to Highlanders in particular. As R. C. MacDonald has pointed out:

> Perhaps there are no race of people better adapted to the climate of North America than that of the Highlands of Scotland. The habits, employments, and customs of the Highlander seem to fit him for the American forest, which he penetrates without feeling the gloom and melancholy experienced by those who have been brought up in towns and amidst the fertile fields of highly cultivated districts.
>
> Scotch emigrants are hardy, industrious, and cheerful, and experience has fully proved that no people meet the first difficulties of settling wild lands with greater patience and fortitude.[143]

They also had a big advantage in ''settling wild lands'' in North America, in that many of their settlements were formed from the outset of whole communities transported intact from Scotland. Clans arrived complete with chief or tacksmen, and ministers, to begin their new life in a strange environment; made less strange, of course, by the familiar company of each other. Most other settlers came as single individuals or families, and ''their adjustments were slowly and painfully made . . . and lacked the group supports enjoyed by the Highland Scots.'' This tendency to settle together enabled Scots to resist many of the disorganizing effects of new social conditions.[144]

The *Encyclopedia Canadiana* of 1968 states that:

> The proportion of people of Scottish origin in Canada is now only 11 p.c. . . . and they are the most evenly distributed group in the Canadian population . . . and Canada's largest city, Montreal, is still facetiously described as ''a city of a million Frenchman ruled by a dozen Scottish bankers.''[145]

As we have seen, this even distribution of the Scottish population in Canada began in the earliest years of colonization, as Scots from the homeland and the United States permeated the British North American continent. By the time of Confederation in 1867, their influence had been felt everywhere in Canada. As communications improved further, so were Scots better able to contact their fellow countrymen around them. In this way, the cohesive feeling of an individual group settlement could be enlarged into a greater Scottish affinity and identity over a larger area. The increase in the formation of Scottish Societies already noted, and the contact between them, was a manifestation of this process.

The Scottish character, then, allied to a broad and well-established pattern of settlement, are factors which enabled the Scots to exert their disproportionately large influence in comparison to their numbers in Canadian history, especially before the twentieth century.

These were, too, part of the reason for an excessive Scottish prominence in sport in Canada during the nineteenth century. For also in the Scottish character, as indicated in chapter 2, was a love of sporting activity which had manifested itself in many ways for centuries in Scotland. It would have been indeed strange if this aspect of their culture had been neglected in Canada, but in fact this was far from being so. The Scottish Societies, like other fraternal orders of immigrant groups, "assisted individuals to hold fast to their native culture and helped to satisfy the nostalgic longings of strangers in a foreign land."[146] Sport was the most common element by which they accomplished this, and Scottish sports accompanied the pattern of settlement in Canada. And the Scots' unique position as an "Establishment" was reflected in the success of their sports in Canada. The reference to the "disproportionately large" Scottish influence in Canadian history in the *Encyclopedia Canadiana*, occurs in a long article entitled: *Scottish Origin, People of*. The article ends with the note: *"See also* Highland *Games."*[147] Other long articles in the *Encyclopedia Canadiana* are devoted to *Curling* and *Golf*.[148] Together with their contributions in other sports, the Scots exerted a disproportionately large athletic influence in Canada, especially in the nineteenth century. As in so many other aspects of Canadian heritage, in sport, too, it was largely a case of "By Way of Scotland."[149]

Notes

1. Gordon Donaldson, *The Scots Overseas* (London: Robert Hale, 1966) pp. 23–32. Also, John Murray Gibbon, *Canadian Mosaic: The Making of a Northern Nation* (Toronto: McClelland and Stewart, 1938), p. 78, states: William Lithgow, writing in the year 1632, says that at about that time there were 30,000 Scots families in Poland."

2. Donaldson, *Scots Overseas*, p. 29–30; Henry Jones Ford, *The Scotch-Irish in America* (New York: Peter Smith, 1941), pp. 2–41; Douglas Hill, *The Scots to Canada* (London: Gentry Books, 1972), pp. 1–2; William C. Lehmann, *Scottish and Scotch-Irish Contributions to Early American Life and Culture* (Port Washington, N.Y.: Kennikat Press 1978).

3. Ford, *Scotch-Irish*, pp. 165–208; Charles A. Hanna, *The Scotch-Irish* (New York and London: G. P. Putnam's Sons, 1902), pp. 6–15. In the nineteenth century, particularly, it was difficult to determine whether emigrants from Ulster should be identified as "Scotch" or "Irish." They were mainly Protestants of Scottish descent living in Northern Ireland, and variously described as "Protestant Irish," "Ulster Scots," "Scotch-Irish," or as simply "Scots" or "Irish." Arthur R. M. Lower distinguishes between "Catholic Irish" and "Ulstermen" or "northern Irish"; see Arthur R. M. Lower, *Colony to Nation: A History of Canada* (Toronto: Longmans, Green and Co., 1959), p. 192.

4. Donaldson, *Scots Overseas*, pp. 33–34; Gibbon, *Canadian Mosaic*, pp. 78–81.

5. The colony was surrendered in 1632 and the small band of Scottish settlers was evacuated. French sovereignty over Nova Scotia was then restored and lasted until 1713. See Donaldson, *Scots Overseas*, pp. 34–38; and Gibbon, *Canadian Mosaic*, pp. 78–81.

6. "But the earliest British visitors were stirred less by climate than by the

brooding heights and crags and the wild torrents that recalled their native land; and it was fitting that a Scot, Simon Fraser from Glengarry, should have named the region New Caledonia, a nostalgic title which was retained until the monopoly of the Hudson's Bay Company was ended, and a separate mainland colony established in 1858.'' Gerald S. Graham, *A Concise History of Canada* (New York: Viking Press, 1968), p. 34.

7. Andrew Dewar Gibb, *Scottish Empire* (London: Alexander Maclehose and Co., 1937), pp. 31–104.

8. An indication of the importance of the Scots in Canadian history is the large number of books dealing specifically with the topic. Indeed, there are many Canadian counterparts to the two works on Scots in America, i.e., George Fraser Black, *Scotland's Mark on America* (New York: The Scottish Section of ''America's Making,'' 1921); and Peter Ross, *The Scot in America* (New York: Raeburn Book Co., 1896). There are two large volumes entitled *The Scotsman in Canada*, published by The Musson Book Company of Toronto, no date given (probably 1911). The author of volume 1 was Wilfred Campbell, and of volume 2, George Bryce. There is also the massive work dealing with Scots in the American colonies before the War of Independence and thereater in Canada: W. J. Rattray, *The Scot in British North America*, 4 vols. (Toronto: Maclear and Co., 1880). Other similar works include: D. Campbell and R. A. Maclean, *Beyond the Atlantic Roar: A Study of the Nova Scotia Scots* (Toronto: McClelland and Stewart, 1974); Charles W. Dunn, *Highland Settler: A Portrait of the Scottish Gael in Nova Scotia* (University of Toronto Press, 1968); John Kenneth Galbraith, *The Non-Potable Scotch: A Memoir of the Clansmen in Canada* (Harmondsworth, Middlesex: Penguin Books, 1967); John Murray Gibbon, *Scots in Canada* (Toronto: Musson Book Co., 1911); J. M. LeMoine, *The Scot in New France: An Ethnological Study* (Montreal: Dawson Brothers, 1881); W. Stanford Reid, ed., *The Scottish Tradition in Canada* (Toronto: McClelland and Stewart, 1976); and James A. Roy, *The Scot and Canada* (Toronto: McClelland and Stewart, 1947). Also, besides Gibb, *Scottish Empire*, there are other works dealing with Scottish emigration all over the world which inevitably emphasize the Scottish contribution in Canada, such as Donaldson, *Scots Overseas*; and Wallace Notestein, *The Scot in History* (London: Jonathan Cape, 1946). To this list may be added the many biographies of famous Scots in Canadian history, e.g., George Brown, Sir John A. Macdonald, William Lyon Mackenzie, Lord Strathcona, and many more. General histories of Canada usually afford the Scots a prominent place; even histories of Scotland necessarily deal with Canada. Historical accounts of exploration, the fur trade, business, education, politics, religion, and sport usually mention Scottish influence as a matter of course. Histories of provinces, countries, cities, and towns in Canada where Scots settled in any numbers also provide information. Much of Canadian fiction has a Scottish flavor; one of the best known novels of this type is Ralph Connor, *The Man from Glengarry* (Toronto: McClelland and Stewart, 1967), first published in 1901. Obviously one cannot list *all* the authors and their works here who have written of the various contributions of the Scots in Canadian history, but an attempt will be made to mention a majority of the most significant.

9. Donaldson, *Scots Overseas*, p. 142.

10. Ibid., p. 38.

11. Pierre Berton, *The National Dream: The Great Railway, 1871–1881* (Toronto: McClelland and Stewart, 1970), p. 192.

12. See chapter 30, entitled ''Scottish Societies in Canada,'' in Wilfred Campbell, *The Scotsman in Canada*, vol. 1 (Toronto: Musson Book Co., n.d.), pp. 407–23; chapter 34, entitled ''Scottish Societies in Western Canada,'' in George Bryce, *The Scotsman in Canada*, vol. 2 (Toronto: Musson Book Co., n.d.), pp. 410–22; and chapter 12, entitled ''The Gaelic Tradition in Canadian Culture,'' by George S. Emmerson, in *The Scottish*

Tradition in Canada (Toronto: McClelland and Stewart, 1976), pp. 232–47. On the Halifax club, see James S. Macdonald, *Annals of the North British Society of Halifax, Nova Scotia* (Halifax, N.S.: "Citizen" Steam Book, Job and General Printing Office, 1868), pp. 5–7. However, it should be pointed out that many more were founded on the continent before the American War of Independence and the later emigration of the United Empire Loyalists. Donaldson, *Scots Overseas*, p. 44, states: "It is remarkable that as early as 1657 a Scots Charitable Society, with twenty-seven members, was established at Boston—surely the first of the many such societies which Scots were to found in all parts of the world." Scots had also established St. Andrew's Societies in Charleston (1729), Philadelphia (1747 or 1749), New York (1756), and Savannah (after 1750); see Donaldson, *Scots Overseas*, p. 44 and 104; and Peter Benedict Sheridan, Jr., "The Immigrant in Philadelphia, 1827–1860" (Ph.D. diss., Georgetown University, 1957), pp. 53–54. Donaldson, *Scots Overseas*, p. 130, also states that "most of the resident members of the Scots Charitable Society of Boston went off to Halifax, carrying the records of the Society with them."

13. Donaldson, *Scots Overseas*, pp. 38–56.

14. Ibid., pp. 47–48. There was another rising in 1708. Three recommended accounts of the Jacobite Rebellions are: George Hilton Jones, *The Main Stream of Jacobitism* (Cambridge, Mass.: Harvard University Press, 1954); Sir Charles Petrie, *The Jacobite Movement: The Last Phase, 1716–1807* (London: Eyre and Spottiswoode, 1950); and Christopher Sinclair-Stevenson, *Inglorious Rebellion: The Jacobite Risings of 1708, 1715 and 1719* (London: Hamish Hamilton, 1971).

15. Donaldson, *Scots Overseas*, p. 57.

16. John Prebble, *Culloden* (Hammondsworth, Middlesex: Penguin Books, 1967), pp. 11–141. Donaldson, *Scots Overseas*, pp. 49–50, states: "The main highland strength of Prince Charles' army lay in a relatively small area—Appin, Glencoe, Lochaber, Lochshiel and Moidart, inhabited largely by Stewarts, MacDonalds and Camerons, who were the hereditary foes of their neighbours, the Presbyterian and Hanoverian Clan Campbell."

17. J. B. Salmond, *Wade in Scotland* (Edinburgh: Moray Press, 1934). On the title page are two lines of verse:

> If you'd seen these roads before they were made,
> You'd lift up your hands, and bless General Wade.

18. James Browne, *The History of Scotland: Its Highlands, Regiments and Clans*, 8 vols. (Edinburgh: Francis A. Niccolls and Co., 1909, 7: 119–80. This is a chapter entitled "The Black Watch." Volumes 7 and 8 deal with nearly 50 Scottish Regiments.

19. Donaldson, *Scots Overseas*, pp. 49–54.

20. Ibid., pp. 52–53. See also: Henry Grey Graham, *The Social Life of Scotland in the Eighteenth Century* (London: Adam and Charles Black, 1969); and John Watson, *The Scot of the Eighteenth Century: His Religion and His Life* (London: Hodder and Stoughton, 1907). Sir Thomas More once made a bitter joke about sheep eating men which "turned out to be truer than he knew"; see Christopher Hill, *The Pelican Economic History of Britain*, vol. 2, *1530–1780, Reformation to Industrial Revolution* (Hammondsworth, Middlesex: Penguin Books, 1969), p. 69.

21. Apart from the American colonies, of course, Scots also went to Australia, New Zealand, and South Africa. See Donaldson, *Scots Overseas*, appendix A, p. 215, for a list of works dealing with Scottish emigration to these countries.

22. John Prebble, *The Highland Clearances* (Harmondsworth, Middlesex: Penguin Books, 1969). Then there is the verse by the anonymous author of the *Canadian Boat Song*:

When the bold kindred, in time long-vanish'd,
Conquer'd the soil and fortified the keep,
No seer foretold the children would be banish'd
That a degenerate lord might boast his sheep.

This apparently first appeared in *Blackwood's Edinburgh Magazine*, September 1829, and has since appeared in many Canadian histories.

23. Donaldson, *Scots Overseas*, p. 53. The kelp industry was concerned with the manufacture of alkali from the burning of seaweed, and was valuable for the manufacture of glass, soap, and alum as a substitute for barilla.

24. D. Campbell and R. A. Maclean, *Beyond the Atlantic Roar: A Study of the Nova Scotia Scots* (Toronto: McClelland and Stewart, 1974), pp. 35–75.

25. Arthur R. M. Lower, *Colony to Nation: A History of Canada* (Toronto: Longmans, Green and Co., 1959), pp. 62–76.

26. Charles W. Dunn, *Highland Settler: A Portrait of the Scottish Gael in Nova Scotia* (University of Toronto Press, 1969), p. 13. The author goes on to state: "they settled peacefully on the island, gained their independence, and prospered; in less than a hundred years the descendants of the original settlers numbered 3,000."

27. Donaldson, *Scots Overseas*, p. 67.

28. *Encyclopedia Canadiana*, 10 vols. (Grolier of Canada, 1968), 9: 248. Gibbon, *Canadian Mosaic*, has a copy of the painting by Charles Sheldon showing "Scots settlers landing from the brig Hector at Pictou, Nova Scotia, in 1773," facing page 81.

29. Lower, *Colony to Nation*, pp. 104–5.

30. *Encyclopedia Canadiana* (1968), 9: 248.

31. Gibbon, *Canadian Mosaic*, pp. 83–86. This is a brief but well-documented account of the Scottish part in the campaign. For a more detailed account, see Browne, *Regiments and Clans*, 7: 300–311.

32. Donaldson, *Scots Overseas*, p. 67.

33. Gibbon, *Canadian Mosaic*, p. 85. This policy was continued after the American War of Independence and War of 1812–14.

34. Lower, *Colony to Nation*, p. 133.

35. Gibbon, *Canadian Mosaic*, pp. 86–87. His book was entitled *Travels and Adventures in Canada and the Indian Territories, 1760–76* (1807). See also chapter 3, entitled "Alexander Henry, Fur Trader," in Edwin C. Guillet, *Early Life in Upper Canada* (Toronto: Ontario Publishing Co., 1933), pp. 24–34.

36. Gibbon, *Canadian Mosaic*, p. 88. See also Marjorie Wilkins Campbell, *The North West Company* (Toronto: Macmillan Co. of Canada, 1957).

37. Ibid. See also Marjorie Wilkins Campbell, *McGillivray: Lord of the Northwest* (Toronto: Clarke, Irwin and Co., 1962).

38. Gibbon, *Canadian Mosaic*, p. 88. The author is quoting from Chester Martin: "For secrecy of action, hard shrewd efficiency and complete unity of purpose, the North-West Company was perhaps the most effective commercial organization that had arisen in the New World."

39. Mackenzie published a *General History of the Fur Trade*, and *Voyage from Montreal through North America*, both in 1801. But more readily obtainable is W. Kaye Lamb, ed., *The Journals and Letters of Sir Alexander Mackenzie* (Toronto: Macmillan of Canada, 1970); and Alexander Mackenzie, *From Sea to Sea* (Don Mills, Ontario: Longman Canada, 1970).

40. Lower, *Colony to Nation*, p. 145; see also J. B. Brebner, *The Explorers of North America* (London: A. and C. Black, 1933).

41. Gibbon, *Canadian Mosaic*, p. 88.

42. A facsimile of the first sheet of the Company's famous charter appears between

pp. 6 and 7 of Sir William Schoaling, *The Hudson's Bay Company 1670–1920* (London: The Hudson's Bay Co., 1920). See also George Bryce, *The Remarkable History of the Hudson's Bay Company* (Toronto: William Briggs, 1900); Douglas MacKay, *The Honourable Company: A History of the Hudson's Bay Company* (London: Cassell and Company, 1937); and E. E. Rich, *History of the Hudson's Bay Company, 1670–1870*, 2 vols. (London: Hudson's Bay Record Society, 1958–59).

43. Donaldson, *Scots Overseas*, p. 137.

44. Gibbon, *Canadian Mosaic*, isolates the Scots' part in the fur trade very well, but for more detailed accounts of the parts played by the French *voyageurs* and the Indians, see H. A. Innis, *The Fur Trade in Canada* (Toronto: University of Toronto press, 1956); and E. E. Rich, *The Fur Trade and the Northwest, to 1857* (Toronto: McClelland and Stewart, 1967).

45. Donaldson, *Scots Overseas*, p. 130. See also A. G. Bradley, *The United Empire Loyalists* (London: Thornton Butterworth, 1932). The usual figures given are between 35,000 and 50,000; see part 3, "The Loyalists' Migrations," in chapter 10 of Lower, *Colony to Nation*, pp. 115–19.

46. Donaldson, *Scots Overseas*, pp. 130–31. For a concise, scholarly account of Scottish settlement throughout Canada, readers are referred to two chapters in *The Scottish Tradition in Canada* (1976); viz., K. J. Duncan, "Patterns of Settlement in the East," pp. 49–75; and Alan R. Turner, "Scottish Settlement of the West," pp. 76–91.

47. Edwin C. Guillet, *Early Life in Upper Canada* (Toronto: Ontario Publishing Co., 1933), pp. 35–47. This is a chapter entitled "The Glengarry Highlanders."

48. *Encyclopedia Canadiana* (1968) 9: 248.

49. Guillet, *Early Life*, pp. 39–46. However, Donaldson, *Scots Overseas*, p. 68, maintains that 520 Highlanders came out in 1785.

50. See John Graham Harkness, *Stormont, Dundas and Glengarry: A History, 1784–1945* (Oshawa, Ontario: Mundy Goodfellow Printing Co., 1946).

51. Donaldson, *Scots Overseas*, p. 131; Gibbon, *Canadian Mosaic*, p. 91.

52. Donaldson, *Scots Overseas*, pp. 64, 90–91, and appendix B, pp. 216–20. The author also states that enthusiastic individuals sometimes produced books or pamphlets praising a particular area, such as one circulating as early as 1773 in Ayrshire, Scotland, declaiming the virtues of Prince Edward Island (p. 91).

53. Ibid., p. 85; see also J. D. Mackie, *A History of Scotland* (Harmondsworth, Middlesex: Penguin Books, 1969), pp. 340–43.

54. Donaldson, *Scots Overseas*, p. 85; Mackie, *History of Scotland*, p. 343.

55. Prebble, *Highland Clearances*, passim.

56. The two excellent chapters, 6 and 7, entitled "Scotland's Changing Industrial Economy" and "Emigration as a Business" in Donaldson, *Scots Overseas*, pp. 81–102, comprehensively describe the events summed up in this paragraph; as do the two chapters 19 and 20, entitled "Unrest and Reform" and "Victorian Scotland," in Mackie, *History of Scotland*, pp. 311–47. A brief and lucid statement has also been provided by Norman Macdonald: "The Industrial Revolution changed the face of Scotland from a sparsely populated agricultural country to one of crowded unsanitary tenements, cotton factories and mills; while the invention of the sewing machine in 1846 made Paisley the centre of the sewing thread industry. That Scotland had too many brittle eggs in one vulnerable basket soon became apparent as foreign competition increased in volume and variety, and raw cotton was difficult to procure. In such a situation, the colonial reformers, advocates of emigration and colonization, found ready listeners and converts among hungry and ambitious Scots." Norman Macdonald, *Canada: Immigration and Colonization, 1841–1903* (Toronto: Macmillan of Canada, 1968), p. 69.

57. Donaldson, *Scots Overseas*, pp. 59, 63, 68, 77 and 91; Dunn, *Highland Settler*, pp. 11–90. The cohesive character of Scottish settlement is an important point which will be referred to again in the text, and the evidence of other authors brought to bear upon it.

58. Donaldson, *Scots Overseas*, p. 68. See also *Encyclopedia Canadiana* (1968) 9: 248; and Alexander Fraser, *The Last Laird of MacNab* (Toronto: Imrie, Graham and Co., 1899).

59. Donaldson, *Scots Overseas*, p. 68; Dunn, *Highland Settler*, pp. 14–19. See also Harkness, *Stormont*, p. 128.

60. Donaldson, *Scots Overseas*, pp. 68–69.

61. John M. Gray, *Lord Selkirk of Red River* (Toronto: Macmillan Co. of Canada, 1963), p. 53. See also George Bryce, *The Life of Lord Selkirk* (Toronto: Musson Book Co., n.d.).

62. Donaldson, *Scots Overseas*, pp. 69–71. Much has been written of this episode by many Canadian historians, but Gibbon, *Canadian Mosaic*, in a graphic account, pp. 99–102, isolates the parts played by individual Scots.

63. Lower, *Colony to Nation*, p. 209.

64. As Professor S. D. Clark has pointed out: "Most of the overseas colonists were Highland Scots and, if they lacked the experience and resourcefulness of the American Settlers, they inherited the traditional close group controls of the clan organization. Their tendency to settle together enabled them to resist many of the disorganizing effects of new social conditions. . . . The great bulk of overseas settlers came in as single individuals or families, and lacked the group supports enjoyed by the Highland Scots. . . . Since 1867, paradoxically, the security of the Canadian nation has depended upon discouraging a too strong Canadian nationalism. Preservation of English and Scots and Irish group loyalties served to perpetuate the colonial attitude of the Canadian people and thus to check the spread of American influence. In the United States the Briton hastened to become a good American: in Canada he has been encouraged to remain a good Briton. . . . The maintenance of the political attachments of Empire or nation depended upon the cultural isolation of the population within the American continental system, and such isolation has been secured most effectively through the preservation of Old World loyalties." S. D. Clark, *The Developing Canadian Community* (Toronto: University of Toronto Press, 1971), pp. 65–66, 195–96.

65. See W. L. Morton, *The Canadian Identity* (Madison, Wis.: University of Wisconsin Press, 1968).

66. Donaldson, *Scots Overseas*, pp. 132–33; see also William Johnston, *History of the County of Perth from 1825 to 1902* (Stratford, Ontario: W. M. O'Beinne, 1903). This has chapters on townships with Scottish names, also, like Downie (pp. 176–95); Fullarton (pp. 196–218); Logan (pp. 323–41); and Wallace (pp. 389–405).

67. See Guillet, *Early Life*, pp. 133–37.

68. C. O. Ermatinger, *The Talbot Regime* (St. Thomas: Municipal World, 1904); Fred Coyne Haniel, *Lake Erie Baron* (Toronto: Macmillan of Canada, 1955). This is, of course, John Kenneth Galbraith's work entitled *The Non-Potable Scotch*, Subtitled "A Memoir on the Clansmen in Canada," and published in 1967 by Penguin Books. (It was previously entitled *Made to Last*, and published by Hamish Hamilton, 1964.)

69. Donaldson, *Scots Overseas*, pp. 133–34.

70. Wilfred Campbell, *The Scotsman in Canada*, vol. 1 (Toronto: Musson Book Co., n.d.), pp. 407–19.

71. Macdonald, *Immigration and Colonization*, p. 35.

72. Ibid., p. 6–7.

73. See note 12.

74. George Bryce, *The Scotsman in Canada*, vol. 2 (Toronto: Musson Book Co., n.d.), pp. 410–12; Campbell, *Scotsman in Canada*, pp. 407–23.

75. Campbell, *Scotsman in Canada*, p. 412.

76. Harkness, *Stormont*, p. 128.

77. Bryce, *Scotsman in Canada*, p. 412–22; Campbell, *Scotsman in Canada*, pp. 408–23.

78. Bryce, *Scotsman in Canada*, pp. 285–99; Campbell, *Scotsman in Canada*, pp. 402–6.

79. Dunn, *Highland Settler*, pp. 74–78. See also the reference to literature in George S. Emmerson, "The Gaelic Tradition in Canadian Culture," in *The Scottish Tradition in Canada* (Toronto: McClelland and Stewart, 1976), pp. 234–38.

80. See J. M. S. Careless, *Brown of the Globe*, 2 vols. (Toronto: Macmillan of Canada, 1959–63).

81. Bryce, *Scotsman in Canada*, p. 421.

82. Dunn, *Highland Settler*, pp. 74–78.

83. Ibid., pp. 79–90. Also, as late as 1892, a purely Gaelic *McTalla* (The Echo) appeared at Sydney in Cape Breton, but ceased publication in 1904; see Donaldson, *Scots Overseas*, p. 147.

84. Donaldson, *Scots Overseas*, pp. 92–96.

85. Ibid., p. 93, quotes McLintock's description of this policy as "the shovelling out of paupers" to places "where they might die without shocking their betters with the sight or sound of their last agony." Dunn, *Highland Settler*, p. 24, quotes from the Surveyor-General of Cape Breton who "vehemently rejected the scheme."

86. Donaldson, *Scots Overseas*, pp. 95–96.

87. Dunn, *Highland Settler*, p. 18.

88. Ibid., Donaldson, *Scots Overseas*, p. 97.

89. Donaldson, *Scots Overseas*, p. 101. Much has been written about the terrible conditions on emigrant ships, but this same author (pp. 98—101) describes them in sufficient detail.

90. Ibid., p. 98.

91. Campbell, *Scotsman in Canada*, p. 417.

92. This is the title of chapter 3 in Macdonald, *Immigration and Colonization*, pp. 30–48, one of the most detailed books on the subject available.

93. Ibid., p. 111. With few exceptions, the colonization companies purchased the land from the railway companies, and the Government stipulated the conditions of settlement and the consequences of failure; see also appendix 3, "Colonization Companies, 1881–1903," pp. 361–69.

94. Joseph Home apparently wrote in 1830 of his Highland neighbors in Nova Scotia: "A curious feature in the character of the Highland population spread over the eastern parts of the Province is the extravagant desire they cherish to purchase large quantities of land." See Dunn, *Highland Settler*, p. 33.

95. Donaldson, *Scots Overseas*, pp. 94, 133–34; Lower, *Colony to Nation*, p. 189. See also chapter 3, entitled "The Canada Company," in Johnston, *History of Perth*, pp. 18–32; and James Young, *Reminiscences of the Early History of Galt and the Settlement of Dumfries in the Province of Ontario* (Toronto: Hunter, Rose and Co., 1880). The New Brunswick and Nova Scotia Land Company, which was founded in 1831, also appealed to Scots.

96. Gibbon, *Canadian Mosaic*, p. 106; Donaldson, *Scots Overseas*, pp. 134–35. Also Johnston, *History of Perth*, pp. 176–218, 323–41, 389–405, has chapters on the settlement of Downie, Fullerton, Logan, and Wallace. For histories of other Scottish set-

tlements, see Rev. W. A. MacKay, *Pioneer Life in Zorra* (Toronto: William Briggs, 1899); and Hugh Templin, *Fergus: The Story of a Little Town* (The Fergus-News Record, 1933).

97. It appears in British Columbia, Manitoba, New Brunswick, Nova Scotia, and Prince Edward Island. (The Scottish name "Dundee" also appears in five Canadian provinces.) See Robert Hamilton Coats and R. E. Gosnell, *Sir James Douglas* (Toronto: Morang and Co., 1910); Derek Pettrick, *James Douglas: Servant of Two Empires* (Vancouver: Mitchell Press, 1969); and Walter Noble Sage, *Sir James Douglas and British Columbia* (Toronto: University of Toronto Press, 1930).

98. Gibbon, *Canadian Mosaic*, p. 105.

99. As quoted in Donaldson, *Scots Overseas*, p. 140. Also, "bands of Scottish overlanders reached the gold fields of the Cariboo in 1862"; *Encyclopedia Canadiana*, 9: 248. A chapter entitled "Scottish Overlanders in 1862" is in Bryce, *Scotsman in Canada*, pp. 241–49.

100. Donaldson, *Scots Overseas*, pp. 140–42.

101. Perusal of the *Dictionary of Canadian Biography* or the Canadian *Who's Who*, with their large number of Scottish names, illustrates the problem. For example, any histories of the fur trade or exploration of the Northwest would include George Simpson and Robert Campbell [see Arthur S. Morton, *Sir George Simpson* (Toronto: J. M. Dent and Sons, 1944) and Clifford Wilson, *Campbell of the Yukon* (Toronto: Macmillan of Canada, 1970), although they have not been mentioned in this text].

102. *Encyclopedia Canadiana* (1968), 9: 250.

103. G. M. Craig, *Upper Canada: The Formative Years* (Toronto: McClelland and Stewart, 1963), p. 93.

104. A great deal has been written by historians about both Macdonald and Mackenzie, but the following should suffice for most purposes: D. G. Creighton, *John A. Macdonald: The Young Politician* (Toronto: Macmillan Co. of Canada, 1952), and *John A. Macdonald: The Old Chieftain* (Toronto: Macmillan Co. of Canada, 1955); and Charles Lindsey, *William Lyon Mackenzie* (Toronto: Morang and Co., 1910).

105. Gibbon, *Canadian Mosaic*, pp. 108–9.

106. James A. Roy, *The Scot and Canada* (Toronto: McClelland and Stewart, 1947), pp. 98–102; Craig, *Upper Canada*, p. 113.

107. Donaldson, *Scots Overseas*, pp. 134, 145.

108. Ibid., p. 145; Gibbon, *Canadian Mosaic*, p. 108; Morton, *Kingdom of Canada*, pp. 195, 223, 228, 286.

109. Campbell, *Scotsman in Canada*, p. 270.

110. Ibid., p. 269.

111. Apart from Campbell, *Scotsman in Canada*, and the individual histories available of many institutions, see also chapter 31 entitled "Scottish Educationalists," in Bryce, *Scotsman in Canada*, pp. 372–82; Gibbon. *Canadian Mosaic*, pp. 111–12; and especially D. C. Masters, "The Scottish Tradition in Higher Education," in *The Scottish Tradition in Canada* (Toronto: McClelland and Stewart, 1976), pp. 248–72.

112. Donaldson, *Scots Overseas*, p. 145.

113. Mackie, *History of Scotland*, pp. 327–29.

114. Clark, *Canadian Community*, p. 116.

115. See Creighton, *John A. Macdonald* (1952 and 1955).

116. Dedication opposite the title page of R. W. W. Robertson, ed., *Sir John A. Builds a Nation* (Burns and MacEachern, 1970).

117. See the letter from Sir John A. Macdonald to Sir John Rose, dated 23 February 1870, in which he states "that to send out an overwashed Englishman, utterly ignorant

of the country and full of crochets, as all Englishmen are, would be a mistake'' (Gibbon, *Canadian Mosaic*, pp. 109–10).

118. Gibbon, *Canadian Mosaic*, p. 109.

119. See D. C. Thomson, *Alexander Mackenzie: Clear Grit* (Toronto: Macmillan Co. of Canada, 1960).

120. Quotation on the title page of Berton, *National Dream*. The other volume which follows, by the same author, is *The Last Spike: The Great Railway, 1881–1885* (Toronto: McClelland and Stewart, 1971). These two works have been praised by many Canadian historians as the most authoritative account of the building of the CPR. See also John Murray Gibbon, *Steel of Empire* (Toronto: McClelland and Stewart, 1935); and Harold Adams Innis, *A History of the Canadian Pacific Railway* (Toronto: University of Toronto Press, 1971).

121. Berton, *National Dream*, and *Last Spike*, brings out this fact strongly throughout his texts, in support of his statement that ''almost every member of the original CPR Syndicate was a self-made Scot.'' (*National Dream*, p. 319).

122. See Berton, *Last Spike*, pp. 326, 354, 413–14.

123. See Beckles Wilson, *The Life of Lord Strathcona and Mount Royal: 1820–1914* (London: Cassell and Co., 1915).

124. Berton, *Last Spike*, p. 1.

125. Ibid., p. 3.

126. Ibid., p. 414.

127. Gibbon, *Canadian Mosaic*, pp. 105–6; Roy, *Scot and Canada*, pp. 72–73.

128. The whole poem is given in Ronald Macdonald, *The Scots Book* (New York: E. P. Dutton and Co., n.d.), p. 6, as well as in other publications.

129. Roy, *Scot and Canada*, p. 73.

130. *Encyclopedia Canadiana* (1968), 9: 249.

131. Roy, *Scot and Canada*, p. 6.

132. Albert Mackie, *Scottish Pageantry* (London: Hutchinson and Co., 1967), p. 15.

133. Ibid., p. 16.

134. Ibid., p. 18.

135. As quoted in Gibbon, *Canadian Mosaic*, p. 78.

136. Creighton, *John A. Macdonald* (1952 and 1955); see also *Canada, 1867–1967: The Founders and the Guardians* (Ottawa: Queen's Printers, 1968), p. 120.

137. See William Thomas Rochester Preston, *The Life and Times of Lord Strathcona* (London: E. Nash, 1914). For primary source material relating to this remarkable man, see the Strathcona Papers in the Public Archives of Canada, in Ottawa, which detail his vast endowments across Canada.

138. *Canada, 1867–1967*, p. 122; W. Buckingham and G. Ross, *The Honourable Alexander Mackenzie* (Toronto: Rose, 1892); Roy, *Scots and Canada*, p. 95.

139. Berton, *National Dream*, pp. 66—67.

140. See D'Alton C. Coleman, *Lord Mount Stephen (1829–1921) and the Canadian Pacific Railway* (New York: Newcomen Society, 1945).

141. As quoted in Berton, *National Dream*, p. 319.

142. Ibid., pp. 319–20.

143. R. C. MacDonald, *Sketches of Highlanders* (St. John, N.B., 1843), appendix, p. ii, as quoted in Dunn, *Highland Settler*, pp. 24–25.

144. Clark, *Canadian Community*, pp. 65–68.

145. *Encyclopedia Canadiana* (1968), 5: 251.

146. Ralph Henry Gabriel, *The Course of American Democratic Thought* (New York: Ronald Press Co., 1940), p. 190.

147. *Encyclopedia Canadiana* (1968), 9: 247–51.

148. Ibid., 3: 171–73; 4: 385–87.

149. This is the title of a chapter in Henry Roxborough, *One Hundred Not Out: The Story of Nineteenth-Century Canadian Sport* (Toronto: Ryerson Press, 1966), pp. 99–111.

4
Curling

*Any game played by three-quarters of a million people
can't be all dull. More Canadians curl than play golf—or any
other sport, for that matter. . . . So there must be more to
curling than sliding a rock down a sheet of ice. And indeed
there is a budding pro circuit, for one. And schools for begin-
ners. And even curling's own fashions and fanatics.*
Paul Grescoe (1971)

E ARLY in the nineteenth century, before curling was
established in Canada, a French-Canadian farmer in Quebec
was somewhat bemused by a form of social activity he had never
seen before:

> Today I saw a band of Scotchmen, who were throwing large
> balls of iron like tea-kettles on the ice, after which they cried
> "Soop! soop!", and then laughed like fools. I really believe
> they ARE fools.[1]

He could not know then that these Scottish antics on the ice
would become commonplace across the continent before the end
of the nineteenth century, participated in by "fools" of many nationalities. Nor could he realize that he had witnessed a sport that
was destined to become one of the most popular in Canada in the
next century, one which Canada would dominate for many years
in international competition. In fact, the event was significant
beyond his derision or imagination. This puzzled farmer had
unknowingly witnessed a very unusual, perhaps unique, phenomenon—the early days of an imported sport which had an en-

104

vironment in its new country more suitable than in its birthplace; and a future before it more glorious than its past. Even the Scots themselves, who were responsible for the appearance and development of curling in Canada during the nineteenth century, were not fully aware of its latent possibilities, especially in the earlier stages. But by 1902–3, it was clear to Scots everywhere that curling represented their greatest contribution to sport in Canada.

A major reason was that the climate and geography of Canada were more suited to the game than were these elements even in Scotland itself. Also, its democratic character was well suited to a pioneering environment, where settlers and soldiers alike could freely indulge this easily organized winter sport. The advance of curling in Canada followed closely the pattern of Scottish settlement, reflected in the organization of clubs and subsequent interclub competition. This was further stimulated by improvements in transport and communications during the nineteenth century, which also assisted international competition with fellow Scots in the United States, and later from Scotland. Although the game was played simply, outdoors and with improvised implements, by many early enthusiasts, yet it was also susceptible of further development and skill. Technical innovations introduced during the nineteenth century, such as the use of indoor rinks with electric lighting, were largely responsible for a more sophisticated game which enjoyed increasing participation, by both sexes. Curling was also promoted by the ubiquitous Scottish Societies and sponsored by many of the most famous Scotsmen in the country. Some governors-general of Canada, in particular, helped the game tremendously by their enthusiastic patronage. For all these reasons, in the period between the formation of the first Canadian curling club in 1807 and the first tour of Canada by a visiting Scottish team in 1902–3, this ethnic imported sport thrived in its new environment in a manner unsurpassed by any other similar diffusion anywhere.

The famous critic of Scotland and its people Dr. Samuel Johnson once referred to that country as consisting of ''stone and water.''[2] Of course this fact, allied with the most rigorous climate in the northernmost part of the British Isles, was largely responsible for the appearance and popularity of curling there. It was on their frozen lochs and rivers that the Scots slid their granite stones. But the winters were unpredictable and ice could not be guaranteed at any definite time, or for any certain period.

Canada also consisted largely of ''stone and water,'' and on a gigantic scale when compared with Scotland. Wherever Scots settled, there was usually water nearby. In fact, most early inland settlements were close by rivers or lakes for purposes of transportation and defense. The Canadian climate ensured that these were frozen for several months every year.

Many historians of curling have been aware of this advantage. When the Reverend John Kerr came to write his prodigious account of the first tour of the Dominion and the United States by a Scottish curling team, he noted that

> in most places in Canada they have four or five months of good ice every winter, that this is so secure that they can draw out a programme of events and publish a calendar for the curling season which has very seldom to be altered.

He referred to this theme again and again, until he added the final apt comment ''and what shall we say more of these winters than to add that they make Canada the Eldorado of the curler?''[3] Creelman agreed with these sentiments, although in his view ''Eldorado'' could be subdivided, and the curling calendar was even more secure in the Prairie Provinces of Western Canada,

> the region in which the game's wondrous possibilities have been given fullest scope for development. There the long, cold, dry winters give assurance that plans for special match games or for successive days of bonspiels can safely be made far in advance of the time specified.[4]

Stevenson maintained that the close ties of Canada with Scotland, ''and her long hard winters,'' were responsible for her being the only country to which curling has been transplanted ''so successfully from its original home that it has acquired nation-wide popularity.''[5] Another book on curling mentions the Fraser Highlanders, after the Siege of Quebec, ''finding ideal conditions in the hard Canadian winters'' to indulge in the sport.[6] Unquestionably, the consistently cold and prolonged winters and the geographical features of Canada were most significant factors in the success of curling. Without these favorable and unique conditions, it is doubtful whether the same ''nation-wide popularity'' could have been attained.

The other major factor, of course, as Stevenson noted, was the close relationship of Canada with Scotland. The widespread and enthusiastic Scots were ready to exploit the ideal conditions to the full in their pursuit of ''the roarin' game.'' The combination of Scotsmen in plenty and abundant and enduring ice provided a ready home in the New World for their traditional sport.

Some historians have suggested that curling began on the North American continent during the Seven Years' War of 1756–63, when Scottish soldiers used the frozen St. Charles River or the St. Lawrence River, or both, for this purpose.[7] This is certainly possible, bearing in mind that there were at least a dozen active curling clubs formed in Scotland before 1760.[8] Kerr has even suggested that

> the eagerness of the Scotch to enlist for active service in Canada during the old contest between England and France is said to have been due to the opportunities there afforded for curling. This may also explain the popularity of Canada as a field for Scottish emigrants.[9]

But as Stevenson has pointed out, this ''is too far-fetched to bear examination,'' betraying an excess of optimistic enthusiasm for the game.[10] Nobody was too eager to enlist in those days, or fight in a foreign country under severe conditions, with a good chance of being killed. As indicated in chapter 3, the reasons for Scottish emigration were far more complex and serious than a desire to curl in a colder clime. Most of the Scottish regiments in the campaign were recruited in the Highlands of Scotland where curling was hardly known at the time. The other assertions made, that Scots were curling in parts of Canada before the end of the eighteenth century,[11] have more merit because of the increased development of the game in Scotland after 1763, and because of the increased immigration of Scots into Canada. Some documentation has been provided for a game taking place in Quebec in 1805,[12] and it can be stated with certainty that the first curling club in Canada was formed in that province in 1807.

Since this club was the first regularly organized sporting club in Canada, the year 1807 was chosen as a starting point for Lindsay's study of nineteenth-century sport in Canada before Confederation, being "more pertinent to the development of Canadian sport than was 1800."[13] In view of the uncertainty of the origins of curling in Canada beforehand, the year of 1807 is also a convenient starting point for an examination of curling in nineteenth-century Canada. Similarly, an extension beyond 1900 in order to view the first Scottish Team's tour in 1902–3 is also desirable, as it formed a fitting and revealing climax to nearly a century of overwhelming Scottish activity and influence on the sport in Canada.

If Kerr's statement that the game followed "the march of Fraser's Highlanders" in Canada is doubtful, one can agree wholeheartedly with these other assertions: "That Scotsmen started it there cannot be denied. It followed the footsteps of the early fur-traders of the North-West."[14] The eastern base of their commercial empire was Montreal, where the first curling club on the North American continent was born:

> A group of Scots who were identified chiefly with the fur trade desired to introduce to Montreal two favourite games of their native land, curling and golf. On January 27, 1807, they founded the Royal Montreal Curling Club at a banquet attended by fifteen charter members. Thus was born the oldest curling club in America. . . . The original members used the River St. Lawrence below what was then known as "the port" for their rink. John Bude took a prominent part in founding the club and Thomas Blackwood, a partner of James McGill, was the first president.[15]

It as not, however, as claimed, "the oldest organized outdoor sporting club on the North American continent,"[16] because other Scots had promoted their other favorite game elsewhere and formed a golf club in Charleston, South Carolina, at least as early as 1795, and in Georgia as well.[17] But the Montreal club was the first curling club in North America and the forerunner of many others, particularly in Canada.

The membership of this first curling club was limited to twenty, and one of its first rules ran as follows:

> The club shall meet at Gillis' on Wednesday, every fortnight at 4 o'clock to dine on salt beef and greens. The club dinner and wine shall not exceed in cost seven shillings and sixpence a head, and any members infringing on this rule, shall be liable to a fine of four shillings. No member shall ask a friend to dinner, except the President and the Vice-President, who may ask two each. . . . The losing party of the day shall pay for a bowl of whisky toddy, to be placed in the middle of the table for those who may chuse [*sic*] it.[18]

Nearly three months after the formation of the club, the members were able to play a game on the river below the harbor as late as April 11 that year. The war of 1812–14 seems to have curtailed the club's activities,[19] although the game survived. From 1820, other curling clubs were formed, particularly in Upper Canada, although one appeared in Nova Scotia by 1825. Wherever there were Scotsmen, in fact, the sport of curling was likely to emerge.

A curling club was formed at Kingston in 1820,[20] and the Quebec Curling Club was formed in the following year.[21] During the winter of 1824—25, a Halifax Curling Club was formed in Nova Scotia, largely through the efforts of a Captain (later Admiral) Houston Stewart, Colonel Graeg, and Dr. Grigor.[22] This was to be the only curling club in the Maritimes area for nearly another twenty years. In fact, the activities of the Halifax, Kingston, Montreal, and Quebec clubs seemed to be the intermittent affairs of a few isolated enthusiasts, or eccentric "fools." Mactaggart, writing of his stay in Canada from 1826 to 1828, even claimed the game was "unknown" there:

> Notwithstanding the numbers of lakes and rivers which abound in Canada, and all the intensity of the winter frost, still the game of curling, the great ice amusement of Scotland, is unknown. There was a curling club formed in Montreal some

time ago, but it seldom attempted the game. The weather is too cold even for the keenest curler to endure; and the ice is generally covered very deep with snow. The "curling stones," if I may use the expression, they have constructed of cast-iron, but as iron is a great conductor of heat, they were not found to answer well, as they stuck into the ice. The surface of the lakes, too, is never what a person knowing the game would call true, that is, level; let no Scottish emigrants then, as heretofore, conceive they will be gratified with plenty of this amusement. Thus it does not follow, that where there are plenty of men, water, and frost, there will be curling.[23]

It was a statement of little faith or vision for a Scotsman to make, even at that time. Clubs had been formed, even if they were forced to use crude cast-iron "curling-stones." Father Macdonell, Selkirk, and others, had already settled hundreds of their countrymen on the continent. John Galt with his Canada Land Company was destined to settle many more in the southern part of Ontario above Lake Erie, a development which greatly affected the progress of curling. The Highland Clearances, and the subsequent various distresses in Scotland's new Lowland industries, ensured a constant supply of Mactaggart's "Scottish emigrants" to all parts of Canada. In fact, not too long after Mactaggart's visit, Scottish coal miners probably brought their curling-stones with them to New Glasgow in Nova Scotia. And many of his countrymen already in Canada had yet to make their indelible mark on events, and become influential patrons of Scottish sports. The spread of Scottish Societies in Canada began after the publication of Mactaggart's book, and many of them sponsored curling clubs. For the Scottish emigrant did not expect to be "gratified" by familiar amusements immediately upon arrival, especially under ideal circumstances. He made his own, often in extremely trying conditions, with enthusiasm and improvisation.[24] Also, Mactaggart could not foresee the later expansion of clubs in Scotland itself, and the formation of the Royal Caledonian Curling Club, to which Canadian clubs would affiliate and thus provide a link for further developments. These developments also included indoor rinks and artificial ice, so that outdoor curling was not the only recourse for enthusiasts when the bitter Canadian climate was often too much of a deterrent. Mactaggart came upon the game in its New World infancy and was hasty in his judgment. In the 1830s it began its career as a popular and highly organized sport.

In a summary of sport in Canada before Confederation, the Howells noted that the names of Scots appeared frequently on the lists of early teams and as organizers of early clubs for sport.[25] Nowhere was this fact more clearly demonstrated than in curling. After Kingston came the Fergus Curling Club, in practically an exclusive Scottish settlement, which was formed in 1834 and was "almost a family affair." It was comprised of the keeper of St. Andrew's Tavern, Hugh Black, his four sons and two sons-in-law, as well as William Buist, James Webster, and James Dinwoodie, who lived seven miles away. "Native dew" was often essential to curler's activities and sometimes the dues of this club were paid in Canadian whisky.[26] Clubs were also formed at West Flamborough (1835), Toronto and Milton (1836), Galt, Guelph and Hamilton (1838), and Scarborough (1839).[27] But again, informal curling activities preceded the formation of clubs, for James Young, Galt's first historian, related that the first game in that district took place in the winter of 1836–37:

> It is not surprising that being so largely settled by Scotsmen, Galt early practised the game of curling so much in vogue in the land of "the mountain and the flood." The first game of which we have been able to find any recollection took place on Altrieve Lake, as it is called, a pretty sheet of water near Mr. James S. Cowan's residence, about two miles west of the town. Among those who took part in it were Messrs. Robert Wallace Sr. (who was on a visit from Brantford), Robert Wallace Jr. of Galt, John Warnock of Beverley, and John Wallace of Dumfries. They made blocks out of the maple tree, putting in pieces of iron as handles, and, although labouring under some disadvantages, the survivors describe it as a jolly and long-to-be-remembered meeting.[28]

Most of these pioneer clubs in Upper Canada first used wooden "stones," an improvisation which enabled the members to enjoy "the roarin' game" in their forest environment.[29]

Interclub matches became more frequent around this time, also, and a classic example of enthusiasm for their sport was set by the Montreal Curling Club when it accepted a challenge from the Quebec Curling Club to play a match at Trois Riviéres, halfway between the two cities, some 180 miles apart, in 1835. The Montreal players left the city on January 7 and 8, some by stage and others by their own sleighs, the first of them arriving at Trois Rivières around noon on January 9. The match took place the next day, with two rinks a side, and the final score was Quebec 31, Montreal 23. The eight Montreal players, as losers, paid £3 2s.6d for the dinner afterwards, and a similar amount for transportation.[30] A good time was had by all, for the two clubs apparently agreed to a return match.[31] The Rebellion of 1837 was responsible for the Montreal Club having no club dinner during 1837–38. Yet it did not prevent the members from constructing a new artificial rink made of wood, and put up under cover in the St. Ann suburb, near the Lachine Canal. This was probably the first closed curling rink in Canada.[32] The Thistle Club, formed in 1842 or 1843, provided the Montreal Club with further competition, as did the 71st Regiment in nearby St. Jean which was also active in the early forties.[33] Two years after its formation, the Thistle Club acquired a convenient site on Craig Street and also constructed an enclosed rink.[34]

The Scots in Montreal had therefore formed the first curling club, and built the first indoor rinks, both highly significant achievements for the progress of the sport in Canada. Yet the pattern of Scottish settlement and the development of railways decreed that later southern Ontario was to be the ''heart'' of Canadian curling for most of the nineteenth century.

Not all of the early enthusiasts used curling irons, or improvised wooden ''stones,'' or imported curling stones from Scotland in these pioneering years. Many Scots were skilled stonemasons, and shaped their own from ''ice-borne boulders of whinstone or granite called hard-heads,''[35] which were left lying around as fields were prepared for cultivation. Granite curling stones were advertised in Toronto in 1839:

To Curlers—Geluque Flumina Constiterent Acuto.
Translation from Horace—"And the rivers are fast set with
nipping frost."

Curling stones may be had on application to the subscriber
who has taken great pains to collect a number of blocks of the
most excellent grain. Several members of the Toronto Club
have already been supplied, and specimens may be seen on the
Bay on Playing Days, or on application to Mr. McDonald at
the City Wharf, or to the subscriber at his residence, 16 New
Street. The price of the stones is eight dollars per pair, according to the handles and finish.

Peter McArthur
(Maker of curling stones).[36]

Thus did McArthur the entrepreneur, in 1839, answer the
gloomy prediction of Mactaggart the author ten years before.

In subsequent years, McArthur probably had a profitable
business, for Toronto was destined to rival any other city in
Canada for curling activity, due to the presence of many enthusiastic Scots in that city.[37] In fact, Stevenson has claimed that
"the erection of St. Andrew's Church in Toronto by the
Presbyterian Scots of that city coincided with the first efforts to
organize the game of curling in Ontario."[38] An early match in
the Toronto area was played between the "Wully Draigles" and
the "Auld Gang Siccars" of the Scarborough (or Scarboro) Club,
during the winter of 1835–36, for the right to meet the Toronto
club. The "Wully Draigles," consisting of J. Gibson (skip), J.
Weir, R. Scott, J. Gibson, J. Green, J. Stobo, J. McCowan, and
W. Miller, won by a score of 27–19, and then represented Scarborough. The Toronto club was represented by Capt. T. Dick
(skip), Dr. Telfer, Alex. Ogilvie, W. Henderson, Alex. Badenach,
J. O. Heward, Hon. Justice Morrison, and G. Denholm, but they
lost to Scarborough by 31 to 16.[39] Thus began a long rivalry between these two curling clubs.

The first book on curling in Canada was published in Toronto, in 1840, and written by the secretary of the Toronto club. This was James Bickett's *The Canadian Curler's Manual; or, An Account of Curling as Practised in Canada, with Remarks on the History of the Games*.[40] Its appearance also did nothing to vindicate Mactaggart's earlier pessimism regarding the sport. Neither did the first Grand East versus West Bonspiel, held at Toronto in 1858, when no less than thirty-two rinks competed.[41] But Kerr maintains that the same contest on the bay at Toronto in the following year, in which forty-two rinks took part, was ''the first big bonspiel on the continent of America.'' It was certainly another indication of Toronto's importance as a curling center. Nearly all the major curling clubs participated, from Bowmanville, Burlington, Guelph, Toronto, Newcastle, Hamilton, Fergus, Ancaster, West Flamborough, Dundas, and London, as well as from Montreal.[42] As Stevenson has noted, the majority of these clubs, and possibly all of them, were begun by Scots.[43] Their enthusiasm was evident by the fact that not only did Guelph, Scarborough, and Toronto muster five rinks each for this bonspiel, but so did the little Scottish township of Fergus. On 28 December 1859 the first covered curling rink erected in Upper Canada was opened by the Toronto club, which obtained possession of

> two sheds in rear of the public building. The floors have been ''puddled'' and banked, and were filled with water to the depth of six inches by the Hose Company on Saturday. By obtaining those covered rinks, the Club will be able to enjoy the ''roarin' game'' in all weathers.[44]

Another covered rink was built for the Heather Curling Club, an offshoot of the Scarborough club, and indoor curling began there on 16 December 1863. This club had been formed by Scots only a year earlier, and their choice of name added another Scottish title to join the many existing ''Thistles,'' ''Caledonians,'' and ''Granites.''[45]

By 1864, there were several curling clubs in the Toronto area.[46] On January 26 of that year, the Buffalo Caledonian Curling Club visited Toronto for a match against the Toronto club,

Curling on the Don River, Toronto, in 1860. Opening of the
Thistle Curling Club rink, in Montreal, 1871.

and a return match was played at Buffalo on February 19. This contact with the Scottish club in the United States resulted in "the great International Bonspiel at Black Rock, Buffalo, in 1865,"[47] in which almost fifty Canadian and United States clubs participated, involving two hundred and forty players.[48] Also in 1865, James Thomson of Toronto and J. Scoville of the Buffalo Caledonian Curling Club, initiated their annual Thomson-Scoville Medal series for competition between their respective clubs.[49] At the international bonspiel, Thomson was a member of a rink, led by a Scot named John Shedden, which acquired the name of the Toronto "Red Jackets" from the brilliant red costumes worn by its members. Thomson was replaced in 1866 by Thomas McGaw, and Shedden retired from curling for business reasons in the following year. His place was taken by David Walker, another Scot who had emigrated to Canada in 1854. This team of McGaw, Walker, and the two original members, Major Gray and Charles Perry, then went on to become one of the most famous rinks in the nineteenth century. A photograph of "The Famous Red Jacket Rink" in Stevenson's *Curling in Ontario, 1846-1946*, shows them wearing tam o'shanters, and the subtitle describes them as the rink "that first put curling on the front pages of the newspapers in America."[50]

Before Confederation in 1867, then, curling was established on an international basis. Of the international bonspiel in 1865, Kerr could exclaim in his Scottish exuberance:

> This grand event stirred the hearts of the people in both countries, and may be said to have given the game an established position as the "King of Games" throughout the whole of North America; and second, it led to frequent friendly matches between the curling clubs of the United States and of western Canada.[51]

The game had also gained ground elsewhere in Canada by this time, although in a less spectacular manner. When news of the formation of the Grand Caledonian Curling Club in Edinburgh reached Canada, the Montreal and Quebec clubs offered their allegiance and were accepted into membership. So was the Thistle Curling Club, formed in 1842, and for a time these three clubs were the only Canadian clubs on the mother club's roll.[52] But then came the formation of the Canadian Branch of the Royal Caledonian Curling Club (R.C.C.C.) in 1852 which was ''an important event in the organization of curling in Canada.'' Clubs were encouraged to join and so become eligible to compete for medals presented by the parent body. The Montreal, Thistle, Quebec, and Stadacona clubs were charter members, and the Bytown and Cobourg clubs joined in the same year. Other clubs quickly followed suit.[53] The hope that affiliation with the famous mother club in Scotland would foster interest was borne out, especially in far Eastern Canada which had few clubs prior to 1852.

In that year, when the Canadian Branch of the Royal Caledonian Curling Club was formed, a Nova Scotia branch was instituted with four clubs, the Halifax, the Pictou, the Thistle, and the Dartmouth club. In 1854, the new Caledonian Club of Pictou and the New Glasgow Club were admitted, and the Antigonish Club became a member two years later. Other curling clubs in the area then were the Fredericton Club of New Brunswick, formed in 1854, and the St. Andrew's Club of St. John in 1856. These two had their first interclub match at Fredericton on 26 February 1857.[54]

In the following year, the Canadian Branch issued its first invitation to the Royal Caledonian Club in Scotland to send out a team to play in Canada. Although the invitation was accepted then,[55] this event did not in fact materialize until the next century, forty-four years later. But the invitation in 1858 was an indication of the game's progress in Canada and of confidence in its future. There were indeed ample grounds for this before 1858, and the subsequent developments until the first team from Scotland did arrive, justified all optimism. Although affiliation with the Royal Club did much to stimulate interest and promote the game in Canada in this period, the absence of a visiting Scottish team was no handicap at all during the nineteenth century. There were many pertinent reasons for the success of curling in Canada before the first invitation went out to Scotland, and before the first international bonspiel—reasons which became more valid as the century progressed.

Some of these have already been noted. Obviously a favorable

climate, plenty of water, and the widespread settlement of enthusiastic Scots was a basic combination for the game's birth and
survival in the earlier days, accompanied by the formation of
clubs. The advent of indoor rinks increased the game's
possibilities immeasurably. But one must look more closely at the
nature of the Scottish influence on this sport in Canada, and the
nature of the game itself, in order to fully understand its subsequent phenomenal development. The coming of the railways was
also a significant feature of Canadian life in this period which
greatly affected sport, and happily coincided with the rise of curling. High-class patronage of the sport was another consistent
feature which assisted its progress.

Although the Scottish influence on curling in Canada was paramount and predominant throughout the nineteenth century, it
was not totally exclusive. It was natural that Scots should be the
first and most serious ambassadors for their sports outside
Scotland. In fact, they were quite determined to enjoy them
wherever they found themselves. In the beginning, the rules of
clubs might state that only Scotsmen were eligible for membership, but this did not last long. To their credit, the Scottish
pioneers of sport did not completely monopolize their games in
any enduring or rigid fashion. More often than not they were
generous in attitude and prepared to allow ''foreigners'' to join
in as well:

> While the Scots are traditionally thrifty they have also been
> very generous in many of their contributions. This has been
> especially evident in the sports world, where some of the most
> exciting games have been gifts from Scottish sportsmen . . .
> particulary curling.[56]

These ''gifts'' were not immediately given or instantly received;
rather they were gradually accepted and assimilated until they
were customary in the new environment. In this way, the Scottish
sport of curling inevitably became less Scottish in Canada,
although this process was far from complete by the end of the
nineteenth century.

However, as early as 1843, the *Toronto Colonist* boldly claimed
that ''Curling may now be considered in this Province, a Cana-

dian rather than a Scottish game.'' The reason for this optimistic statement was that a Canadian, William Reynolds, had won the Denham Medal competition in that year. Credit was also given to the Toronto Club for its encouragement of participation by those other than natives of Scotland.[57] But Toronto was not alone in this kind of stimulation. A clipping from another Canadian newspaper ''illustrates vividly the progress of curling among the non-Scottish . . . as far back as 1854'':

> The great event of the past week was the monster curling match. Scotchmen had challenged all who came not from the north of the Tweed to beat them at their national game. The challenge was instantly responded to by the curlers of Quebec or Barbarians, as they facetiously styled themselves, and immense excitement ensued. Sir James Alexander, A.D.C., acted as umpire. The game commenced at 1 o'clock, and continued with great zeal until half past four. The scene on the river was novel and interesting; hosts of ladies and gentlemen and many gay equipages surrounded the rinks; bursts of merriment, snatches of broad Scotch, cries of ''Soop him, soop him'' resounded on all sides; curling stones with red or blue ribbons came gliding towards the tee, now quietly, anon with thundering force, as the skips directed; the curlers, besom in hand, seemed all absorbed in the game, occasionally coaxing on some favourite stone with honied expressions, as though their very lives depended on the issue, and not infrequently a great player would lose his footing in the excitement of the moment, to the infinite amusement of the bystanders. In the background arose the fortress of old Stadacona, whose cannon were manned by a company of artillery at target practice, and firing, as it were, a royal salute to the curlers. The playing was keen, aye, as keen as the N.W. wind which forced many of the fair admirers unwillingly from the spot, and the result of the game has clearly proved that the Barbarians are but little behind their civilised brethren in this manly sport. Scotchmen, 94; Barbarians, 83.[58]

Similar contests became common throughout the curling fraternity. In Chatham, for example, where the Curling Club was formed in 1862, the inaugural encounter on the river ice was between the ''Benedicts'' (married men) and ''Bachelors.'' Before the end of 1863, this club had been recognized by the Canadian

Branch of the R.C.C.C. (one of only nineteen Canadian member clubs); and it had taken part in the celebrated International Bonspiel at Buffalo in 1865. By 1870, it had also won a commendable total of three Caledonian medals in interclub competition; and a native son, David Walker, had also curled as a member of the famous Toronto Red Jackets rink.[59]

The Montreal and Quebec city clubs also established annual "bachelors versus married" contests, a well as "Canadians versus Scots."[60] It was reported in the *Morning Chronicle* of 9 January 1861 that Benjamin Rousseau, "a true French-Canadian," had won the Quebec Curling Club Annual Gold Medal Competition. The Hadlow Club also had regular matches between French Canadians and British Canadians.[61] Apparently fewer French Canadians now regarded Scotsmen on ice as "fools," or else they were willing to appear foolish themselves. Yet it is true for the most part that "the majority of French Canadians continued to display little interest in following sports of such British tradition."[62]

In 1869, a curling match took place in New Brunswick between "Home-Born Scots" and the "Native-Born."[63] Many Britons other than Scots came to the sport during the nineteenth century, in fact, either at home[64] or in Canada. Perusal of the 626 pages of Kerr's mammoth work on the history of curling reveals that British surnames other than those of Scottish origin appear more frequently in accounts of clubs' activities as the nineteenth century progressed, although Scottish names certainly predominated throughout.[65] The Scottish settlement of Lindsay, Ontario, provides an example of this trend, where the first curling club was organized in 1876:

> From the beginning, curling took a foremost place in the affections of the town's best citizens, for the average Canadian has a great love for a personal enjoyment of outdoor sport. A feature of the game in Lindsay was, that it caught in its rings the men whose forebears came from Ireland and England, and they became just as enthusiastic and as skilful as those of Scottish birth or descent. No skip is more worthily known in Canada today than Mr. J. D. Flavell, one of the early members of the Lindsay Club, and an Irishman.[66]

One of the expert players when the St. Mary's Curling Club was formed was Thomas Iredale, "an English underhand bowler at cricket." Most of the people who wished to curl in Canada were naturally Scottish, but the fact that others were able to participate if they wished, and indeed were encouraged to do so, ensured that the game did not suffer from too rigid ethnic boundaries in its development. Curling retained its Scottish flavor (even until today) without ever becoming unpalatable to those who were not born "North of the Tweed."

But the leading pioneers, players, and officials of the sport in the nineteenth century were naturally Scottish. Evidence of this is provided by Stevenson's chapter entitled "Famous Curlers," in which twenty persons are listed. No fewer than eleven of these were born in Scotland, viz., Rev. J. Barclay, John Ferguson, Robert Ferguson, James Ferguson, G. H. Gillespie, Peter Gow, Dr. James Hamilton, Lt. Col. James Moffat, J. S. Russell, David Walker, and T. G. Williamson. Four were born in Canada of Scottish descent: James A. Macfadden, Alexander Ferguson MacLaren, John Alexander McMillan, and William Rennie. It is probable that William Badenach, Thomas McGaw, and Thomas Thauburn, were also of Scottish descent.[67]

It is more than fitting that the game should be open to all nationalities, since its inherent character was essentially democratic and traditionally open to all classes. Curling, in fact, was regarded as one of the most democratic of all sports in nineteenth-century Canada, a fact which certainly did not hinder its progress in the frontier society of the New World.

Throughout the centuries that curling was played in Scotland, it was renowned for its democratic tendencies.[68] A parody of Robbie Burns's verses has been used to indicate its democratic nature, and many humorous stories attest the fellowship of all classes of people during a game.[69] An English inspector of prisons, during an official visit to Dumfries in the winter of 1836, was greatly impressed when he discovered the convenor of the county and the sheriff engaged in curling with their tenants, friends, and neighbors.[70] An early encyclopedia stated that "peers, peasants, clergymen, farmers, country gentlemen, tradesmen and artisans all meet hilariously and familiarly for the occasion.''[71] Curling literature of all types testifies to the democratic quality of the game,[72] an example being this by the Ettrick Shepherd:

> Here Peer and peasant friendly meet,
> Auld etiquette has lost her seat,
> The social broom has swept her neat,
> Beyond the pale o' Curling.[73]

These principles of open good fellowship on the ice, regardless of status, were well maintained in Canada, also. The *Toronto Examiner* of 11 March 1840 reported a match between sixteen married men and sixteen bachelors, with eight men to a rink. These curlers included ''a noted legislator,'' ''a judge,'' ''one of Toronto's Mayors,'' ''a descendant of the House of Lauderdale,'' ''a sea captain and later proprietor of the Queen's Hotel,'' ''a famed preacher,'' as well as a chemist, schoolteacher, tobacconist, apothecary, baker, upholsterer, shipbuilder, grocer, and Bank of Upper Canada clerk, together with a few men of leisure listed as ''gentlemen.''[74] Similar diversity obtained at Montreal fifteen years later, when a recorder of one particular bonspiel observed:

> Amongst the players we noticed the Merchant and the Mechanic, the Soldier and the Civilian, the Pastor and his Flock, all on an equal footing for the game of curling levels all ranks.[75]

While there appears to be no reason to doubt the verdicts of such eyewitnesses of more than a hundred years ago, it has been pointed out that around this time most matches were normally played on weekdays, ''a fact which restrained most labouring men from participation.'' Thus many civilian curlers were either professional or self-employed men, with a certain amount of free leisure time available.[76] Despite the 1855 quote above from the *Montreal Gazette*, for example, it has been maintained that three curling clubs there, the Montreal (1807), the Thistle (1842/43), and the Caledonia (1850) remained among the most exclusive throughout the nineteenth century.[77] Military personnel of the garrisons, of course, of whatever rank, seemed to enjoy abundant unstructured time for recreation, regardless of the day of the week.

Indeed, rank meant nothing on the ice, where the game was all-important. Kerr relates an amusing story of how a Colonel Dalrymple of the 71st Highlanders suffered at the hands of a private who apparently was partial to "copious libations" before a game, but nevertheless "as skip was king of the rink, and knew his authority . . . and placed his shots with great skill." The colonel, however, was unnerved by his subordinate's condition and played badly, and "the spectators were convulsed with laughter, as the private proceeded to give his superior a lecture on how to play, and kept it up till the day's match was over."[78] In Canada, as in Scotland, it was a case of "the spruce tailor, the burly stonemason, the active weaver, the quiet-thinking minister, the humble voter, and the M.P. are all on a level. The grand test is who curls best."[79] This democratic characteristic was held to be greatly responsible for the acceptance and development of curling throughout North America during the nineteenth century. Eventually all nationalities and classes of people were able to participate in a simple game which added to the enjoyment of winter. As Hedley later observed in 1892:

> It is a democratic game. As in the old country, according to Norman McLeod's delightful curling song, we find "the master and servants, the tenant and laird" coming together o'er the brown heather to the curler's gathering, so on this side of the Atlantic we may see the millionaire and the artisan, the banker and his clerk, the university professor and his pupil, the dominie and the clergyman, all met in fine frosty weather and, if not as loving as Norman would have them, still all civil, all gleeful, all equally free.[80]

And it is interesting to note that the editor of *The Dominion Illustrated* for March 1891, claimed that "curling has spread through the land from Dan to Beersheba" because of its democratic qualities.

But although persons of rank could not exercise any power beyond curling ability while on the ice, their enthusiasm for the sport was consistent. Before Confederation, many important and famous persons had been involved from earlier years in the rise of curling in Canada, either as participants or spectators. Since the activities of influential people inevitably attracted much notice, the sport derived benefit from their association. Naturally enough, the majority of well-known figures were Scots, pursuing an interest in their native sport. Some of these promoted and sponsored it in very direct fashion and greatly assisted its development. There were too many notables involved in curling before 1867 to mention them all, but some examples can illustrate their interest. In particular, the viceregal support of Scottish governors-general, which began in the period, was a significant asset which then continued throughout the century.

The Quebec City Curling Club has had some distinguished names on its rolls, including the Earl of Dalhousie, Governor of Canada, who was a member in 1828.[81] The Hon. Adam Fergusson was the founder of Fergus, the Scottish settlement in the township of Nicholl, and he was also the organizer and first president of the Fergus Curling Club, formed in 1834. Of the large bonspiel held in Toronto six years later it was reported:

> The governors of Canada have usually taken an active interest in the game, and at this match the spectators included the Governor-General, Lord Sydenham, and the Lieutenant-Governor of Upper Canada, Sir George Arthur.[82]

One of the first *Annuals* published referred to the interest taken in curling by His Excellency Sir George Arthur.[83] Lord Elgin had become patron of the Montreal Thistle Club in 1847, but after the critical reception of the Rebellion Losses Bill in 1849, his name was removed from its list of members—an action approved by resolution at a meeting of the Quebec Stadacona Club.[84] Politics has always been traditionally a forbidden subject in curling, and never allowed to interfere with the fellowship of the sport. Fines were often imposed against offenders who introduced a political topic while on the ice, as well as against other forms of impropriety, such as swearing or wagering.[85] This unusual action by the Canadian clubs, therefore, revealed their very strong feelings on the subject.

Sir James Alexander, A.D.C., acted as umpire for the game already mentioned between the Scotsmen and the ''Barbarians'' at Quebec in 1854,[86] and four years later, during the annual competition for the Gold Medal of the Montreal Curling Club, ''Sir W. Eyre was present during the greater part of the day, and took a great interest in the manly game.''[87] One can readily agree with Kerr's statement that:

There is no doubt that the progress of curling in Canada has been in great measure due to the almost continuous support received from the Governors-General of the Dominion.[88]

The Dominion, of course, came into being after 1 July 1867, and certainly the impact of Scottish viceregal patronage, as well as that of other important persons, was greatest in the post-Confederation period of the nineteenth century. However, the game was also undoubtedly nurtured by nobility and the famous from its pioneering days.

It also benefited from the advent of railways, another factor which tremendously affected the spread of this sport, and others, for the rest of the century. But curlers had special reason to be grateful for this technological advance, and to take advantage of it, since their heavy curling-stones and brooms had to accompany them upon any journey for competition, a fact which often posed serious problems.[89] As we have seen, true enthusiasts persevered despite the hardships involved. An enterprising group from the Toronto Club even made use of the lord mayor's carriage and four for a trip to Hamilton in January, 1855![90] Before railways, such a trip was a three-day affair; one to travel the forty miles by sleigh, another to play the match, and a third for the return journey.[91] For this reason, most interclub curling competition naturally reflected local rivalries, such as between Hamilton and Dundas, Montreal and Thistle, Paris and Galt (described as ''positively ferocious'' at times),[92] and Toronto and Scarborough. Transport difficulties were indeed ''a major deterrent to the spread of competition during the forties.''[93] To return to the topic of class participation in sport around this time, Guillet has noted:

It was usually only wealthy gentlemen who could afford the time and expense because inter-club games, particularly in cricket and curling in the 1830's and 1840's through the difficulties of transportation, placed such competition in the category of a half-week's holiday.[94]

In this respect, therefore, the subsequent spread of the railways may be regarded as a ''democratizing'' influence, also.

The great expansion of railways began after 1850; up to that year less than a hundred miles of track had been laid.[95] But by the time of Confederation in 1867, a varied network of over two thousand miles of rail linked the major cities and towns of Ontario in particular, Quebec, and the Maritimes.[96] With this increase came the opportunity for more regular competition with neighboring towns and ''one-day'' events, allied with a general reduction in the amount of traveling time. Also, conditions in the railway carriages themselves gradually improved, basic fares became cheaper over the years, and excursion and special fares were offered to groups by the railway companies.[97] These facts undoubtedly ''made large bonspiels more feasible'' before 1860, such as the Grand East-West affairs of 1858 and 1859.[98] And at a Montreal meeting of the Canadian Branch, also in 1859, it was reported that nearly all the curling clubs of Upper and Lower Canada were represented.[99]

These railways also provided a base for the exceptional increase in the number of curling clubs in the post-Confederation years of the nineteenth century. By 1858, the Great Western had a total length of 345 miles and linked Toronto, Hamilton, Galt, Guelph, Harrisburg, Windsor, and Sarnia. The Grand Trunk had 872 miles by 1860, also serving Toronto, Guelph, London, and Sarnia, but also reaching many other communities as well, including Stratford, Oshawa, Brockville, Montreal, Sherbrooke, Richmond, Quebec, and Kingston among others. The many other smaller railways also linked various communities.[100] As we have seen, curling clubs had been formed in some of these places by hardy enthusiasts before the railways, but the railways undoubtedly contributed to subsequent club development. In the 1860s there were at least eight new curling clubs in the Ontario region,[101] and

at least twice this number again in the 1870s.[102] The numbers of
new clubs then tapered off slightly until 1900.[103] The effect of the
railways can be seen in the rise of many clubs in those places newly
served by their iron roads.

Apart from the two largest railways, the Grand Trunk and the
Great Western, one example is provided by the Port Hope, Lindsay and Beaverton Railway. This was opened on 30 December
1857, and by January 1870 it consisted of eighty-nine miles of
track, linking Port Hope, Lindsay, Millbrook, Peterborough, and
Beaverton.[104] The Port Hope Curling Club was probably formed
sometime between 1862 and 1865;[105] the Lindsay and Peterborough Clubs in 1876; and the Beaverton Club in 1884.
Another example is the Brockville and Ottawa Railway which
which opened in 1859, and linked Brockville to Almonte, and
Smith's Falls to Perth. The Almonte Curling Club was actually
formed in 1855, but the railway provided easy access for competition with the clubs that were later formed in Perth (1875) and
Smith's Falls (1879). The Cobourg and Peterborough Railway
opened its fourteen miles to Harwood in May 1854, and three
years later there was a curling club in Cobourg. Barrie and Col-
lingwood were other communities which were joined by the Northern Railway in 1855 and formed curling clubs in later years.[106]

Southern Ontario was ''full of Scotchmen''[107] who were not
slow to respond as it became well served by hundreds of miles of
railways, by using them well in pursuit of their sports. For the
second East-West bonspiel at Toronto in 1859, the *Globe*
reported:

> Every train which arrived at the Union Depot brought its
> quota of players, accompanied by their curling stones and
> brooms, and upon the arrival of the cars from Hamilton, shortly
> before twelve o'clock, a special train was in waiting to convey
> the curlers to the vantage ground.[108]

The railways ushered in a new era of comfort and cooperation. At
the International Bonspiel at Buffalo in 1865, it was reported that

> through the courtesy of the Great Western Railway, a special
> car was prepared for the curlers, and indeed this company

deserves great credit for the manner in which they have acted towards those who participated in the match.[109]

Then the 10 February 1866 edition of the *Globe* pointed out that the completion of the Grand Trunk Railway from Montreal to Toronto ten years earlier, and the construction of the Great Western Railway in the Lake Erie region, had given many ardent curlers the opportunity to compete in annual bonspiels, held at numerous centers along the railway connections. (Perhaps the fact that many of the directors and officers of the Great Western Railway at this time were Scots had a lot to do with its favorable treatment of the curlers.)[110]

Although basic fares were becoming cheaper, the expense of increasing travel commitments disturbed sporting organizations; and in the 1870's and early 1880's, officials of such organizations began to press the railways for some special fares or discounts for their members, with considerable success. A notable example was that of the Ontario Branch of the Royal Caledonian Curling Club. In 1882—83 the Grand Trunk; Northern; Northwestern; Midland and Credit Valley Railways conceded a rate of one and one-third single fare for the return journey to members of the Branch who were going curling or travelling to an annual meeting. By 1884 there was a flat rate of two cents per mile for a single journey from station to station for parties of not less than eight persons travelling to and from curling matches.[111]

Before the railways, sportsmen travelled overland by other means already mentioned, or by water. In fact, steamboats preceded the locomotives as instigators of intercommunity sport in many parts of Canada,[112] and curlers used them where possible. In 1855, the *Novascotian* stated that ''the steamboat company ought to be very much obliged to the curlers for increasing the travel across the Ferry.''[113] But in the month before this statement, the Nova Scotia Railway was opened, which consisted of 217 miles by the time of Confederation.[114] Also, the opening of the railroad from Halifax to Windsor in the spring of 1858 improved intercolonial travel, as trains ran to and from Halifax twice a day, except Sundays.[115] Through these developments the curlers in the Maritimes also obtained benefit. Curlers there in future could also visit more than one town on a weekend trip and play a series of matches, as did some from Fredericton in 1880, when they travelled to St. John to play against the Thistle Curling Club before continuing to St. Andrew's the next morning for further competition.[116]

Obviously railways greatly affected life generally, especially in trade and commerce, and had many social ramifications which affected all sports. Yet their initial expansion and profusion in areas of concentrated Scottish settlement, at a time when Scots were pioneering their sports, was crucial to the success of those sports. The significance of this was again evident in the spread of Scottish Highland Games in Canada during the same period, as we shall see in the next chapter.

Another railway was responsible for the new and significant direction in the development of curling in Canada after Confederation. Elements which had contributed previously, such as the formation of clubs, interclub competition, high-class patronage, and indoor rinks, continued to affect the sport in an increasingly decisive fashion. Women's participation in the sport was an important new element at this time, also. But the second half of the nineteenth century was dominated by the completion of Canada's first intercontinental railway, the Canadian Pacific. As it shaped the geography and life of the new nation, so it also formed the future of Canadian sport, including curling. As the ''old'' Eastern base was further developed and made secure, more pioneering was necessary as the game followed the CPR west. Scots had brought their ''roarin' game'' across the continent to the Pacific.

By the time the last spike of the CPR was driven home by Donald A. Smith (later Lord Strathcona and Mount Royal) at Craigellachie, in the mountains of British Columbia, in 1885, the railway had served to keep that province in the Confederation; and it permanently shaped the map of Canada as it eventually created and developed some eight hundred communities that stretched across the three prairie provinces alone.[119]

The eventual route stretched from Winnipeg through Portage la Prairie, Brandon, Regina, Moose Jaw, Swift Current, Medicine Hat, Calgary, Banff, Kamloops, and later to Port Moody and Vancouver. The earlier route surveyed by another Scot, Sandford Fleming, who had "made the first practical suggestion for a Pacific railroad nearly a quarter of a century before," had been abandoned in favor of this more southern route.[118]

The acquisitive, energetic, and enterprising Scots were active in these new communities as they had been elsewhere in the Dominion. Apart from their dominant influence in the CPR itself, one Scottish writer has been moved to claim:

> Perhaps the crowning success of Scottish nationality in Western Canada is the spread of the great Scottish game of curling.

The fact that the writer, George Bryce, was a former skip of the Winnipeg Granite Curling Club gave him "peculiar pleasure in recording the remarkable influence exercised by the game of curling in the west." Despite the possible bias, it was not altogether an exaggeration, and the facts bear out his further contention:

> Almost every railway town in Western Canada early in its history erects a commodious building, which is flooded on the interior ground floor and forms an ice sheet which lasts, with some addition, for three or four months.[119]

In 1871, a St. Andrew's Society was organized in Winnipeg, and Donald A. Smith was its first president. Many other Scottish Societies were formed there in subsequent years, a development which can be traced back to Lord Selkirk's original Red River settlement.[120] Curling became organized in Manitoba a few years later, and Smith became a patron of the sport, using some of the wealth gained from his railway enterprises to donate the Strathcona Cup and sponsor the sport in other ways, also.[121] Writing in *Outing* magazine in 1895, Henry J. Woodside observed that "Sir Donald A. Smith, K.C.M.G., donor of the Royal Caledonian Tankard" was

> among the most eminent patrons and curlers of the Northwest. . . . His home is now in Montreal, but he has a

warm feeling for the Province in which the most of his busy life was spent. He is an ardent friend of the Bonspiel and of the game.[122]

Woodside also claimed:

Curling has been more or less in vogue in the Red River settlement since the early part of the century, and has been regularly played in Winnipeg since before the eighties.[123]

However, it was not until 11 December 1876, that "the first official game" was played at the Winnipeg rink of the Manitoba Curling Club.[124] Subscriptions from the seventy members had made the erection of the rink possible, and before the year had ended "arrangements had been made to curl by artificial light." The game lasted two hours and the losers donated their prize, a barrel of oatmeal, to the hospital.[125]

Such charity was not uncommon in Scottish sports, but it must be recorded that another common feature was a generous prize list in their competitions. Monetary prizes, and items of considerable value, were the ultimate objects of such Scottish sporting endeavor in Canada, as they were in Scotland. Certainly many true enthusiasts also participated without any form of profitable inducements, but prizes were a noticeable feature, particularly in curling and the Highland Games. Rewards usually increased in number and value as their sports developed.

By 1889, for example, sixty-two rinks gathered at the Winnipeg Bonspiel for three days of competition "for magnificent trophies and numerous gold and silver medals."[126] Largely through its generous prizes the Winnipeg Bonspiel "was the curlers' delight." In 1901 some of the "loot" included:

First Prize: Challenge Cup, value $250, to be held for one year, and four diamond pins, value $100 each.
Second Prize: Four pearl-handled umbrellas—$50 each.
Third Prize: Four brass kettles—$50 each.
Fourth Prize: Four Bronze statuettes—$30 each."

Other events awarded diamond horseshoe scarf pins; mens' and ladies' gold watches; gold lockets; French bronze onyx clocks; ivory opera glasses; Morris reclining chairs; solitaire opal pins; travelling cases; cups; silver four dishes; alligator cigar cases; gold-headed canes; silver-mounted pipes; bronze lamps; boxes of cigars; and field glasses. Each prize bore a value tag.[127]

The developments towards such opulence were quite spectacular. In fact, the seventy charter members of the Manitoba Curling Club in 1876 initiated perhaps the most prodigious and successful growth of any single sport, associated with a particular area, anywhere in the world. In the late nineteenth century the CPR established Winnipeg; in the twentieth century the province of Manitoba was established as the world center for the sport of curling. This position was being determined before the Scottish curling influence in Canada was gloriously climaxed by the first tour of a Scottish team in 1902–3.

February 13, 1884, "was a red-letter day in the curling history of Manitoba when a grand Provincial Bonspiel was opened." The play lasted two days and ended with a "sumptuous banquet" enjoyed by the members of clubs from Brandon, Emerson, Portage la Prairie, Stonewall, Stony Mountain, and Winnipeg. Other curling clubs, such as those at Carberry, Clearwater, and Morden, were also formed within the next few years.[128] Like their countrymen before them who had crossed to Buffalo for competition in 1865, the Manitoba men followed suit:

> The year 1888 first saw the international border line ignored in a truly sportsmanlike spirit at St. Paul, where nine Manitoba rinks were pitted against American rinks and in all but one contest were victors. The best skill of Portage, Wis.; of Milwaukee, Chicago, Fargo, Wanpaca, St. Paul and Minnesota failed to stay the swift advance of their Northern invaders from over the imaginary line.[129]

Throughout the nineteenth century, in fact, the Scots often treated the international border as "imaginary" while in pursuit of their national sports, especially with regard to the Highland Games.

The success at St. Paul led directly to the formation of the Manitoba Branch of the Royal Caledonian Curling Club, instituted on 6 December 1888, at a meeting in the rooms of the Winnipeg Granite Club.[130] This branch was noted as "having for its territory a district larger than many a world-famous kingdom—from Port Arthur to Calgary, nearly fifteen hundred miles."[131] In years to come, the area was to become equally distinguishable by its numbers of participants. In fact, by 1896, the "Winnipeg Granites were numerically, the strongest curling club in all Canada."[132] Four years earlier Hedley had observed:

> People in Ontario consider that province in an especial degree the home of curling. Many of them will be surprised, however, on learning what strides the game has taken in the far West, and how active and enterprising its votaries are. There are fifteen clubs in Manitoba and eight in the territories of Assininboia and Alberta, the active membership of which twenty-three clubs is over 1,200. The two Winnipeg curling clubs, the Granite and the Thistle, boast respectively 150 and 116 members, and one of their rinks possesses five sheets of ice.

He went on to give membership details of smaller clubs, and to point out that "the citizens of Winnipeg subscribed the sum of $800 for the trophies alone" in a recent bonspiel. (These were the Grand Challenge Cup, the Tuckett Trophy, the Grand International Trophy, the Grand Points Competition Prize, and the Walkerville Tankard.)[133]

From the first donation of a barrel of oatmeal in 1876, to the formation of the Manitoba Branch of the Royal Caledonian Curling Club in 1888 and the subsequent success of the Winnipeg Granites and Thistles in the next decade, it is obvious that there was a large Scottish presence in the sport in Manitoba. Many Scots had migrated there from Ontario, in fact, when it became a wheat-growing province. When Kerr and his party of Scottish curlers visited Winnipeg in 1903, they were able to meet many of the Scottish pioneers of curling in the Northwest.[134]

Ontario had about a hundred clubs in the 1890s against approximately half that number in the rest of Canada.[135] During the

nineteenth century the center stage of curling had passed from
Montreal to Toronto, which had six curling clubs, "all in
excellent working order," by 1884, and had become the headquarters of curling in Ontario.[136] One of the original members of
the Toronto Granite Club, formed in 1875, was no less a person
than Sir John A. Macdonald, accompanied by other eminent
public figures.[137] But by the turn of the century the spotlight was
moving inexorably towards Winnipeg. The historian Kerr was
also captain of the visiting Scottish team to Canada in 1902–3,
when all the party were much impressed by the palatial premises
owned by the Toronto curling clubs.[138] Kerr observed there that
"it seemed to him that the interest in curling increased the father
they went west."[139] And when the team eventually did proceed
"Far West to Winnipeg,"[140] his tendency to use superlatives in
praise of Scottish sport knew no bounds.

"Undoubtedly," said Kerr, "Winnipeg is the very fireplace or
hearth of the game in the Dominion." Significantly, he went
much further: "Winnipeg was indeed the mecca of curlers all
over the world," where curling was "conducted on a scale un-
equalled anywhere else in the world," and the place where "one
meets the finest curlers and sees the finest curling in the world."
Finally, and it was another large and generous admission for an
ambassador of the mother club in Scotland to make, "Winnipeg
was the summit and acme and climax of all."[141] If this were true
then, it was certainly confirmed later. By 1950, Winnipeg had
more curling clubs than Montreal and Toronto combined; and
Manitoba had more curling clubs than in the whole of Ontario
and Quebec. In the 1949–50 season, the Flin Flon Curling Club
claimed to be "the largest individual curling club in the world,
with 121 regular men's and 40 ladies' rinks." The bonspiel entry for the Manitoba Curling Association in 1948, its Diamond
Jubilee Year, was a world record, when 454 rinks competed on
eighty-nine sheets of ice. In 1888, 62 rinks had competed.[142]

Before it became "the very fireplace or hearth of the game in
the Dominion" by 1903, Winnipeg was the springboard by
which curling was taken further west, via the rails of the Canadian Pacific Railway. Under the heading of "Curliana," the
Calgary Herald of 30 November 1883 asked: "Would it not be

well for those of our citizens who participate in the 'roarin' game' to meet together and discuss the propriety of forming a Curling Club?'' A curling club was formed in 1885, and plans were made to form a joint stock company which would sell shares to finance the erection of an enclosed rink. The stock company was registered as the Alberta Rink Company, and the new rink was completed in 1890.[143] In the meantime the curling club had used the Star Skating Rink, and competed in the Winnipeg bonspiel.[144]

Western newspapers at this time were far less sophisticated and detailed than their eastern counterparts, so it is difficult to assess the number of Scots involved in the Calgary Curling Club. However, it is safe to assume some Scottish membership at least, judging from a notice in the *Calgary Herald* in 1889, calling ''The Sons of Scotia'' to a New Year game of shinty on the Elbow River.[145] Also, the *Edmonton Bulletin* in 1884 had reported a curling match in Prince Albert East, in which ''Canada scored 29 against Scotland 26,''[153] indicating a Scottish presence there. A group of Scots were definitely the founders of the Edmonton Curling Club. The *Edmonton Bulletin* of 1 December 1888 announced there would be ''A public meeting for the purpose of organizing a skating and curling club . . . to be held in McDonald's & McLeod's office tonight.'' The same newspaper also carried a report of what was described as ''The first curling match in Northern Alberta'' by a group of Scots celebrating St. Andrew's Day:

> A large number of spectators, many of them ladies, witnessed the game, and much enthusiasm was shown. The following were the rinks played: G. J. Kinnaird, D. G. McQueen, J. Johnson, G. Hislop, skip—15. H. S. Young, T. B. Henderson, James Martin, Jas. McDonald, skip—12. After the game a meeting of the St. Andrew's Society was held in H. S. Young's office when the officers elected on the 23rd were installed.

Whatever may have happened in McDonald's & McLeod's office, it was the gentlemen of the Edmonton St. Andrew's Society who formed a club, for almost a year later the *Edmonton Bulletin* recorded that:

The monthly meeting of the Edmonton Curling Club was held in the club room of the rink of Friday night, M. McCauley presiding. The management committee reported . . . having appointed Rev. D. G. McQueen, Chaplain, and F. Oliver and H. S. Young, club representatives . . . The Secretary reported having 60 names on the membership roll . . . The contractors completed the curling rink building this week . . . It is said to be the best building of the kind in the Territories.[147]

This club also affiliated with the Manitoba Branch of the Royal Caledonian Curling Club and competed in the Winnipeg bonspiel of 1889.[148]

Other curlers were on the river at Medicine Hat in 1889, although a club was not formed until 1896.[149] Also in 1896, curling was taking place in Banff, where a club was formed by 1900.[150] A Lethbridge Curling Club ''was organized in 1889,'' which opened an indoor rink, complete with electric light, eight years later.[151] The Fort Macleod Club also opened its new rink in 1898,[152] and a curling club was formed in Anthracite in 1899.[153] The Calgary bonspiel of the latter year had rinks competing from Edmonton, Fort Macleod, Fish Creek, Lethbridge, Innisfail, and Golden, British Columbia.[154]

The Golden Curling Club had been formed during the winter of 1895–96, along with others at Nelson and Sandon. These were preceded only by a club consisting of sixteen members at Kaslo, who obtained their rocks from Winnipeg.[155] Elsewhere in British Columbia:

The first curling in Armstrong, January 1897, was held in a cattle barn built by Wood Cargill Co. The ''rocks'' were turned by Mr. Norman McLeod from a birch log and handles put in by the blacksmith. Some very interesting games were played with the wooden rocks.[156]

The Kootenay Curling Association was organized at a meeting in the Allan Hotel at Rossland, on 12 February 1898, with J. B. McArthur of Rossland as president. This meeting took place during ''the first bonspiel to be held in British Columbia,'' when eighteen rinks representing Rossland, Sandon, Kaslo, and

Revelstoke took part. Ten years later this association became the British Columbia Curling Association and affiliated with the Royal Caledonian Curling Club of Scotland.[157]

As already stated, the editor of *The Dominion Illustrated* for March 1891 claimed that "curling has spread through the land from Dan to Beersheba."[158] Certainly by the end of the century indoor curling was established as a Dominion wide sport. And during its remarkable progress in the West, it had certainly not lapsed to the east of Winnipeg, either, where other important developments had taken place.

A eulogy of sport in British Columbia, written by a gentleman in 1898, mentioned "the roaring game played by the inferior sex" in that province.[159] It was indicative of an attitude toward women at a time when usually "men performed on the tourney fields of sport under the approving and admiring gaze of ladies." But in the second half of the nineteenth century a favorable change in the attitude of society towards women's participation in sport became apparent, emerging as society itself experienced dramatic changes under such influences as advanced technology and social reform.[160] One of the sports in which women gained their athletic emancipation was curling.

It has been suggested that the consumption of "copious quantities of whisky during the matches" was a very good reason that curling was initially a game for men only, and that ladies became enthusiastic spectators as this habit began to wane.[161] The men began to encourage their presence as spectators, also. In 1890, a Montreal club sponsored a gala ladies' night to which it invited one hundred ladies, and "dainty hands clapped warmly to encourage the players."[162] But by this time many dainty hands had also steered bicycles, thrown basketballs, held hockey sticks and wielded golf clubs,[163] so it was not long before the ladies also participated in curling. One female supporter observed:

> I was much amused the other day, to see the expression of a man's face, when I was telling him that some women had been curling at Galt. He is a Scotchman and pretty well known among the curling fraternity for his proficiency in the game, and his face was a study when he heard that "Some of us

women'' were actually beginning to think that we could
''curl.''

I don't profess to know anything about the game and have
never seen it played, but surely a woman should know better
than a man how to ''sweep'' and how to ''curl.''[164]

It cannot be stated with certainty when or where ladies first pro-
pelled a curling-stone, iron, or wooden block along Canadian ice,
but the first ladies' curling club was formed in Montreal, in
1894, through the efforts of a Mrs. E. A. Whitehead who became
its first president.[165] This stimulated the growth of other ladies'
clubs, mainly in the East, in Lachine, Ottawa, Arnprior, Toronto,
and Kingston, though one club was reported as far away as
Revelstoke, British Columbia.[166] Ladies were curling in Banff and
Edmonton, and probably elsewhere in the West, by 1900.[167] Kerr
and his Scottish party were certainly delighted with the hospitality and competition they enjoyed from lady curlers during their
tour of Canada in 1902-3, and several photographs of the
members of the ladies' clubs involved are included in his book of
the tour.[168] And a women's rink from Quebec City defeated the
visitors, causing Kerr to point out that they used small iron
stones about half the size and weight normally used by the
Scotsmen.[169] On his return home to Scotland, Major Scott Davidson reported that ''the ladies were particularly attentive,'' and
read out telegrams received from the lady curlers of Canada to
support his statement.[170] Curling was not the first sport participated in by women in Canada, nor did it require any radical
attire likely to arouse controversy in the nineteenth century, as
did others. But the advent of women's curling clubs was another
indication of the game's popularity, reflecting social changes that
also opened up other future possibilities for the game's development.

A distinguished lady, the Marchioness of Dufferin, had
previously provided much useful evidence of the support given to
curling by her husband, during his term as governor-general from
1872 to 1878. Lady Dufferin's Canadian diary for the period
recorded many of the earl's curling matches, nearly always with
Scotsmen.[171] His active patronage of the game exceeded that of

Lord Dufferin and party curling at Rideau Hall, Ottawa. (National Photography Collection, Public Archives of Canada, PA 8498)

his predecessors, and shortly after his arrival in Canada, he had a curling rink built at his own expense at Rideau Hall. Despite the many political difficulties during his tenure, the rink subsequently "never lacked for use," as Lord Dufferin formed a Vice-Regal Curling Club and played often and well.[172] In 1892, one Scot, James Brown, vividly recalled playing against His Excellency:

Dae ye mind yon match at the Thistle ice in 1875—four Fredericks, Dufferin, skip, against four Jamies, Macdougall, skip, when the Earl beat us, much to the chagrin of 'The Boss Miller'? Man! there's only twa o's Jamies left. Tempus fugit, and is ever changing, but we may live to meet yet and hae a chat o'er the auld days. Gude grant it.[173]

Lord Dufferin also instituted the Governor-General's Prize, which became one of Canada's most coveted curling trophies, and was first awarded in 1880.[174] On his departure from Canada, the curling clubs of Quebec presented him with a picture of a Canadian curling match, which featured "faithful portraits of many of Canada's keenest curlers, and some of His Excellency's most attached friends." In fact, so enamored of curling was Lord Dufferin that in his next post as British Ambassador to Russia, he endeavored "to establish a curling rink at St. Petersburg on the Canadian principle."[175] Without doubt he was "an avid curler" and "gave a most decided impetus to Scotland's ain game."[176]

This impetus was largely sustained for the remainder of the century by the five succeeding governors-general, three of whom were Scottish and not unfamiliar with the game.[189] Lord Dufferin's curling rink was, of course, a permanent fixture at Rideau Hall and winter sports were established as a social feature there.[178] The Vice-Regal Curling Club continued, also.[179] When the Marquis of Lorne went to meet Princess Louise (the Marchioness of Lorne) at Halifax on her return from England in 1880, he accepted an invitation from the Halifax Curling Club to play on their rink at Tower Road. "The spectators were deeply interested in the games and noticed that His Excellency was a skilled and careful player."[180] The Haligonians finally won a close match by a score of eleven to ten, in what was described as "the red letter day for the Halifax Curling Club."[181] The Marquis of Lansdowne also promoted the game by awarding prizes and became a keen curler during his tenure from 1883 to 1888.[182] J. S. Russell, the Scot whom Kerr regarded as the greatest authority on curling in Canada in 1904, and Stevenson described as the Grand Old Man of the curling world of Ontario, was of the opinion that Dufferin, Lorne, and Lansdowne, "occupying the highest position in the Dominion, greatly promoted the game of curling, and gave it a 'standing' in public estimation it had not previously held."[183]

Their successor, Lord Stanley (1888–93), an Englishman, was at Rideau Hall when ''sport figured more prominently than ever before,'' but curling was featured less, and Kerr does not deign to mention his Lordship. However, as the donor of the Stanley Cup for hockey, his place in Canadian history is assured. The wife of the next governor-general was also apparently ''fascinated by the game of hockey,'' but her husband, Lord Aberdeen (1893–98), was true to his Scottish title and ''eagerly took part in the curling.''[184] The next Scot in office, the Earl of Minto (to whom Kerr dedicated his book of the Scottish Tour), actually ''devoted his spare time more to skating than curling,'' and founded the Minto Skating Club, from which there later emerged a Canadian world champion in the sport, Barbara Ann Scott.[185] His Excellency also established the Minto Cup for lacrosse and, reflecting the general rise of sport in society, again it could be said that ''sport now played a more prominent part in the life of Rideau Hall than before.''[186] Despite the apparent downgrading of curling, Lord Minto's nationality no doubt redeemed him in Kerr's eyes, and besides, ''no one was more anxious to see our Scottish team out in Canada and no one showed us more kindness than His Lordship.''[187] Also, in his younger days in Canada, when he was a military secretary, he had apparently taught the Marquis of Lansdowne the rudiments of curling.[188]

Many people apart from His Lordship were anxious to receive a visit from a Scottish curling team, and had been for years. Scots in Canada were naturally proud of the game's tremendous progress, of their indoor rinks, and of their own ability. They had a natural desire to exhibit their facilities and skills to their countrymen in ''auld Scotia,'' the home of the royal club. As time went by, and curling became more and more established in Canada, their invitations to Scotland became more challenging, more personal, and more urgent.

It was in 1858 that the curlers of Upper Canada ''were so pleased with their skill on the ice that they sent a challenge to the Royal Caledonian Curling Club, but it evoked no response.'' In succeeding years, more clubs were formed in Canada; international matches were played against the United States; indoor rinks began to multiply; the railways helped to spread the game further; and the Ontario Branch of the R.C.C.C. was formed in 1874, largely due to the initiative of Scots J. S. Russell and David Walker. Scots at home were obviously going to find it more difficult to ignore the requests of their curling brethren in the largest Dominion. At its first meeting, the Ontario Branch agreed to ask Dr. Barclay, the Scottish Reverend of St. Andrew's Church in Toronto from 1842 to 1872, to attend the annual meeting of the R.C.C.C. and request its members "to enjoy with us the admirable conditions under which the game is carried on in Canada." Dr. Barclay acceded to this request, "and had spiced his invitation to the curlers of Scotland to send a team to Canada, with an undertaking that they would meet their match in Ontario." The members of the R.C.C.C. were no less confident of their curling ability, and proclaimed their willingness "to meet us in friendly encounter, and beat us too."[189] But no Scottish visit to Canada resulted from this repartee.

Within the next few years after Dr. Barclay's return to Canada, interprovincial curling became common, thanks to the railways, and more indoor rinks were built. In 1880, a Manitoba team traveled to Ontario for games, and in the following year Nova Scotia defeated Manitoba in Winnipeg.[190] Members of the Ontario Branch also decided "to emphasize their achievement of complete autonomy" from the R.C.C.C., by changing its name to "The Ontario Curling Association," at the annual meeting held on 18 October 1892.[191]

At this time, curlers in Canada had many clubs scattered far and wide, provincial associations, cooperative and convenient railways, and excellent facilities with a guaranteed suitable climate. They had competition at every level, and a large number of annual trophies and prizes. They enjoyed consistent and beneficial high-class patronage of their sport, which also enjoyed an increasing amount of space in the newspapers and journals of the time. There had been differences over the years, certain unavoidable growing pains,[192] but no sport in Canada was in better shape or seemed to have a better future. And they had also achieved a degree of autonomy from the Royal Club in Scotland. Yet they were all united in wanting what they still lacked—a chance to display their wonderful achievements to representatives from the birthplace of the sport. As children obtaining independence seek to impress their parents, so the Scottish curlers in Canada consistently entreated the mother club to visit them.

They especially requested departing governors-general to do whatever they could to bring about a Scottish tour to Canada, upon their arrival back in Britain. Lord Dufferin, Lord Lorne, and Lord Lansdowne faithfully passed on their wishes to the R.C.C.C. in Scotland.[193] Lord Meglund, later Lord Minto, was

> not only a very ardent curler but he was President-elect of the Royal Caledonian Curling Club and he bestirred himself zealously to back a renewed invitation to the curlers of Scotland to send at least two or three rinks for a curling tour in Ontario but it did not evoke the response which had been hoped for.[194]

In 1896, the Scottish author George Bryce was present at the annual meeting of the Royal Club, held that year in Perth, Scotland:

> As representing the Canadian branch, the writer in speaking issued a challenge to a number of Scottish curlers to make a playing trip through Canada, suggesting also that the Canadians might be able to set an example as to how the game should be played, even in the presence of those who were adept at the Scottish sport.[195]

Obviously, Scottish pride could not endure such challenges for long, and no doubt the curiosity of curlers in Scotland was being stretched to the limit by accounts of the game's remarkable progress in Canada. Dr. Barclay of Montreal again ''renewed, in a pressing manner'' the invitation from the Canadian Branch when he went across for the annual meeting of the Royal Club in 1901, but

> . . . the best fillip to the Scottish tour was given by Mr. Hugh Cowan, who, in an interesting article in the *Scotsman* of March 17, 1902, in a description of Winnipeg as a ''curler's paradise'' finished his remarks by saying: ''For many years a

visit from a Scottish team has been eagerly looked for. Four years ago it was promised and then abandoned, to the great regret of all. Ever since they hoped, from year to year, to see the promise fulfilled. The interest in this is not confined to Manitoba. Toronto and Montreal are just as eager, and an extended tour should be taken; but the officials of the Manitoba branch have asked the writer to voice their feelings. . . .''

In Kerr's words, ''Mr. Cowan fairly set the ball rolling'' at last. Kerr himself, then chaplain of the Royal Club, immediately endorsed the suggestion wholeheartedly by also writing to the *Scotsman*, stating towards the end of his letter ''we shall be unworthy of our national game if we do not take action.'' Three days later, another letter was published in the same newspaper from the Rev. Gavin Lang of Inverness, a former chaplain of the Montreal Curling Club, who recalled that Lord Dufferin had played his first game on the club's rink. The Reverend went on:

One of the pictures in my modest collection of which I am especially proud, is that which Mr. William Notman, of Montreal, contributed to a Paris Exhibition, in which he depicts a curling scene on the River St. Lawrence and under the shadow of Mount Royal. In the forefront stand Lord and Lady Dufferin, attended by Mr. George Denholm, a veteran curler, broom in hand, and nearly all the notables of Canada, including Sir John A. Macdonld, Sir Hugh Allan, Colonel Dyde, A.D.C. to the late Queen, etc., etc., are either players or spectators. It is an honour that I exceedingly prize that the artist represents me as one of the two, the other being a Quebec champion, in the act of playing our turn. By all means send a Scottish team to Canada, and let the extended tour sketched by Mr. Cowan be carried out.[196]

Other letters pressed the point, special meetings were held on both sides of the Atlantic, arrangements were finally made, and the long-awaited tour was ''on.''[197]

Many notables in both countries were pleased at the prospect, including Lord Strathcona, who responded to his circular from the Royal Club by offering ''such service as I can render, either personally or as High Commissioner.''[198] Cowan had previously pointed out that the journey would prove no difficulty, since "the steamboat and railway companies would always be willing to give special facilities for the tour."[199] The Ontario Curling Association was extremely pleased at the prospect of the proposed tour, but for one item. When the itinerary revealed that only nine days out of the six-week tour of Canada were scheduled for the territory under its jurisdiction, the association felt compelled to point out to the Royal Club "that Ontario was the greatest stronghold of curling in Canada," and its representations resulted in an extension to thirteen days.[200]

The tour was a great success, and a most apt and fitting tribute to the influence of the Scottish curling pioneers in Canada throughout the previous century. At the very first rink the tourists entered in Canada, at Halifax, there was displayed the Scottish flag with the lion rampant, as well as the Union Jack, and a large sign with a Gaelic motto: "Caed mille failthe o Alba uir do shean Alba" ("A hundred thousand welcomes from new Scotland to old Scotland"). Such scenes and sentiments became commonplace as the tourists progressed from Halifax to St. John (New Brunswick), and then to Quebec City, Montreal, Ottawa, Peterborough, Lindsay, Toronto, Hamilton, Guelph, Stratford, St. Thomas, Windsor, and Winnipeg. Everywhere their hosts pledged their loyalty to Scotland, "the auld mither," and the British Crown, while also praising Canada and taking evident pride in being described as "Scoto-Canadians," or simple "Canadians." Scots from places not included in the tour, such as Alberta, Victoria in British Columbia, and even Dawson City in the Yukon, pleaded with the tourists to extend their visit in order to play with their curling clubs.[201] All had to be reluctantly declined, including "a truly Scottish invite" from the Brandon Club of Manitoba, which began:

Rev. Mr. Kerr,
Captain o' oor Mither Curlers frae Hame.

REV. SIR—Ooor curler freens up here i' "The Wheat City" are anxious tae hae an end or twa wi' ye an' yer Cronies, an' tae that end we extend ye a herty welcome tae Brandon. We're plantit doon here i' the hert o' the Manitoba Wheat Belt,

The Scottish Curling Team that toured Canada, at Winnipeg, 1903. (National Photograph Collection, Public Archives of Canada. C81312)

whaur we hae No. 1 Hard Wheat in Autumn and No. 1 Hard Ice in Winter.[202]

Only one unpleasant incident occurred in the whole tour, when a Reverend Dr. Milligan of Toronto took the Scottish tourists to task from his pulpit for an outing on the Sabbath. He had expected better, he said, ''than the spectacle of Scotsmen, with a minister at their head, on a Sunday jaunt to Niagara Falls.''[203] The Reverend John Kerr, Captain of the Scottish team, replied that they had all regularly attended church since their arrival in Canada, ''and surely a day off to worship the Almighty at such a

magnificent shrine might be permitted us''; and he ended by
paraphrasing Wordsworth:

> One impulse from Niagara,
>   Will teach you more of man,
> Of moral evil and of good,
>   Than Dr. Milligan.

Much debate ensued concerning the matter,[204] but it remained an
isolated incident, and it was with great reluctance that the party
left Winnipeg, and Canada, to continue their tour with a shorter
visit to the United States.

Perhaps the happiest outcome of all was that it inspired the
Reverend Kerr to produce his *Curling in Canada and the United
States*, an unsurpassed record of its development in both countries up to 1903, especially with its profuse and valuable illustrations. Together with the faithfully recorded ''Impressions of the
Team,'' it provides the most valid example of the supreme Scottish influence on this sport in Canada, and has guided the other
authors whose works subsequently complemented but never surpassed it.

The secretary of the Boston Curling Club suggested in 1891
that ''one often hears it said that Scotchmen keep the Sabbath
and everything else they can lay their hands on that is worth
keeping.''[205] They certainly laid claim to curling as ''Scotland's
ain game,'' but equally certainly it was not kept to themselves.
The very year that the Scottish touring team arrived, in 1902,
Munro sensed the transition:

> There was something of romance in those winter nights
> when, with torches, stuck in the snow banks at the rink-side,
> their Scottish accents floated out through the shadows of the
> trees towering up through the surrounding darkness—''Play
> the broom, Geordie,'' ''Anither o' the same, Psalms o'
> David,'' ''Yer fer a curler; come up an' look at it yersel',
> mon.'' Now all this has changed. The romance of the pioneer
> has given place to the comforts of civilization. Even the Scot-
> tish accents are fading out of the game and in clear-cut Cana-
> dian the skip's orders ring out; in stately rinks and on sheets of

pebbled ice as level as a billiard board the games are played while the electric lights have turned the outside darkness into a second edition of the day. Yes, all is changing save the game itself. "Elbow oot" and "Elbow in" may now be "Out turn" and "In turn"; "A wheen more bona" may now be "A little more ice," and the Scotch-bonnetted red-sashed shouter may have given place to a quieter and more carefuly groomed player, but the old game with its same old fascination is there still. And while it lasts and the frost holds Canada will never lack for curlers.[206]

By the time Kerr and his party returned to Scotland the following year, the message was clear. Scotland represented the glorious past of curling, and Canada promised it a brilliant future. Early in his prodigious account of the tour, the Reverend Captain himself expressed the hope that

> it will prove to be a solid and reliable basis for any future history that may be written of Curling in the land of its adoption, where the game has such a glorious future before it, and where it is destined to play a most important part in the evolution of a great race.[207]

Scotland had been the parent of curling, Canada was now its "Eldorado," and Winnipeg—almost exactly in the center of the Dominion—was the "Mecca" of the sport.[208] One can only wonder at what Kerr's feelings might have been had he been able to read in *Maclean's* magazine, seventy one years after the great Tour, that:

> Curling claims to have 800,000—that's one in every 27 Canadians. Its popularity is still growing but even now it probably comes closest to being our true national sport.[209]

If the Scots had done nothing more than bring curling to Canada, and develop it, their place in the sporting history of the nation would be significant and secure.

In fact, they did much more. Other sports were also traditional in Scotland besides "the roarin' game," notably the Highland

Games and golf. (Kerr and his party celebrated their first tourists'
annual reunion at Elie, in Fife, by playing golf.)[210] Although curling represents the most important aspect of Scottish influence on
sport in Canada during the nineteenth century, the other athletic
endeavors of Scots in this period were also significant and successful ventures.

Notes

1. John McNair, *The Channel Stane, or Sweeping Frae the Rinks*, 4 vols.
(1883–85), 1:73–74, as quoted in Edwin C. Guillet, *Pioneer Days in Upper Canada*
(Toronto: University of Toronto Press, 1970), pp. 208–9.

2. This was on the Island of Mull, in conversation with Sir Allan McLean, who had
boasted that Scotland had an advantage over England by its having more water. Johnson
replied "Sir, we would not have your water, to take the vile bogs which produce
it. . . . Your country consists of two things, stone and water. There is, indeed, a little
earth above the stone in some places, but a very little; and the stone is always appearing. It
is like a man in rags—the naked skin is still peeping out." See F. V. Morley, ed., *James
Boswell: The Life of Samuel Johnson and The Journal of a Tour to the Hebrides with
Samuel Johnson, LL.D.* (New York: Harper and Row, 1966), pp. 564–65.

3. The Rev. John Kerr, *Curling in Canada and the United States: A Record of the
Tour of the Scottish Team, 1902—3, and of the game in the Dominion and the Republic*
(Toronto: The Toronto News Co., 1904), pp. 107, 605.

4. W. A. Creelman, *Curling Past and Present* (Toronto: McClelland and Stewart,
1950), p. 142.

5. John A. Stevenson, *Curling in Ontario, 1846–1946* (Toronto: Ontario Curling
Association, 1950), p. 23.

6. Robin Welsh, *Beginner's Guide to Curling* (London: Pelham Books, 1969) p.
131.

7. Gerald William Bowie, "The History and Trends of Curling" (M.S. thesis,
Washington State University, 1962), p. 60, states: "It is held by many historians that
curling began on the North American continent around 1760 when the sick and the
wounded of Fraser's Regiment, or the Seventy-Eighth Highlanders, who fought at Ste.
Foy under General Murray in the Seven Year War of 1756–1763, curled on the ice of
the St. Charles River during the days of their convalescence," Henry Roxborough, *One
Hundred—Not Out: The Story of Nineteenth-Century Canadian Sport* (Toronto: The
Ryerson Press, 1966), p. 100, states: "Curling was an early import into Canada. Some
historians give its birth as the winter of 1759/60 when Wolfe's soldiers at Quebec melted
down French cannon and moulded the metal into irons for curling."

8. John Kerr, *History of Curling: Scotland's Ain Game, and Fifty Years of the
Royal Caledonian Curling Club* (Edinburgh: David Douglas, 1890), pp. 114–15. These
clubs were in Berwick, Dumbarton, Fife, Lanark, Perth, Stirling, and perhaps Midlothian.

9. Ibid., p. 323.

10. Stevenson, *Curling in Ontario*, p. 23.

11. Ibid.; Bowie, "Trends of Curling," p. 60; Guillet, *Pioneer Days*, p. 207; Kerr,
History of Curling, p. 324, and *Curling in Canada*, p. 143.

12. Peter Leslie Lindsay, "A History of Sport in Canada, 1807–1867" (Ph.D. diss.,
University of Alberta, 1969), pp. 22–23.

13. Ibid., p. vii.

14. Kerr, *History of Curling*, p. 323.

15. *Montreal Star*, January 1934.

16. Stewart Alexander Davidson, "A History of Sports and Games in Eastern Canada Prior to World War I" (D.Ed. diss., Columbia University, 1951). p. 30.

17. John Allen Krout, *Annals of American Sport 15, The Pageant of America Series*, 15 vols. (New York: United States Publishers' Association, 1929), p. 281. This is a section entitled "The Scottish Influence," and the author gives a reproduction of a notice in the *Charleston City Gazette*, 13 October 1795, advertising the anniversary of the golf club.

18. As quoted in Stevenson, *Curling in Ontario*, pp. 23–24.

19. Ibid., Guillet, *Pioneer Days*, pp. 207–8, Roxborough, *One Hundred—Not Out*, p. 100. It is possible that only the other social activities ceased while curling continued. Stevenson quotes the secretary of the club, after a resolution to dine before and at the end of the season, adding: "This was adopted because the club had not met to dine for more than 6 years, partly occasioned by the war in which we were engaged with the United States." Roxborough maintains: "Through the years of the War of 1812–14 the Montreal Club curtailed some of its social functions, but the curlers still continued their matches."

20. *Annual of the Ontario Curling Association for 1968–1969*, volume 94 (Toronto: Maclean-Hunter, n.d.), p. 134; hereafter referred to as Annual of the O. C. A.

21. Creelman, *Curling Past*, p. 136; Stevenson, *Curling in Ontario*, pp. 24–26. The charter members of the Quebec Curling Club, showing the predominant Scottish influence, were: Andrew Paterson, Robert Paterson, Andrew Weir, William Findlay, A. Moir, William Pemberton, M. McKenzie, William Phillips, L. P. MacPherson, J. C. McTavish, James G. Heath, George Pemberton, and Thomas Greegan. See also the letter signed "A Curler" in the *Montreal Gazette*, 5 January 1841, with reference to curling in Quebec "occasionally, before 1807," and a club being formed there "several years after the formation of the Montreal Club."

22. John Quinpool, *First Things in Acadia* (Halifax, N.S.: First Things Publishers, 1936), p. 85: Creelman, *Curling Past*, p. 127. However, Kerr, *Curling in Canada*, p. 81, gives 1825 or 1826 as the date of the founding of the Halifax Curling Club, while Phyllis R. Blakeley, *Glimpses of Halifax, 1867–1900* (Halifax, N.S.: The Public Archives of Nova Scotia, 1949), states: "Curling in Halifax owed its popularity to the presence of officers of the army and navy and to other loyal sons of Scotland. Organized first in 1825 by Captain Houston Stewart R. N., games were played in the open, chiefly on ponds near Tower Road and on the Dartmouth Lakes."

23. John Mactaggart, *Three Years in Canada, 1826–1828* (London: Henry Colburn, 1829), pp. 11, 222.

24. Creelman, *Curling Past*, pp. 127–28.

25. Nancy Howell and Maxwell L. Howell, *Sports and Games in Canadian Life: 1700 to the Present* (Toronto: Macmillan of Canada, 1969), p. 55. Also, Kerr, *Curling in Canada*, passim, provides the names of literally hundreds of Scots connected with curling clubs in Canada.

26. Hugh Templin, *Fergus: The Story of a Little Town* (Fergus: Fergus News Record, 1933), p. 261. See also Stevenson, *Curling in Ontario*, p. 23.

27. *Annual of O. C. A.*, pp. 133–37. For an extensive description of early curling in Scarborough, which gives details of early clubs and members up to 1896, see David Boyle, ed., *The Township of Scarboro, 1796—1896* (Toronto: William Birggs, 1896), pp. 241–50.

28. James Young, *Early History of Galt and the Settlement of Dumfries* (Toronto: Hunter, Rose and Co., 1880), p. 127.

29. Guillet, *Pioneer Days*, p. 209; Roxborough, *One Hundred—Not Out*, p. 101. See also Stevenson *Curling in Ontario*, between pp. 36–37, for photographs showing "the development of the curling stone in Ontario between 1835 and 1870."

30. Guillet, *Pioneer Days*, p. 208; Kerr, *Curling in Canada*, pp. 144–45.

31. *Montreal Gazette*, 22 December 1836.

32. Guillet, *Pioneer Days*, p. 208.

33. Kerr, *Curling in Canada*, p. 145; *Montreal Gazette*, 11 December 1848.

34. *Montreal Gazette*, 5 December 1844.

35. Kerr, *Curling in Canada*, p. 336.

36. As quoted in Roxborough, *One Hundred—Not Out*, p. 101.

37. Kerr, *Curling in Canada*, pp. 332–44.

38. Stevenson, *Curling in Ontario*, p. 26.

39. Boyle, *Township of Scarboro'*, pp. 241–43.

40. For a lengthy review of this book at that time, see the *Montreal Gazette*, 9 January 1841. The unidentified writer hoped the book was "destined to find its way into many successive editions; and thus afford both instruction and amusement to the lovers of curling in the CANADAS now happily united by law, as we hope soon to find them by an interchange of mutual challenges and contests in the noble, and, we may add, national science of 'Curling.'" This is probably the first (though somewhat oblique and optimistic in 1841) reference to curling as a national game in Canada.

41. *Globe*, 19 February 1858.

42. Kerr, *Curling in Canada*, p. 336.

43. Stevenson, *Curling in Ontario*, pp. 23–42, 165–226.

44. *Globe*, 27 December 1859.

45. Boyle, *Township of Scarboro'*, pp. 247–48.

46. "In 1862 we find the following new clubs organized and in active operation within the range embraced by the Toronto district, viz.—Vaughan, Scarborough, Ancaster, Dundas, Bowmanville, and Newcastle; Markham was added in 1863, and Port Hope in 1864," Kerr, *Curling in Canada*, p. 337.

47. Ibid. But there was a smaller contest between Canadian and American curling clubs before this date. A match at West Troy, in northern Vermont, was referred to as being a Canada versus United States game in the *Montreal Gazette*, 12 January 1861. "Canada" was represented by Dr. Hamilton, and Messrs. Beattie, Betts, and Gillespie.

48. *Globe*, 7 January 1865.

49. *Globe*, 4 February 1865; 16 and 17 January 1866.

50. Stevenson, *Curling in Ontario*, pp. 68–69, 172–75, 222–24.

51. Kerr, *Curling in Canada*, p. 338.

52. Bowie, "Trends of Curling," p. 62.

53. Lindsay, "Sport in Canada, 1807 to 1867," pp. 31–32. The Bytown Curling Club was formed in 1851, and many artifacts, documents, and photographs pertaining to the club's history can be seen today at the Bytown Museum, in Ottawa, including some early curling irons and stones.

54. Ibid., p. 34; Kerr, *Curling in Canada*, p. 84. Creelman, *Curling Past*, p. 131, gives 1855 as the founding date for the St. Andrew's Club of St. John. It is interesting to note that the St. Andrew's Society of St. John, New Brunswick, is one of the oldest Scottish Societies in Canada, being formed on 8 March, 1798. Campbell has devoted several pages to the history of this Society but gives no clue to the date of the formation of a curling club associated with it [Wilfred Campbell, *The Scotsman in Canada*, vol. 1 (Toronto:

The Musson Book Co., n.d.), pp. 412–18]. Also, J. Hedley, "Curling in Canada," *Dominion Illustrated Monthly* 1 (1892): 177, suggests that "Curling was first practised in New Brunswick by officers of the 'Black Watch' Highland regiment, stationed at St. John in 1853."

55. *Globe*, 3 December 1858. See also Stevenson, *Curling in Ontario*, p. 30.

56. Roxborough, *One Hundred—Not Out*, p. 99.

57. As quoted in the *Montreal Gazette*, 2 March 1843.

58. As quoted in Kerr, *History of Curling*, p. 326.

59. Robert Douglas Day, "Impulse to Addiction: A Narrative History of Sport in Chatham, Ontario, 1790–1895" (M.A. thesis, University of Western Ontario, 1977), pp. 169–76.

60. Lindsay, "Sport in Canada, 1807 to 1867," pp. 29–30.

61. *Morning Chronicle*, 8 February 1862.

62. Lindsay, "Sport in Canada, 1807 to 1867," p. 40.

63. Creelman, *Curling Past*, p. 131.

64. For accounts of curling in other parts of Britain than Scotland during the nineteenth century, see Kerr, *History of Curling*, pp. 308–20; and Welsh, *Guide to Curling*, passim.

65. Kerr, *Curling in Canada*, passim.

66. Ibid., p. 294. Also, curling seems to have been the first organized sport in Paris, Ontario, when a group of twenty-three Parisians formed the Paris Curling Club in 1843. Not all of them were Scots, but most of them were, "and very proud of it." D. A. Smith, *At the Forks of the Grand* (Paris, Ontario: Walker Press, n.d.), p. 189.

67. Stevenson, *Curling in Ontario*, pp. 45, 207–26.

68. "The Curler's Annual," *Chambers' Edinburgh Journal* 3 (1844): 120–22.

69. Welsh, *Guide to Curling*, pp. 177–78.

70. Kerr, *History of Curling*, p. 311.

71. *Chambers Encyclopedia* (1860–68), 3:368, as quoted in Guillet, *Pioneer Days* p. 207.

72. The works of Creelman, Kerr, and Welsh, as quoted, provide many examples.

73. As quoted in Welsh, *Guide to Curling*, p. 168.

74. Roxborough, *One Hundred—Not Out*, p. 102. More details of these individuals are given in Kerr, *Curling in Canada*, pp. 333–36.

75. *Montreal Gazette*, 10 January 1855.

76. Day, "Sport in Chatham," pp. 171–72.

77. Alan Metcalfe, "Organized Sport and Social Stratification in Montreal: 1840–1901," in Gruneau and Albinson, eds., *Canadian Sport: Sociological Perspectives* (Don Mills, Ontario: Addison-Wesley Canada, 1976), p. 80.

78. Kerr, *Curling In Canada*, pp. 228–29.

79. Guillet, *Pioneer Days*,p. 207.

80. J. Hedley, "Curling in Canada," *Dominion Illustrated Monthly* 1 (1892):117.

81. Creelman, *Curling Past*, p. 135; Stevenson, *Curling in Ontario*, pp. 24–25.

82. Guillet, *Pioneer Days*, pp. 209–12.

83. Kerr, *Curling in Canada*, p. 148; idem, *History of Curling*, p. 327. The *Annual* referred to is probably James Bicket's *The Canadian Curler's Manual: or an Account of Curling as Practised in Canada, with Remarks on The History of the Game* (Toronto, 1840).

84. *Montreal Gazette*, 30 April 1849.

85. Kerr, *History of Curling*, passim; Stevenson, *Curling in Ontario*, pp. 176–77; Welsh, *Guide to Curling*, p. 176. This was another argument used in support of the

CURLING

sport's democratic nature, for it meant that political or religious opponents could theoretically enjoy curling in each other's company without recourse to differences between them.

86. Kerr, *History of Curling*, p. 326. Quoting from the same clipping in his *Curling in Canada*, however, Kerr states that "Sir James Alexander, A.D.C., acted as Mayor." Whatever the correct title attached to his duties, Sir James obviously took an active part in the proceedings.

87. *Montreal Gazette*, 23 January 1858.

88. Kerr, *Curling in Canada*, p. 148.

89. In winter, the wheels of carriages were replaced with runners, and the "cutter" and carriole were suitable passenger sleighs. The stagecoach for passenger travel was usually drawn by four hourses and accommodated about nine persons with luggage, mail, and light freight. See C. P. de T.Glazebrook, *A History of Transportation in Canada*, vol. 1 (Toronto: McClelland and Stewart, 1964), pp. 32–131. As late as 1890, two Prince Albert rinks traveled to Qu'Appelle on sleighs, hauling their curling stones behind them on a toboggan, and then continued by train to the Winnipeg bonspiel (Roxborough, *One Hundred—Not Out*, p. 103).

90. *Globe*, 20 January 1855. The party consisted of Messrs. A. Morrison, J. Hutchinson, J. Helliwell, J. Ewart, J. Dick, D. McBride, A. McPherson, and G. Ewart.

91. Guillet, *Pioneer Days*, p. 211.

92. Stevenson, *Curling In Ontario*, p. 52.

93. Lindsay, "Sport in Canada, 1807–1867," p. 30.

94. Guillet, *Pioneer Days*, p. 10.

95. Glazebrook, *Transportation in Canada*, p. 153.

96. Ibid., vol. 2, p. 94; Alexander M. Delisle, *Railroad between Quebec, Montreal, Bytown and Georgian Bay* (Montreal: W. Salter and Co., 1853); William Michaud, *Pioneer Railways of Central Ontario* (Toronto: Canadian National Railways, 1964).

97. Ian F. Jobling, "Sport in Nineteenth Century Canada: The Effects of Technological Changes on its Development" (Ph.D. diss., University of Alberta, 1970), pp. 34–38.

98. Lindsay, "Sport in Canada, 1807–1867," p. 32.

99. *Morning Chronicle*, 20 January 1859.

100. J. M. and Edw. Trout, *The Railways of Canada for 1870-1* (Toronto: Monetary Times, 1871), pp. 35–36.

101. These were situated at Keene (1861), Chatham (1862), Sarnia (1864), St. Mary's (1866), Belleville (1867), Hamilton (1867), and Arnprior (1868). See *Annual of O. C. A.*, pp. 133–38. The Hamilton Thistle Curling Club began in 1853; the one formed in 1867 was the Hamilton Victoria Club. *The Minutes of The London Curling Club*, 3 vols., 1849–1940, are situated in the Library, University of Western Ontario.

102. These were situated in Elmvale (1870), Orillia (1873), and Renfrew (1874). Curling clubs were formed in Kincardine, Owen Sound, and Perth in 1875. In the following year, clubs were formed at Brant, Brantford, Lindsay, Meaford, Pembroke, Peterborough, and Seaforth. Then followed Lakefield (1877), Churchill (1878), and Smith's Falls (1879). See *Annual of O. C. A.*, pp. 133–38.

103. At least fifteen new curling clubs were formed in the 1880s in Ontario, and at least another ten in the 1890s. See *Annual of O. C. A.*, pp. 133–38.

104. Trout, *Railways of Canada*, p. 36.

105. Strangely, neither Creelman, Kerr, Stevenson, nor even the *Annual of O. C. A.* gives the founding date for the Port Hope Curling Club. However, Stevenson, *Curling in Ontario*, p. 31, states: "The next five years, i.e., after 1862, saw the admission of nine

additional clubs: Chatham, Hope (Port Hope), Thames of London, Ayr, Otonabee (Keene), Galt, Thamesville, New Dominion (Ayr), and Cobourg Waverley, which replaced the defunct Cobourg Club, and this expansion of membership in Upper Canada impelled the governing authorities of the Branch to increase the number of R.C.C.C. medals alotted to it to seven.'' This indicates that Port Hope Club could have been formed between 1862 and 1867. But a Port Hope "club" took part in the International Bonspiel at Buffalo in 1865 (*Globe*, 7 January 1865), so it was probably formed sometime between 1862 and 1865.

106. *Annual of O. C. A.*, p. 133—137; Trout, *Railways of Canada*, pp. 35—36.

107. John K. Munro, "Curling in Canada," *Canadian* 18 (1902):529. For this reason, the author goes on, "[curling] clubs sprang up on all sides."

108. *Globe*, 9 February 1859.

109. *Globe*, 7 January 1865.

110. See the chapter entitled "Great Western Railway" in Trout, *Railways of Canada*, pp. 87–102.

111. Stevenson, *Curling in Ontario*, p. 78.

112. Jobling, "Technological Changes," pp. 14–24.

113. *Novascotian*, 5 March 1855.

114. Trout, *Railways of Canada*, p.36.

115. As quoted in Jobling, "Technological Changes," p. 33.

116. *Reporter and Fredericton Advertiser*, 11 February, 1880.

117. Pierre Berton, *The National Dream: The Great Railway, 1871—1881* (Toronto: McClelland and Stewart, 1970), passim; and *The Last Spike: The Great Railway. 1881—1885* (Toronto: McClelland and Stewart, 1971), passim. And, of course, in this way too, it was the CPR which largely determined where sport would flourish in Canada. See also George M. Grant, "The Canadian Pacific Railway," *Century Magazine, October 1885, pp. 882—89.*

118. Berton, *Last Spike*, pp. 2, 16–21.

119. George Bryce, *The Scotsman in Canada*, vol. 2 (Toronto: Musson Book Co., 1911), pp. 417–18.

120. *Constitution of the St. Andrew's Society of the City of Winnipeg* (Winnipeg: Walker and May, 1886), p. 8. It was organized when "Scotchmen and descendants of Scotchmen" met at the Davis Hotel, Winnipeg, on Tuesday, 7 November 1871, when the name of the Society was actually the Selkirk St. Andrew's Society of Manitoba in honor of the noble lord who landed the first band of Scottish Colonists in the Red River Settlement. It was reorganzied as the "St. Andrew's Society of Winnipeg" in 1879. The above *Constitution* and other documents pertaining to the society, are located in the Public Archives of Manitoba, Legislative Library, Legislative Buildings, Winnipeg, Manitoba.

121. A photograph of this cup is in Kerr, *Curling in Canada*, p. 471. The Strathcona Papers are in the Public Archives of Canada, Ottawa. Strathcona Papers, M.G. 29, D. 14, vol. 19, D. 52, gives details of his annual donations to the Manitoba Curling Club, as well as many other subscriptions. Kerr, *Curling in Canada*, p. 464, gives details of Lord Strathcona's gift of $500 for the Winnipeg bonspiel in 1903, and on pp. 209–10 states that Lord Strathcona was Patron of the Lachine Curling Club, and "on hearing of the visit of the Scottish Curlers sent the club a handsome donation to defray expenses." See also: Gerald Redmond, "Apart from the Trust Fund: Some Other Contributions of Lord Strathcona to Canadian Recreation and Sport," *Canadian Journal of History of Sport and Physical Education*, December 1973, pp. 59–69.

122. Henry J. Woodside, "Curling in the Northwest, Part II," *Outing*, March 1895, p. 498.

123. Henry J. Woodside, "Curling in the Northwest, Part I," *Outing*, February 1895, p. 422.

124. Roxborough, *One Hundred—Not Out*, p. 103.

125. Creelman, *Curling Past*, pp. 142–43; Roxborough, *One Hundred—Not Out*, p. 103. *The Winnipeg Free Press*, 21 March 1877, reported the installation of a gas-lamp reflector system. See also Fred C. Lucas, *An Historical Souvenir Diary of the City of Winnipeg, Canada* (Winnipeg: Cartwright and Lucas, 1923), pp. 226.

126. Woodside, "Curling in the Northwest" (I), p. 423. Also, Hedley, "Curling in Canada," p. 180, states: "The scale on which these western men arrange their bonspiels is something princely. The tankards, and the gold medals by the dozen, offered as prizes, would bankrupt many an eastern club."

127. Roxborough, *One Hundred—Not Out*, p. 103.

128. Creelman, *Curling Past*, p. 143.

129. Woodside, "Curling in the Northwest" (I), p. 423.

130. Creelman, *Curling Past*, p. 143.

131. Woodside, "Curling in the Northwest" (I), p. 423.

132. Roxborough, *One Hundred—Not Out*, p. 103.

133. Hedley, "Curling in Canada," pp. 178–79.

134. Kerr, *Curling in Canada*, pp. 443–509.

135. Hedley, "Curling in Canada," pp. 118, 173. It is difficult to calculate the exact number of curling clubs in Ontario at this time. Kerr's *History of Curling* was published in 1890, and he cites J. S. Russell—" who is the best authority on the subject of Canadian curling at the present day"—secretary to the Ontario Branch, who maintained that there were ninety-nine clubs affiliated to the branch then (p. 338). Munro, "Curling in Canada," p. 528, writing in 1902, maintained that there were eighty-one clubs in the Ontario Curling Association at that time.

136. C. Pelham Mulvany, *Toronto: Past and Present* (Toronto: W. E. Caiger, 1884), pp. 121–22. These clubs were the Caledonia Curling Club; the Caledonian Curling Club; the Granite Curling Club; the Moss Park Curling Club; the Parkdale Curling Club; and the Ontario Branch of the R.C.C.C. This was formed ten years before, with its headquarters in Toronto (Stevenson, *Curling in Ontario*, pp. 38–39). Also, R. C. Whittet, "Curling," *Outing* 19 (1891):365, states: "Toronto, Ont., is indeed the Curlers' Capital of the Continent."

137. Stevenson, *Curling in Ontario*, pp. 190–91. Macdonald was also first president of the Ottawa Rowing Club, formed in 1867.

138. After a reception and luncheon by the Ontario Curling Association, they were guests of the Granite Curling Club, the Toronto Curling Club, the Parkdale Curling Club, the Lakeview Club, the Caledonian Curling Club, the Prospect Park Curling Club, and the Queen City Club. A vivid account of the Scottish team's visit to Toronto, which also includes several photographs of the excellent facilities of the curling clubs there, is in Kerr, *Curling in Canada*, pp. 298–351.

139. Ibid., p. 304.

140. Ibid., pp. 443–510. This is the title of Chapter 11.

141. Ibid., pp. 452–86.

142. Creelman, *Curling Past*, pp. 144–45.

143. *Calgary Herald*, 9 January 1889; 1 October 1890. The building was 175 feet by 73 feet, with two sheets of ice, a clubroom, a spectator gallery, and large windows. The installation of electric light enabled the curlers to play in the evenings under excellent conditions.

144. Ibid., 9 January 1889; 6 March 1889.

145. Ibid., 9 January 1889.

146. *Edmonton Bulletin*, 9 February 1884.

147. Ibid., 9 November 1889.

148. Ibid., 17 February 1889.

149. *Medicine Hat Times*, 26 November 1896. Creelman, *Curling Past*, p. 149, states that a curling club was formed in Medicine Hat in 1900.

150. This information is contained in a scrapbook of newspaper clippings and photographs, entitled ''Billy Mather and Other Pioneers,'' located in the Archives of the Canadian Rockies at Banff, Alberta. Unfortunately, the exact dates of the newspaper clippings are not given, but it is clear from the material that curling took place in Banff in 1896, and ''in 1899, the first rocks were bought, and a club started by John Walker, Dave Whyte Sr., Frank Beatty, Dr. Brett, William Mather Sr., Ike Byers, who then ran the *Crag and Canyon* [the local newspaper], Mr. Galsetty, and Dr. White, partner in the Brett Sanitarium. The first curling ice was in front of the sanitarium, somewhere near the south side of the bridge across the Bow River.''

151. Creelman, *Curling Past*, p. 149; *Lethbridge News*, 9 January 1895.

152. *Macleod Gazette*, 16 December 1898.

153. Creelman, *Curling Past*, p. 149.

154. *Calgary Herald*, 26 January 1899.

155. Creelman, *Curling Past*, p. 151.

156. Johnny Serra, *The History of Armstrong, British Columbia* (Armstrong Branch of the Okanagan Historical Society, n.d.), p. 18.

157. Creelman, *Curling Past*, p. 151.

158. *Dominion Illustrated Monthly*, 21 March 1891, p. 278.

159. Thomas L. Grahame, ''National Sport: Pastimes in British Columbia,'' *Canadian Magazine*, March 1898, p. 464.

160. Peter L. Lindsay, ''Woman's Place in Nineteenth Century Canadian Sport,'' *CAHPER Journal*, September–October 1970, pp. 27–28.

161. Margaret Ann Hall, ''A History of Women's Sport in Canada prior to World War I'' (M.A. thesis, University of Alberta, Edmonton, 1968), p. 101.

162. *Montreal Gazette*, 21 February 1890.

163. Hall, ''Women's Sport in Canada,'' p. 102.

164. ''The Women's Pages,'' *Athletic Life*, April 1896, p. 172.

165. *Standard*, Canadian Winter Sports Number, February 1909, p. 8, as quoted in Hall, ''Women's Sport in Canada,'' p. 102.

166. *Globe*, 22 November 1901.

167. ''Billy Mather and Other Pioneers'' Scrapbook (see note 150). *Crag and Canyon* (Banff), 3 May 1935, mentions lady curlers there in the 1890s. See also John E. Reid, ''Sports and Games in Alberta Before 1900'' (M.A. thesis, University of Alberta, 1969), p. 69.

168. Kerr, *Curling in Canada*, pp. 170–71, 204–8.

169. Jean Cochrane, Abby Hoffman, and Pat Kincaid, *Women in Canadian Life: Sports* (Toronto: Fitzhenry and Whiteside, 1977), p. 27.

170. Welsh, *Guide to Curling*, p. 152. Examples of the telegrams included ''Absence makes the heart grow fonder'' (from Maudie, Halifax); ''Will ye no' come back again? All hearts bowed down'' (from lady curlers, Montreal); and ''None but the brave deserve the fair'' (from Ethel, Winnipeg).

171. Marchioness of Dufferin, *My Canadian Journal, 1872-1878* (London: John Murray, 1891), pp. 123–34. See, for example, the colorful account of the curling match between the Vice-Regal Team and the Thistle Curling Club of Montreal, in the *Canadian Illustrated News*, 23 February 1878, p. 119.

172. R. H. Hubbard, *Rideau Hall: An Illustrated History of Government House, Ottawa* (Ottawa: Queen's Printer, n.d.), p. 33; Kerr, *Curling in Canada*, p. 149.

173. Hedley, "Curling in Canada," p. 180.

174. Kerr, *Curling in Canada*, p. 149; Munro, "Curling in Canada," pp. 531–32; Stevenson, *Curling in Ontario*, pp. 40–41. Earlier, in 1874, Lord Dufferin had also presented medals for inter club competition (*Globe,* 20 November 1875).

175. Kerr, *Curling in Canada*, pp. 150, 320.

176. Howell and Howell, *Sports in Canadian Life*, p. 88; Kerr, *Curling in Canada*, p. 149.

177. These were the Marquis of Lorne (1878–83); Lord Aberdeen (1893–98); and the Earl of Minto (1898–1904). But even the Earl of Dufferin (1872–78), often described as "Irish," could be termed an Ulster Scot, and was related to the noted Scottish Blackwood family of Edinburgh. See *Canada, 1867—1967: The Founders and the Guardians* (Ottawa: Queen's Printer, 1968), pp. 82—92.

178. Besides skating, a huge wooden toboggan slide, with stairs, was also installed in the grounds. See Hubbard, *Rideau Hall*, pp. 30–45, and plates 46, 47, 49.

179. "The very first year after Lord Lorne's arrival we find the Vice-Regal Club winning a royal medal from the Caribou Club, His Lordship, according to the report of the Match, playing a fine lead" (Kerr, *Curling in Canada*, p. 150). The Marquis of Lorne was also a former president of the Royal Caledonian Club (Kerr, *History of Curling*, p. 336).

180. Blakeley, *Glimpses of Halifax*, p. 145.

181. Ibid., *Citizen and Evening Chronicle*, 31 January 1880.

182. Kerr, *Curling in Canada*, p. 150.

183. Ibid., pp. 332–36; Stevenson, *Curling in Ontario*, p. 220.

184. Hubbard, *Rideau Hall*, pp. 75–84; Stevenson, *Curling in Ontario*, p. 93.

185. John Cowan, *Canada's Governors-General: Lord Monck to General Vanier* (Toronto: York Publishing Co., 1965), p. 80; Kerr, *Curling in Canada*, p. 150.

186. Hubbard, *Rideau Hall*, p. 102. On this page (plate 159) is a photograph of this trophy.

187. Kerr, *Curling in Canada*, p. 151.

188. Stevenson, *Curling in Ontario*, p. 79.

189. Ibid., passim; Kerr, *Curling in Canada*, p. 3.

190. *Free Press* (Winnipeg), 14 January 1880; 2 March 1881.

191. Stevenson, *Curling in Ontario*, p. 83.

192. For example, when only three of the forty clubs enrolled in the Ontario Branch entered for the first competition for Lord Dufferin's gold medal, it was considered at Rideau Hall to be a poor response to his initiative. The explanation offered was that many of the clubs in Ontario played on outdoor rinks, and the members considered themselves handicapped against indoor curlers. It was also felt by some that indoor curlers "channelled" the ice by grooving the surface, and so provided a fixed course for the stone. Also, the fact that curlers in Quebec used solid iron blocks, weighing from forty-six to eighty pounds, while those in Ontario used the traditional granite stones, caused some dissension and lessened curling intercourse between them. (See Guillet, *Pioneer Days*, pp. 209–10; and Stevenson, *Curling in Ontario*, pp. 24–92). However, it can be said that none of the disagreements adversely affected the development of curling in Canada to any great or permanent extent.

193. Kerr, *Curling in Canada*, pp. 4, 7.

194. Stevenson, *Curling in Ontario*, p. 79.

195. Bryce, *Scotsman in Canada*, p. 420. It is strange that Kerr makes no mention of this 1896 challenge in his *Curling in Canada*; but perhaps he was busily engaged in his

Golf Book of East Lothian, which was published in 1896.

196. Kerr, *Curling in Canada*, pp. 5–10.

197. Ibid., pp. 11–48; Stevenson, *Curling in Ontario*, pp. 100–101.

198. Kerr, *Curling in Canada*, pp. 19–20. Other people to receive the same circular included Lord Minto, Sir Wilfred Laurier, Mr. Chamberlain, Lord Mountstephen, Lord Elgin, Lord Mansfield, Lord Balfour of Burleigh and Lord Breadalbane.

199. Ibid., p. 6.

200. Stevenson, *Curling in Ontario*, pp. 100–101.

201. Kerr, *Curling in Canada,* passim. The many after-dinner speeches usually followed the same pattern, of praising Scotland and Scottish kinship first, while next pledging absolute loyalty to the British Crown and Empire, before pointing out the remarkable contribution Scots had made to Canada, and finally emphasizing the glorious future which lay ahead in the Dominion.

202. Ibid., p. 506.

203. Stevenson, *Curling in Ontario*, p. 103.

204. Ibid., Kerr, *Curling in Canada*, pp. 425–31.

205. Whittet, "Game of Curling," p. 364.

206. Munro, "Curling in Canada," p. 534.

207. Kerr, *Curling in Canada,* p. viii.

208. Ibid., pp. 468, 605.

209. Jack Ludwig, "Rocks of All Ages," *MacLean's*, February 1974, p. 26.

210. Kerr, *Curling in Canada*, pp. 750–53.

5

The Caledonian Games

Highland Games, Highland dancing and pipe bands are now so characteristic of the Canadian scene that they are for many as much Canadian as they are Scottish. They are primarily maintained by the Canadian descendants of Scottish immigrants and their attainments are salutary, the standards achieved being comparable to the best anywhere and often better.

George S. Emmerson (1976)

THE revival of the Highland Games in Scotland toward the end of the eighteenth century and subsequent Scottish emigration led to their appearance on the North American continent. In Canada and the United States they became known as "the Caledonian Games," being sponsored mainly by Caledonian Clubs, whose main function was the promotion of these annual Gatherings. But other Scottish Societies also celebrated these Games, which became immensely popular, especially in the post-Civil War and post-Confederation period. As in curling, Scots in both countries did not allow the international border to interfere with the pursuit of their sports, and competition and cooperation through Caledonian Games was a consistent policy, aided by the improved communications and transportation facilities. Famous people patronized and attended the Games, and prominent athletes came from Scotland to compete in them. From a local ethnic holiday festival, the Caledonian Games emerged as a national and international sporting occasion, open to all, which included events and sports more indigenous to their new environment than in Scotland. In Canada, as in the United States, the

Scots who promoted and participated in the Games were a significant influence on the later development of track and field athletics. This development, allied with the appearance and popularity of other sports, contributed to a decline in the popularity of Caledonian Games in the late nineteenth century, especially in the United States. These Games survived better in Canada, where they have flourished to the present day.

It is not definitely known when or where Scottish Highland Games were first celebrated on the North American continent. The Games enjoyed an era of tremendous popularity in the United States for about twenty years after the Civil War, when they became a nation wide institution, and attracted large crowds in numerous American cities, which were unsurpassed in any other country.[1] The Highland Society of New York held its ''first Sportive Meeting'' in 1836; and the ''first of the Caledonian Clubs was organized in Boston, March 19, 1853, and its earliest games were held later in the same year.''[2] The Scots in Boston had apparently met for their traditional Games for several summers previously, however, before an official club was formed.[3] Still, Highland Games were held in Canada before the 1836 Meeting in New York, and a Canadian Caledonian Club was formed several years before the Boston Caledonian Club. Whether or not this Scottish initiative inspired their countrymen south of the border to similar action is uncertain, but their Games, which were destined to become so popular all over the continent, first appeared in several localities in British North America. Later contact between all the pioneer clubs celebrating Highland Games was maintained on a north-south basis between the Maritimes, Quebec and Ontario, and the Midwest and New England States in America. This was enlarged from east to west in both countries as the Caledonian Games spread westward in due course.

As seen in chapter 2, one of the first occasions of Caledonian Games on record in Scotland was that organized by the St. Fillans Highland Society in 1819, and it has been claimed that ''by the 1820s Highland Games were in full swing throughout Scotland.''[4] Scotsmen in Canada were certainly not far behind their countrymen at home in fostering this element of their sporting heritage, for in the same year as the St. Fillans Gathering in Scotland,

> Rev. Father Macdonald with William MacGillivray, John Macdonald of Garth and others had been instrumental in organizing a Highland Society in Glengarry in 1819 with Sir Peregrine Maitland, K.C.B., as President, the Reverend Alexander Macdonell, Colonel the Honourable Neil McLean and Lieutenant-Colonel Donald Greenfield Macdonell as vice-Presidents, Alexander Fraser, Esq., as Treasurer, Archibald McLean, Secretary, and Roderick McLeod, Alex McLean and Alexander Wilkinson as directors.

Unfortunately, "After many successful gatherings," this Highland Society of Glengarry "was allowed to lapse."[5] But a start had been made, and later Scottish Societies which sponsored Highland Gatherings were more successful, although it could not be claimed that they were in full swing throughout Canada until several years after Confederation.

Father Macdonald's enterprise may have been the first Highland Society formed in British North America, but is was by no means the first Scottish Society to be formed. This distinction belongs to the venerable "North British Society or Scots Club" of Halifax, which was instituted on 26 March 1768.[6] Another Scottish Society was also formed in the eighteenth century, namely the St. Andrew's Society of St. John, New Brunswick, at a meeting held in that city on 8 March 1798. Forty-four years later "the New Brunswick branch of the Highland Society" was founded there by Lieutenant-Colonel Roderick Charles Macdonald, but like its counterpart in Glengarry, it was short-lived. But other Scottish Societies formed around this time endured, and were the forerunners of many successful institutions, such as the St. Andrew's Societies of Montreal and Quebec, both founded in 1835.[7] Scots were also celebrating St. Andrew's Day in Bytown as early as 1838, and from these celebrations there evolved the St. Andrew's Society of Ottawa.[8].

The consistent immigration of Scotsmen already noted provided the members of the societies, and of the many others which sprang up not many years afterwards. Although their main function was to celebrate St. Andrew's Day, and to assist fellow countrymen and their descendants in any sort of distress, these societies also held annual picnics at which Scottish Games were featured, and these events became very popular with all nationalities in later years. The statement made about the St. Andrew's Society of Ottawa could be applied equally well to them all:

> The members of the Society in addition to the charitable work carried on by them have, in various ways, endeavoured to keep alive and foster the cherished memories of the land across the sea, and in furtherance of that object, its picnics and games held from time to time, its excursions to New York, Niagara Falls, Montreal and other cities, and especially its entertainments on St. Andrew's Day, whether by dinner, ball or concert have been very helpful. These entertainments, which are always looked forward to with the greatest interest, have, in no small degree, been the means of promoting good fellowship and a friendly feeling, not only among Scotchmen, but also with other nationalities, whose representatives have always been honoured guests on these occasions.[9]

In fact, the annual Games became so popular and profitable, that for many Scottish Societies, their athletic endeavors gradually superseded other considerations. The St. Andrew's Society of Montreal was responsible for the formation of the Montreal Caledonian Society in 1855, "for the purpose of fostering and maintaining a love for all that is best in Scottish customs, literature and song." This action then allowed the St. Andrew's Society to devote all its time and energies to its charitable work.[10] As far as the members of Caledonian Clubs and Societies were concerned, the "best in Scottish customs" involved Scottish sports, which gradually occupied much more time than any devoted to Scottish "literature and song."

It is generally supposed that "Highland Games have been a Canadian attraction since 1838, when the Caledonian Club of Prince Edward Island was organized."[11] This Caledonian Club survived to the present day, when athletics, dancing, and piping are still featured at an annual Highland Gathering each August, held at Charlottetown Race Track.[12] In 1845, the patriotic Scots of the North British Society of Halifax

> celebrated the anniversary of Bannockburn, 24th June by a Procession and Picnic in which they were joined by the Highland Society, and the display of Scottish costume in the Procession joined with the splendid new banners, made it one of the most brilliant exhibitions ever witnessed in Halifax. The Picnic was a most triumphant success.[13]

No further details are given, but these picnics were traditional occasions for participating in Scottish Games, and in view of the fact that the Highland Society was also present, it is reasonable to assume that Highland Games were also a part of the celebration. Ten years after the Prince Edward Island Caledonian Club held its first Games,

> The Caledonian Society of Cape Breton organized Highland Games at Sydney in 1848. For many years they included track and field events as well as as piping and dancing, but they were eventually discontinued.[14]

However, the cause was taken up in more lasting fashion elsewhere in the Maritimes. A Halifax Caledonian Club was formed in 1860, which ''gave added impetus to regular athletic sports in that city,'' and was formed just in time to entertain the Prince of Wales during his visit to the city, with a nineteen-event program.[15] In the following year, the Highland Society of the County of Sydney was formed at the Courthouse in Antigonish, on 22 August 1861.[16] The name was due to the fact that Antigonish village was then the county seat of the county of Sydney; when there was a redivision of the province, the name of the shiretown was extended to the newly created county of Antigonish, and subsequently the Highland Society became the Antigonish Highland Society.

This Society was formed

> for the preservation of the culture of the Gael as exemplified in the language, music, dances, games, and antiquities of the

Highlands; for the relieving of the distressed among the Highlandmen; and the assistance of newly arrived settlers of Highland origin to the country.[17]

From then until now, the Antigonish Highland Games have probably been the most genuine counterpart ever to the Highland Games in Scotland, situated in the most Gaelic-speaking part of Canada, where the Highland way of life predominated throughout the nineteenth century. Nowhere else in the world, in fact, has "the culture of the Gael" been preserved intact for so long. [18] Certainly the Antigonish Highland Games became the most famous tourist attraction of the many Canadian versions of the Games which still exist today, largely because of their authentic nature, in an environment where the people tenaciously retained their Scottish traditions.

But this important and thoroughbred outpost of Scottish culture was a microcosm set apart from the mainstream of Scottish influence in nineteenth-century Canada. Indeed, its relative isolation served to maintain its solidarity in this respect. Curling clubs had multiplied in Ontario because it was "full of Scotsmen,"[19] and for the same reason this region became the main area for Caledonian Games in Canada. Scots in Montreal, too, were not idle in promoting their athletic festivals. And the railway contact from Montreal and various places in Ontario, to the Midwest and New England regions of the United States, enabled Scots in both countries to attend each other's Games, as officials or competitors, and carry news of developments back and forth.

The *Montreal Gazette* of 11 July 1840 reported that "the Highland Games at Lancaster, on the 30th ultimo, went off with great spirit," as if it was not the first occasion upon which they had been held there. They were suggested and promoted by a Colonel Carmichael, and the prize list was Scottish in every detail:

The first prize, a handsome Highland Sword, was awarded to Captain James McDonnell (of the Glen) as the best thrower of a twenty-four pound shot.

A Highland purse was awarded to Mr. Urquhart, of the River Raisin, as the second best thrower of a twenty-four pound shot.

A Highland sword to Capt. McDonnell, as the best thrower of a twenty-five pound hammer.

A plaid to Mr. James Williams of Lancaster, as the second best do.

A pair of steel pistols to Mr. Duncan McLennan of Lancaster, as the best runner of half a mile.

A handsome silver mounted dirk, to the same gentleman, as the best leaper.[20]

A few years later, in 1847, a very successful Highland Games meeting was held in Toronto, with all the pageantry that was customary to a Highland Gathering. The initial marshaling in the city center, followed by the procession to the ground by the Scots in their colorful national costume, accompanied by their unique bagpipe music, was a sight that attracted and intrigued spectators and became an eagerly awaited annual event in many places. After the sports, too, there were usually other social events, sometimes a feast and a return procession. The Toronto Gathering of 1847 followed a pattern which became fairly general in future years:

The Gathering, according to notice, came off on Wednesday the 15th instant, in presence of a large concourse of spectators, both in the field and the City Hall.

The procession moved from the City Hall, headed by the President Captain Stewart, supported by the vice-Presidents The MacNab and Ronald MacKinnon, Esq., followed by the banner of the Society and a number of the Members, in their national costume, among whom we were delighted to see the gallant Knight of Dundurn, and here we must confess, that we have seldom seen a finer specimen of Highlander, the completeness of whose costume would have entitled him to the first prize, had he not kindly waived his right in favour of the other competitors.

On the procession reaching the ground, the contest for the following games, viz., throwing the hammer, putting the stone, throwing the cabbar [sic], the leap, and 400 yard race, took place, all of which were carried on with that frank good humour which evinced no bad or envious feeling among the competitors. These sports were conducted personally by the President of the Society, a worthy representative of the house of Garth.

When the outdoor games were concluded the procession was reformed and returned to the City Hall in the same order as before, when the competition for the bagpipe, Highland fling, sword dance, singing, and the best dressed Highlander were keenly contested for, and afforded particular pleasure to the numerous fair visitors present.

Some of the ''fair visitors'' participated in the proceedings, also, as one of the prizes was ''the Ladies Purse for the best singer of a Gaelic Song.'' It was customary to have events for boys at Highland Games, too, and at this meeting there was a prize awarded to ''the best dressed boy in Highland costume.''[21]

Shortly after this successful gathering in Toronto, a Highland Society was officially formed there for the purpose of ''promoting the good old games of Scotland.''[22] How long this society functioned is uncertain, for in 1859, another first Highland Games meeting was reported in Toronto, this time under the auspices of the ''Canadian Highland Society'':

The first great gathering of the Canadian Highland Society took place at the Caer Howell College Avenue, at two o'clock. There were a large number of spectators on the ground, a great portion of whom were ladies, and the proceedings appeared to excite unusual interest. The spectators occupied the balcony of the hotel, and also the rising ground around the bowling green. The games consisted of ''putting the light and heavy stones,'' ''running leap,'' ''throwing the light and heavy hammers,'' ''tossing the caber,'' ''Ghillie Callum,'' or the sword dance, ''high leap,'' ''Highland fling,'' etc. . . . A successful throw of the hammer, or an inch higher leap, drew down thunders of applause from the onlookers. Several of those who entered the

lists appeared to be old hands at the business, and their performances would not have disgraced either Strathallan or
Braemar . . . . The sword dance and Highland fling were well ex-
ecuted by A. C. Carlyle and J. W. Barrie; the dancing of the
latter, who is admitted to be the first Highland dancer in Upper
Canada was rapturously applauded.

But these Games were certainly unlike any at Strathallan or
Braemar, or anywhere else in Scotland, in one essential respect.
In fact, they were probably unique in the annals of Highland
Games history, for it was also reported that ''there were several
competitors, *and although no prizes were given* [author's italics],
each athlete strove to the utmost to win his spurs.''[23] Although
there have been isolated incidents of athletes in Scotland and
North America winning events but then declining to accept the
prize,[24] it was unusual in the extreme for there to be no prizes
awarded at all at a Highland Games meeting. For example, three
years before these peculiar Toronto Games, the first ''Caledonian
Games'' were held at Guilbault's Gardens in Montreal, when
nearly two thousand spectators witnessed a program of sixteen
events, every one of which carried a monetary prize or two. Actually, the total prize money for this first occasion amounted to
only £13 10s. 0d., a paltry amount when compared to sums in
future years.[25] For example, the much smaller community of
Lucknow, in Ontario, offered ''more than $1,000 in prizes'' at
the Caledonian Games held twenty-four years later.[26] But a
twenty-shilling first prize was still valuable in 1856, and the
events at Montreal in 1856 were keenly contested. The first prize
for Putting the Heavy Stone was 15s., with 7/6d. for the runner-
up, and only two inches separated the two winners! Only four
inches meant a difference of ten shillings in the prize money
awarded to the first and second competitors in the Throwing the
Heavy Hammer event.[27]

Also in 1856, in the predominantly Scottish area of Zorra in
Ontario, the Embro Highland Society was formed there on March
18. No details of its first program were provided, but it was also
formed ''for the purpose of preserving the language, martial
spirit, dress, music, literature, antiquities, and games of the

ancient Caledonians.'' This gave way in time to the Zorra
Caledonian Society, which still holds an Annual Gathering
today.[28] The Caledonian Games at Zorra may not have been
among the biggest or best known in the land, but before the nineteenth century was ended, a Scottish tug-of-war team from the
township had become world-famous.[29] The tug-of-war was a
popular event in Canada during the century, especially at Caledonian Games, and Scotsmen were described as ''ardent tuggers''
in this period, as well as the most successful.[30] It was an event for
big, strong men and therefore Scottish hammer-throwers and
stone-putters were as common in tug-of-war ranks in Canada, as
they were in their native land.

In passing, it is interesting to note that the highest prize awarded
at the first Montreal Caledonian Society Games of 1856 was for
quoits, value twenty-five shillings.[31] In fact, earlier that year, the
Society had already sponsored a quoits match against two
American opponents for a wager of a hundred dollars a side, when
the Montreal representatives won each of the three games.[32] It
has already been pointed out in chapter 2 that quoits was popular
in Britain for centuries, particularly in Scotland, ''for the game
thrived north of the border and eventually was carried overseas by
pioneering Scotsmen.''[33] The Scots indulged in the game enthusiastically in many parts of Canada during the nineteenth century, and it was frequently a very popular activity at Caledonian
Games, and often the first event on the program. Part of figure
7, for example, features a game of quoits at the Hamilton Caledonian Games in 1875.[34]

There were twice as many spectators for the Second Annual
Games of the Montreal Caledonian Society in 1857, when ''the
Glengarry men took all before them in throwing Weights and
Quoits,'' in the presence of John Sandfield Macdonald, then
member of Parliament, ''who looked well and seemed to enjoy
himself exceedingly.''[35] A dozen years later the enthusiasm was
such that ''ticket sellers were driven to despair by the demand for
tickets'' at the Fourteenth Annual Montreal Games. And in
1872, there were more than eight thousand spectators there, including Sir George Etienne Cartier. Two years before, in Toronto,

The Caledonian Games at Decker Park, Montreal, on Dominion
Day, 1871.

Crowds of strangers poured into the city from the earliest hour by steamboats, rails and vehicles of all descriptions until, with local citizens, the grounds around Crystal Palace were packed with at least 12,000 persons awaiting the Games.[36]

This enthusiasm and patronage was maintained in Canada during the nineteenth century, and new Caledonian Societies were still being formed well into the twentieth century for the purpose of holding Annual Games.[37] Also in Ontario, the St. Andrew's Society of London began to hold annual picnics and Scottish Games in the 1860s;[38] and the St. Andrew's Society of Ottawa held the first of its Annual Games meetings in 1863, when "the usual games, foot races, quoits, hop, step and leap, etc.," took place and prizes were awarded. About five hundred people witnessed the Games at Ottawa in the following year, when prizes between $2.00 and $4.00 were awarded for fifteen events.[39] The *Ottawa Citizen* of 21 June 1867 fully reported the society's Games of that year as "The Caledonia Gathering," stating it to be "a most decided success," and expressing the hope that "it will not be long before our Caledonian friends will afford us a similar treat." They were not disappointed, for in succeeding years the greater attendance figures, the patronage of the famous, and the increase in the value of the prizes all combined to make the Annual Games of the St. Andrew's Society of Ottawa a splendid affair.

In fact, situated as it was in the capital city, where so many Scots were prominent in government and business, this St. Andrew's Society was the most prestigious in Canada. Its Annual Ball was looked upon as the social event of the season, regularly attended by governors-general, prime ministers, cabinet ministers, and other notable persons of rank.[40] In its history, it is casually recorded that "at a meeting of the Society on November 4th, 1869, a communication was received from Sir John A. Macdonald, K. C. B. asking to become a member of the Society, and along with a number of other applicants he was duly elected."[41] Among the many other famous members were people like George Brown, Sandford Fleming, and another prime minister, Alexander Mackenzie. The Society's Annual Games became a prestigious event, also, well patronized and sponsored by many celebrated figures. Apart from the numerous Scottish merchants involved, Sir John A. Macdonald himself donated silver cups as prizes for this annual athletic event, while Sandford Fleming donated money prizes. The Hon. George Brown, too, was a president of the Toronto Caledonian Society, who presented a gold medal as first prize for the winner of the "Throwing the 56 lbs. weight" event at the Society's Games in 1872.[42]

An example of how the Ottawa Games prospered can be seen in the program for 19 August 1875, when "the necessary arrangements were all in order, such as swings for young people, booths and tents and other paraphernalia," and the total value of the prizes amounted to over $350. By 1889, the St. Andrew's Society could afford to pay $50, $20, and $10 prizes for first, second, and third positions in one event alone, as well as $100 for an exhibition of swordsmanship. There were prizes of $80, $40, and $10 for only one event in the following year. The records of the St. Andrew's Society of Ottawa reveal that the holding of its Annual Games was usually a profitable occasion, as it was for similar institutions elsewhere in Canada during the nineteenth century.[43]

Other St. Andrew's Societies were formed in Quebec City, Toronto, Montreal, Hamilton, Barrie, Brantford, Chatham, Guelph, Galt, Brockville, Cornwall, and Kingston in the nineteenth century. (Before he joined the society in Ottawa, John A. Macdonald had been first vice-president of the Kingston Society formed in 1840.)[44] Annual picnics at which Highland Games were celebrated were also featured by these societies.[45] At Chatham, for example, "the first structured Scottish Games" were organized there by the St. Andrew's Society in 1862, following a game of shinty.[46] It was natural that the largest crowds attended Caledonian Games at the biggest urban centers, such as Montreal and Toronto, where the Caledonian Societies in turn became most prominent. But apart from the places already mentioned, Caledonian Games were also held in Central and Eastern Canada at many other places, usually under the auspices of a Caledonian Society or a St. Andrew's Society. The *Scottish-American Journal* reported Highland Games during the 1870s and 1880s from such places as Brussels, Dundas, Ingersoll, London, Lucknow, St. Catherine's, Stratford, and Woodstock in Ontario, and Fredericton in New Brunswick.[47]

Scottish Highland Games were also celebrated in Western Canada sooner than is generally realized. For example, the statement that "in the Prairie Provinces, Highland Games date from 1906 at Winnipeg," which appears in the *Encyclopedia Canadiana*,[48] is erroneous, since it overlooks the fact that a St. Andrew's Society held successful annual Games there from 1880.

This society was organized by "Scotchmen and descendants of Scotchmen" at a meeting in the Davis Hotel, Winnipeg, on Tuesday, 7 November 1871, when it was known as "the Selkirk St. Andrew's Society of Manitoba, in honor of the noble lord who landed the first band of Scottish colonists in the Red River Settlement." Its first president was none other than Donald A. Smith, later to be a "noble lord" himself, i.e., Lord Strathcona. The society was reorganized and renamed, as the "St. Andrew's Society of Winnipeg," in 1879, and in the following year, "the first annual games under the auspices of the Society took place on Dominion Day, in the old Winnipeg Driving Park. Sports were held in the afternoon and a promenade concert and fireworks in the evening. Proceeds $135.76." This first athletic venture was evidently a success, and the second Games were patronized by the governor-general:

> The annual games were held in the old Driving Park, Aug. 3rd, 1881, in commemoration of the visit of the Marquis of Lorne. He visited the grounds, witnessed the games, and accepted an address from the Society and replied thereto. He presented the prizes to successful competitors the same evening in the musical pavilion, where a grand concert was held under the auspices of the Philharmonic Society.

From then on, the annual Highland Games of the St. Andrew's Society of Winnipeg became greater affairs. In 1882 it was stated that "the Scottish Games in Dufferin Park on Dominion Day were probably the most successful ever held by the Society."

But even their growth worried the canny Scots, for next year it was recorded:

> The Games were held in Dufferin Park, and were again a great success. The outlay, however, was so large that the surplus was only something over $200.

However, in the following year, "a surplus of $800 was realized from the games on Dominion Day," and in 1885, also, the Games "proved a financial success, the sum of $434.32 having been realized therefrom."[49] Unless bad weather interfered, a handsome profit usually resulted from these popular Scottish sports, despite the increasing expenditure necessary to accommodate the enthusiastic crowds and offer an imposing prize list.

Similar athletic contests had spread even further west before they were promoted by the St. Andrew's Society of Winnipeg, however, as "the fur traders and early missionaries both witnessed and participated in foot races."[50] The Reverend John McDougall, after winning a race against several Indians in 1863, commented: "That race opened many a lodge and the heart of many a friend in subsequent years."[51] But the Scottish reverend did not only take part in foot races, for he also describes jumping and throwing contests against a party of métis from Lac-la-biche, whom his party met on a trip to Fort Garry:

> At one of our evening encampments one party challenged the other to a contest in athletic sports, and we beat them badly, my man Baptiste leaving their best man easily in a footrace .... Then in the jumping and throwing of the stone we were far ahead and my men were greatly pleased at our victory. I confess to feeling well-pleased myself, for I delighted in these things at that time.[52]

Nor was McDougall alone in his delight, for "The North West Mounted Police and the Hudson's Bay Company posts were the scenes of the early athletic meets."[53] At a meeting organized by the Fort Macleod police garrison in 1876, Indians, civilians, and the police competed in running, jumping, and throwing events, for cash prizes totaling $280.[54]

Young competitors, Caledonian Games, 1889. (Public Archives of Canada, C110081)

Seventeen years earlier, athletics took place on the Queen's birthday, at Queensborough, in 1859, when the events included foot and hurdle races, shot-putting, hammer-throwing, high and long jumps, and tossing the caber, as well as boxing, wrestling, and boat races." No doubt the caber was also tossed at the "Caledonian Picnic" described by the *Daily Colonist* of 26 June 1865:

The Caledonian Society, with a number of their friends, will go up the Arm this morning to some available spot, where they will indulge in dancing, athletic games, and other sports. Mr. Sandrie will provide the music. The boats will start from the Ferry from 8 to 10 o'clock and all intending to joining the party are requested to be punctual.

Another ''typical Caledonian meet''[56] was held at Victoria four years later, when there was a 25-cent entrance fee, and the first prizes ranged from $2 to $5.[57] The *Scottish-American Journal* reported a ''Gathering in British Columbia'' in 1877, when:

> The Caledonian Society of Mainland, B.C., having its head-quarters in New Westminster gave its first annual games last month at Langley. It was quite successful, many spectators having gathered from great distances to enjoy a Scotch day.[58]

From then on, Gatherings became annual events in various parts of British Columbia during the nineteenth century, the largest being in Vancouver.[59] Scottish Highland Games were therefore a nationwide occurrence, from Cape Breton Island to Vancouver Island, before Confederation in 1867, and still being initiated and celebrated throughout the Dominion before and after 1900.

However, Caledonian Games did not have a monopoly on such athletic activity in Canada during the nineteenth century, despite their great extent and popularity, and of course not all athletic meetings were held under the auspices of a Scottish Society. What has been described as ''the earliest record of an organized track and field meeting'' was the report of the ''Toronto Athletic Games'' on 11 September 1839. Before this, ''only foot races, either conducted by garrisons or additions to horse race meetings, received public notice.''[60] Pedestrian challenge races, in fact, were reported as early as 1808 in Nova Scotia, and continued to be regular events in most parts of British North America, as well as the United States.[61] Howell and Howell have provided an apt summary of other athletic activity, under the title of ''Track and Field'':

> In the early pioneer days, when ''bees'' were both necessary and popular, various contests of strength and endurance were held. Among these were foot-races, jumps, stone-throwing,

and so on. When organizations such as the Caledonian Society, the St. George's Society, and the Irish Protestant Benevolent Society were formed in Canada, their annual picnics always featured athletic events. The King's birthday or a town's annual festival were celebrated with races and athletic competitions. Many of the events, such as wheelbarrow races, sack races, climbing a greased pole, rolls and treacle, greased-pig races, and blindfold races are now considered children's activities, but in this period they were seriously contested, with the inevitable wagers on the side. The names of other events, the "Running high leap," the "running long leap." and "vaulting," for instance, have changed through the years.

The largest part of the Howells's track and field section prior to Confederation, however, is devoted to a full report of "The Grand Annual Gathering of the Caledonian Society in Guilbault's Gardens, Montreal, in 1857."[62] Davidson has also commented on the terminology used for the various events at early athletic meetings in Canada, again under the heading of "Track and Field":

> Early newspaper accounts of track and field events are interesting to the sports historian, as they report the results of events in which our athletes still participate today. For some events, the nomenclature was different, with the running high jump known as the "running high leap." The "running long leap" was the descriptive title given to the running broad jump, with a distance of seventeen feet six inches being recorded in 1857.

> "Vaulting" was also engaged in, with heights of seven feet two inches reported in the same year. This was probably the equivalent of the pole-vault. The weight events consisted of throwing the hammer and putting the stone. The heavy stone weighed twenty-one pounds and the light stone sixteen pounds. Events which we consider novelty events, such as the sack race or wheelbarrow race, had a definite place in "The Games" in those early days.

The distances and heights referred to are also from the Montreal Caledonian Games of 1857. In fact, Davidson footnotes the above quotation: "For an account of a track and field meet held in 1857, see Appendix E"; and Appendix E is the report from the *Montreal Weekly Gazette* of the Caledonian Games there.[63]

The fact was that not only the "nomenclature," but the majority of events themselves, in early track and field meetings and other societies' picnics, were identical to those in the Caledonian Games. Cox and the Howells, Davidson, Lindsay, and Roxborough, in common with other historians of Canadian sport, have recognized the affinity between the popular and widespread Caledonian Games of the period and the development of track and field.[64] Day begins his "Track and Field" section with the comment that "the Scots, predisposed to athletic sports, undoubtedly added a significant stimulus to sport in Chatham."[65] Historians who have investigated these Games in the United States, too, have regarded them as a significant influence on the development of track and field athletics there.[66] Although the panoply of Scottish bagpipes, kilts, Highland flings, and tossing the caber, may serve to disguise the fact, Caledonian Games were really a professional form of track and field.[67]

The picnics of other ethnic societies mentioned tended to be much smaller replicas of the Caledonian Games:

> During the sixties, track and field activities thrived, largely due to their adoption by groups following the examples set by the various Caledonian Societies.

In Montreal, for example, the Ladies' Benevolent Society, the Irish Protestant Benevolent Society, and the St. Patrick's Society all instituted annual picnics at which athletics were featured.[68] A comparison of relative importance can be seen in the reports of the *Montreal Gazette* in 1871 regarding the Dominion Day celebrations there. The twenty-eight events of the "Caledonian Society's Picnic" were reported in a hundred and seventy-one lines, in contrast to the ten events of the "St. Patrick's Society's Picnic" in only fifty-one lines.[69] Apart from the difference in the value of the prize-list, an "Irish Jig" was substituted for the Highland fling in the St. Patrick's Society Picnic, otherwise the events were common to Caledonian meets. In fact, no other track and field meetings anywhere in Canada in the nineteenth century

The "Ghillie Callum" at the Montreal Caledonian Games, 15 August 1872.

could match the Caledonian Games in their extent or organization, their consistently high attendance figures, or their valuable prize lists. Nor should this be in any way surprising, since the widespread Scots were simply celebrating a very genuine aspect of their culture, a traditional festival which was part of the fabric of Scottish life. No other ethnic group which followed the Caledonian example in track and field ever had regular international meets with fellow countrymen in the United States, or regularly entertained athletes from the homeland overseas, or formed an international association for the promotion of athletic games, as did the Scottish organizers of the ubiquitous Caledonian Games in the nineteenth century.

However, apart from these distinguishing characteristics pertaining to their own Games, Scottish athletes were also prominent in other meetings which featured similar athletic activity. This was not surprising, either, considering their athletic heritage, and in view of the fact that other nationalities were participating in the Caledonian Games. The Allardice tradition in pedestrianism, for example, was well maintained by Captain Angus Cameron of the 4th Battalion Incorporated Militia in 1840. Sponsored by Captain Henderson of the same regiment, who had taken a wager of £50 ''that he would find a man, on or before the first day of May, to walk two miles in sixteen minutes, . . . within seven miles of Kingston,'' Cameron accomplished the task at his second attempt in fourteen minutes and forty-five seconds. The *Montreal Gazette* waxed lyrical about his performance:

> We believe seven minutes is the shortest record time a mile has been walked in England. If this opinion be correct, Capt. Cameron's last mile in six minutes forty-nine seconds, is the greatest feat in the annals of walking, when it is taken into consideration that the road was slippery, and the walker completely saturated with water, giving him at least an additional weight of six pounds to carry three-fourths of the time. We should think the whole performance unequalled in any country. Captain Cameron is now a resident of Kingston, and is now ready, for any sum, from £500 to £1000, to walk against the ''tallest'' traveller on this continent.[70]

Cameron was said to have deliberately walked slowly on the first day in order to obtain bets against his second attempt, however, and the whole affair was seen as a fairly typical exploitation of the public urge for gambling.[71]

Three years later, the same newspaper announced that the "Montreal Athletic Games" would take place on Thursday the 28th and Friday the 29th of September:

> The first day will be occupied by rifle-shooting, running and standing high vault, leaping, throwing the hammer, foot-racing, throwing the cricket-ball, and climbing the pole: the second day, boat-race, putting the ball, hop-step-leap, wrestling, and others—all old English games, calculated to draw forth every variety of athletic skill, and to develop that muscular strength and nervous vigour, which have contributed so much to make our race pre-eminent among the nations of the earth.[72]

As Lindsay has aptly commented in a footnote: "This reflects the very British attitude which prevailed towards most sport of the time";[73] and actually "British" games would have been a more accurate description. Or, considering the events, and the history of the Highland Games briefly outlined in chapter 2, the adjective "Scottish" could have been used with equal merit. (For example, eight years before, in Braemar, Scotland, there had also been a "boat race" and "rifle practice" at the Highland Gathering there.)[74] In any case, many nationalities participated, and the *Gazette* afterwards expressed pleasure the "competitors, whose paths of life, and even race and language, are so diverse, met in amicable contest."[75]

In 1844, the title of this meeting was changed to the "Montreal Olympic Games."[76] This was no doubt so named after the ancient Olympic Games of Greece, as so many athletic clubs were in the nineteenth century. But it is interesting to note at this point that probably the greatest authority on ancient Greek Games, the late Professor E. Norman Gardiner, writing of the athletic contests mentioned by Homer, stated that "the nearest parallel to them is to be found in the sports of the Highland Clans."[77] However, the great Scottish authority of Highland

Games in the nineteenth century, Charles Donaldson, had disputed any similarity to the Olympic Games nearly thirty years earlier, with typical nationalistic fervor:

> No part of this great competition had the remotest similitude to Scottish Highland Games, which, although on a much smaller scale than the meetings among the Greeks, are more romantic and pleasing to the Scotsman in all climes than a dozen Olympic games, even if they were instituted by Hercules in honour of Jupiter.[78]

Whatever the degree of similarity, it is hard to disagree with a later English authority who maintained that "the Scots, also, have played a big part in keeping the athletic ideal of the Greeks alive."[79] In any event, they definitely played a big part in the Montreal Olympic Games of 1844, held under the patronage of the governor-general, Sir Charles Metcalf.

Lindsay has summarized this meeting thus:

> The two-day programme contained twenty-nine events, including five lacrosse matches. Members of the Montreal Olympic Club won the bulk of the track and field events, though they were pressed by Sergeant McGillivray of the 93rd Highlanders, who took honours in hammer throwing (15 pounds) and ball putting (9 pounds and 24 pounds).[80]

Actually, the men of the 93rd Highlanders were prominent throughout these Games. As well as Sergeant McGillivray, other successful competitors included Private A. McPherson, "Ross of the 93rd," Private Peter McDonald, and Private John McLeod. And when the twenty-nine official events had been completed, "a private match between men of the 93rd at the Running High Leap" took place, which was won by David Ross, with the redoubtable McGillivray second, and James Gow coming third. As the report of the proceedings aptly concluded:

> The fine Band of the 93rd Regiment enlivened the amusements, and contributed much to the enjoyment of the spectators; and it is due to this fine Regiment to state, that in

almost every game someone of their number put the skill and metal of the civilian competitors to a severe test.

Some of the "civilian competitors" were probably Scottish, too, such as "Mr. Boyd" and "John McDonald."[81]

Again, it was natural that Scots should excel in such familiar sports, and be "canny" enough to use their ability to carry off many prizes at various athletic meetings. Lindsay proceeded to correctly point out that "increased Scottish participation in Athletic Games during the forties is evidenced by the names of winners at these meetings: McDonald, McDonnell, McLeod, McGillivray, McKay, McCallum, McMillan, and others." The same author, in his "Track and Field" section, maintains that "the highlight of the fifties was the first annual Games of the Montreal Caledonian Society, held in Guilbault's Gardens, Montreal, on Tuesday, September 2, 1856," when two thousand spectators watched a fifteen-event program.[82] Obviously Scottish athletes were dominant figures at their own Caledonian Games, but in the fifties, too, they were successful competitors in other similar Athletic Games, as they had been in the previous decade.

An example of this was provided only two weeks after the first Montreal Caledonian Society's Games, when "The Beauharnois Athletic Games" took place. The events held were Lacrosse matches, Dancing the Highland Fling in Costume, Quoits, Throwing the Hammer (heavy and light), Putting the Stone (heavy and light), Running (Long Race, Short Race, Sack Race, and Wheelbarrow Race), Leaping (Running High Leap, Standing High Leap, Running Long Leap, Standing Long Leap, Running Hop, Step and Leap, and Standing Hop, Step and Leap), and Cricket Ball Throwing. Algonquin and Iroquois Indians, French Canadians, and Britishers all took part; but in such a Caledonian program, it is not surprising to find Duncan McCuaig winning first prize in throwing both hammers, first prize in putting the heavy stone, and second prize in putting the light stone, and obtaining $23.50 for his efforts. Other successful athletes with Scottish names were A. R. McDonald, Robert Alexander, and John Murray.[83]

The advent of regular, annual Caledonian Societies' Games brought consistency to the sport. As we have seen, until the first Games of the Montreal Caledonian Society, athletic meetings were sporadic affairs:

> Organized track and field meetings were held irregularly in Montreal until 1856, when the annual Caledonian Society Gatherings were inaugrated.[84]

This fact did not only apply to Montreal; indeed, from 1856 on and for the remainder of the nineteenth century, the organizers of Caledonian Games were the sponsors of most track and field activity in Canada.

One of the outstanding all-round Scottish athletes during the fifties and beyond was Alexander Muir, who was also a noted educator, artist, orator, and musician.[85] Born in Lesmahagon, Lanarkshire, Scotland, he came early to Canada and was educated at Queens University. This was one of the most Scottish of the many famous educational institutions in nineteenth-century Canada which were founded by Scotsmen.[86] From his student days there onwards, Muir "especially excelled in those games having Scottish origins," and "ran, jumped and threw the sledge" with success at many Caledonian gatherings.[87] The speciality of this extremely versatile resident of Scarborough, however, was quoits:

> The first club was organized in 1858, and was the outcome of a championship contest held in Toronto, under the auspices of the Caledonian Society, when Messrs. David Johnston and A. Muir, both Scarboro men, carried off the medal. Instead of deciding as between themselves, they very public-spiritedly undertook to form a club, placing it in possession of the medal, to be held against all comers.

This club subsequently competed against quoit clubs in other Scottish communities, such as Ayr and Galt, with results reported as "invariably in favor of Scarboro,"[88] no doubt largely due to Muir's skill. In fact, he went on to become the quoits champion of both Canada and the United States.[89] He was also the first secretary-treasurer of the Scarboro Cricket Club and held office in other clubs devoted to curling, draughts (i.e., checkers), rifle-shooting, and rowing.[90]

Muir was a Scot who felt patriotic towards the country in which he lived. He was a member of the Highland Company of the Queen's Own Rifles, fought at Ridgeway during the Fenian invasion, and later became president of the Army and Navy Veterans' Society. Roxborough has compared him to "his compatriot, Dr. George Beers," the "father of lacrosse," but he surpassed even Beers in nationalistic fervor, being the composer of both lyrics and music for "The Maple Leaf Forever," which then "became accepted as Canada's national anthem."[91] Roy has described this as "the song which made Canada articulate," and Muir created it in Confederation year of 1867.[92]

It was on 1 July 1867 that Canada became a Dominion, and the people "could find no better way to celebrate than through attendance or participation in sporting events." In Montreal, Ottawa, Toronto, Kingston, Hamilton, and many other places, athletic games and other sports were the patriotic order of the day.[93] Yet on this very special Canadian day, some of Muir's athletic fellow countrymen were involved in another pertinent sporting event south of the border. This was the first "Great International Caledonian Games," held at Jones Wood, New York City, on 1 July 1867. A magnificent color painting of this splendid affair can be seen today in the J. Clarence Davies Collection, at the Museum of the City of New York.[94] Scottish curlers from both countries had participated in an international bonspiel at Buffalo two years earlier, of course, and this first international Caledonian Games meeting in New York may not seem particularly significant, but developments three years later proved otherwise.

The ground for the first international Caledonian Games had been laid on 7 September 1866, when "a meeting of representatives from the various Scottish organizations throughout the United States and British Provinces" convened at the headquarters of the New York Caledonian Club, at 118 Sullivan Street, to discuss matters of mutual concern and cooperation. At this meeting there were representatives from Caledonian Clubs in

New York, Boston, Philadelphia, Brooklyn, Scranton, Pittston, and Montreal; and it was "resolved to have a grand international gathering of the clans in the year 1867." It was not surprising that this took place in New York, where the Caledonian Club was the largest and richest in North America throughout the nineteenth century.[95]

Such international cooperation and competition was a natural result of the tremendous growth and popularity of Caledonian Games in both countries, at a time when travel across the border was facilitated by the various and increasing number of railways. Scots from both countries attended each other's Games in delegations consisting of officials, competitors, and spectators. Since there were so many Caledonian Games in the many American cities, however, it was more common for Canadian athletes to travel south and seek their fortune in the larger American circuit, than vice versa. At the Twelfth Annual Games of the New York Caledonian Club, for example, in 1868, "Mr. William McRobie of Montreal" was one of the judges, when "the successful competitor of the day was Mr. Peter Fraser of Montreal, who carried off seven prizes, and would probably have won others, only he was disabled from taking part in the games during the latter part of the afternoon."[96] But even this feat was surpassed by the Canadian Fraser, who also reaped rich rewards at New York. In its report of the Sixteenth Annual Gathering of the Montreal Caledonian Society, the *Canadian Illustrated News* stated that "Robert Fraser, from Glengarry, famous as the man who took fourteen prizes in New York in one day, was invincible, and carried off the first prize for everything he entered for."[97] Another competitor at New York in 1868, J. R. Brindley, "one of the Canadian lacrosse players," was involved in a dead-heat finish of the mile race, in front of ten thousand spectators.[98]

An all-round Canadian athlete, Duncan E. Bowie of Montreal, did well at the Sixteenth Annual Games of the New York Club, also, winning the mile race, the hop, step and jump, the long race and short race, and coming second in the running long jump:

All the races were very meritorious, and Bowie the clever young Canadian Scot, sufficiently signalised himself to take his

Putting the shot, Caledonian Games, 1889. (Public Archives of Canada, C110082)

stand as a member of whom the Montreal club ought to be proud. We especially admired his cool way in the mile race of allowing his two leading opponents to race with each other for the lead, and then quietly passing them on the last lap, of running in an easy winner with any distance to spare.

The prize money for these Games amounted to $1,500, of which $1,000 was awarded in cash prizes and $500 "in goods consisting of part of the Highland costume." The value of the prizes won by Bowie amounted to $90.[99]

But if such Scottish sporting intercourse across the international boundary was not unusual, the same could not be said for the society formed by Caledonian Clubs from both countries only three years after the first Great International Caledonian Games were held in New York. In 1870, a convention took place "at which delegates from nearly all the Caledonian Clubs in the United States and Canada were present." A major item on the agenda was the standardization of implement specifications, measurement procedures, and rules governing the various events:

> Since there had been little standardization of the weight of hammers and stones, methods of measuring the distances these objects were thrown, measuring how far or high, the athlete jumped, or, for the specifications of the equipment, an attempt was made to overcome these diverse obstacles at this meeting. The convention also attempted to standardize the rules governing the events at the games.[100]

The rapid growth of Caledonian Games in both countries had made such proposals necessary. As the communications and contact between the many Caledonian Clubs increased, these discrepancies were further revealed and some action seemed prudent, if only to avoid the "constant wrangling betwixt officials and competitors" at Caledonian Games, where at times, "the officials were incompetent and the athletes were selfish."[101]

In fact, as early as 1858, Mr. D. Ross of Toronto had written to the *Globe* to urge the importance of having a uniform weight for hammers and stones at Highland Games in Britain and North America. He cited examples of differences in the weights of hammers used at Boston and New York, and concluded by saying that "with such material differences, it is impossible to decide as to the relative strength of competitors at a distance."[102] Perusal of the many newspaper accounts of Caledonian Games in Canada and the United States bears out Ross's contention, before and indeed long after 1858. "Heavy" hammers ranged from 12 lbs. in weight to 22 lbs., and "light" hammers from 7 lbs. to 16 lbs. "Heavy" stones could weigh as little as 21 lbs. or as much as 28 lbs., while "light" stones varied from 9 lbs. to 18 lbs.[103] However, despite individual and official concern, such differences

tended to persist in the nineteenth century, in Scotland as well as
in North America, and in the length and weight of the wooden
cabers as well as the hammers and stones. Local organizers tended
naturally to favor their own traditional implements.[104], and it
could well be argued that their parochialism in this regard served
to obtain some consistency in local records, at least. It was the rise
of amateur track and field in the countries involved, together
with its concomitant clubs and national associations, which provided the biggest stimulus toward the standardization of athletic
equipment of all types.[105]

Apart from the attempt to standardize equipment and rules at
the Caledonian Club's Convention of 1870, however, another
important decision was made. At the conclusion, the Clubs
federated in a North American United Caledonian Association,
and for the remainder of the nineteenth-century Caledonian Clubs
in Canada and the United States followed the Association's rules
at their annual Games.[106] A major concern of all the Caledonian
Clubs and Societies in both countries was the promotion of their
annual Games, and this was the first international organization of
their sport. Its birth was further proof of the popularity of these
international Games and the financial benefits of consistently
large, public patronage.

The formation of the North American United Caledonian
Association, three years after Confederation, was also a significant indication of Scottish cultural pride in North America,
which in this case transcended national considerations. The Scots
concerned did not form two separate national associations, one in
Canada and one in the United States, as one might have expected.
Instead of an ''American'' or ''Canadian'' Society, it was a
''North American'' Society, but the crucial adjectives in its title
seem to have been ''United'' and ''Caledonian.'' Many Scots
might well have agreed with Muir's sentiments expressed in
''The Maple Leaf Forever'' (especially those, like Sir John A.
Macdonald, who helped to bring Confederation about), but as far
as their Caledonian Games were concerned, an international and
Scottish outlook prevailed whether they lived under the Maple
Leaf or the Eagle. The ethnic pride in their cultural identity
superseded any national pride which might have existed in 1870.

The *Scottish-American Journal*, in fact, was in reality a "Scottish-North American Journal" since it circulated among the Scottish population of both countries, and reported all aspects of Scottish culture in Canada and the United States, besides always having a large section devoted to news from Scotland itself. And it was published in New York, from 1857 to 1919,[107] a period which assured it of a regular audience from newly arrived immigrants as well as an established clientele, and one which coincided fortuitously with the greatest era of the Caledonian Games. For these reasons, Caledonian Games should be regarded as a North American phenomenon in the nineteenth century, and a sporting product of Scottish self-esteem throughout the continent. One cannot look at the development of these Games in Canada alone, or only in the United States, during the nineteenth century, without an imbalance in historical perspective.

The mutual concern and cooperation in the promotion of Caledonian Games in both countries, under the auspices of the North American United Caledonian Association, was evident after 1870. Also, the amount of space devoted to them by the American and Canadian press indicated their popularity and importance. Apart from the lengthy newspaper reports, for example, illustrations of Caledonian Games were featured in the leading journals as well. The Montreal Games were so featured on the front pages of the *Canadian Illustrated News* in 1871 and 1872, the Hamilton and Toronto Games in 1875, and the International Games at Montreal in 1879 (see figures 5, 6, 7, and 8).[108] In the United States, illustrations of Caledonian Games appeared in *Harper's Weekly* and *Frank Leslie's Illustrated Newspaper*.[109] (It is very probable that they were featured in other journals not available or readily accessible to historians.)

When the Eighth Annual Games of the Brooklyn Caledonian Club were advertised in 1874, it was laid down that

> The following rules will control the sports of the day:
> The games are open to all sister clubs in the United States and Canada.
> Members of sister clubs will be required to show a certificate of membership, signed by the Chief and Fourth Chieftain of

their respective clubs, before being allowed to compete in the games.[110]

These requirements might have been fairly standard procedure, although such a certificate was rarely mentioned in reports of the Games. They may have been enforced, for instance, at the Eighteenth annual Games of the New York Caledonian Club, held two weeks after the Brooklyn Games, but no mention is made of the fact. The crowd then was estimated at some twenty thousand people, and "a number of Scottish visitors from different parts of the United States and Canada were in attendance."[111]

At the Sixth Annual Convention of the North American United Caledonian Association, held in Toronto, it was felt by the delegates that the "International Highland Games" held in conjunction with the conventions were a great success. Satisfaction was also expressed at the $23,000 cash balance and largest membership of the New York Club.[112] However, it was obvious that all was not well. Another urgent meeting of the Association was held several days later in Albany, New York, when the *New York Times* reported:

> At the meeting of the North American United Caledonian Association held here, the proposition to amend the bye-laws so that "all competitors at annual games must be members of Caledonian clubs or societies, and no honorary member shall have the right to compete in the games of any club" was, after a long discussion, defeated.[113]

The reference to a "long discussion" seems to indicate that the Caledonians concerned were far from "united" on this point. Quite clearly, all competitors at Caledonian Games in the past had not been members of Scottish clubs. Was this policy to continue? Despite the qualms of many of its members, the highest Caledonian authority of all now officially sanctioned their Games as open to all. In this case, financial motives held the day against considerations of pedigree. As Berthoff has observed:

> Americans as well as Scots soon flocked by the thousands to Caledonian Games in cities the country over. If the Scots

Top: The Caledonian Games at Toronto, July, 1875. *Bottom:*
The Caledonian Games at Hamilton, August, 1875.

frowned on these motely crowds, they welcomed the flood of silver at the gates and soon threw the competitions open to all athletes, be they Scots, Americans, Irish, Germans or Negroes. Down to the 1870's, however, practised Scotsmen won most of the prizes.[114]

The crowds actually flocked to Caledonian Games all over the North American continent, at admission prices which usually ranged from twenty-five to fifty cents. Another statement in the *Scottish-American Journal* in 1875 referred to the usual Fourth of July celebrations in the United States, but could equally well be applied to Dominion Day celebrations in Canada, and aptly summed up the aims and hopes of the promoters of Caledonian Games:

> On Monday, when the "Glorious Fourth" will be celebrated, a good number of the Caledonian Clubs throughout the country will hold their annual out-door gatherings. We wish these . . . pleasant weather, a happy day, troops of visitors, and substantial additions to their funds.[115]

In ten years' time, however, an article in the same journal severely censured Caledonian Societies for conveniently ignoring ethnic qualifications in pursuit of the dollar.

Meanwhile, Caledonian Games continued as an international North American affair, which all nationalities could legitimately enjoy as participant or spectator. A group from Hamilton, Ontario, was among delegations from other cities at the Boston Games of 1878, before proceeding to the New York Games a few days later, where they were joined by fellow Scots from Toronto.[116] The following year the International Caledonian Games were held at the Montreal Lacrosse Grounds in Canada.[117] In 1880, when "a great crowd gathered to see one of the best athletic exhibitions ever given in New York" at the Caledonian Club's Annual Games, competitors from Ottawa, Montreal, and Toronto were among the prizewinners.[118] Four years later there was a delegation from Prince Edward Island at the Boston Caledonian Games.[119] Spectators from Hamilton, Ontario, travelled to the annual Games of the St. Andrew's Society of Buffalo, New

York, in July 1885; and in September, at the New York Caledonian Club's Games, it was reported that ''the honors of the day
were shared pretty evenly by the visitors and members of home
athletic organizations, a goodly number of the prizes going to
Boston and Canada.''[120]

Before this, many of the prizes had even gone to Scotland. The
famous Donald Dinnie, and his travelling companion-athlete,
James Fleming, as well as other athletes from Scotland, made profitable tours of the North American Caledonian Games circuit in
the 1870s.[121] Promoters realized the value of having such
famous names from their homeland at their Gatherings to attract
the crowds.[122] But this practice was often resented by local, less
proficient, or less professionally minded athletes. In a letter to the
Scottish-American Journal in 1875, the Boston quoits champion,
John Brown, addressed himself to the delegates attending the
Sixth Annual Convention of the North American United Caledonian Association:

> Before concluding, I would like to call the attention of the
> Caledonian delegates to Toronto, to the growing nuisance of
> travelling athletes who make a business of flying from place to
> place during the season, and hope some means will be adopted
> so as to handicap these gentry, or stop their movements
> altogether, so that amateurs may have a chance.[123]

Brown's hopes were in vain, and seven years later another letter
of protest signed from ''Canadian Athletes'' appeared in the
Scottish-American Journal of 18 May 1882, in which they expressed concern at the impending visit of Dinnie, George Davidson, and W. Cummings to Highland Games meetings in Canada,
since ''. . . other athletes will find it impossible to make it
remunerative to attend the games.'' This was yet another indication of the mercenary element which was characteristic of Caledonian Games. Famous athletes undertook arduous tours of several
Games because it was profitable, organizers booked them for the
same reason, and others resented the practice since it lessened
their own prospects of financial reward.

Three years after the Canadian athletes' letter, there appeared a

The Bagpipes of the Fifth Royal Scots—The Sword Dance—The High Leap; Caledonian Games, 1889. (Public Archives of Canada, C110083)

long and significant article in the *Scottish-American Journal* which indicated that the greatest era of the Caledonian Games in North America was coming to an end, for a number of valid reasons. As the first really discordant and pessimistic note in the Scots' own newspaper, a journal which did more than any other in the nineteenth century to promote and report Scottish sports, it is worth quoting from at length:

> The season for the Caledonian Games in this country and Canada may now be considered as almost over. Lucknow, Wingham, etc., have still to be heard of. . . .
>
> Financially the games have been by no means as successful as those of last year. New York, Boston, Newark, Jersey City, Philadelphia and Rochester had large gatherings; so had Montreal, London, Stratford, Woodstock and other places in Canada; but the amount of money realized was smaller than before, and in some cases the balance seems to have come out on the wrong side. In Brooklyn, and in one or two other cities, the games fell quite flat; and at Albany, Hartford, and elsewhere the weather interfered. . . . At the same time, making all due allowances for weather, counter-attractions, and other incidentals, we question very much if it is now possible to make Scottish games in this country such financial successes as they were ten years ago. The novelty has worn off these festivals, similar sports can be seen everywhere at frequent intervals during the summer, and the pic-nic features, which used to be so enjoyable, have been abandoned. . . . People are getting tired of seeing the everlasting Highland Fling and Sword Dance, to the exclusion of all others.
>
> In view of the general results of the year, we think that Caledonian Clubs and Societies should not now depend for financial assistance upon their annual games, as they have done in the past. The expenses attending such meetings are very great, and seem to be increasing every year, and the consequences of failure are more disastrous than ever. We could name a long list of clubs which have started under brilliant auspices, with every prospect of lengthened and useful careers, but which were hopelessly wrecked because their first games turned out financial failures. Clubs, like children, must learn to

"creep afore they gang." A pleasant pic-nic, with a few games thrown in, costs but little, yet affords much fun. . . . Some organizations, unfortunately, could hardly afford to be content with such an inexpensive demonstration at present; the New York Club, for instance. . . . One or two other Clubs are in the same position; but it is a position which is opposed to all sound business principles, and should be abandoned as quickly as possible. Most of our Societies have been managed as though money-making were the sole reason for their existence, and the sooner this idea is departed from the better for all concerned.

The writer goes on to suggest that Games be held every two years, and that "more mirth-provoking competitions . . . should form the bulk of the sports." In conclusion, he expressed the view that "attention to these matters will make our games in the future, as they have been in the past, productive of much pleasure to the Scottish residents of this country and Canada, and in the realization of this pleasure is found their true mission and their original design—at least on this side of the Atlantic."[124] But eight years later there came another plea in the *Scottish-American Journal* to exclude competitors of other nationalities and make the Games Scottish again.[125] In 1896, these sentiments were echoed by Peter Ross in his book, *The Scot in America*. In 1885, it had been claimed that "similar sports can be seen everywhere at frequent intervals during the summer,"[126] but Ross was more specific:

All over the country, during the season, games are held under the auspices of local athletic clubs, and these games are nearly all very similar to those which might be witnessed at Hawick or Inverness.

The similarity did not end there, for Scottish rules were also "really the basis on which all athletic contests here are conducted." The result was that Caledonian Clubs were outnumbered by local amateur athletic clubs, whose more frequent meetings supplied the public demand. Ross also felt that it had been a mistake to throw the Games open to competitors of all nationalities, and suggested a return to the traditional and exclusive conventions of the past.[127]

There can be little doubt that the concerned writer(s) of the *Scottish-American Journal* articles, and Ross, were correct in their judgment. The Caledonian Games had begun early in the century as a traditional festival for Scotsmen alone. Soon the organizers were surprised at the crowds which attended them, and the substantial amount of gate receipts, and were encouraged to open the Games to all nationalities. As this policy prospered and brought remarkable profits, their Games became more lavish and expensive productions, and experienced an era of great popularity. Some Caledonian Clubs, however, did not prosper in their efforts to emulate other larger and successful clubs, at a time when attendance and financial returns began to decrease. A major reason for this was the concomitant rise of amateur sport in Canada and the United States, especially track and field athletics, and the subsequent appearance of national associations governing amateur sports in both countries.[128]

The first amateur track and field athletic club in the United States was the New York Athletic Club, formed in 1868, and eleven years later there were approximately one hundred such clubs in the New York area alone.[129] By 1883, there were about one hundred and fifty amateur athletic clubs in the United States.[130] In post-Confederation Canada, the Montreal Pedestrian Club was formed in 1873, and other amateur sport clubs subsequently held track and field meetings, until the formation of the Montreal Amateur Athletic Association in 1881.[131] Then track and field "began to take on a new dimension" as the M.A.A.A. held regular meets which "were strictly for amateur competitors and officials."[132] The Amateur Athletic Union of Canada was formed on 14 December 1883, for "the advancement and improvement of amateur athletic sports."[133] What has been described as "the first specifically track and field association in Canada,"[134] however (the Ontario Amateur Athletic Association), was not formed until April 1900. In the United States, meanwhile, the National Association of the Amateur Athletes of America was formed in 1879; and the Amateur Athletic Union of the United

The International Caledonian Games at the grounds of the Montreal Lacrosse Club, in 1879.

States was formed in 1888. The New York Athletic Club was a leader in the progress towards this formation of the A.A.U., but another well-known athletic club involved was the Scottish-American Club.[135] This was organized in 1875 by Scottish athletes who broke away from the New York Caledonian Club because they were concerned about their amateur status.[136]

These developments in both countries were not without some Scottish influence,[137] but ironically they also greatly contributed to the decline of Caledonian Games. Similarly, amateur sport was fast gaining in popularity in American and Canadian educational institutions, including track and field. Again, its appearance on many campuses owed much to Scottish influence, yet its development also represented a counterattraction to Caledonian Games.

The University of Toronto undergraduates had an annual track and field meeting in the 1860s which became known as "the Games" during the nineteenth century, and which naturally included such Caledonian events as hammer-throwing, stone-putting, standing and running high and long jumps, three-legged races and sack races.[138] McGill University of Montreal held annual interfaculty meets from 1872 which were also identical to a Caledonian Games program.[139] Not surprisingly, in both institutions there was an abundance of Scottish names among the event winners, for example, McDougall, McKenzie, Campbell, McMurchy, Lindsay, Bruce, Maclean, McKendrick, McNally, and many more.[140] In 1873, the same Duncan E. Bowie who did so well at the Sixteenth Annual Games of the New York Caledonian Club in the previous year, represented McGill University and won the first intercollegiate footrace in the United States. This was a two-mile race at Springfield against representatives from Amherst College and Cornell University.[141] In this year, also, the Scottish director of the Gymnasium at Princeton University, George Goldie, initiated the "Caledonian Games" there. These were so named in his honor and became an annual event.[142] Other colleges and universities followed suit with similar programs.[143] In 1875 delegates from several of these institutions formed the Intercollegiate Association of Amateur Athletes of America. Its first athletic meeting was held the next year, and won by Goldie's pupils from Princeton.[144] (Goldie went on to become the first director at the famous New York Athletic Club from 1885 to 1893, before returning to Princeton and his subsequent retirement.)[145] In Canada, a conference between McGill and Toronto University delegates in 1898 resulted in "the first official inter-collegiate meet" being held between their institutions on 21 October 1899, again referred to as "The Games."[146]

This rise of track and field catered for amateur principles, and offered a similar and more frequent alternative attraction to the Caledonian Games for competitors and spectators alike, without the trappings of Scottish pageantry and peculiar Scottish events like caber-tossing and Highland dancing.[147] As the ethnic custom of a minority immigrant group, Caledonian Games tended to become superfluous to the national associations of sport in Canada and the United States. Paradoxically, though, they were the most important pioneer and professional form of the later amateur athletics meetings which served to make them obsolete. As Leonard and Affleck have stated, the Caledonian Clubs "may be considered the precursors of our modern amateur athletic clubs,"[148] an opinion shared by Berthoff among others. It was by the 1870s, he maintained, that "Caledonian clubs had to compete for public favor with American imitators. In fact, the modern American Track and field meet evolved directly from the games of the Scottish immigrants."[149] As mentioned previously, historians of sport in Canada have also agreed that the Canadian track and field meet evolved in the same way.

Yet, although the rise of amateur track and field contributed to a decline of the Caledonian Games in both Canada and the United States, there were important differences. In the same way as there were more Caledonian Clubs, and therefore Games, in the much more heavily populated southern Republic than in the northern Dominion, so too there were more track and field clubs there. And as the professional Caledonian athletes from Canada had gone south to compete in richer pastures, their amateur successors followed suit. Athletes of Scottish descent were among those from Canada who were members of leading American track and field clubs.[150] Probably the most famous of these was George Reginald Gray, a member of the New York Athletic Club, from Coldwater, Ontario. Before he retired from athletics in 1902, Gray had been the champion sixteen-pound shot-putter of Canada and the United States for seventeen years. He also won titles in Britain, and a total of 188 medals and trophies, all "firsts," during a career in which he established over twenty world records.[151]

A look ahead into the twentieth century reveals that amateur track and field and the Caledonian Games became largely incompatible in the United States. Each went their separate ways; the former became a major sport in which Americans excelled in international competition, while the latter declined in comparison to the former glory of the post–Civil War era.[152] In view of the fact that the United States had long since been independent of any British relationship, and indeed was the "melting-pot" for immigrants from all over the world, this is not so surprising. Today Highland Games are still held in several places in the United States, such as Boston (Massachusetts), Linville (North Carolina), Media (Pennsylvania), San Francisco (California), and Stamford (Connecticut), organized by Americans who remain proud of their Scottish heritage.[153]

In contrast, the advent of amateur track and field in the Dominion of Canada represented only a temporary distraction to the Highland Games, to which an adjustment was easily made without too much divergence in a country where the Scottish tradition was so firmly rooted. Although the glorious years of the post-Confederation era, when expansion and enthusiasm were greatest, could never be totally recaptured, no serious decline was ever noticeable or permanent. The two forms of athletic activity have coexisted happily to date. The affinity and relationship of the old, established and professional Scottish form with the newer, amateur and nonpartisan form, was continued without undue embarrassment to either side. In fact, provincial amateur track and field championships in various parts of Canada have usually and regularly been held in conjunction with Highland Games meetings. New Caledonian Clubs and Highland Games Societies were still being formed in Canada, also, late into the twentieth century, to take their place alongside the many other established Gatherings which have not only survived but flourished to the present day.

For example, the 1906 Winnipeg Games had fourteen events for amateurs and fourteen events for professional athletes, and although the events changed over the years, the practice of holding the amateur track and field championships in a joint meeting with Highland Games continued.[154] The first official Highland Gathering at Banff, Alberta, was in 1927, and held under the auspices of the Calgary St. Andrew–Caledonian Society and the Banff Amateur Athletic Association.[155] For many years the Provincial Track and Field Championships were held at the Banff Highland Gathering, and the Rules of the Amateur Athletic Union of Canada governed them.[156] In 1929, the Edmonton Olympic Club took over the supervision of the athletic portion of the Edmonton Highland Gatherings in Alberta. Right up to the present day in Canada, from Vancouver Island to Prince Edward Island, Highland Games are still held with track and field as an integral part of the proceedings.[157] For many years past, the excellent published program of the Antigonish Highland Games in Nova Scotia has carried a double center-page with the heading: "The Highland Games Program of Track and Field Events."[158] The International Gathering of the Clans took place with great pageantry in Nova Scotia in 1979 when these Games were held from July 7 to 15, with Track and Field Championships being contested as an integral part of the proceedings on the Thursday, Friday and Sunday.[159] It is difficult to find evidence of serious decline, too, considering that twenty-seven thousand people attended the Glengarry Highland Games in Ontario, in 1948, opened by Prime Minister Mackenzie King; and that new Scottish Societies which held Highland Games were still being formed in various parts of Canada.[160] The long tradition of political patronage was continued by former prime minister the Rt. Hon. John Diefenbaker, when he attended the Glengarry Highland Games in 1975, appropriately dressed in a kilt.[161]

It is certain that the North American United Caledonian Association was still the governing body in 1902,[162] but it is not known when the association became extinct. The *Scottish-American Journal*, for so long the oracle of information on Scottish affairs in North America, including Caledonian Games, unfortunately ceased publication in 1919. However, Scots and their descendants are still "united" by the Highland Games wherever they are held. As international travel has become easier, they have attended each other's Games in their respective countries. Many take an annual pilgrimage from North America to the Braemar Royal Highland Games Society's Gathering in Scotland to take part in the celebrations.[163] Similarly, twentieth-century Scots have followed the path of Dinnie and his contemporaries, and attended their Games in other countries besides their own.

But, outside Scotland, nowhere else in the world is the tradition of Highland Games maintained so dutifully or successfully as in Canada. No other country besides Scotland has nearly so many

Gatherings, as Scottish visitors and others will testify. Also, no other country has sent more competitors to the various Games in Scotland than this Dominion. Beginning in 1911, when the great Canadian athlete, Walter Knox, distinguished himself before royalty at Braemar, Canadians have been the most prominent overseas visitors in Scottish competitions, as Scots will verify.[164]

Could it be, in fact, that history will repeat itself in this respect? We have seen how curling developed until it became more popular, established, and successful in Canada than in any other country, even Scotland itself. A Canadian Gold Medal winner at the World Highland Dancing Championships, held in Scotland in 1964, maintained that Canadians were much keener about Highland dancing than the Scots, and that there were always more entries for the competitions in Canada.[165] Perhaps a historian of the future who can observe the remainder of the twentieth century in Canada and Scotland will provide the answer.

In the meantime, it is certain that the great success of the Caledonian Games during the nineteenth century, and their enthusiastic presence in the Dominion still, is yet another significant indication of the enduring Scottish influence on sport in Canada. It is a reflection of the Scottish tradition inherent in Canadian life, which exists on a scale unparalleled in any other nation outside of the land which gave it birth.

Notes

1. Fred Eugene Leonard and George B. Affleck, *The History of Physical Education* (Philadelphia: Lea and Febiger, 1947), p. 282; Rowland Tappan Berthoff, *British Immigrants in Industrial America* (Cambridge, Mass.: Harvard University Press, 1953), pp. 151, 167; Gerald Redmond, *The Caledonian Games in Nineteenth-Century America* (Rutherford, N.J.: Fairleigh Dickinson University Press, 1971), pp. 42–98. See also: R. T. Berthoff, "Goldie and the Caledonian Games," *Princeton Alumni Weekly*, 23 May 1952, p. 6.

2. *Emigrant and Old Countryman*, 19 October 1836. The Meeting was held "to review the sports of their Native Land" at the Elysian Fields in Hoboken, and may have been confined to games of caman or shinty, and Highland Dancing to bagpipe music. Leonard and Affleck, *Physical Education*, p. 282.

3. R. E. May, in an article in the *Boston Scotsman*, 7 April 1906, states: "Scottish games were no doubt held in Boston many years before 1849, but that is the first year for which there is authentic record, as the surplus resulting therefrom was that year donated

to the Charitable Society and for several years thereafter.'' A letter from a Scot who came to Boston in 1848 was included in the *Boston Scotsman*, 16 February 1907, in which the writer stated: ''At that time there were quite a number of Scotsmen about Boston who were interested in Scottish games, such as curling, quoiting, throwing the hammer, etc., and frequently met for a day during the season to enjoy playing those games. There was no regular organization among them, but for two or three years the formation of a club was constantly the subject of conversation at all these meetings, social and otherwise.''

4. David Webster, *Scottish Highland Games* (Glasgow: William Collins Sons and Co., 1959), p. 14.

5. John Graham Harkness, *Stormont, Dundas and Glengarry: A History, 1784-1945* (Oshawa, Ontario: Mundy-Goodfellow Printing Co., 1946), p. 128.

6. James S. Macdonald, *Annals of the North British Society of Halifax, Nova Scotia* (Halifax, N.S.: ''Citizen'' Steam Book, Job and General Printing Office, 1868), p. 7.

7. Wilfred Campbell, *The Scotsman in Canada*, vol. 1 (Toronto: Musson Book Co., n.d.), pp. 408-18.

8. *MG 28, 1, 40, vol. 10, Public Archives of Canada*. Among these records of the St. Andrew's Society of Ottawa is a handwritten manuscript entitled ''The St. Andrew's Society of Ottawa, 1846-1897: Sketch of the First Half Century,'' written by John Thorburn; and also an enlarged version of the same, typewritten, entitled ''The St. Andrew's Society of Ottawa, 1846-1946: History of the First Century,'' by John Thorburn and A. E. Cameron.

9. Ibid., p. 14.

10. This information is contained in *The Caledonian Society of Montreal, Programme for 1964-65*.

11. Robert Meyer, Jr., *Festivals, U.S.A. and Canada* (New York: Ives Washburn, 1967), p. 207.

12. *Encyclopedia Canadiana*, 10 vols. (Toronto: Grolier of Canada Limited, 1968), 5:124.

13. Macdonald, *North British Society*, p. 143.

14. *Encyclopedia Canadiana* (1968), 5:124.

15. *Novascotian*, 2 July 1860, 23 July 1860; Peter Leslie Lindsay, ''A History of Sport in Canada, 1807-1867'' (Ph.D. diss., University of Alberta, 1969), p. 147.

16. *Encyclopedia Canadiana* (1968), 5:124. The Antigonish Highland Society produces a large booklet as a program for its annual Highland Games. In the 1965 and 1966 issues are facsimiles ''of the minutes of the first and founding meeting of the Highland Society in 1861.'' (The pages in these booklets are not numbered.)

17. *The Antigonish Highland Society, Program for 1966*.

18. See D. Campbell and R. A. MacLean, *Beyond the Atlantic Roar: A Study of the Nova Scotia Scots* (Toronto: McClelland and Stewart, 1974); and Charles W. Dunn, *Highland Settler: A Portrait of the Scottish Gael in Nova Scotia* (Toronto: University of Toronto Press, 1968). See also: *Scottish-American Journal*, 4 October 1877.

19. John K. Munro, ''Curling in Canada,'' *Canadian Magazine* 18(1902): 529.

20. *Montreal Gazette*, 11 July 1840.

21. *Globe*, 22 September 1847. Nine years earlier, on 17 October 1838, the ''Toronto Olympic Games'' were held at the Caer Howell Grounds with a program of 11 events similar to a Caledonian Games meeting. The umpire was Colonel Mackenzie Fraser, the secretary was John Maitland, and the prizes were ''Silver Medals, Blue Bonnetts and Money.''

22. *Morning Chronicle*, 18 October 1847.

23. *Globe*, 25 May 1859.

24. See Webster, *Highland Games*, p. 39; and *Porter's Spirit of the Times*, 2 October 1858.

25. *Montreal Gazette*, 4 September 1856.

26. Henry Roxborough, *One Hundred—Not Out: The Story of Nineteenth Century Canadian Sport* (Toronto: Ryerson Press, 1966), p. 110.

27. The results were: Putting the Heavy Stone: 1st prize, 15s. to D. Robertson, Distance 22 ft. 6 ins.; 2nd prize, 7/6d. to James Munogue, Distance 22 ft. 4 ins. Throwing Heavy Hammer: 1st prize, 20s. to W. B. Johnston, Distance 50 ft. 3 ins.; 2nd prize, 10s. to Murdoch McKenzie, Distance 49 ft. 11 ins. (*Montreal Gazette*, 4 September 1856).

28. *The Zorra Caledonian Society, Program for 1956.*

29. Roxborough, *One Hundred—Not Out*, pp. 186–89. This will be discussed more fully in chapter 7.

30. Ibid., pp. 108–9.

31. *Montreal Gazette*, 4 September 1856.

32. Ibid., 19 June 1856.

33. Roxborough, *One Hundred—Not Out*, p. 108. Quoits will also be mentioned more fully in chapter 7.

34. For an account of this meeting, see the *Canadian Illustrated News*, 28 August 1875.

35. *Montreal Gazette*, 5 September 1857.

36. Roxborough, *One Hundred—Not Out*, p. 110.

37. *Encyclopedia Canadiana* (1968), 5:125.

38. *Minute Book of the St. Andrew's Society of London, 1860–1875*. This is located at the General Library, Lawson Memorial Building, the University of Western Ontario, London, Ontario.

39. *MG 28, 1, 40, vol. 10, Public Archives of Canada.*

40. So it was in Montreal, too. The *Canadian Illustrated News* of 7 December 1878, p. 361, features a large illustration, in six parts, of the St. Andrew's Ball there, one of which shows the governor-general dancing a Strathspey Reel, observed by (Sir) John A. Macdonald.

41. *MG 28, 1, 40, vol. 10, Public Archives of Canada.*

42. Charles Donaldson, *Men of Muscle, and the Highland Games of Scotland, with Brief Biographies of the Leading Athletes of the Last Fifty Years, with Portraits* (Glasglow: Carter and Pratt, 1901), p. 119.

43. *MG 28, 1, 40, vol. 10*. The surplus of receipts over expenditure for the Games varied from $25 to $650. Weather was an important factor which often affected attendance, and a fine day was hoped for by the organizers. An unusual deficit, of $60.81, occurred in 1890, when the Society seems to have been overgenerous in the amount of prize money awarded.

44. Campbell, *Scotsman in Canada*, pp. 407–23. St. Andrew's Societies were also formed in the United States, of course, which also celebrated the Highland Games; see *Scottish-American Journal*, 1 July 1875; 8 July 1875; 15 July 1875; 22 July 1875; 4 October 1877; 11 October 1877; 18 October 1877; 14 July 1881, 29 June 1882; and 23 July 1885, for some examples.

45. *Scottish-American Journal*, 1 July 1875, and passim to 18 August 1897. See, for example, the *Scottish-American Journal*, 15 July 1875, which gives an account of the St. Andrew's Society of Barrie, Ontario, holding Highland Games on Dominion Day of that year.

46. Robert Douglas Day, ''Impulse to Addiction: A Narrative History of Sport in

Chatham, Ontario: 1790–1895'' (M.A. thesis, University of Western Ontario, 1977), p. 187.

47. *Scottish-American Journal*, 8 July 1875; 2 June 1881; 15 September 1881; and 29 September 1881.

48. *Encyclopedia Canadiana* (1968), 5:125.

49. *Constitution of the St. Andrew's Society of the City of Winnipeg* (Winnipeg: Walker and May, 1886), passim; hereafter referred to as *Constitution from Winnipeg*. This booklet, together with other documents, correspondence, and programs, from 1879 to 1952, and also a scrapbook from 1867 to 1952, is located in the Public Archives of Manitoba, Legislative Library, Legislative Buildings, Winnipeg, Manitoba.

50. John E. Reid, ''Sports and Games in Alberta before 1900'' (M.A. thesis, University of Alberta, 1969), p. 57.

51. John McDougall, *Saddle, Sled and Snowshoe: Pioneering on the Saskatchewan in the Sixties* (Toronto: William Briggs, 1896), pp. 52–53.

52. Ibid., pp. 136–37.

53. Reid, ''Sports in Alberta,'' p. 58. See also: Penelope Dawn Routledge, ''The North-West Mounted Police and Their Influence on the Sporting and Social Life of the North-West Territories, 1870–1904'' (M.A. thesis, University of Alberta, 1978).

54. Allen Elton Cox, ''A History of Sports in Canada, 1868–1900'' (Ph.D. diss., University of Alberta, 1969), pp. 179–81.

55. *Daily Colonist*, 30 May 1859, as quoted in Lindsay, ''Sport in Canada, 1807 to 1867,'' p. 146.

56. As quoted in Nancy Howell and Maxwell L. Howell, *Sports and Games in Canadian Life, 1700 to the Present* (Toronto: Macmillan of Canada, 1969), p. 18.

57. Cox, ''Sports in Canada, 1868 to 1900,'' p. 178; *Daily Colonist*, 10 June 1869.

58. *Scottish-American Journal*, 18 October 1877.

59. Ibid., 15 September 1881; *Encyclopedia Canadiana* (1968), 5:125.

60. Lindsay, ''Sport in Canada, 1807–1867,'' p. 138.

61. *Nova Scotia Royal Gazette*, 8 March 1808; 15 March 1808; Cox, ''Sports in Canada, 1868 to 1900,'' pp. 177–96; Lindsay, ''Sport in Canada, 1807–1867,'' pp. 138–48. See also: Foster Rhea Dulles, *A History of Recreation: America Learns to Play* (New York: Appleton-Century-Crofts, 1965), pp. 143–44; and John Allen Krout, *Annals of American Sport 15, The Pageant of America Series*, 15 vols. (New York: United States Publishers' Association, 1929), pp. 186–87.

62. Howell and Howell, *Sports in Canadian Life*, pp. 52–53.

63. Stewart Alexander Davidson, ''A History of Sports and Games in Eastern Canada prior to World War I'' (D.Ed. diss., Teachers' College, Columbia University, 1951), pp. 48–49.

64. Cox, ''Sports in Canada, 1868 to 1900,'' p. 176, states: ''The vigorous Scottish people, who contributed so much to Canadian society during the nineteenth century, must be given much of the credit for the early developments of track and field in Canada.'' See also Howell and Howell, *Sports in Canadian Life*, pp. 52–56, 89–95; and Davidson, ''Sports in Eastern Canada,'' pp. 48–49, 87–90, appendix E. On page 90, Davidson states: ''During all this period, track and field sports held a very secondary position, and were largely centred in annual or district Caledonian celebrations or special Highland games, or as additional attractions at lacrosse games.'' Lindsay, ''Sport in Canada, 1807–1867,'' p. 144, states: ''During the sixties, track and field activities thrived, largely due to their adoption by groups following the examples set by the various Caledonian Games.'' On page 382, the same author states: ''Track and field activities, as well as curling and golf, were indebted to early Scottish influence. Irish Benevolent Societies and military garrisons conducted athletic games, but it was the Caledonian Societies that

organized annual track and field carnivals in Montreal, Toronto, and Halifax, beginning in Montreal in 1856." See also Roxborough, *One Hundred—Not Out*, pp. 99, 109–11. Among other historians, Ian F. Jobling, "Sport in Nineteenth Century Canada: The Effects of Technological Changes on its Development" (Ph.D. diss., University of Alberta, 1970), p. 375, states: "The Caledonian Societies had helped to promote the sport, i.e. track and field, from the mid-century on." See also Wm. Perkins Bull, *From Rattlesnake Hunt to Hockey: The History of Sports in Canada and of the Sportsmen of Peel, 1798 to 1934* (Toronto: George J. McLeod, 1934), pp. 151–59.

65. Day, "Sport in Chatham," p. 95.

66. See Berthoff, *British Immigrants*, pp. 151–52, 167–68; C. W. Hackensmith, *History of Physical Education* (New York: Harper and Row, 1966), pp. 177, 343; Robert Korsgaard, "A History of the Amateur Athletic Union of the United States" (Ph.D. diss., Teachers' College, Columbia University, 1952), pp. 22–29, 32, 68; Leonard and Affleck, *Physical Education*, p. 282; Emmett A. Rice, John L. Hutchinson and Mabel Lee, *A Brief History of Physical Education* (New York: Ronald Press Co., 1969), p. 188; Peter Ross, *The Scot in America* (New York: Raeburn Book Co., 1896), pp. 426–27.

67. For example, Augustus Maier, "Physical Training in Athletic Clubs" (thesis, Springfield College, 1904), p. 11, admitted that "the Caledonian societies participated in athletic games before any of the other clubs," but maintained that "their games were of a different type from those we have today, and were peculiarly adapted to the participants." In similar fashion, Duncan Edwards, "Life at the Athletic Clubs," *Scribner's*, July–December 1895, p. 4, admitted that, before the New York Athletic Club was formed in 1868, Scots "tossed the caber, ran footraces, and drank good Scotch whiskey in honor of Robbie Burns and the domestic affections." See also George J. Fisher, "Athletics Outside Education Institutions." *American Physical Education Review*, June 1907, p. 112.

68. Lindsay, "Sport in Canada, 1807–1867," p. 144.

69. *Montreal Gazette*, 3 July 1871. But of course, some Scots had control of the press (as did George Brown, editor of the Toronto *Globe*). See in particular chapter 29, entitled "Scotchmen in Literature, Journalism, and Art," in Campbell, *Scotsman in Canada*, pp. 402–6.

70. *Montreal Gazette*, 16 May 1840.

71. Lindsay, "Sport in Canada, 1807–1867," pp. 139–40. It is interesting to note that Colonel Angus Cameron, a retired officer, "was both originator of, and first instructor in, physical training at Queen's." See D. D. Calvin, *Queen's University at Kingston: The First Century of a Scottish-Canadian Foundation, 1841-1941* (Kingston, Ontario: The Trustees of the University, 1941), pp. 277–79.

72. *Montreal Gazette*, 20 September 1843. The *Scottish-American Journal* devotes much space to rifle-shooting among the Scots in North America during the nineteenth century, and separate rifle-shooting clubs were formed. For example, see *Scottish-American Journal*, 1 July 1875, 8 July 1875, and 22 July 1875. Most reports were carried under a special column entitled "The Rifle."

73. Lindsay, "Sport in Canada, 1807–1867," p. 140, footnote.

74. Sir Iain Colquhoun and Hugh Machell, *Highland Gatherings* (London: Heath Cranton, 1927), p. 140.

75. *Montreal Gazette*, 29 September 1843.

76. Lindsay, "Sport in Canada, 1807–1867," p. 140.

77. E. Norman Gardiner, *Athletics of the Ancient World* (London: Oxford University Press, 1967), p. 27. It should perhaps be pointed out that Professor Gardiner does go on to say "but it is probable that, if we knew more, other parallels might be found wherever a similar state of society has existed."

78. Donaldson, *Men of Muscle*, p. 2.

79. Lt. Col. F. A. M. Webster, *Olympic Cavalcade* (London: Hutchinson and Co., 1948), p. 19.

80. Lindsay, "Sport in Canada, 1807–1867," p. 140.

81. *Montreal Gazette*, 29 August 1844 (report of the first day's proceedings), 30 August 1844 (report of the second day's proceedings).

82. Lindsay, "Sport in Canada, 1807–1867," pp. 141–42.

83. *Montreal Gazette*, 16 September 1856. Apart from the events, there was another Scottish aspect to these Beauharnois Athletic Games, for the report also stated: "At the entrance stands the Scotch Presbyterian Church, a small stone building against the gable of which the grandstand was erected."

84. Lindsay, "Sport in Canada, 1807–1867," p. 141.

85. Ibid., p. 143; Roxborough, *One Hundred—Not Out*, pp. 174–75.

86. See D. D. Calvin, *Queen's University*, pp. 273–77. This refers to the strong Gaelic tradition at Queen's, and the author concludes "and there will always be Highlanders at Queen's. Do not the very sports-scribes call our teams 'The Gaels'?" See also the other work of which he was co-author, T. R. Glover and D. D. Calvin, *A Corner of Empire: The Old Ontario Strand* (Cambridge: University Press, 1937). On page 126 it is stated: "it is noticeable how many Canadian universities have Scottish names or at least Scotsmen among their founders"; and on page 127: "Queen's College was a Scottish and Presbyterian foundation, and there are those (we are told) who thought in 1839 of so naming it, the Scottish Presbyterian College." See also notes 132 and 133 in chapter 3.

87. Roxborough, *One Hundred—Not Out*, p. 174. For example, he won the running high jump and the running leap at the Canadian Highland Society's first gathering at Toronto, in 1859 (*Globe*, 25 May 1859); and won the high leap again "in 1860 at the games that were planned as entertainment for the Prince of Wales" (Roxborough, *One Hundred—Not Out*, p. 175).

88. David Boyle, ed., *The Township of Scarboro, 1796–1896* (Toronto: William Briggs, 1896), p. 250.

89. Roxborough, *One Hundred—Not Out*, p. 175.

90. Ibid., pp. 174–75; Boyle, *Township of Scarboro*, pp. 241–60.

91. Roxborough, *One Hundred—Not Out*, pp. 174–75.

92. James A. Roy, *The Scot and Canada* (Toronto: McClelland and Stewart, 1947), p. 112.

93. Lindsay, "Sport in Canada, 1807–1967," pp. 322–24.

94. A reproduction of this can be seen between pp. 202 and 203 of Dulles, *History of Recreation*, although no mention is made of the Caledonian Games in the 446-page text.

95. *Minutes of the New York Caledonian Club, 5 November 1862 to 18 December 1866.* These and other documents up to 1875 relating to the club are located in the Second Presbyterian Church., West 95th Street, New York City. See also the *Scottish American Journal*, 15 September 1866. The assets of the New York Caledonian Club in 1875 totalled $23,977.23. Much of this came from the profit from holdings its annual Games in New York, where crowds of more than twenty thousand were not uncommon and admission charges varied from 25 cents to 50 cents. Nearly $2,000 was cleared after expenses as early as the 1868 Games, an amount that was often exceeded in future years. The Club's premises were always luxurious, also, each location in the nineteenth century becoming more grand than the previous quarters. The new premises in 1879 were "built and furnished at an expense of over $30,000"; and the famous Scottish-American millionaire, Andrew Carnegie, opened the new palatial club premises on 7th Avenue in 1898. A common practice of the prudent Scottish officials of the New York Caledonian

Club was to regularly purchase U.S. 5/20 Savings Bonds for $1,000 each. See also the articles entitled ''Historical Sketches of the Scottish Organizations in New York, Parts VII and VIII: The Caledonian Club,'' in *Scottish-American Journal*, 1 July 1875 and 22 July 1875; also John L. Wilson, ''The Foreign Element in New York City, IV, the Scotch,'' *Harper's Weekly*, 28 June 1890, pp. 513–16; and 5 July 1890, p. 522.

96. *New York Times*, 4 September 1868.

97. *Canadian Illustrated News*, 8 July 1871. However, it is possible that ''Peter Fraser'' and ''Robert Fraser'' were one and the same person, although one was apparently from Montreal and the other from Glengarry, since the prize-winners' list in the report refers to ''P. Fraser''. But with so many Frasers in both places it is difficult to be sure.

98. *New York Times*, 4 September 1868.

99. *Scottish-American Journal*, 12 September 1872.

100. Korsgaard, History of A. A. U.,'' pp. 27–28.

101. Schroeder, ''History of the AAU of the US'' (thesis, Springfield College, 1912), p. 2. The author's first name or initial is not indicated, nor what degree was awarded.

102. *Globe*, 9 October 1858.

103. As well as the newspaper accounts already quoted, see Jobling, ''Technological Changes,'' pp. 176–78; and Korsgaard, ''History of AAU,'' p. 24, for examples of varying weights of hammers and stones at Caledonian Games. As late as 1888, the *Scottish-American Journal*, 1 August 1888, lamented that: ''the weights of the hammers, stones, etc., have seldom been officially authenticated, and are rarely true.''

104. For example, Malcolm W. Ford, ''Shot-Putting,'' *Outing*, July 1892, p. 287, states: ''John D. McPherson . . . is here represented in Highland costume with a stone in his hand, for from the old-time Scotch game, putting the stone, came putting the shot; and even at this day a number of Caledonian Clubs in America give competitors a stone to put in place of an iron or lead sphere.'' Also, Webster, *Highland Games*, passim, cites many examples of local cabers, hammers, and stones being traditionally used. Perhaps the most famous example is ''the world famous Braemar Caber which measures 19'3'' and weighs 120 lbs.'' Most cabers are around 17 feet in length and 100 lbs. in weight.

105. See Korsgaard, ''History of AAU,'' pp. 32–68; Krout, *Annals of American Sport*, pp.185–205; Roberto L. Quercetani, *A World History of Track and Field Athletics, 1864-1964* (London: Oxford University Press, 1964), passim; Schroeder, ''History of AAU,'' pp. 2–114; and Melvyn Watman, *History of British Athletics* (London: Robert Hale, 1968), passim.

106. *Scottish-American Journal*, 8 September 1870 and passim to 6 August 1902; *Spirit of the Times*, 10 September 1870.

107. Berthoff, *British Immigrants*, pp. 215–17.

108. See *Canadian Illustrated News*, 8 July 1871, 24 August 1872, 28 August 1875, and 30 August 1879.

109. See *Harper's Weekly*, 10 July 1867, 2 November 1867, 28 June 1890, and 5 July 1890; and *Frank Leslie's Illustrated Newspaper*, 20 July 1867 and 18 September 1869.

110. *New York Times*, 11 August 1874.

111. Ibid., 4 September 1874.

112. *Spirit of the Times*, 7 August 1875. The convention was also advertised in the *Scottish-American Journal*, 1 July 1875 and 8 July 1875.

113. *New York Times*, 17 August 1875.

114. Berthoff, *British Immigrants*, p. 151.

115. *Scottish-American Journal*, 1 July 1875.

116. *Boston Daily Globe*, 30 August 1878. See also the *Globe* (Toronto), 29 June

1878, for an account of Canadian athlete E. W. Johnston winning events at Scottish Games in Baltimore and Philadelphia; and the same newspaper for 19 June 1879, for an account of the exploits of Hugh McKinnon in North America. *New York Times*, 6 September 1978.

117. *Canadian Illustrated News*, 30 August 1879.

118. *New York Times*, 3 September 1880.

119. *Boston Daily Globe*, 29 August 1884.

120. *New York Times*, 4 September 1885; *Scottish-American Journal*, 23 July 1885. At the Detroit Games of 1890, many athletes from Canada competed, including "a herculean athlete from Ridgetown, Ontario," who won the 16 lb. shot-putt, hammer-throw, tossing the caber, and throwing the 56 lb. weight. See the *Globe*, 25 August 1890.

121. Donaldson, *Men of Muscle*, passim. See especially the chapter entitled "Donald Dinnie of Aboyne," pp. 22–32; and the chapter entitled "James Fleming of Ballinbrig," pp. 33–37. And on pp. 119–20 is an account of Dinnie and Fleming competing at the Caledonian Games in Toronto in 1872.

122. For example, an advertisement for the Twelfth' Annual Games of the Hudson County Caledonian Club, in the *Scottish-American Journal*, 29 June 1882, proudly announced: "DONALD DINNIE WILL POSITIVELY APPEAR."

123. *Scottish-American Journal*, 15 July 1875.

124. Ibid., 9 September 1885.

125. Ibid., 26 July 1893.

126. Ibid., 9 September 1885.

127. Ross, *Scot in America*, pp. 426–27.

128. For Canada, see Cox, "Sport in Canada, 1868 to 1900," passim; Howell and Howell, *Sports in Canadian Life*, pp. 67–143; Jobling, "Technological Changes," passim; and Roxborough, *One Hundred—Not Out*, passim. For the U.S.A. see Dulles, *History of Recreation*, pp. 148–286; and Krout, *Annals of American Sport*, pp. 148–307.

129. Krout, *Annals of American Sport*, p. 186. The first meeting of the New York Athletic Club was described as "handicap Scottish Games" (Berthoff, *British Immigrants*, p. 151), largely because the New York Caledonian Club, founded twelve years earlier, participated in the meeting. One authority described it as "an International match—America against Scotland"; see Frederick William Janssen, *A History of American Athletics and Aquatics, 1829-1888* (New York: Outing Co., 1888), p. 126. Korsgaard, "History of AAU," pp. 32–33, 50.

130. Albert B. Wegener, *Track and Field Athletics* (New York: A. S. Barnes and Co., 1924), p. 147.

131. Cox, "Sports in Canada, 1868 to 1900," pp. 176–97; Howell and Howell, *Sports in Canadian Life*, pp. 89–95; *Montreal Gazette*, 23 June 1873. This was actually the revival of a club which had been formed in 1866 (*Montreal Gazette*, 22 October 1866) but only lasted a short time before being disbanded. Also in 1881, "the Hamilton Athletic Club conducted its first annual track and field meet." [Roxborough, *One Hundred—Not Out*, p. 154]. See also Jobling, "Technological Changes," pp. 383–85, for more details pertaining to Canadian Athletic Clubs.

132. Cox, "Sports in Canada, 1868 to 1900," p. 189.

133. *Globe*, 3 January 1884.

134. Cox, "Sports in Canada, 1868 to 1900," p. 196.

135. Korsgaard, "History of AAU," pp. 37–68; Schroeder, "History of AAU," pp. 2–64.

136. *Spirit of the Times*, 5 December 1874, devoted an editorial to the intention of

Yale University to award cash prizes at its Annual Games. It warned that the amateur standing of the participants could be jeopardized, and called attention to the Scottish Inter-University Games of 1873, when a University of Aberdeen student was disqualified from running in an amateur meet because he had previously competed against Dinnie, Fleming, and other Caledonian athletes.

137. For example, Cox, "Sports in Canada, 1868 to 1900," pp. 176–77, states: "In the sixties and seventies the majority of organized track and field meets were conducted by the numerous Scottish societies in Canada, with the Caledonian Society leading the way." Jobling, "Technological Changes," p. 375, states: "There were many discrepancies in the track and field meetings and competitions held in Canada, and it was not until associations were organized that regular, well-conducted meets were held. The Caledonian societies had helped to promote the sport from the mid-century on, but the formation of the Montreal Amateur Athletic Association of Canada in 1883, gave the most impetus to its development." Regarding the Amateur Athletic Union of the United States, Korsgaard, "History of AAU," p. 68, states:

> The house of the AAU was literally built upon the bricks of the early pioneers who came from Europe, particularly England, and carried with them their love for sports and games . . . and the athletic-loving Scotchmen who pursued their native games at the Caledonian outings and provided entertainment for more spectators at any single track meet than any other organization had been able to do until well into the twentieth century.

138. T. A. Reed, *The Blue and White: A Record of Fifty Years of Athletic Endeavour at the University of Toronto* (Toronto: University of Toronto Press, 1944), pp. 2, 71, 147–55.

139. Davidson, "Sports in Eastern Canada," pp. 88–89. See also: *Montreal Gazette*, 20 October 1876; and McGill *Gazette*, 1 November 1876. The University of Trinity College, Upper Canada College, and a number of high schools, also held track and field meets in the nineteenth century; Howell and Howell, *Sports in Canadian Life*, pp. 93–95. See, for example, the account of the "annual games" at Bishop's College, Lennoxville, in the *Montreal Gazette*, 1 July 1871; and the details of track sports in *A History of the Ottawa Collegiate Institute, 1843–1903* (Ottawa: The Mortimer Co., 1904), pp. 111–12.

140. Davidson, "Sports in Eastern Canada," p. 88; Reed, *Blue and White*, pp. 147–55.

141. Probably the longest and most detailed account of this race is found in the student magazine of Cornell University, *Cornell Era*, 12 September 1873. Roxborough, *One Hundred—Not Out*, p. 124, refers to "D. E. Boivie" as the winner of the race, and states that he won a $500 trophy as such. A picture of this "Bennett Cup" can be seen in the *Canadian Illustrated News*, 20 June 1874.

142. Frank Presbrey, *Athletics at Princeton: A History* (New York: Frank Presbrey Co., 1901), p. 29; *Scottish-American Journal*, 26 June 1873.

143. Rice, Hutchinson and Lee, *Physical Education*, p. 188, states:

> From the Scottish Caledonian Games, brought to America in the early nineteenth century, developed the track and field sports today. The boys at Princeton were introduced to the Caledonian Games in 1873 by their Scotch physical director, George Goldie (1841-1920) and their popularity then spread into other Colleges and down into the lower schools.

Also, two editorials in the Amherst student magazine in the year following the first Princeton Caledonian Games are indicative of the Scottish influence:

The Scotch have shown great ingenuity in devising such games, and we can imagine nothing more interesting to the public, or beneficial to the whole college, than the institution of a grand field-day, for the exhibition of skill and strength in such sports under the stimulus of a few small prizes in each department. . . . Princeton has the advantage of an accomplished athlete at the head of her gymnasium who, himself, has won many a prize at the annual Scottish games of the Caledonian Club in Philadelphia. Shall Amherst retire and leave the place to others?

See *Amherst Student,* 7 October 1874 and 31 October 1874.

144. Krout, *Annals of American Sport*, p. 188; Leonard and Affleck, *Physical Education*, p. 283; Presbrey, *Athletics at Princeton*, p. 404. But again, probably the most detailed account of the formation of the I.C.A.A.A.A. is found in a student magazine, *College Argus*, 18 December 1875.

145. Presbrey, *Athletics at Princeton*, passim. See also: Walter Kershaw, "Athletics in and around New York," *Harper's Weekly*, 21 June 1890, for an account of Goldie's work as director at the New York Athletic Club; and also his obituary in the *New York Times*, 25 February 1920.

146. Cox, "Sports in Canada, 1868 to 1900," p. 194; Reed, *Blue and White*, p. 154. The continual use of the word "Games" to describe track and field meets in North America is another aspect of the Caledonian legacy. In Britain, track and field was generally known as "athletics," and "meetings" were held. The term "Games" was almost exclusively reserved for ball-sports involving teams.

147. As Berthoff, *British Immigrants*, p. 151, has stated: "American athletes appropriated the favorite sport of the Scottish immigrants . . . they abandoned some two peculiarly Scottish events like caber tossing."

148. Leonard and Affleck, *Physical Education*, p. 282.

149. Berthoff, *British Immigrants*, p. 151.

150. Cox, "Sports in Canada, 1868 to 1900," p. 190.

151. This information on Gray was kindly supplied by Mr. H. M. Reid, first curator of Canada's Sports Hall of Fame in Toronto, where there is a magnificent display of Gray's medals. A photograph of this display can be seen in Adelaide Leitch, *The Visible Past: The Pictorial History of Simcoe County* (Ontario: County of Simcoe, 1967), p. 197. See also Cox, "Sports in Canada, 1868 to 1900," pp. 190–91; and Roxborough, *One Hundred—Not Out*, p. 236.

152. Krout, *Annals of American Sport*, pp. 185–205.

153. Gordon Donaldson, *The Scots Overseas* (London: Robert Hale, 1966), pp. 127–28. See also issues of *The Pibroch*, which is published in April and October of each year, by the St. Andrew's Society of the State of New York, as this sometimes gives details of Highland Gatherings.

154. *Encyclopedia Canadiana* (1968), 5:125; *The Scottish Athletic Association of Manitoba, Programme for 1906.* I am also grateful for information provided on this point, and others following by Mr. R. T. Lund of Queen's University.

155. *Crag and Canyon* (Banff), 2 September 1927, 9 September 1927.

156. Ibid., 4 September 1931. Also, in the Archives of the Canadian Rockies at Banff, Alberta, is a file which contains newspaper clippings and programs of the earliest Banff Highland Gatherings. The programs are magnificent little booklets, sponsored by the Canadian Pacific Railway.

157. Highland Gatherings are still held today at the following places in Canada: Antigonish, Charlottetown, Southport, Eldon, St. Ann's, Pugwash, Dartmouth, Glace Bay, Amherst, Embro, Thunder Bay, Kincardine, St. Catherine's, Windsor, Cobourg, Dutton, Fergus, Maxville, Orillia, Oshawa, Sault Ste. Marie, Toronto, Brantford, Renfrew, Ed-

monton, Moose Jaw, Saskatoon, Winnipeg, Vancouver, Victoria, Duncan, Port Alberni, Calgary, Saanich, and very probably in other places as well. See Donaldson, *Scots Overseas*, p. 151; *Encyclopedia Canadiana* (1968), 5:124–25; and Meyer, Jr., *Festivals*, pp. 206–8.

158. I am grateful to Dr. John Dewar, Judge Hugh MacPherson, and Dr. Brian Mutimer for sending me a selection of programs for the Antigonish Highland Games, from 1929 to 1979.

159. *Program for the Antigonish Highland Games, 1979*.

160. For example, the Dartmouth Scottish Society of Nova Scotia in 1950; Amherst St. Andrew's Society, Nova Scotia (1950); the Kinloch Highland Gathering, Ontario (1953); the Saskatoon Highland Dancing and Piping Association, Saskatchewan (1954). Highland Games were also begun at Sault Ste. Marie (1955), Cobourg (1963), and Renfrew (1963), all in Ontario.

161. *Edmonton Journal*, 5 August 1975.

162. *Scottish-American Journal*, 6 August 1902.

163. Perusal of *The Annual Book of the Braemar Gathering* confirms this fact.

164. Henry Roxborough, *Great Days in Canadian Sport* (Toronto: Ryerson Press, 1957), pp. 78–79. A photograph of Knox in his prime is also featured in Leitch, *Visible Past*, p. 197, with more details of his athletic career.

165. In 1971, the *Observer Colour Magazine*, 7 November, in the United Kingdom, featured a photograph with the caption:

Two girls who this year danced away with prizes at that most Scottish of Highland occasions, the Argyllshire Gathering in Oban, were not Scots at all. Margot Guest (right) and Christine Vasey took the part in their Highland dress, but they are in fact a couple of 19-year old Canadians from Edmonton.

See also the *Canadian Weekend Magazine*, 31 October 1964.

6
Golf

*A recent writer has stated that golf is the most popular
game in Canada, but there are other games that attract more
general attention and are played by a greater number of people. No other sport, however, so thoroughly absorbs the time
and enthusiasm of those who follow it. Once a man has
begun to play golf he usually loses interest in all other forms
of amusement and recreation.*

Joseph T. Clark (1905)

GOLF has been described as "Scotland's Gift"[1] and
certainly its appearance and subsequent development in
Canada during the nineteenth century, like curling and the
Caledonian Games, were due almost entirely to the influence of
Scots. It became one of the Scottish sporting "boons to
mankind" mainly in the twentieth century, when many nationalities adopted the game at one time or other.[2] Which Scots in
Canada actually played it first, and where, remains a matter of
conjecture. Clark has stated that the introduction of golf to
Canada dates back to Scottish officers in General Wolfe's army,
who played the game outside the walls of Quebec City.[3] It is possible, remembering that golf was established in Scotland before
1759, but as Roxborough states, it is also "debatable":

Indeed, it seems that if so many firsts in Canadian sport can
be traced back to Wolfe's soldiers, it is difficult to comprehend
how they found time to pursue their military duties.[4]

Others have found some Canadian sporting origins in the contests and feats of the *coureurs de bois* and the *voyageurs.*[5]

214

Kavanagh, in his *History of Golf in Canada,* includes an intriguing quote from a CPR publicity brochure of 1918, which suggests that the fur traders of the seventeenth century may have imported golf to Canada:

> In days lang syne the distant posts of the Hudson's Bay Company . . . were almost all manned by Scotchmen . . . Many of them undoubtedly brought out with them their golf clubs with which to enjoy even in a most primitive fashion the exhilarating swing and the ''fair follow through'' so dear to the heart of the golfer . . . What more likely then that the Scotch factors of ''The Governor and Company of Adventurers of England trading into Hudson's Bay''—Pro Pelle Cutem—nearly four centuries ago were the pioneer golfers of America? That the strident ''Fore'' was first heard in the spacious West and that its echo, centuries old, has travelled Eastward only of recent years? Supposition is strongly in favor of this contention. Proof of course there is none![6]

Imagine the Orkneymen and Highlanders of the Old Company teeing up their featheries in the vast emptiness of the Northwest Territories in the seventeenth century. It is a thought to boggle the minds of many, comfort some, and possibly disturb others. The suggestion is made even more intriguing by Kavanagh's statements elsewhere that the first municipal course in Canada opened in Edmonton, Alberta, on 156 acres originally owned by the Hudson's Bay Company, and that ''Western Canada took the lead in establishing public courses.''[7] Bearing in mind that it is a well-documented fact that golf was being pioneered by Scotsmen in Eastern parts of the United States before 1800[8], there are obviously still many unanswered questions regarding the game's origins on this continent. Unfortunately, no similar documentation for the suggestion pertaining to the Scottish soldiers under Wolfe's command has been provided by its authors.

References to golf in both countries, in fact, are few and far between even in the first half of the nineteenth century, as any earlier activity in the previous century obviously did not survive. Strangely, although golfing activity seems to have been more common south of the border before 1800, the formation of established golf clubs in the nineteenth century began in post-Confederation Canada, several years earlier than in the United States. There are, therefore, large "gaps" in the history of golf on the North American continent. However, since "the founding of the Royal Montreal Golf Club in 1873 marked the official beginning of the game in Canada,"[9] its progress afterwards was assured and rapid. Within a few years, many other golf clubs were formed in various parts of the Dominion. Before the end of the century, interclub and interprovincial golf matches had taken place, the Canadian Amateur Golf Championship had been initiated, international matches against the United States were held, and ladies as well as gentlemen were enthusiastic participants in the sport.

Roxborough has also maintained that "just as curling was a wintertime gift from early Scottish settlers, so golf at a later period was a warm-weather boon from Scotland to Canadian sportsmen."[10] Ironically, though, the first mention of golf in Canada in the nineteenth century refers to a game played during the winter of 1824, on Christmas Day:

> The first trace of Canadian golf which we find is contained in the following extract, which is taken from a Montreal newspaper bearing the date of December, 1824:—"To Scotsmen—A few of the true sons of Scotia, eager to perpetuate the rememberance of her customs, have fixed upon Dec. 25th and Jan. 1st for going to the Priests' Farm, to play golf. Such of their countrymen as choose to join them will meet them before ten o'clock a.m., at D. McArthur's Inn, Hay Market. Steps have been taken to have clubs provided." Though aside a little from the text it is worth noting the time of year to which this clipping refers. It is Christmas and New Year's Day. It is commonly heard that even the Canadian winter is not what it used to be in the good old days of our grandfathers, but I imagine that the cold and snow of today would be enough to induce the most fiery of Scotting golfers to perpetuate the rememberance of his country's customs in some other way than playing golf on Christmas.[11]

These sentiments were expressed by Kerr in 1901, and Roxborough shared them sixty-five years later. To him, also, Christmas Day seemed ''an unlikely season for a field game.''[12] But in fact, as Lindsay has pointed out, the weather was relatively mild then, and ''it would have been possible for golf to have been played during that Christmas period of 1824.''[13] It is also possible that the Scots concerned were connected with the fur trade in Montreal, and had tried to introduce golf there earlier, as they had done with curling.[14]

Some rather vague references have been made to golf having been played in the Montreal area, on a common called Logan's Farm[15] in the 1850s. Uttley has stated that German mechanics in old Kitchener (Berlin) were interested in golf at this time, too, but as they had no proper clubs available, they practiced putting with garden hoes.[16] Herein lies a partial answer to the question of golf's comparatively late development. As we have seen in chapter 2, golf was a sport which required a variety of specialized clubs to play properly. Even by the first half of the nineteenth century, clubs had been divided into the four categories of drivers, spoons, irons, and putters. Then the introduction of the harder gutta percha ball in 1848 necessitated further changes in the manufacture of clubs, and players required even more clubs as the game became more sophisticated. An average set of eight clubs could be selected from some thirteen varieties available. So, until enthusiasts could afford or obtain the necessary equipment, putting was usually the simplest form of golf that could be indulged in.

In addition to the comprehensive and requisite equipment, of course, the proper game of golf also demanded time and space. Participants needed to have fairly considerable leisure time available to devote to golf, especially when their enthusiasm became ardent and they spent an increasing number of hours on the golf course. Unlike some other sports of the day, golf was not exhausting or likely to lead to bodily injury, and it usually took place in pleasant surroundings, so it was quite easy and enjoyable to while away hours in its pursuit. Moreover, a suitably laid out golf course required far more space than other contemporary sports, usually several acres. Until this ideal was reached, however, devotees of golf had to improvise with inferior equipment which they used over makeshift courses. It was not until late in the nineteenth century that sufficient leisure time, equipment and cultivated space were available, so that golf clubs began to proliferate and the sport became established.

Meanwhile, the first makeshift courses on record were the three-hole affairs in the 1860s mentioned by Roxborough, and apparently introduced by officers on ships from Scotland. They were located in Montreal and Quebec City.[17] It has also been recorded that, "as far back as 1869, golf was regularly played in the outskirts to Toronto by a few enthusiasts, chief of whom was Mr. J. Lammond Smith, father-in-law of Mr. E. B. Osler, M.P., himself a devoted player and supporter of the game."[18] To Mr. Lammond Smith belongs the distinction of being the founder of the Toronto Golf Club, in 1876, and its first captain.[19]

But the honor of the establishment of the first golf club in Canada, and indeed what the *Encyclopaedia Britannica* describes as "the first permanent golf club in the western hemisphere,"[20] reverts to Montreal. This was the Montreal Golf Club, formed in 1873. Roche quotes from the first page of "an old book of rules belonging to the club," regarding its origin:

> A meeting convened to arrange the preliminaries of a golf club, for playing the royal and ancient game of golf on Mount Royal Park, was held on the fourth day of November, 1873, when it was resolved that the club be called "The Montreal Golf Club." The officers for the year were appointed: Alex Dennistoun, president; W. M. Ramsay, vice-president; D. D. Sidey, treasurer; Jos. Collins, secretary. The rules of St. Andrew's Club (Scotland) were adopted. According to the club minute-book there were also present at this initial meeting Hon. M. Aylmer, J. G. Sidey, H. McDougall, and T. Holland.[21]

Mr. Alexander Dennistoun, the Club's first president, was a Scot from Edinburgh who had since been referred to by authors as "the father of golf in Canada."[22] He had played in his younger days over the famous links at St. Andrews and Musselburgh, and

The Royal Montreal Golf Club, 1882. (National Photography Collection, Public Archives of Canada C46491)

was a member of several other leading clubs in Britain. Dennistoun presented the Scratch Medal, "the most coveted trophy in the possession of the club,"[23] and was resident in Canada for many years until he died in Edinburgh, Scotland, shortly before Roche wrote his article entitled "Canadian Golf" in 1898. In it the author also provided a list of other "early players" of the Montreal Golf Club, showing the predominance of Scots:

... the Hon. Geo. Drummond, J. K. Oswald, F. Braidwood, Eric Maim, Jno. Taylor, Homer Taylor, Rev. Dr. Campbell, Rev. Canon Ellegood, C. C. Foster, and R. M. Esdaile. Among the younger generation may be mentioned Mr. W. Wallace Watson, the president captain; Rev. Dr. Barclay, F. Stancliff, W. J. S. Gordon, J. R. Meeker, K. R. Macpherson, J. Hutton

Balfour, G. W. MacDougall, J. L. Morris, Q. C., A. H. Harris, W. A. Fleming, Alex. Macpherson, Rev. W. W. McCuaig, A. A. Wilson, Rev. Mr. Dobson, Jno. Dunlop, Fayette Brown, Dr. Macdonald, Dr. Andrew Macphail, and A. Piddington.[24]

But in golf, as with other Scottish sports in the New World, other nationalities soon took part as well, although Scots remained in the forefront as initiators and organizers of the sport in the nineteenth century. Like their curling brethren, the Montreal golfers also had social occasions featuring ''beef and greens'' dinners and Scottish anecdotes.[25]

The first course of the Montreal Golf Club was Fletcher's Field, situated on the eastern side of Mount Royal.[26] There were no holes, apparently, and the object of the game at first was simply to hit the ball around the predetermined course.[27] Six holes and ''greens'' of packed sand were soon prepared, although the length of the grass on the fairways depended upon the appetite of the resident sheep in pasture. These sheep were prevented from invading the putting greens, however, by surrounding moats, ''adding to the already high number of natural hazards.''[28]

In the beginning, the membership of the Club was limited to twenty-five, and the fees were fixed at five dollars a year. Governor-General Dufferin became Patron of the Club in 1876, and during these early years ''a comfortable and somewhat picturesque club house was built, and everything went well.''[29] So well, in fact, that in 1884, Governor-General Lansdowne received permission from Queen Victoria to use the prefix ''royal'' in the club's title.[30] The next twelve years were prosperous ones for the Royal Montreal Golf Club, and 1896 it was relocated on a property of one hundred and twenty acres, nine miles from the city. Before then, golf had been well developed elsewhere in the Dominion during the interim period.

Not surprisingly, the next golf club appeared in Quebec City, in the year following the formation of the Montreal Golf Club, and it resulted from enthusiasm and initiative:

The organization of the Quebec Club was due to a Scotsman, a Mr. Hunter of Glasgow, who was visiting the city. He began to play and spread the fever to some other gentlemen, among them Mr. W. A. Griffith, and the late Mr. C. Farquharson Smith.[31]

Other people involved in the origin of the Quebec Golf Club were James Stevenson and H. Stanley Smith; and it has been suggested that its course at Cove Fields was used as early as 1869 by golfing enthusiasts.[32]

In 1876, the two pioneer golf clubs competed against each other at Montreal in the first golf-club match on record in America.[33] The *Montreal Gazette* was used to publicize the game beforehand:

> A golf match between six or seven players of the Quebec Club against an equal number of the members of the Montreal Club will take place today, at noon, on the golf ground of the club, near the top of Dorchester Street.[34]

From then on, competition between these two clubs was keen and consistent. The *Scottish-American Journal* reported an astonishing victory for the Quebec Club in 1877:

> GOLFING AT MONTREAL—The members of the Golfing Clubs of Montreal and Quebec met on the grounds of the former on Saturday last, and played a club game—nine men a side. The Quebec men secured an early victory, they having won 45 holes, while their opponents secured only 2.[35]

As the weekend trips between the two clubs became popular, the Montreal members received railway concessions from the North Shore Railway. In 1880, they paid three dollars each for return tickets to Quebec, and the secretary obtained the use of a Pullman sleeping car for the whole party for sixteen dollars.[36] In this same year, in addition to an article entitled "Golf: A Royal and Ancient Game," the *Canadian Illustrated News* carried a full page of drawings depicting "The Golf Match Between the Montreal and Quebec Golf Clubs, on Fletcher's Field, Montreal."

Pictures of the Dennistoun Challenge Medal, the magnificent challenge trophy initiated in 1877, and a Montreal Golf Club

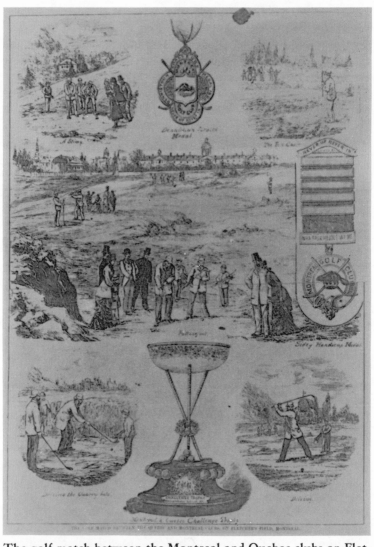

The golf match between the Montreal and Quebec clubs on Fletcher's Field, Montreal, 1880.

Medal, were included. The Scottish influence was evident by the inscription on the latter: "WHA DAUR MEDDLE WI ME."[37] It was certainly apparent in the Quebec Golf Club, too, which adopted what can only be described as a truly "Scottish-Canadian" emblem:

> The Quebec Club adopted a unique coat of arms, which included two crossed clubs, a ball and the date 1874; to the right was a maple leaf, to the left a thistle, and the whole surrounded by a beaver. In a garter surrounding the entire design was a motto reading Ne Timere, nec timidie.[38]

Hunter, writing in *Athletic Life* in 1895, revealed that the golfing rivalry between Montreal and Quebec was still prominent and keenly contested:

> The great golfing fixture in the Province of Quebec is the Montreal and Quebec semi-annual matches played in Quebec on the Queen's birthday, and in Montreal in October. These matches have been played almost continuously since 1877 and Quebec now stands three matches to the good and as both Montreal and Quebec Clubs are noted for a generous openhanded hospitality to visitors, great anxiety is shown to be on the team.

By 1895, the Quebec Golf Club had about eighty members. John Hamilton was captain of the club, and Major H. C. Sheppard was the Hon. Secretary. The club prizes were "the Silver Medal," and "the Championship Gold Medal."[29]

But the outstanding characteristic of the Quebec Golf Club by this time, commented on by many writers, was the unique and unparalleled beauty of its links. It was not always so, and Roxborough tells us that "The first Quebec course was crude and tough."[40] However, the environment was such that subsequent development of the golf course obviously complemented its natural surrounds. Hunter, for example, was moved to declare:

> The Quebec Links are beautifully situated and in the highest degree picturesque, covering that historic ground known as

the ''Cove Fields,'' facing on the St. Lawrence River and lying between the citadel and the Plains of Abraham. From the old French bastion ''one of the hazards'' an impressive view of Quebec scenery is obtained. The old time houses of lower town at your feet, the St. Lawrence in sight for miles passing through that most beautiful section of French Canadian country below Quebec, with the distant mountains, beyond the further shore, standing out against the sky . . .These Links are most diversified in character, nature having provided with no sparing hand, every possible hazard or bunker with the exception of sand, but the want of ''sand'' is seldom felt by clubs playing against Quebec. The course runs over and across the old French forts and earth works, the hazards being deep precipices, old fortifications, gullies, moats, rocks, swamps, and bogs. The writer has frequently heard these hazards highly commended as being the golfer's sporting ideal, leaving nothing further in that way to be desired. These Links are noted for the fine velvety grass and elastic turf; as a consequence the putting greens are excellent.[41]

The eminent Scottish historian of golf, H. G. Hutchinson, writing in Britain, was equally moved to eloquence regarding the merits of the Quebec golf course, in the sixth edition of his book entitled *Golf*, published in 1898:

But of all places of interest, other than golfing interest, on which golf is played, the most entrancing is far away on the other side of the Atlantic, where the Quebec Golf Club plays beside the Plains of Abraham. Here the delving niblick may disinter a musket ball, heavy with history, the devious driver may find a grave in the St. Lawrence, far below him; he who is both far and sure may carry at a drive, as by a forlorn hope, the 'Old Forts.' There are suggestions of poetry, war, and even golf, in the very names; for indeed the golf is good, with dire penalties for the erratic and feeble, and justly earned rewards for the strong and skilful.[42]

By 1895, the Quebec Golf Club was also the longest in Canada, extending over two miles, with fifteen or sixteen holes, two or three of which were played again to complete the full round. The shortest hole was 130 yards, and the longest hole was an impressive 450 yards.

Another reference to the Quebec links in 1898 is of interest, since it alludes to the formal attire customarily worn by the golfers:

> Quebec's golf links form part of the historic battleground, the Plains of Abraham. Scarlet coats are still numerous there, where Wolfe and Montcalm led, but the contest is now a bloodless one.[43]

The members of the Montreal and Quebec Golf Clubs, and probably others in nineteenth-century Canada, were required to wear red coats, white flannel trousers, and caps of the "fore-and-aft" style. Rules stipulated that opposing captains made the initial drives for their teams wearing white gloves, after which they were removed.[44] Ties were also worn, and severe fines were imposed upon any members who were improperly dressed.[45] A picture of J. G. Sidey, "One of the Pioneers of Golf in Montreal" and captain of the Royal Montreal Club in 1890-91, is featured in Clark's article published in 1905, in which he is wearing one of the caps mentioned. But the Scottish influence came through again in the picture of John L. Morris in the same article, who was captain from 1894-96, and is shown wearing a Highland tam o' shanter bonnet.[46]

A rather informal golf club was organized at Toronto in 1876, the year when "Messrs. Lamond [sic] Smith, R. H. and George Bethune, and the two Messrs. Scott were enjoying the old Scottish game on the slopes of Norway Heights.[47] A picture of the same J. Lamond Smith is featured in Clark's article of 1905, with the caption "Father of Golf in Toronto. Played as early as 1869. First Captain Toronto G.C. 1876." Only a small group were involved with him in this enterprise, which also played at the Woodbine, until the Toronto Club "was regularly formed"[48] in 1882, the year in which the records of the Club begin. For the next eleven years the Club had a somewhat precarious existence (in 1888 the membership was thirty-five), until 1893, when new property was acquired at Fernhill, and "the erection of a substantial and comfortable club house was proceeded with.'' This structure stood on rising ground a hundred feet above Lake Ontario and commanded magnificent views. By the end of the following year, the membership of the Toronto Golf Club had risen to the limit of one hundred and sixty.[49]

In 1877, a golf club was formed at Niagara, mainly through the efforts of Charles Hunter, who held the office of president for the remainder of the century.[50] Two years later there was a golf club at Brantford (where the players also wore red jackets trimmed with brass buttons) and the game was beginning to take hold over a larger area. Another club was formed at Kingston, in 1886; and golf was obviously being played much further west in Winnipeg before 1890, although the date of the first golf club organized there is usually suggested as 1894.[51] The *Winnipeg Free Press* of 24 May 1889 gave details of the links at Stony Mountain:

> The starting point, or in Golf phraseology, the teeing ground, is immediately opposite Col. Bedson's residence. The course is then due west toward the railway station; thence south along the line of the C.P.R. until you reach the fourth or Joe's (Sabiston) hotel; then south east across the spur line, to the track hole, on to the brickyards and Dr. Sutherland's cottage, where the course turns north. The last stretch of link; crossing the ditches and big ploughing, landing you at the eighth hole on the breast of the hill, the last drive being over boulders and badger holes (pretty pronounced hazards) and down the same hill west to the first putting green.

It was in the 1890s, however, that golf experienced a tremendous Dominion wide expansion, aided again by the CPR, so that it could be maintained that ''by the turn of the century, most cities across Canada had at least one golf course.''[52] Its popularity in the last decade, as well as its largely exclusive nature, was obvious from the following observations:

> So popular has this newly imported game become that one is almost tempted to spell it with a capital G, for it will be by all odds the most fashionable game indulged in by lovers of the exclusive. Society folk break out into athletic fads only at inter-

vals. Polo was one sport that the rich alone could afford but it had the great disadvantage of barring women folk; and sport nowadays must be a pastime for both sexes. Very properly golf has caught the fancy of the rich, for it is of necessity an exclusive game, requires acres of ground specially adapted, expensive sticks and costumes, which are not to be had for the asking."[53]

It had been "newly imported" from Scotland, of course, and Scots were again never far removed from the ensuing action in the progress of golf in Canada during the last ten years of the nineteenth century. It was a period, too, when the active enthusiasm of women for the new sport became most apparent.

The first of the many new golf clubs to be formed in the 1890s was in the capital city: "The Ottawa Golf Club was instituted in April 1891, through the efforts of the late J. Lloyd Pierce and Hugh Kenwick, of Castle Park, Lanark, Scotland.'"[54] Play was begun in the fields near the Rideau rifle ranges, and on Sandy Hill. A clubhouse was erected on land donated by a Mr. Magee, and "in a very short time the club numbered seventy members." Again, the surnames of many of the members suggest that Hugh Kenwick did not lack Scottish company. Lord Aberdeen, the governor-general, became Patron of the Ottawa Golf Club in 1894, "the year that saw golf spring forward into popular favour;" according to Kerr.[55] Events across the Dominion indicate that he was correct in his judgment. For example, the first amateur championship of Canada was held in June 1895, on the links of the Ottawa Golf Club, for which "His Excellency had given a magnificent silver challenge cup," won by Mr. T. H. Harley,[56] The winner came from Kingston, Ontario. Other winners of the championship in the nineteenth century were Stewart Gillespie of Quebec (1896); W.A.H. Kerr of Toronto (1897); George S. Lyon of Rosedale, Toronto (1898); and Vere C. Brown, also of Rosedale (1899).[57]

Other golf clubs had been formed in Toronto before the first amateur championship. The second club in Toronto, named Deer Park Golf Club, opened a nine-hole course east of Yonge Street, and within easy reach of the city in 1892.[58] The established

Toronto Golf Club was holding regular Saturday competitions in the following year,[59] when the Rosedale Golf Club was organized and became "a great nursery for golf," as subsequent championships proved. Writing in 1901, Kerr described the Rosedale Club as being in a "very flourishing condition," with "a fine brick club-house, and, like the Toronto, [it] employs a Scotch professional."[60] The Spadina Golf Club also flourished for a time before amalgamating with the Rosedale Club in 1903, because it could not secure its own permanent links. Before this happened, the High Park, Highlands, and Lambton Golf Clubs had also been active in the Toronto area.[61]

It is possible that some of this growth was stimulated by an extensive article which appeared in the Toronto *Globe* in 1890. The article was one of several features on different sports which appeared in the *Globe* during the 1890s. In fact, it can be noted here that George Brown's "Scotsman's Bible," aside from its political bias, actually did a great deal to promote Canadian sport, giving "excellent sporting coverage under such headings as 'Sporting Amusement Notes,' 'Sports and Amusements,' 'Sporting Intelligence,' and 'Sports of a Day.'" In addition, the Toronto *Globe*[11] pioneered illustrations and photographs, especially of a sporting nature."[62] Several line drawings were included in the article on golf in the 1890 Saturday edition. In view of the phenomenal success of the Caledonian Games and curling, it is hardly surprising that the headline in bold type at the type of this article proclaimed: "Another Scotch Athletic Exercise Becomes Popular." The writer gave details of the game and the organization of the Toronto Golf Club in an entertaining way, as the following excerpt shows:

> How many people in the city know of the existence of the Toronto Golf Club or know anything of the game its members play? Golf! What is it? You ask a golfer, and he will carry you off your feet with his talk of "puts" [*sic*], "niblicks," and "tees." As well may the greenhorn attempt to translate the vernacular of the curling rink as gleaned from a golfer, except at great expenditure of pertinacity and patience, an understanding of the beauties of this other Scottish game. For golf has a language of its own, like all other long established devices for

athletic entertainment and exercise. In this attempt to explain
the game to the readers of THE GLOBE . . . if I succeed in
showing that the game is far removed from plebeian
"shinny," [golfers] may extend forgiveness, for, be it known,
and take warning, you cannot hurt the Golfer more cruelly
than by exclaiming with a glow of sudden intelligence suffus-
ing your countenance, "oh yes, I understand; it's a sort of
shinny."[63]

But there were probably more than enough golf enthusiasts
around with Scottish blood in their veins to explain the intricacies
of golf (or curling) to the uninitiated, judging by the names of the
persons responsible for the formation of the golf club in Hamilton
four years later.

It was October 1894 that the Hamilton Golf Club was organized, under the auspices of Senator D. McInnis, A. G. Ramsay,
G. Hope, A. D. Stewart, H. D. Braithwaite, P. Banker and M. Pattison.[64] The members first played in a field adjoining the Jockey
Club,[11] the use of which was generously granted free of charge by
Mr. William Hendrie." In 1895, a nine-hole course was mapped
out along the line of the Hamilton and Dundas railway.[65] Jobling
has explained the affinity of golf courses with railway lines:

It was important that golf courses be in areas where large
segments of land could be purchased at reasonable cost so they
were usually situated on the outskirts of cities and towns.
However, in order to encourage people to use them, they were
usually located close to railway lines.[66]

The course of the Toronto Golf Club, for example, which was
constructed in 1882, was easily accessible by 1896 using either
the King Street cars or the Midland train of the Grand Trunk
Railway. These conveyed golfers right to the golf course
entrance.[67] The Lambton golf and Country Club was situated at
Lambton Mills, about seven miles from the center of Toronto, but
was situated on the main line of the CPR, and the new electric
road to Hamilton passed its gates.[68] Golf had spread to the Atlantic and Pacific Coasts of Canada before 1900, and there was a golf
club in Victoria, British Columbia, formed on 7 November 1893:

It is situated at Oak Bay, distant some three miles from the city. The grounds are reached by the electric railway, which runs to a point within a quarter of a mile of the links.[69]

Until the automobile was developed in the next century, in fact, golf club members were largely dependent upon public forms of transport and most golf clubs throughout the Dominion were situated near railways.

Apart from this Victoria Golf Club, the *Inland Sentinel* of 26 July 1895 reported that many golf clubs had been formed in British Columbia, a statement verified by the fact that the British Columbia Amateur Golf Championship was held in the same year.[70] In fact, there were many golf clubs across the whole of Canada by this time. And before the turn of the century, in addition to all the golf clubs already mentioned, others had been organized at the following places: Brockville, Calgary, Cobourg, Edmonton, Fort Macleod, Fredericton, Halifax, Kincardine, Lindsay, Lennoxville, London, Medicine Hat, Murray Bay, Oshawa, Peterborogh, Port Hope, Sherbrooke, Simcoe, St. Catharines, St. John, and Vancouver.[71] As seen in previous chapters, many of these places were also conspicuous by Scottish names and settlement, where Caledonian Games and curling clubs had been established. It is not, therefore, surprising that the other Scottish sport of golf should appear in these areas, also.

Nor was it surprising that in 1895, the writer of an article in a British Columbia newspaper should suggest the following attire as suitable for the numerous lady golfers, considering the often-quoted Scottish ancestry of the sport:

A golf suit is recommended that has about it a suggestion of Scotland, possibly of hand made homespun from the Highlands. The full skirt is the most comfortable as it gives the necessary room for play. Beneath the skirt is worn a garment much like ordinary riding breeches. Over the skirt waist or sweater . . . should be worn as an Eaton jacket or golf cape. In the way of golf stockings . . . the latest is the blue and green plaid, known as the ''Rockaway Hunt.''[72]

Actually, golf was traditionally a Lowlands game in Scotland, but outside of that country there has ever been a tendency to identify things Scottish as being from the Highlands. In any case, this imaginative ensemble was hardly the common fashion in Canada, as an article published seven months later about the recent involvement of ladies in the Toronto Golf Club indicated:

> An account of the club without reference to ladies, is a poor and imperfect thing; but it would need an article by itself to describe their links and their matches.
> The fair golfers, albeit most of them clad in violently red blouses . . . add a picturesqueness and interest to the scene; for such pretty faces and graceful figures triumph over violently red blouses.[73]

The lady golfers of Toronto were obviously emulating the dress of their male counterparts mentioned earlier.

It is not known when or where women first played golf in Canada, as Hall indicated in her history of women's sport in Canada,[74] but they were certainly active golfers and club members during the 1890s. Their participation invoked either the sort of masculine approval just noted, indifference, or resentment at female intrusion in what had previously been a male domain. As early as 1869 in Britain, Tulloch had written a satirical article about golf in *Belgravia* magazine, entitled "A New Game for Ladies," in which he stated that:

> Golf, or goff, is originally and emphatically a Scotch, and, we may add, in its full and perfect form a gentleman's, game . . . that has now begun to be played by ladies, and which gives fair promise of rivalling in attraction the charms of Aunt Sally and croquet.

He went on to describe in detail the play for the golf medal of the ladies club at famous St. Andrews in Scotland,[75] indicating that female participation in the sport was quite well established by this time. Yet the complete acceptance of women on the golf course was long delayed. Twenty-seven years after Tulloch's article, Lord Wellwood wrote of British women, "if they choose to play at times when the male golfers are feeding or resting, no one can object. But at any other time . . . they are in the way.''[76] However, by 1896, Canadian women were certainly very well established in the new sport. In fact, it is difficult to find mention of a golf club anywhere in Canada that did not have lady members in surprising numbers in the late nineteenth century. In the same way as they took to the other Scottish sport of curling, at around the same time, women in Canada enthusiastically adopted golf.[77]

Probably the first women's golf club in the Dominion was the ladies' branch of the Royal Montreal Golf Club, formed in 1892.[78] The wife of George A. Drummond became first president, and in addition to Mrs. Drummond, other ladies involved were: Mrs. H. V. Meredith, secretary; Mrs. W. Wallace Watson; Mrs. Halton; the Misses P. Young, A. Lamb, and A. Paterson.[79] The Montreal Club had moved to new premises at Dixie in 1896, after ''collisions with passing pedestrians were of such frequent occurrence that it was found necessary to seek other grounds.''[80] The following year, no fewer than one hundred and fifty lady members ''built themselves a club-house adjoining that of their husbands and brothers at Dixie.''[81] And after another year had passed, Roche reported these same lady golfers as ''even more enthusiastic than the men.''[82]

A Quebec Ladies Golf was also formed in 1892 or 1893; and the Ottawa Golf Club had ''25 lady associate members'' in 1894.[83] Four years later this total had risen to forty-eight, and these lady members could use the links every morning except Saturday, and on Monday, Tuesday, Thursday, and Friday afternoons.[84] This practice was not uncommon,[85] because it reserved the links for men's weekend use, but there were exceptions. At Winnipeg, competitions were held every Saturday afternoon where two sets of golf, silver, and bronze buttons were awarded to each of the three ladies and gentlemen with winning scores.[86] In 1896, a *Winnipeg Free Press* sportswriter commented:

> The numbers of the fair sex who play at golf is small when compared to the men, but each day new recruits are enlisted. By many it is supposed that golf is a game requiring too much physical exercise to become popular among women, but a

diligent inquiry as to facts would overthrow that theory. . . . At all tournaments of importance nowadays special competitions are arranged for the so-called weaker sex. As a general rule, women are not strong in long driving, but their direction is usually certain. In the short game they are wonderfully accurate.[87]

The High Park Golf Club of Toronto also allowed women to play on Saturdays in 1900.[88]

It was in 1896, too, that the Oshawa and Sherbrooke Golf Clubs came into being, and both had ladies' clubs attached within two years.[89] Also, by 1898, the Victoria Golf Club of British Columbia was ''nearly equally divided between the two sexes,'' whilst at Hamilton in Ontario, the lady golf-club members actually outnumbered the men.[90] And at the Brantford Golf Club by the turn of the century, there were more female members than male, the reported figures being thirty-nine gentlemen and forty-eight ladies.[91] Lady golfers were also coping successfully with railway cuttings, a dry moat, dikes, rifle pits, long grass and other hazards, at the Niagara Golf Course.[92] It cannot be denied that feminine enthusiasm for the game was manifest through Canada, as Kerr pointed out in 1901:

> The enthusiasm of the Toronto ladies about golf may be guessed when it is known that there is a huge waiting list. Progress up this is painfully slow owing to the fact that a golfer having once driven off never stops till death forces her to hole out, and that only occurs at a fabulous age, as the game itself is an elixir of life. Some Toronto mothers, the owners of little daughters, whom they wish one day to play golf, are said to have added their children's names to the waiting list, so that ten years from now they may stand some chance of being members.[93]

Four years later, Clark vigorously endorsed golf as a game for women, stating that ''as strength does not count for so much as accuracy and skill, it is possible for some women to play better than most men.''[94] The other Scottish sport of curling had similar attributes, and the Scots deserve great credit for having introduced at least two sports into Canada which could be played by both sexes, at all levels and almost all ages. Of course, by the late nineteenth century, the social emancipation of women was not confined to golf, or indeed exclusive to sport, as Lindsay has noted, and as Gourley reported in 1896:

> The Canadienne has, as a rule, magnificent health, the reward (as is much of her beauty) of her fondness for the open air. She is as happy on the tennis court or golf ground, as in the ball room; as much at home in the canoe, or the saddle, as in the opera box or at five o'clock tea.[95]

Golf was but one important facet of ''the Canadian woman's new outlook on life,''[96] but women's nationwide presence, which has been briefly outlined, meant that they were never far behind in the other important developments in the ancient Scottish sport, which made great progress in the last decade of the nineteenth century.

Annual interprovincial matches between Ontario and Quebec began in 1893, when the first contest took place on the links of the Ottawa Golf Club. These continued into the next century, and other interprovincial matches were played in Montreal and Toronto as well.[97] The first interclub matches in Ontario began at Toronto in 1894, when the Deer Park Golf Club played against the Toronto Golf Club, with twelve players each side. Toronto G.C. won by thirty-one holes,[98] and press reports of interclub games increased after 1896. The ladies of the Toronto Golf Club also played what was probably the first ladies' interclub match in Canada in 1896, when they opposed the ladies of the Rosedale Golf Club, with ten players on each side.[99] In October of the following year, interprovincial competition among the ladies commenced when fifteen lady golfers from Toronto met an equal number from Montreal and Quebec.[100]

The first Canadian Amateur Golf Championship referred to earlier, held in 1895, was actually held under the auspices of the newly formed Canadian Golf Association. Within a year, this Association was also permitted the use of the word ''Royal'' in its title. With several golf clubs in existence then, it was felt that "if the sport was to be kept pure and in good repute it was essential that some central organization be formed for the government of the game." The individual driving force behind the founding of the R.C.G.A. seems to have been the energetic secretary of the Ottawa Golf Club, Mr. A. Simpson, who was also runner-up to T. H. Harley in the first Canadian Championship.[101] The enthusiastic George A. Drummond of Montreal became first president of the Association in 1896. Other presidents in the nineteenth century were John Hamilton, of the Quebec G.C. (1897); Col. George A. Sweny, of the Toronto G.C. (1898); and Lt.-Col. D. T. Irwin, of the Royal Ottawa G.C. (1899). The new century was then begun with W. Wallace Watson, of the Royal Montreal G.C. in the office of president.[102]

Examples were given in chapter 2 of edicts in Scotland against golfers who played the game on Sundays, many of whom were forced to make public amends by occupying the Seat of Repentance at the local church. In Canada, also, throughout the nineteenth century,

> The Lord's Day Act exerted a restrictive influence on the development of recreation and sport. In the urban centres, where the act was more rigorously enforced, Sunday became a day of inactivity.[103]

However, around the time of the inception of the Canadian Golf Association, an interesting precedent was set in 1895 when a High Court Judge ruled that the playing of golf on Sundays did not contravene the Lord's Day Act and subsequently afforded the sport a peculiar legal testimonial. Four golfers on the links in East Toronto were summoned to appear before a magistrate, who fined them five dollars each plus costs. But the case was appealed in the High Court, where it was claimed that golf was a game of clubs and not ball, and that as no noise resulted from its practice, it should not be included under the ban.[104] The judge reserved his decision for a few days until he had considered the evidence, but then ruled in favor of the golfers, stating:

> This game of golf is not a game within the meaning of the

law. It is not noisy. It attracts no crowds. It is not gambling. It is on a parallel, it seems to me, with a gentleman going out for a walk on Sunday and, as he walks, switching off the heads of weeds with his walking stick.[105]

Cox has stated that from this time on golf was one game which could openly be played on Sundays, an advantage which many other sporting activities did not enjoy in the nineteenth century.[106]

Fifteen years after the formation of the Montreal Golf Club, Scottish influence was also responsible for the formation of the first permanent golf club in the United States. In 1888, ''Robert Lockhart, a native Scot who had prospered in his adopted country,'' visited Scotland, including the St. Andrews golf course. He returned to the United States with a number of golf clubs and gutta percha balls, which since 1848 had supplanted the ''featheries,'' and collaborated with his friend John Reid and others in the founding of the St. Andrew's Golf Club of Yonkers on 14 November 1899. Another Scot in Chicago, Charles Blair Macdonald, had tried unsuccessfully to introduce golf there since 1878. He had played at the St. Andrews course in Scotland. The World's Fair at Chicago in 1893 provided him with support at last: ''To the city on the shores of Lake Michigan it opened up many new vistas and among them was the ancient Scottish game.'' It was at this time that the Chicago Golf Club at Belmont was formed. This club, together with the St. Andrew's Golf Club (Yonkers), the Shinnecock Hills Golf Club (Long Island), the Brookline Country Club (Massachusetts), and the Newport Golf Club (Rhode Island), very quickly formed the Amateur Golf Association of the United States in 1894. Charles Blair Macdonald himself won the amateur title in 1895, and for many years it was a case of ''The Scots Supreme'':

In the early tournaments of the national organization which soon took the name of the United States Golf Association, the Scots drove down the fairways to victory with monotonous regularity. Native players with more energy than skill strove in vain to prove their mastery of the game.

Women golfers of Scottish descent also dominated the early tournament play in the United States.[107]

With the game well established by Scots on both sides of the international border, the first golf match between American and Canadian golf clubs took place at Niagara in 1896, when the Chicago Golf Club played against the Niagara Golf Club. The winner of the individual trophy was a seventeen-year-old youth, R. H. Dickson, the son of the Niagara captain. His score at the end of seventeen holes was 86 strokes, a record for the course.[108] Two years later, international matches between teams represent ing Canada and the United States were inaugurated at the Toronto Golf Club. The Canadian team on the first occasion was: A. Smith, W. A. Kerr, and D. Blage (Toronto); G. S. Lyon, V. Brown, and F. Hood (Rosedale); F. Pattison (Hamilton); J. Gillespie (Quebec); and J. Taylor (Montreal). However, the strong United States team won the match by 27 holes to 7.[109]

George Seymour Lyon, of the Canadian team, who was Canadian amateur golf champion eight times between 1898 and 1914, and also one of Canada's best curlers,[110] deserves special mention for his all-round sporting ability. The *Toronto Sunday World*, 25 September 1904, reported of him in a news story:

> He is one of the best all-round sportsmen in Canada. Not only did he excel in golf and cricket but he was a good football, baseball and tennis player and pulled a strong oar. At cricket, he was one of the finest bowlers in the game and held the best batting average in the Canadian Cricket Association three years ago. In 1895, he was captain of the Canadian International Cricket Team.

But one of George Lyon's greatest claims to sporting fame was the fact that he won a gold medal for Canada in the Scottish game of golf, which was included in the Olympic Games at St. Louis in 1904.[111]

A national element was introduced into ladies' golf competitions by 1900, a year in which lady golfers from Canada also competed successfully in the United States.[112] The first Open Championship for ladies in Canada was held at the Royal Montreal Golf Club, in 1901, when competitors came from Hamilton, Montreal, Quebec, Toronto, and St. John.[113] Miss Lily Young, of the home club, was the eventual winner, and Miss Mabel Thomson was runner-up, although she subsequently won the championship five times. Miss Dorothy Campbell of Hamilton, Ontario, "dominated the ladies game before the First World War," having previously "learned her game on the dunes and moors of North Berwick" in Scotland.[114] She was an apt pupil, for she became the first lady to win the United States and British titles in the same year. Altogether, Dorothy Campbell won the Canadian Championship three times, the United States Amateur Ladies Championship three times, and the British Ladies title twice.[115] Not all the champion women golfers of Canada in the twentieth century were of Scottish descent, of course. Florence Harvey, also of Hamilton, who won the Canadian Ladies Open Championships of 1903 and 1904 and founded the Canadian Ladies' Golf Union (now called the Canadian Ladies Golf Association), was born in England.[116] In any case, the term "Canadian" became more appropriate and meaningful in the twentieth century. But the earlier Scottish influence on golf is strongly hinted at in the names of the only two Canadian women golfers to be elected to the Canadian Golf Hall of Fame, i.e., Miss Ada Mackenzie, and Marlene Stewart Streit (later Mrs. J. Douglas Streit).[117]

Some Scottish influence lingers on among the names of the presidents of the Royal Canadian Golf Association from 1901 to the present, such as Balfour, Crerar, Wilkie, McCall, Campbell, Gould, Rankin, Ferguson, Robertson, Blair, Johnston, Forbes, McLean, and even Brown, Wilson, Harris, and Taylor.[118] Much stronger evidence is provided, however, by the widespread tendency to employ Scottish professionals at golf clubs in both Canada and the United States, where their traditional knowledge of the old game lent an "old-country" atmosphere which was valued at the time. An article in 1901 about "the largest golf store in the world," in New York, proudly described the manager, John Duncan Dunn, as "a genial Scotchman, famous golfer and thorough businessman,"[119] indicating commercial possibilities of a genuine Scottish presence. In Canada in the same year, as noted, Kerr reported that the Rosedale Golf Club, like the Toronto, employed a Scotch professional.[120] Actually, the Scot at Toronto became more famous, being one of only four men who have been elected to the Canadian Golf Hall of Fame. This was George Cumming, and his fellow Hall of Fame members were George Seymour Lyon, Charles R. Murray, and C. Ross (Sandy) Somerville.[121]

Cumming was born on 20 May 1879, at Bridge of Weir, in Scotland, and at ten years of age caddied at the Ranfurly Castle Golf Club. At the age of fourteen he joined the Forgan firm at Glasgow to learn club-making, and two years later was sent to Dumfries Golf Club as professional, where he remained for four years. In October of 1899, he met and played golf with Stewart Gordon, who was then the honorary secretary of the Toronto Golf Club. This meeting led to a professional contract with the Toronto Golf Club, and on 20 March 1900, George Cumming arrived in the Canadian city. Canadian golf was indebted to his subsequent successful career:

> Affectionately known as "Dean of Canadian golf professionals," George had an active service record of 50 years at Toronto Golf Club. His genial smile and humor, his uprightness and unique personality endeared him to the thousands who came in contact with him during his half century of work at Toronto Golf Club.
> Many caddies trained by him and who now hold important positions in the business world, attribute their success largely to his careful training. The assistant professionals who worked under him, carried his teachings with them and undoubtedly their thorough training by George did much to raise the profession to the high spot it occupies today in Canada.[122]

Cumming died on 26 March 1960. Another Scottish contemporary colleague of his from Vancouver, British Columbia, "held in very high esteem by the golfing fraternity," was David L. Black, who was born on 15 September 1883, at Troon, in Scotland. He left there in 1906 and became professional at the Outremont Golf and Country Club, Montreal; in 1910, he moved to the Rivermead Golf Club at Hull, Quebec; and then in 1920, he became professional at the Shaughnessy Heights Golf Club, Vancouver, until he retired in 1945. Like Cumming, he also had a distinguished golfing career, winning the Canadian Professional Golfers' Championship four times, and being for a time a director of the Canadian Professional Golfers Association. In 1929, in an exhibition match at the Point Grey Golf Club in Vancouver, he and Duncan Sutherland beat the great Walter Hagen and Horton Smith.[123]

Seven years before this George Cumming had played in an exhibition match to celebrate the opening of the new clubhouse at the prestigious Weston Golf Club of Toronto. This club had risen to prominence over the years since it was founded by a newly arrived Scottish immigrant:

> In 1909 Mr. John Lindsay arrived from Scotland to take up his residence in Weston, and he immediately set out to interest some friends in starting the royal and ancient game here. With the help of some ardent followers such as his brother Martin, Bert Church, and Richard Dawson, it was not long until they had a course of four holes established on the Wadsworth Flats.
>
> By the summer of 1913, there was so much enthusiasm and interest in the game being shown locally, that these gentlemen felt that the time was ripe to form a proper club.

A club was formally organized in 1914, which very soon had "over sixty gentlemen and some twenty ladies" as members, and "enjoyed phenomenal growth," until it was described twenty-three years later as "one of the largest and best equipped clubs in Ontario."[124]

At Banff in Alberta, in 1911, a garbage dump was converted into a golf course by an expert from Scotland, called in by the Canadian Pacific Railway for the purpose. Like his pioneer fellow-countrymen curlers who had long before been derided by the amazed French Canadian who believed they were fools, his antics also caused mirth: "This fellow in knickerbockers was always hitting a ball wherever we saw him. We all thought he was crazy."[125] It had caused mirth earlier south of the border, too. The *Scottish-American Journal* carried a report, in 1873, on the Chicago Scot who "returned from a visit to Scotland with a knobbly set of golf sticks and commenced knocking the 'gutty' balls around a field . . . to the amusement of his neighbors and the joyous sneers of the hoodlums.''[126] But before the century ended, there were more than a hundred golf clubs in the United States, several of them started by Scots, and many employed Scottish professionals.[127] As we have already seen, the sport was also well established in Canada before the uninitiated were amused by the Scottish golf expert at Banff. Dorothy Campbell herself played on the new Banff Springs Golf Club Links in 1912, which became a great attraction for CPR Hotel guests, residents and tourists alike.[138]

It has been the Scotsman's lot, in fact, to pioneer his sports in the New World in the face of some adversity and ridicule. His early attempts to introduce golf, the Highland fling, caber-tossing, and curling were often accompanied by a fair share of criticism and mirth. The same is true of his national characteristics, epitomized by the kilt, Scotch whisky, the bagpipes, a solemn demeanor and rigid religion, and an alleged propensity for meanness. The amazement of foreigners had to be endured with some degree of stoicism, until most of the mirth gradually subsided. Enemy soldiers have tended to laugh at tartan-skirted Scottish soldiers—before the battle. Although some Scottish elements are still regarded as humorous or strange in many places, Scots and people of Scottish descent are entitled to look back on their record in sports with quiet pride and satisfaction. They are able to contemplate the pleasure which millions derive from those sports today, now that the early derision of the few has been transformed into mass participation. This is particularly true in Canada, because of the success of the Highland Games, curling and golf.

It has already been pointed out in the previous chapter that there are more Highland Games meetings all over the Dominion than anywhere else outside of Scotland, and that Canadians are probably the most successful outside competitors at the Games in Scotland. Canada has also been the largest and most successful curling nation in the world for some time, replacing Scotland in this respect. The *Canadian Magazine* of 6 March 1971, in an article entitled ''Any Game Played by 750,000 People Can't Be All Dull,'' reported that ''more Canadians curl than play golf—or any other sport for that matter.[128] No one would claim that Canada is the most successful golfing nation in the world, although she has had a fair share of success, for this honor would undoubtedly go to the United States. But this reference to curling also implied the great popularity of golf in Canada, an implication sustained by the evidence. Jones has provided evidence to show that, as early as 1920, ''golf had developed into one of Canada's most popular sports. The main problem was still an insufficient number of courses for the masses of people wishing to participate.''[130] The *Encyclopedia Canadiana* in 1968 reported more than six hundred Golf Clubs in Canada.[131] The Report of the President of the Royal Canadian Golf Association for 1971 stated that there were 843 golf clubs as members of the association, ''an increase of 26 over 1970.''[132] By 1972 this had increased to 846, with other statistics showing that ''more than one million men and 250,000 women in Canada play golf.''[133]

Perhaps when the milestone of one thousand golf clubs in the Canadian Golf Association is reached, someone may propose a toast to the pioneer golfers who were mainly responsible—from Alexander Dennistoun, ''the father of golf in Canada,'' to George Cumming, ''the Dean of Canadian golf professionals.'' Whatever ensues, the Scots who introduced and promoted their traditional sport in the Dominion, and enabled so many others to subsequently share their pleasure, should not be forgotten. As Roxborough has said,

> Canadian sportsmen during the nineteenth century were greatly indebted to those sons of Scotland who participated in and sponsored a great variety of games.[134]

Golf was certainly one of those games. Its late development and enduring popularity meant that many Canadian sportsmen during the twentieth century had comparatively recent cause for gratitude. Still, it was no great mystery to John P. Roche, writing on ''Canadian Golf'' in an American magazine before the nineteenth century ended:

> The generally accepted idea is that golf is as Scotch as curl-

ing; and there is never a loyal Scot, and Canada is full of them, but will lay claim to a first mortgage on these two finest pastimes the ingenuity of man ever invented.

But that is not the question for discussion here. Golf in Canada is the subject. It is no wise strange, seeing how deeply tinctured with Scotch, who are still actuated and moved to a greater or less extent by the traditions of the British Isles, Canada is, that golf should have found an early home there.[136]

Notes

1. See Joseph S. F. Murdoch, *The Library of Golf: 1743–1966* (Detroit, Mich.: Gale Research Co., 1968), p. 304.

2. Murdoch, *Library of Golf*, passim; Henry Roxborough, *One Hundred—Not Out: The Story of Nineteenth Century Canadian Sport* (Toronto: Ryerson Press, 1966), p. 99.

3. Joseph T. Clark, "Golf in Canada," *Canadian Magazine*, November 1905, p. 43.

4. Roxborough, *One Hundred—Not Out*, p. 105.

5. David Lavender, *Winner Take All: The Trans-Canada Canoe Trail* (Toronto: McGraw-Hill Book Co., 1977), passim.

6. L. V. Kavanagh, *History of Golf in Canada* (Toronto: Fitzhenry and Whiteside, 1973), pp. x–xi.

7. Ibid., pp. 147–48.

8. See Foster Rhea Dulles, *A History of Recreation: America Learns to Play* (New York: Appleton-Century-Crofts, 1965), p. 52; and John Allen Krout, *Annals of American Sport 15, The Pageant of America Series*, 15 vols. (New York: United States Publishers' Association, 1929), p. 281.

9. *Encyclopedia Canadiana*, 10 vols. (Grolier of Canada Limited, 1968) 5: 385.

10. Roxborough, *One Hundred—Not Out*, p.105.

11. W. A. R. Kerr, "Golf in Canada," *Canadian Magazine* 17 (1901): 342.

12. Roxborough, *One Hundred—Not Out*, p. 105.

13. Peter Leslie Lindsay, "A History of Sport in Canada, 1807–1867" (Ph.D. diss., University of Alberta, 1969), pp. 113–14. The *Montreal Herald*, 1 January 1925, reported that the Christmas Day temperature was twenty-eight degrees, which had risen to thirty-six degrees by New Year's Day, with practically no snow upon the ground.

14. *The Montreal Star*, 13 January 1934, reported that "a group of Scots who were identified chiefly with the fur trade desired to introduce to Montreal two favorite games of their native land, curling and golf."

15. Kerr, "Golf in Canada," p. 342; John P. Roche, "Canadian Golf," *Outing*, June 1898, p. 260. See also Frank G. Menke, *The Encyclopedia of Sports* (New York: A. S. Barnes and Co., 1953), p. 425.

16. W. V. Uttley, *A History of Kitchener, Ontario* (Waterloo, Ontario: Chronicle Press, 1937), p. 107.

17. Roxborough, *One Hundred—Not Out*, p. 105.

18. Clark, "Golf in Canada," pp. 43–44.

19. Kavanagh, *History of Golf*, p. 57.

20. *Encyclopedia Britannica*, vol. 10 (London: William Benton, 1968), p. 551.

21. Roche, "Canadian Golf," p. 261.

22. Ibid., Kerr, "Golf in Canada," p. 343.

23. Kerr, "Golf in Canada," p. 343.

24. Roche, "Canadian Golf," p. 261.

25. Charles Hunter, "Golf in Canada," *Athletic Life,* February 1895, p. 63.

26. Ibid., p. 62; Ian F. Jobling, "Sport in Nineteenth-Century Canada: The Effects of Technological Changes on its Development" (Ph.D. diss., University of Alberta, 1970), p. 273.

27. R. Bruce Forbes, "Golf, The Royal and Ancient Game," *Merit News,* July 1965, p. 2. This is published by the I.A.F. group of companies, 1320 Graham Boulevard, Montreal 16, Quebec.

28. Ibid., Jobling, "Technological Changes," p. 273.

29. Kerr, "Golf in Canada," p. 343.

30. Ibid., *Canadian Sport Monthly*, June 1949, p. 35.

31. Kerr, "Golf in Canada," p. 343.

32. Hunter, "Golf in Canada," p. 64; Kavanagh, *History of Golf*, p. 69.

33. Roche, "Canadian Golf," p. 262.

34. *Montreal Gazette*, 10 October 1876.

35. *Scottish-American Journal*, 18 October 1877.

36. Jobling, "Technological Changes," p. 53.

37. *Canadian Illustrated News*, 16 October 1880.

38. Roxborough, *One Hundred—Not Out*, p. 106.

39. Hunter, "Golf in Canada," pp. 64–65.

40. Roxborough, *One Hundred—Not Out*, p. 106.

41. Hunter, "Golf in Canada," p. 64.

42. Horace G. Hutchinson, *Golf* (London: Longmans, Green and Co., 1898), p. 332.

43. Hunter, "Golf in Canada," p. 64, says "sixteen" and "twice," while Roche, "Canadian Golf," p. 262, says "fifteen" and "three times."

44. *Canadian Sport Monthly*, June 1949, p. 35.

45. Forbes, "Ancient Game," p. 3. See also Roxborough, *One Hundred—Not Out*, p. 106.

46. Clark, "Golf in Canada," pp. 41–46.

47. Kerr, "Golf in Canada," p. 346.

48. Clark, "Golf in Canada," pp. 40–44.

49. Kavanagh, *History of Golf*, p. 57; Kerr, "Golf in Canada," p. 346.

50. Janet Carnochan, *History of Niagara* (Toronto: William Briggs, 1914), p. 260.

51. Forbes, "Ancient Games," p. 2; Kavanagh, *History of Golf*, p. 59; Roche, "Canadian Golf," p. 263; Roxborough, *One Hundred—Not Out*, p. 107.

52. Jobling, "Technological Changes," p. 275.

53. As quoted in Roxborough, *One Hundred—Not Out*, p. 107.

54. Hunter, "Golf in Canada," p. 65.

55. Kerr, "Golf in Canada," p. 347; Roche, "Canadian Golf," p. 263.

56. Roche, "Canadian Golf," p. 263.

57. Clark, "Golf in Canada," p. 47.

58. Roxborough, *One Hundred—Not Out*, p. 107.

59. *Globe*, 8 May 1893 and passim.

60. Kerr, "Golf in Canada," p. 347.

61. Clark, "Golf in Canada," pp. 44–45.

62. Jobling, "Technological Changes," pp. 106–8.

63. *Globe*, 17 May 1890. The Journalist also stated that "a disgruntled tennis player, when asked what he thought of golf, replied: 'Confounded game; knock a ball into a bush and hunt for it all day.' "

64. Roche, "Canadian Golf," p. 264.

65. Kerr, "Golf in Canada," pp. 347–48.

66. Jobling, "Technological Changes," p. 65.

67. *Globe*, 7 November 1896.

68. Clark, "Golf in Canada," p. 45.

69. Kavanagh, *History of Golf*, p. 41; Kerr, "Golf in Canada," p. 349.

70. Nancy Howell and Maxwell L. Howell, *Sports and Games in Canadian Life: 1700 to the Present* (Toronto: Macmillan of Canada, 1969), p. 104.

71. Kerr, "Golf in Canada," pp. 347–49; Roche, "Canadian Golf," pp. 263–66.

72. *Inland Sentinel*, 26 July 1895.

73. *Athletic Life*, January 1896, p. 29.

74. Margaret Ann Hall, "A History of Women's Sport in Canada prior to World War I" (M.A. thesis, University of Alberta, 1968), p. 104.

75. W. W. Tulloch, "A New Game for Ladies," *Belgravia* 8 (1869):79–84.

76. As quoted in Ernest A. Bland, *Fifty Years of Sport* (London: The Daily Mail, 1946), p. 283.

77. Jean Cochrane, Abby Hoffman, and Pat Kincaid, *Women in Canadian Life: Sports* (Toronto: Fitzhenry & Whiteside, 1977), pp. 27–28.

78. Kerr, "Golf in Canada," p. 343.

79. Roche, "Canadian Golf," p. 262.

80. Hunter, "Golf in Canada," p. 63.

81. Kerr, "Golf in Canada," p. 343.

82. Roche, "Canadian Golf," p. 262. The same thing was said by *Athletic Life*, April 1895, p. 188, concerning the Winnipeg Golf Club: "ladies were as numerous on the links as the men, and, if possible, more enthusiastic."

83. Hunter, "Golf in Canada," p. 65; Kerr, "Golf in Canada," p. 343; Roche, "Canadian Golf," p. 262.

84. Roche, "Canadian Golf," p. 263.

85. Hall, "Women's Sport in Canada," pp. 103, 158.

86. *Athletic Life*, April 1895, p. 188.

87. *Manitoba Morning Free Press*, 24 September 1896.

88. *Globe*, 14 May 1900.

89. Roche, "Canadian Golf," p. 264.

90. Kerr, "Golf in Canada," p. 349.

91. Kavanagh, *History of Golf*, p. 59.

92. Carnochan, *History of Niagara*, p. 269.

93. Kerr, "Golf in Canada," p. 346.

94. Clark, "Golf in Canada," p. 43.

95. Reginald Gourlay, "The Canadian Girl," *Canadian Magazine*, October 1896, p. 509; Peter L. Lindsay, "Woman's Place in Nineteenth Century Canadian Sport," *Journal of the Canadian Association for Health, Physical Education and Recreation*, September–October, 1970, pp. 25–28.

96. Jobling, "Technological Changes," p. 362.

97. Clark, "Golf in Canada," p. 47; Allan Elton Cox, "A History of Sports in Canada, 1868 to 1900" (Ph.D. diss., University of Alberta, 1969), p. 131; *Globe*, 8 October 1894; Hunter, "Golf in Canada," p. 65.

98. *Globe*, 5 November 1894.

99. Cox, "Sports in Canada, 1868 to 1900," p. 132; *Globe*, 8 June 1896.

100. *Canadian Magazine*, November 1897, p. 93. It was also stated that "Golf as a ladies' game is par excellence."

101. *A Concise History of Golf in Canada* (Toronto: Royal Canadian Golf Association, n.d.), p. 2; Kerr, "Golf in Canada," p. 349.

102. *Royal Canadian Golf Association: Report of the President and Board of Governors, 1971*, p. 2; hereafter referred to as *R.C.G.A. Report*.

103. Jobling, "Technological Changes," p. 346.

104. *Globe*, 7 October 1895.

105. As quoted in Wm. Perkins Bull, *From Rattlesnake Hunt to Hockey: The History of Sports in Canada and of the Sportsmen of Peel, 1798 to 1934* (Toronto: George J. McLeod, 1934), p. 183.

106. Cox, "Sports in Canada, 1868 to 1900," p. 135; Jobling, "Technological Changes," pp. 345–46.

107. Krout, *Annals of American Sport*, pp. 282–84, 292–94; see also Dulles, *History of Recreation*, p. 242.

108. *Globe*, 5 September 1896.

109. Ibid., 3 October 1898.

110. Cox, "Sports in Canada, 1868 to 1900," pp. 133–35.

111. *Globe*, 26 September 1904. See also Roxborough, *One Hundred—Not Out*, p. 247.

112. *Globe and Mail*, 25 April 1900; Hall, "Women's Sport in Canada," pp. 157–58.

113. *Globe*, 15 October 1900.

114. Forbes, "Ancient Game," p. 3; Krout, *Annals of American Sport*, p. 293. Two photographs of Dorothy Campbell are featured on this page, also.

115. Forbes, "Ancient Game," p. 3.

116. Quoted from biographical material pertaining to Miss Harvey kindly provided by Mr. L. V. Kavanagh, then Secretary-Treasurer and Manager of the Royal Canadian Golf Association, accompanied by a letter dated 21 February 1972.

117. *R.C.G.A. Report*, p. 18.

118. Ibid., p. 2. There are numerous Scottish surnames among the Board of Governors and other officials, too.

119. As quoted in Carl T. Felker, "Golf—From First Feather Ball to Modern Solids," *The Sporting Goods Dealer*, May 1969, p. 100.

120. Kerr, "Golf in Canada," p. 347.

121. *R.C.G.A. Report*, pp. 18–19.

122. Quoted from biographical material pertaining to George Cumming provided by Mr. L. V. Kavanagh.

123. Quoted from biographical material pertaining to David L. Black provided by Mr. L. V. Kavanagh.

124. F. D. Cruickshank and J. Nason, *History of Weston* (Weston, Ontario: Times and Guide, 1937), pp. 153–54.

125. As quoted in Brad L. Kilb, "Sport in Banff before 1914" (term paper, Department of Physical Education, University of Alberta, 1967), p. 90.

126. *Scottish-American Journal*, 7 August 1907.

127. Ibid., 14 July 1897, 5 January 1898, and 22 May 1907. See also Krout, *Annals of American Sport*, p. 291: "Amateur Golf in the United States is deeply indebted to the professionals. . . . In the early days, they were generally Scots, who laid out the courses,

interpreted the rules, exemplified the etiquette of the game, and instructed club members in the technique. Their number was gradually augmented by many native-born Americans who had mastered the game sufficiently well to become teachers.''

128. *Crag and Canyon* (Banff), 4 May 1912, 6 July 1912, and passim.

129. *Canadian Magazine*, 6 March 1971, p. 7.

130. Kevin G. Jones, ''Sport in Canada, 1900 to 1920'' (Ph.D. diss. University of Alberta, 1970), p. 135.

131. *Encyclopedia Canadiana* (1968), 4:385.

132. *R.C.G.A. Report*, p. 7.

133. Kavanagh, *History of Golf*, p. 4.

134. Roxborough, *One Hundred—Not Out*, p. 111.

135. Roche, ''Canadian Golf,'' p. 260.

7

The Scots and Some Other Sports

> *There is more than a probability that Canada has derived at least one of its national games from the Gaels, namely ice hockey. The most popular Scottish Gaelic game is shinty, played with sticks or clubs and a wooden ball. In some parts of the Highlands the word Shinty was corrupted to ''shinnie'', and it is an interesting fact that ''shinnie'' was played upon ice in Canada before the word ''hockey'' was used of the game.*

> George S. Emmerson (1976)

T HE Caledonian Games, curling, and golf were traditional sports which had been popular in Scotland for centuries. It is natural that these sports were the ones most associated with emigrant Scots, as they in turn participated in them with enthusiasm and success wherever they settled. For this reason, these sports were accepted as Scottish wherever they appeared.

Yet there were other sports, as demonstrated in chapter 2, that had also been part of social life in Scotland for many years, such as cricket and football. These were common to other parts of Britain as well, especially England, where the most important events in their development occurred. Such British sports were also pioneered successfully in Canada, mainly due to English and Scottish influence.

There were new sports, too, that were developed in Canada during the nineteenth century, such as lacrosse and ice hockey. The Canadian climate encouraged all inhabitants to take part in other activities such as skating, snow shoeing, and tobogganing for several months of the year. People of all nationalities were involved in and contributed to this Canadian development in sport, and among them were the ubiquitous and sport-loving Scots. Although not equaling the absolute achievement epitomized by the success of Scottish sports in Canada, their influence in other sports was by no means negligible. When it is combined with their efforts detailed in previous chapters, in fact, a more complete and significant Scottish contribution to sport in Canada during the nineteenth century is revealed. Since one cannot discover, at this point in time, the names of *all* the Scotsmen who were involved in *every* club for *each* sport in Canada, nor determine exactly the nature of their influence, a complete and total exposition is unattainable. Nevertheless, enough examples can be given in several sports to sustain a conviction that the Scots were indeed influential, in varying degrees, in other than the traditional Scottish sports.

The two British sports of quoits and tug-of-war have already been mentioned in connection with the Caledonian Games, as they were usually featured in the programs. David Webster, author of *Scottish Highland Games*, describes the tug-of-war as "one of the truly great spectacles at Highland Gatherings" in Scotland.[1] In the chapter entitled "By Way of Scotland," in his book on nineteenth-century Canadian sport. Roxborough deals with only five sports: Caledonian Games, curling, golf, quoits, and tug-of-war. There is no doubt that although the last two sports were not unknown in England as well, their development in Canada has been dominated by the Scots. In fact, it is very interesting to note that in his chapter on the English influence on Canadian sport, entitled "There Always Was an England," Roxborough confines himself to only five sports again: archery, cricket, hunting, pugilism, and rifle shooting.[2] Scotsmen and other nationalities participated in these sports, too, but Roxborough is correct in that the English influence predominated. In the same way, the Scottish influence was paramount in quoits and tug-of-war, as Roxborough and others have noted.

Quoits has already been mentioned in chapter 5, since a quoiting contest was nearly always included in a Caledonian Games program in Canada, and usually opened the proceedings as the first event. Roxborough has stated that this British game "thrived north of the border and eventually was carried overseas by pioneering Scotsmen."[3] Much of this pioneering was accomplished through the consistent appearance of the game at the popular and widespread Caledonian Games. The first contest at the inaugural Games of the Montreal Caledonian Society in 1856, and the one which carried the highest prize money of twenty-five shillings, was quoits.[4] Subsequent programs elsewhere followed a similar tendency. For example, the Games of the St. Andrew's Society of Ottawa, in 1867, began at 11:00 A.M. with a quoits contest. The first prize was a silver cup, the second prize $2, and the third prize was a pair of steel quoits.[5] W. McRobie won the first prize of a "silver quoit medal" at the first event in the Montreal Games of 1871.[6] Quoits was a keenly contested event at the Hamilton Games of 1875, also[7]. Bull devotes a chapter to "Quoits and Horseshoes" in his history of sport in Peel County, mentioning two famous father-and-son quoiters, Joseph and John Lawson:

> Testimony to Dr. John's pitching prowess is offered by the cup which stands in his surgery, and which he won at the Scottish Games of 1893.[8]

Without doubt, the sport of quoits was greatly promoted and popularized at many "Scottish Game" meetings throughout Canada.

But it was a sport in which clubs were formed, too, and it was pioneered in this manner also, outside of the Caledonian Games. Not surprisingly most of these clubs were situated in areas of Scottish settlement, and Scots were the protagonists. It is possible that Scarborough was the place where quoits really began in earnest. Boyle, writing in 1896, reports that "this game has been played in the Township with enthusiasm for upwards of sixty years,"[9] indicating some quoiting activity there at least as early as 1836. It was included in the program for the Toronto Athletic Games of 1839,[10] and Boyle also stated that "among the earliest quoiters in the township was John Torrance, who won a championship Silver Medal at the Athletic Games in Toronto, in 1840, and which is still in the possession of his descendants."[11] There were actually two quoiting contests at these Games, the other being won by John Muir of Scarborough, who "dominated the contests at Toronto during these early years."[12] Strangely, however, the first club at Scarborough for quoits was not formed until 1858. This was the outcome of a championship contest held in Toronto, under the auspices of the Caledonian Society, when Alexander Muir and David Johnston, both of Scarborough, "carried off the medal. Instead of deciding as between themselves, they very public-spiritedly undertook to form a club, placing it in possession of the medal, to be held against all comers."[13] This was the same Alexander Muir mentioned in chapter 5, who composed "The Maple Leaf Forever," and had many talents. This Scot was elected first president of the Scarborough Quoit Club, and later achieved fame as the quoits champion of both Canada and the United States.[14] Possibly the quoiters of Scarborough were also inclined to organize themselves into a formal club at this time, however, by the existence of other quoits clubs long before 1858.

The first quoit club reported was in Montreal, which existed by 1841, when a match was announced at St. Pierre between the club's bachelors and its married members.[15] "Quoiting" opened the second day's events at the "Montreal Olympic Games" of 1844, and was won by Second Private John McLeod of the 93rd Highlanders.[16] Meanwhile, the bachelor versus married contests continued as annual affairs, until a Thistle Quoit Club was mentioned in 1846. At this time, as Lindsay has pointed out, "it was evident that members of curling clubs were playing quoits as a summer substitute for their organized winter activities," so it is possible that the Thistle Club was formed before 1846, when it played a match against the Montreal Club.[17] Quoiting was indeed the curler's summer pastime, and Boyle includes in his book photographs of Andrew Fleming ("The Duke"), Walter Glendinning, James Findlay, Archd. Glendinning, William Purdie *and* "a Wm. Purdie," under the heading "Curlers and Quoiters." It is therefore understandable why quoits clubs were situated in those places which had curling clubs, and where Caledonian Games were held. The Scarborough Quoit Club had a long rivalry with clubs from Ayr and Galt, in fact, which Boyle maintains "resulted invariably in favor of Scar-boro."[18] Quoiting was not widely reported in the press in com-parison with curling, but it is not unreasonable "to assume that other curling centres had established quoit clubs as well."[19]

In 1847, the Thistle Quoit Club announced a two-rink match between its Scottish members and those born in Canada. The Scots managed to win by only one point, "which indicated that the Canadians were approaching the game with increasing en-thusiasm and skill."[20] The Caledonian Curling Club was formed in 1850, and the Caledonian Quoit Club began its activities the following summer, arranging annual matches with another club, the Montreal Union Quoit Club.[21] These two clubs competed at Guilbault's Gardens in 1853, when no less than fifty players represented each group.[22]

Other quoit clubs were reported from Hamilton and West Flamborough. The Quoit Club of Hamilton was confident enough to issue a challenge to the rest of Upper Canada in 1848, but "especially [to] a club in Flamborough West,"[23] although any result of this challenge is not recorded. Several weeks before its first Games of 1856, in which quoits was prominently featured, the Montreal Caledonian Society had promoted a quoits match against two American opponents for a wager of $100-a-side. The Montreal representatives won each of the three games. [24] Bearing in mind that Alexander Muir was the American champion as well, the United States does not seem to have had much success in quoiting competitions against Canadian teams, for Boyle also stated that, "in an international match against a picked team from various noted quoiting centres in the United States, Scar-boro won by 365 points."[25]

Before 1860, other quoit clubs had been reported in Halifax, Toronto, Bowmanville, Burlington, Dundas, and Hamilton (the Maple Leaf Club, 1858); and "the sixties witnessed a further spread of competition, with matches reported from Quebec, Yorkville, Lachute, St. Andrew's, Ottawa, Whitby, and Victoria."[26] As they had adopted other Scottish events during similar athletic Games at their annual picnics, other ethnic societies also featured quoits at their outings. The St. George's Society of Toronto, for example, organized a quoits competition in conjunction with the Toronto Fair of 1859, when John Scott of Toronto won the fourteen-dollar first prize and S. Ferguson of Hamilton won the second prize of four dollars.[27] In 1862, W. Bell won a Knockout Competition, from twelve entrants, at the Irish Protestant Benevolent Society Picnic in Montreal.[28] The following year, the *Morning Chronicle* of Quebec advertised a competition for a "Gold Quoit," which was subsequently won by John Murray from a large number of entrants.[29] The prizewinners' names—Scott, Ferguson, Bell and Murray—again suggest a strong Scottish presence in the sport.

The Studley Quoit Club of Halifax, formed on 24 August 1858, seems to have been the foremost club in the Maritimes region:

> The membership had increased to one hundred by the turn of the century and the Club had become famous for its punch and its hospitality to the officers of the Services and to distinguished visitors such as the Marquis of Dufferin, the Earl of Aberdeen, and Prince George of Wales, later King George V, who visited the club once in 1883 when he was a midshipman and twice in 1890 while in command of H.M.S. *Thrush*.[30]

An annual competition of this club for "the governor-general's medal" was reported in the *Montreal Gazette* of 11 September 1877, probably presented by the Marquis of Dufferin, who was in office between 1872 and 1878.

Seventeen years earlier, the *Daily Colonist* (Victoria) had provided evidence of the game on the West Coast, under the unusual heading of "Hitting a Chinaman with a Quoit." It was recorded that some sailors and marines were playing at quoits near a Chinaman's house, at Esquimault, when a marine named Dennis McEvoy "struck a Celestial with one of the quoits." The "Chinaman" complained to a public judge, but McEvoy's officer stated in court that he had been punished by his order, and the case was dismissed.[31] Another match at quoits was reported in the same newspaper five years later,[32] and it is clear that it may be considered as another nationwide pre-Confederation sport.

As with curling, there "was much sociability associated with quoiting," of which Roxborough has provided examples, stating that most quoiting pitches were situated close to inns, "where refreshment was convenient." He goes on to emphasize the influence of the Scots regarding quoits in Canada:

> Constantly there were reminders of Scottish traditions and customs. For instance, participants in the 1880 Dominion Championships were expected to appear in their special costumes. It was also announced that the awards would be a grand gold medal valued at $50 and a silver medal valued at $15, together with "cash and goods which are now being collected from friends and storekeepers adjacent to the West Toronto grounds."[33]

Again, it is possible that these substantial money prizes attracted many Scots to the sport, and represented a partial reason for the predominance of Scottish names among the most successful exponents of the art of pitching a quoit. For it was an art which *could* be profitable, not unlike other athletic abilities of the time. Some examples of money prizes for quoits have already been mentioned, notably the $100-a-side international contest at Montreal in 1856, but there were other instances of lucrative rewards for quoiting skill. The Toronto *Daily Globe* of 27 October 1879 reported a "Challenge Quoit Match" for $50-a-side at Galt, between a Mr. Walter I. Reid and Mr. Walkinshaw. Boyle reported in 1896 that "the largest prize which has come to Scarboro for quoiting supremacy was won by Wm. Purdie, jun., in a Toronto contest, when he carried off a $50 prize—$42 cash and a pair of steel quoits."[34]

Although it received far less publicity than many other sports, quoits was reasonably popular and widespread in the nineteenth century (a club was organized in Chatham as late as 1887, particularly among Scottish curlers,[35] until it was superseded by the related activity of horseshoe pitching).As Bull reported in 1934:

> Many were the keenly-fought inter-community matches during the later years of the nineteenth-century. Only in recent years has quoit-pitching gone the way of so many of the

earlier sports of the people and almost disappeared from the villages and roadsides of the country.

Its place has been taken by its sporting cousin, horseshoe-pitching.[36]

Dulles has stated that the sport of quoits in the United States, also, was replaced by horseshoe pitching.[37] This remains a seldom-reported "Cinderella" sport today in both countries (although there does exist an American Horseshoe Pitching Hall of Fame), as its forerunner of quoits was in the nineteenth century. But there is no doubt that whatever popularity quoits enjoyed then in the Dominion was due in greatest measure to the enthusiastic participation of the Scots.

The same can be said of the tug-of-war, another event included in Roxborough's chapter "By Way of Scotland," and also popularized to a great extent by the Caledonian Games:

> Still another sport with a Scottish background was the familiar tug-of-war. In Canada's pioneer days pulling on a rope was frequently an after-supper pastime at bees; it was also an event on many picnic programmes where there was as much fun in choosing sides as in the actual contest. However, as rivalries developed, villages, counties, provinces and even nations engaged in tugging competitions. It became the big attraction at police games, Caledonian Games, fairs and army exercises.[38]

One difference is that there were no official or formally organized "tug-of-war clubs," as in quoits, but there were teams which regularly pulled together, which were able to gain local, provincial, or even national recognition. The most renowned of these was composed of Scots, again participating in a sport which was often featured at Highland Gatherings in their native land,[39] who managed to obtain an international title in the sport.

The tug-of-war was a contest of sheer strength, and the caber-tossers, hammer-throwers, and shot-putters of the Caledonian Games meeting were well suited for the ordeal. Apart from the earlier and more informal activity mentioned at bees, the greatest era of the sport was during the last quarter of the nineteenth century. Apart from its popularity at Caledonian Games, elsewhere too "it was the crowd-puller in the 1880's and 1890's. Whenever the police, firemen, or militia held their annual field-days, the most esteemed and popular of all competitions was the tug-of-war."[40] Judging from the Toronto Police tug-of-war team of 1883, described as "a mountain of flesh," the Scots made their presence felt at Police Games, also. Its members were con-stables Macrae, 195 lbs.; Cusick, 200 lbs.; Patterson, 205 lbs.; McDonald, 210 lbs.; Anson, 240 lbs.; and Stormont, 260 lbs.[41] Bull also confirmed the great popularity of the tug-of-war among communities in the eighties and nineties:

> The Cheltenham team was regarded for several years as unbeatable, having on its strength such stalwart rope-men as Spencer McDonald, stone-mason, William H. McKechnie, farmer, John Patterson, stone-mason, and John Foster, thresher. Such men, it is said, would often prolong a tug until the rope was broken.[42]

But it was a team of Scottish farmers from Oxford County in On-tario which was destined to become the most famous tug-of-war team in nineteenth-century Canada, and provide one of the memorable *Great Days in Canadian Sport.* In the book of this ti-tle, a whole chapter was devoted to this team under the Scottish heading of "They'll No Tak' Zorra."

As seen in chapter 3, Zorra was settled by Highlanders from Scotland who seemed typical of their breed, being described as "devout, thrifty and thirsty for knowledge." Before the end of the nineteenth century the settlement had produced clergymen, doctors, lawyers, inventors, college presidents, U.S. senators, millionaires, and cabinet ministers. C. W. Gordon, who wrote novels under the pseudonym of "Ralph Connor," also came from Zorra. The residents of Zorra have been described as fiercely competitive, as well as "tall, well-proportioned and powerful."[43] Tales of strong men abounded in these pioneer communities. Bull tells us of Archie McGregor of Caledon, "said to have been, from 1830 to 1840, the strongest man in the five townships." Frank Horan of Albion was another who "had a similar reputation for great feats of strength.''[44] One of the well-proportioned Zorra men was credited with throwing a rampaging young bull into a brush-heap. Although these feats have probably been embellished over the years, the exploits of such men in tug-of-war contests were more factual, and witnessed and verified by many spectators. No exploits, however, surpassed those of the Zorra Scots.

Nearly every township in Oxford County had its own tug-of-war team by the 1880s and Zorra was no exception. When the members first assembled in 1880, their ages varied from twenty-eight to thirty-eight years:

> The team was composed of five tall, sturdy farmers, and their captain. The smallest of the five was Billy Munro, who stood six feet one inch and weighed 188 pounds; Ira Hummason was six feet two inches and weighed 199 pounds; Sandy Clark statured six feet two inches and scaled 206 pounds; Bob MacLeod, the tallest of the quintette, was six feet two-and-one-quarter inches and weighed 197 pounds; while anchorman Bob MacIntosh, the heaviest of all, was six feet one inch tall and weighed 215 pounds. Ed. Sutherland, the team captain, was also a strapping six-footer. In combination, the five pullers weighed over half a ton, but each was tall and carried his poundage without any trace of surplus flesh. They were men truly equipped to pull their weight.

Their first success was against a Dereham Township team, which outweighed them by about twenty pounds a man, but which Zorra defeated four times. The men of Zorra then challenged the Lucknow Giants, pride of Bruce County, and were again victorious. Another victory came against a team from Brant County, earning the Zorra team a considerable reputation. People travelled many miles to see them perform at Fairs and Games throughout the Province.

The Royal Chief of the Scottish Clans of America organization in 1888 was James Sutherland, the federal member for North Oxford and later a cabinet minister, who was also much impressed by the Zorra team. His position enabled him to obtain an invitation for the team to compete in the North American Tug-of-War Championship, held in Buffalo during August of 1888. It was quite a step from provincial championships to an international contest on foreign soil, but the Zorra men defeated all opposition in front of ten thousand spectators to become the North American champions.[45]

A famous Chicago Highland Association tug-of-war team disputed the title, however, and claimed that the Buffalo event had only attracted Eastern teams and was therefore not truly representative. The Zorra team agreed to compete against the Chicago team in August 1890 in Chicago. The Chicago team won the contest, but there were protests that the team had used a starting trick that was unknown to and unexpected by the Canadians.[46] A return match was arranged a few weeks later, on 10 October 1890, at the Fair of the Embro and West Zorra Agricultural Society. It was "an event of international import."[47] which attracted people from all over the province, including its Scottish premier, Sir Oliver Mowat. It was well established before the contest began that victory would go to the first team to win two heats. The Zorra men easily won the first pull, but the second developed into a titantic struggle lasting thirty-five minutes, until the bagpipes were used not for the first time to inspire sons of Scotland:

> As the struggle continued without any sign of an imminent decision, an inspired Zorra supporter was intrigued by the thought that men who bore such illustrious Scottish names as Sutherland, Munro, MacLeod and McIntosh could be inspired by music. So in the hope that haunting brooding bagpipes melodies might ensure victory, a couple of pipers were instructed to play tunes that had given fire and fearlessness to Scotia's sons. Immediately, and almost magically, the marker on the manila rope began inching toward the strong hands and belt of anchorman McIntosh. Soon the required length was gained. The five Canadians, plus a pair of hard-blowing pipers, had saved Zorra and recaptured the North American tug-of-war championship.[48]

The *Toronto Mail* afterwards gloated in a Scottish manner, declaiming that "the Chicago team will need to live a little longer on oatmeal before they can succeed in pulling the rope from the

Zorra boys.''[49] The intriguing and unanswered question, of course, is why did not the bagpipes also inspire an American team with the Scottish name of the Chicago Highland Association?

Three years later, when four of the Zorra team were in their forties and Ira Hummason was over fifty years old, they decided to compete in the World Tug-of-War Championship to be held at the Chicago World's Fair. This was truly an international affair, ''for Britain, France, Belgium, Germany, Canada and the United States had entered their best tuggers.''[50] After the preliminary heats and semifinals, it was again a case of ''America versus Canada,'' as the two remaining unbeaten teams were Humboldts of the United States and Zorra of Canada. The final was held on the American national holiday of July 4, 1893, in the Chicago Baseball Grounds. Zorra won the first pull in a time of six minutes, the Humboldts won the second, and ''the stage was set for the final round, which began as the sun was setting in the mammoth Chicago Stadium.'' Zorra triumphed, and a newspaper dispatch recorded the whole event:

> This afternoon, five brawny sons of Zorra, neither young nor handsome, but possessing the strength and endurance of Hectors, listlessly strolled into the Chicago Baseball Grounds. There, in the presence of many thousands, they wrested the tug-of-war championship of the world from the famed Humboldts.
>
> Crowned by such a halo of victory, surrounded by an excited throng of admirers, the welkin ringing with their praises, the Zorra's oldest and proudest member, Ira Hummason, age fifty-one, was carried from the field.[51]

All the members of the Zorra team lived into their eighties, except Ira Hummason, who was injured in that final pull at Chicago. Before the nineteenth century ended they had proved themselves ''The World's Best''[52] in one of the world's most strenuous sports.

Another attraction featured at the Caledonian Games, in addition to quoits and tug-of-war, was the game of lacrosse, which was certainly indigenous to Canada.[53] It had its origins in the North American Indian game of *baggataway*, and was not adopted by the white man until the early 1840s. The participation of whites was somewhat sporadic until the game experienced a tremendous expansion in the Confederation Year of 1867, when lacrosse clubs multiplied at a tremendous rate in Montreal, Toronto, and elsewhere, and the National Lacrosse Association of Canada was formed. Dr. George Beers, who had individually promoted the game in so many ways, and particularly as a national game for Canada, was elected secretary of the association. Today he is referred to as the "Father of Modern Lacrosse."[54]

The game was popularized to some extent, in the early years of its adoption by European settlers, by its appearance at Caledonian Games and other similar meetings, when the developing game was provided with exhibition arenas attended, during its infancy, by large audiences.[55] The Indians were mostly featured in early exhibitions as naturally the most skilled players, and they used their prowess in a professional manner. On the first day of the Montreal Olympic Games on 28 August 1844, Caughnawaga Indians entertained the crowd in this way after a foot race:

Game of La Crosse

The race was followed by the Indian game of La Crosse, much resembling the game in Scotland termed "shinty." A purse of $10 was made up for the winners among the spectators, who appeared to be highly gratified by the agility displayed.[56]

No doubt the Indians were further gratified by more purses on the second day, when no less than four more lacrosse games took place, two of them against whites.[57] The reporter was obviously acquainted with shinty, which was also brought to Canada by Scots, and later supposed to resemble ice hockey and golf as well. In 1856, at the Beauharnois Games, Iroquois Indians defeated a team of Algonquins for a purse of $40 in a lacrosse game.[58]

It was in 1856, also, that the Montreal Lacrosse Club was formed by athletes from the disbanded Olympic Club. The members of this "first organized white team to play the game" were: T. Blackwood J. Bruneau, A. Charrier, P. Christie, T. Coffin, F. Dowd, G. Kerrick, H. MacDougall, W. MacFarlane, and G. Redpath.[59] It is more than likely that some of these men were Scots, aside from the suggestion of their Scottish names, considering the evidence which has already been presented of the Scottish presence and sporting activity in Montreal. But the list presents a problem which confronts any student of nineteenth-century sport in Canada, for whom it is not always possible to determine the nationality or ethnic loyalty behind a name. As far as the Scots are concerned, the Howells have correctly stated that ''they too entered into the sporting life of the new country, and their names appear frequently on the lists of early teams and as organizers of early clubs for sport.''[60] In fact, the statement can be equally well applied to the list of later teams, and to organizers of later clubs for sport, throughout the nineteenth century. This is not to say that Scottish names were the only ones to appear, only that they were exceedingly numerous. Apart from reports of Caledonian Games, curling, golf, quoits, and tug-of-war, where they logically predominated, a plethora of Scottish names of every description appeared in nineteenth century chronicles of other sports in Canada as well. They appeared from the beginning, with consistent repetition, in every sport, from Nova Scotia to British Columbia, like a roll call of Highland Clans or Lowland families.

The problem is, How many Scots were involved in an influential manner? Or rather, for the historian of today, what's in a name? Given the undisputed Scottish fact in Canadian history, it is not unreasonable to presume a Scottish influence in sport by the appearance of so many Scottish names where individual and personal details are not availabe. But some names, of course, may represent a person a generation or two removed from any Scottish origins; on the other hand, it may have belonged to a genuine Scot newly arrived in Canada.[61] The reader cannot be sure, and the example of Tommy Burns, the Canadian World Heavyweight Boxing Champion, is hardly reassuring. He was born in Hanover, Ontario, on 17 June 1881, of parents of Italian descent, and his real name was Noah Brusso. He did not adopt the very Scottish name of Burns (related to the Campbell of Argyll clan) until after 1900 when he began his boxing career.[62] This is obviously an extreme example, but one which indicates a necessary caution when confronted with a profusion of Scottish names. Nevertheless, given the Scottish tradition in sport, the consistent emigration and widespread group settlement of Scots in Canada, the network of many Scottish Societies, and their influence in so many aspects of Canadian life, it is certainly not presumptuous to assume that a large number of these names—the exact proportion cannot be determined—represented people who were Scottish in nature and fact. The Zorra tug-of-war team members were often described as ''Canadians,'' but their life-style in the Scottish community, and their famous response to the bagpipes, revealed their Scottish nature. Within the abundance of Scottish names, however, there were some definite examples which denoted that the Scots were indeed significantly involved in other sports beyond their own.

They were certainly members of the Montreal Lacrosse Club.[63] Another club in Montreal, the Caledonia Lacrosse Club, also no doubt had Scottish members, just as the Montreal Shamrocks were mostly Irish.[64] Many curling clubs were called after the Scottish emblem of the thistle, and the Scottish township of Fergus had a Thistles Lacrosse Club.[65] After the example given in the previous paragraph, however, one dare not be dogmatic about whether ''Robert Burns,'' the man who organized the Halifax Lacrosse Club, was a Scot, or even about the lacrosse club which was also founded in New Glasgow. But it is certain from the article ''Lacrosse in the Maritime Provinces,'' published in 1892, that many Scots were indeed skilled exponents of the game there.[66] In fact, articles were written on lacrosse in Canada by other authors with very Scottish names, such as W. Cruikshank, John K. Munro, and Ross Mackenzie.[67] The last named was himself one of the most famous players in the nineteenth century.[68] MacKenzie played with a Toronto Club, however, and so was not included in the Montreal Lacrosse Team which toured Britain (including Scotland) in 1876, and which consisted of: R. Summerhays, F.C.A. McIndoe, Dr. W. G. Beers, Henry Joseph, D. E. Bowie, T. D. Ralston, S. Massey, S. McDonald, J. K. Green, H. W. Becket, S. G. Hubbell, W. D. Ross, Angus Grant, and T. Hodgson.[69] Among the Scottish names, Duncan E. Bowie can be identified as the Scot who excelled at Caledonain Games, won the first intercollegiate footrace in the United States,

and was a member of the McGill Football Club and Montreal
Snow Shoe Club as well. Of H. W. Becket, Wise and Fisher have
written:

> Becket, who in 1882 was vice-president of the Montreal
> Snow Shoe Club, was the archtype of the nineteenth century
> Montreal sportsman. His father, John C. Becket, had come to
> Montreal from Scotland in 1832, and founded the city's print-
> ing industry. As well, the elder Becket operated a stationery
> and bookstore, was a long-time president of the St. Andrew's
> Society, the founder of the first Oddfellows Lodge in Montreal
> and a leading Presbyterian layman. From this overwhelmingly
> respectable past came Hugh Wylie Becket; also beyond
> reproach and an athlete as well.[70]

It was probably the presence of Scots in the Montreal Lacrosse
Club which obtained the use of the club ground for the International Caledonian Games there in 1871.[71] Thirty years later, it
was definitely the Scottish governor-general, the Earl of Minto,
who presented a silver cup for competition among the champion
teams of recognized senior lacrosse leagues in Canada.[72]

From its early beginnings as a white man's game to the first
game for the Minto Cup, the Scots were actively involved with
others in the development of a truly Canadian sport. In fact, during the expansion of the sport in Confederation Year, there was
probably a "Canadian" influence on sport in nineteenth-century
Britain, for J. Weir of the Montreal Lacrosse Club, in the spring
of 1867 "found himself in Glasgow, Scotland, and proceeded to
organize a lacrosse club."[73] And the *Illustrated London News,* 16
October 1875, announced that: "The late General Sir James
Lindsay expressed a great desire to see the game introduced into
our public schools."[74] His wish was fulfilled, although in
England lacrosse became particularly popular as a ladies' game.[75]

As stated, Duncan Bowie, who also toured Britain again with a
Canadian lacrosse team in 1883, was one of many Scots who
belonged to the Montreal Snow Shoe Club, of which H. W.
Becket wrote the *History* in 1882.[76] This was formed in 1840,
the pioneer of many subsequent clubs whose members enjoyed
what became a very popular sport in the nineteenth century.

These snow shoe clubs "were famed for fun and sociability," besides offering competition in snowshoe races from a hundred yards to several miles. Often their members would participate in long tramps over the countryside, sometimes in torch-lit processions by moonlight. People of all nationalities were snowshoers, including Indians who were skilful exponents of the art, and as in lacrosse, used their prowess for financial benefit.[77] The Scottish presence was consistent and prominent in the Montreal Snow Shoe Club in particular, and Bowie and his countrymen were often among the medal- and money-winners as well.[78] Scots obviously enlivened some of the social gatherings, too, when "McGregor gave the highland fling, Stewart, the sword dance, then followed the many songs with grand choruses." [79] Often parts of the route of a club outing read like a Scottish itinerary, as one member described, "headed usually by Angus Grant and his dog Munday, we would go west on Sherbrooke Street as far as the McGill College Grounds; . . . we would land on McTavish Street, then up past the reservoir to the stone fence at Ravenscrag then the residence of Sir Montagu Allan, . .. and across McKenna's Farm." As with lacrosse, many of the snowshoe clubs were also organized and named along ethnic lines, with names like Le Canadien, St. George, Emerald, and Huron.[80] It was in 1875 that a former member of the Montreal Snow Shoe Club resigned to form another club with a Scottish title:

> QUARTER MILE—open, dash,—prize, gold medal—was trial between R. Summerhayes of the "Montreal" and John Davey of the "Caledonia." Davey was a member of "ours" this season but resigned and formed the club dignified by the Scottish cognomen.[81]

Other snowshoe clubs that were also dignified by a "Scottish cognomen" were the Argyle, Gordon, and Royal Scots Snow Shoe Clubs.[82] Clubs such as the Alexandra, Aurora, and Dominion boasted such "notable Snowshoe Athletes" as Hartland MacDougall, D.R. McCord, C. Peers Davidson, and P.S. Ross.[83] And when the Scottish Curling Team visited Montreal in January 1903, they were entertained by "an old-fashioned snowshoe turnout,'' when three hundred trampers assembled outside their hotel:

> They had a piper to lead them and the sound of his pipes brought all the Scotsmen and many others on the scene, the hotel rotunda being virtually packed before the march-out took place.[84]

Ten years after the bagpipes had inspired the Zorra team to pull harder, they had obviously inspired others to tramp across the snow.

Like everyone else who lived in Canada, the Scots participated in other winter sports apart from snowshoeing, such as ice hockey and skating, although their most significant participation was in curling. But even ice hockey and skating owed something to Scottish influence in their development as popular sports. Shinty was one of the forerunners of ice hockey, a sport that was codified mainly at McGill University, and indoor curling rinks were often used as ice-hockey arenas and skating rinks.

The origin of ice hockey in Canada has been the subject of considerable debate among historians, and will not be settled here. R. Tait Mackenzie in his article ''Hockey in Eastern Canada,'' written in 1893, observed that there were two causes for the popularity and permanence of the game, the climate and the covered rinks. These were, of course, reasons for the favorable development of curling earlier. Mackenzie was also confident that:

> Hockey, as at present played, has been evolved from an old Scottish game, ''Shinty.'' It was first played in Canada at Montreal, by a club of McGill College students, one of whose number had played it in Glasgow. It was then played in an open air rink on the St. Lawrence, but for some years little progress was made.[85]

Shinty, or ''shinny,'' was played in various parts of Canada before Confederation. As they had done in Scotland, Highlanders in the County of Antigonish used their shinty sticks at traditional

Christmas and New Year social occasions.[86] Organized shinty games began in Kingston, Ontario, in 1839, on New Year's Day, and the following year a Camac Club was formed. In January 1843, a shinty match took place between Scotsmen born in the counties of Argyle and Ross, which lasted three hours.[87] The soldiers at British garrisons are said to have played the game at Kingston, also.[88] Day has reported that at Chatham: "The Scots made their presence felt during the winter months"; and in 1848, the sons of "Old Scotia" played several games of shinty on Christmas Day, "with great gusto," according to a report in the *Chatham Gleaner*.[89]

Other derivations for ice hockey in Canada have been suggested, ranging from "bandy," and "hurley," to "ricket."[90] But as Lindsay has pointed out: "Shinty was the most popular game, and it is most probable that games of 'hockey,' referred to during the pre-Confederation period were of this nature."[91] Orlick has studied the problem of when ice hockey properly emerged, and stated succinctly:

> The question is not when the games of field hockey, hoquet, hurley or shinny started, but rather, when and where did hurley or shinny develop into the game of Ice Hockey as we know it today? . . . we are not looking for the origin of "shinny" and if we were, we could trace it back to Scotland where it was played many centuries before it was played in Kingston.

Many authorities agree with Orlick's evidence, which suggests that: (1) the first game definitely called ice hockey was played in Montreal at the Victoria Skating Rink on 3 March 1875, in which two teams captained by J.G.A. Creighton and F. W. Torrance took part; and (2) that two McGill students, R. F. Smith and W. L. Murray, and an ex-McGill student, W. F. Robertson, subsequently rewrote the rules and invented modern ice hockey in 1879. Altogether Orlick details twenty-six "McGill contributions to the origin of Ice-Hockey" to support his thesis, which remains the most feasible explanation to date.[92] Roxborough has agreed that "no institution or club made a greater contribution to the origin and growth of ice-hockey than did the Montreal Students."[93]

One of the early "Gaels" teams of Queen's University. (National Photography Collection, Public Archives of Canada, C29648)

Considering the number of other ''firsts'' in Canadian sport at Montreal already noted, the birth of modern ice hockey there should not be wondered at; nor should the fact that Scots were among the eager participants in the sport. Apart from students who played at the universities, McGill, Queen's, and Toronto in particular, there were Scots in other hockey teams elsewhere. The first two hockey teams in Toronto, in fact, were the Caledonians and the Granites.[94] In 1893, Lord Stanley of Preston, the English governor-general, donated the Stanley Cup to be awarded to the ''champion hockey team in the Dominion of Canada.''[95] It was first won by a Montreal team which consisted of: T. Paton, goal; James Stewart, point; Allan Cameron, coverpoint; Alex Irving, Havilland Rovth, Archie Hodgson, J. Lowe, A Kingan and Billy Barlow, forwards.[96] It seems likely that there was a genuine Scot or two on this team; and perhaps this member of Osgoode Hall ice hockey team was Scottish too.

> J. F. Smellie, captain of the team, who has been playing the game since he wore short trowsers [sic] and a Scotch cap, is one of the most effective forwards playing in Toronto today. His strength, endurance and shooting powers are more than extraordinary.[97]

What was described as an ''extemporaneous team from Saskatchewan'' had four McPhees as members: ''Mary, Donald, Little and Big Angus,'' in the 1890s.[98] Further west, the first two hockey teams to be organized in Edmonton were the Thistles and the Shamrocks.[99] Around 1892, also, in Hamilton, Ontario, an ice-hockey club was organized under the Scottish name of the Thistle Hockey Club:

> It was organized late last season by Messrs. Rupert Watson and W. E. Boyd. These prime movers were handicapped at first by a lack of interest in the pastime and by the further fact that ''The Thistle Curling Rink,'' where the game is played, was designed simply for a curling rink.[100]

Although it is difficult to identify all the Scots who played ice hockey among the usual abundance of Scottish names in hockey

Another of the many teams in Canada that featured Scottish names and/or emblems: the famous "World Champions" Kenora Thistles Ice Hockey Team, (National Photography Collection, Public Archives of Canada, PA50700; courtesy of Canada's Sports Hall of Fame)

teams, and evaluate their influence exactly, it is certain that the existence of indoor curling rinks benefited the development of ice hockey in its early stages. Curling rinks were far from ideal for ice hockey, or even for skating, but at least they provided an area of *indoor* ice which could be used until hockey was sufficiently well established to obtain separate and more suitable facilities.

For example, not only did the Hamilton Thistle Hockey Club use the curling rink, but so did the Edmonton Thistles. The Edmonton Thistle rink was an outdoor structure built next to the covered curling rink, but many hockey games were played indoors.[101] The Caledonians and Granites of Toronto have already been mentioned as the first hockey clubs in that city, and the *Daily Mail* of 23 January 1888 showed how the Caledonian Curling Club's rink was involved:

> About two weeks ago the Toronto Athletic Club authorized Secretary Orr to make whatever arrangements were possible for the introduction of hockey to the citizens of Toronto, and as a direct result of his negotiations, the Caledonian Curling Club agreed to permit members of the athletic and lacrosse clubs to practice in their rink, and two very good practices have taken place on that excellent rink. The Caledonian rink having taken the initiative, the next step towards the goal of a public exhibition of this excellent winter game was the formation of Granite Hockey Club.

The first hockey match recorded at Chatham took place at the Covered Skating and Curling Rink on 24 January 1891; and two of the ''leaders in Chatham's ice hockey movement'' were Donald M. Christie and George F. H. Rispin.[102] This practice of using curling clubs' facilities for ice hockey became widespread. and Hedley reported in 1892 that curling rinks ''are now so much in request for the game of hockey on skates.''[103]

Of course, a few enclosed rinks were provided for skating only long before ice hockey became popular, the most notable being the Victoria Rink in Montreal, opened on Christmas Eve, 1862. Halifax, St. John, Hamilton, Quebec, and Toronto all had indoor skating facilities of this type before Confederation, although the Toronto Skating Rink was also under the management of the Toronto Curling Club.[104] As early as 1875, hockey enthusiasts were reported using skating and curling rinks in Montreal.[105] Cox has stated, in fact, that quite a few curling clubs solved the problem of mortage payments on their buildings by providing separate facilities for skating.[106] The rink at Galt, for example, had two sheets of ice for curling, 80 feet by 156 feet, on either side of a skating area, which was 136 feet by 40 feet.[107] When Kerr and his party visited Ottawa in 1903, they were greatly impressed by a hockey match they watched between Ottawa and Montreal, begun by his Excellency Lord Minto. Kerr mentioned the popularity of the game throughout the Dominion at that time, stating that "even curling alongside of it does not come in for such prominent notice in the local newspaper."[108] The affinity of curling clubs and ice-hockey teams was mentioned also by Eskenazi in his book on hockey, with a different Scottish connotation:

> For want of a better name, the places where ice hockey games were staged were called "rinks." The word "rink" actually is Scottish and means a "course." Over the years it came to refer specifically to a place where curling competition was staged. Since curling was played on ice, in confined area, the British-oriented Canadians started to call ice hockey sites rinks, and the name has remained.[109]

As we have seen, "the British-oriented Canadians" actually played early indoor ice hockey in the rinks of curling clubs, a more likely explanation of why the term "rink" came to be applied to ice-hockey arenas.

However, the Canadian climate was a disadvantage to those sporting enthusiasts of British stock in Canada who wished to play football in their adopted land. In Britain, it was possible to play soccer and rugby throughout the winter for most seasons, but in the Dominion it was a case of playing again when the snow departed in the spring of the following year, and before the summer sports began. But in the end this did not deter them from pursuing a traditional sport here. As noted in chapter 2, forms of football were popular in the British Isles for centuries before 1800, until the two distinct forms of soccer and rugby emerged in the nineteenth century. It is not known when the first game of football, of whatever type, was played in Canada, but Britons established both soccer and rugby here also.

Since all people of British descent pioneered football, Roxborough wisely excluded soccer or rugby from his chapters pertaining directly to English and Scottish influence, in his book on nineteenth-century Canadian sport.[110] The Scots were significantly involved with other Britons, and their enthusiasm for these games in Canada was compatible with their endeavors in the homeland, remembering that it was a Scotsman who established the English Football League and the rugby tradition in Scottish schools, and was responsible for the success of the Scottish soccer and rugby teams in international matches.

An early game of football was recorded during the Christmas festivities at York Factory in 1822, when "several vigorously contested matches were played" by the men of the Hudson's Bay Company. Considering the large number of Scots known to be in this company's employ, it is likely some took part, just as the "Mr. McTavish" who offered a prize of a two-gallon keg of gin was probably a Scot. In subsequent years, other forms of football were recorded at bees, fairs, military garrisons, and various societies' picnics.[111] According to McDougall, who called soccer "the national game of the North West,"[112] Hudson's Bay Company forts were the scenes of early soccer games also. The first reference was in 1862, stating: "The next day we had dog-races, and foot-races, and football, and the fun was fast and furious."[113] Football was also widely featured at Caledonian Games before Confederation. For example, "a Game of Football" was included in the Games of the St. Andrew's Society of Ottawa, Ontario, in 1864, and at the annual picnic of the Caledonian Benevolent Society in Victoria, British Columbia, in 1865.[114] It was in the latter year, also, that yet another "first" was recorded for Montreal, when the Montreal Football Club was formed.[115] It was after Confederation, however, that reference to football became more frequent, and three distinct forms emerged: soccer, rugby, and what is now known as Canadian football, which was a derivation from rugby and a product of American influence. An international intercollegiate football match took place in 1874 between McGill University and Harvard at Cambridge, Massachusetts, played under the American rules (a form of Association Football). (The second game between the two universities was the more famous rugby encounter).[116]

Dennis Signy, in his *Pictorial History of Soccer*, declares, without further elaboration, that "Scottish immigrants introduced football to Canada in 1880, the year the Western Association was formed, but little real progress was made until the early

1950's.''[117] Canadian football eventually surpassed both British football games in popularity during the next century, and in this respect dwarfed any comparative ''progress'' of soccer and rugby. Nevertheless, both were popular games throughout the Dominion in the nineteenth century, and have survived to the present day. Scots were among those who introduced, pioneered, promoted, and preserved them.

Signy's brief statement is borne out to the extent that ''in the early 1880's western Ontario was a soccer hotbed,''[118] and it was indeed played in many of the numerous Scottish townships in that area. It was popular in the Border cities of Ontario, also, whose first opposition was a team of Scottish stone masons from Detroit:

> These Scots were a bit too much to handle: they returned to their homeland each winter to play professional football and obviously outclassed the scrub team of local residents.[119]

But it was played by other nationalities besides the Scotch, and it is difficult to be categorical about who introduced the game to Ontario. Certainly football of both types was popular before 1880, as the following request in the Toronto *Globe*, 28 October 1879, indicated:

> *Football*—Notice to Correspondents—Secretaries of football Clubs, and others who send us intelligence of the game, will confer a favour by stating in all cases whether matches are played according to Association or Rugby Union Rules. In the case of newly organized clubs and challenge matches this is particularly desirable.

A move had been made at the University of Toronto in 1876 to form a soccer club, also, under the rules of the Scottish Football Association, which had been formed in Scotland in 1873. This was organized three years later when James Chisholm became its first president. The sports historian of the University, T. A. Reed, recalled an important event in 1880:

> A great impetus was given to Association Football by the formation of the Western Football Association. The influence

both direct and indirect, of that organization upon football in Canada in general, and our University in particular, can hardly be over-estimated.

The University of Toronto Soccer Club subsequently enjoyed a keen rivalry with Knox College, in which many Scottish players were involved. A Central Football Association was formed sometime before 1884, and this association first played against the Western Association in 1886, for a trophy known as "the Caledonian Cup," which became the premier soccer prize in subsequent years.[120] The donor or donors of this trophy have not been discovered, but its name adds more substance to Signy's assertion of Scottish influence. So does the fact that the members of the Toronto Scots soccer team were described as "the Champions of Canada" in the *Globe*, 20 August 1890, when playing against the Marlboros for gold medals offered by the Sons of Scotland Society.

Scots were among other "old countrymen" who were playing soccer in Winnipeg in the 1870s, and later in Alberta[121] and British Columbia. By 1890, Victoria had no less than eight soccer clubs, two of which were the United Scots and the Thistles.[122] The sport was also stimulated by the presentation of medals for provincial championships donated in 1890 by the St. Andrew's and Caledonian Society.[123] Bull reported many Scots playing soccer in his favorite Peel County, including another Thistle team in Caledon East, organized about 1888. Among its members were: Donald McKay, Neil McDevitt, Thomas McDevitt, Joseph McDevitt, John Gray, Archie McQuarrie, W. H. McKinnon, Archie McKinnon, Duncan Baxter, Dr. Allan J. McKinnon, Richard Baxter, Robert Elliott, Alexander McFarlane, Robert McFarlane, and Charles Lamont.[124] It was in 1888, too, that a Canadian Soccer Team, which included players from the University of Toronto and was managed by Scot David Forsyth (sometimes known as the "Daddy" of Canadian soccer), successfully toured England and Scotland.[125] Another similar tour was made from August 1891 to January 1892, when a combined American and Canadian team played 58 games. Much of the subsequent praise upon the team's return was reserved for one of the Scottish players:

> Munro played outside left all the time he was with us. He plays the waiting game and centres very accurately. The fact that he played for Scotland versus England in 1888 speaks for itself.[126]

The England versus Scotland soccer rivalry was carried on in Canada, too;[127] but it was the combined influence of enthusiasts from both countries which was responsible for the emergence and progress of the game in the Dominion. Looking ahead at that progress in this century, it is interesting to note that the administrator who probably did ''more than any man in Canada to raise the standard of Canadian soccer and promote it abroad'' was George Anderson, who was born in Aberdeen in 1890 and emigrated to Canada at the age of eighteen; and that the person named in 1950 as ''Canada's outstanding soccer player of the half-century'' was another Scot, from Edinburgh, by the name of David Turner.[128]

English and Scottish influences were mainly responsible for the development of rugby in Canada, also. In a letter to the editor of the Toronto *Globe* in 1875, R. D. McGibbon remarked that rugby had been played at McGill University for ''the last ten or twelve years.''[129] It had been played on an interfaculty basis in 1873. The versatile Duncan E. Bowie, obviously an all-round athlete of distinction, was a member of the McGill team which played against Harvard University in 1874, the second game of which series ''was the first game of Rugby ever played in the United States.''[130] Rugby Union rules were also introduced at the University of Toronto in 1877 by J. H. Mayne Campbell, who had played the game at Loretto School, near Edinburgh, in Scotland, and was the first captain of the university team. (It will be remembered from chapter 2 that many Scottish schools, such as Edinburgh Academy, Fettes, Merchiston, and Loretto, had played rugby matches in the 1860s.) Campbell's brother, Graham, who was also educated at Loretto, was captain in 1881.

His younger brother, Archibald H. Campbell, succeeded him in 1882.[131] Before 1880, rugby football was also played at Upper Canada College, Trinity, and Queen's, and interuniversity games had taken place.[132] These three educational foundations, as well as McGill and Toronto, were all founded by Scotsmen, and there can be no doubt that Scots were among others who promoted rugby in these institutions. There were also no doubt some Scottish members in various rugby clubs in the 1880s and 1890s reported from Ontario and Quebec, such as in Hamilton, London, Ottawa, Kingston, Peterborough, Sarnia, Brampton, Galt, Dundas, and elsewhere.[133]

The Winnipeg Football Club was formed by a group of old countrymen in 1879, which used to play on a vacant lot at the corner of Broadway and Hargrave streets.[134] Rugby was developed in subsequent years, and another Campbell was among the Scots who contributed:

> Among the pioneers of Rugby were the following men. J. A. Campbell, a splendid player who learned the game in Scotland and who became the first president of the Manitoba Rugby Football Union, in 1892, Lieutenant-Colonel H.W.A. Chambre, P. A. Macdonald, Keith Blanchard, H. Kyall, E.W.H. Armstrong, H. G. Wilson, W. Clark, G. Norquay, A.R.D. Paterson and B. P. Dewar.[135]

Other rugby-playing Scots in Manitoba had learned the game in Scotland, too, such as at least two members of the Eastern Assiniboine team which defeated Winnipeg in 1890, whom the *Manitoba Free Press* described in the following terms: "Back—Bellhouse, Fettes, Scotland, good collar and kick . . . Half—H. Moore, Loretto, beautiful tackle and very quick." But the cosmopolitan nature of these early teams is revealed by the description of another member of the same team: "Forwards—Van Millingen, Constantinople, the only Turkish trained forward in the country."[136] Further west, it is difficult to believe that there were not some Scots in the following Victoria rugby team, of British Columbia, which played against fifteen men from Her Majesty's Fleet at Esquimault, as early as 1877: J. J. Alexander, A. Maxwell, R. McKenzie, J. C. Keith, J. W. Finlayson, W. Tolmie, Rev. H. H. Mogg, C. R. Brodie, J. L. Raymur, S. Wooton, R. Ward, W. B. McKenzie, Jas. Tolmie, and A. W. Jones.[137]

Similar civilian versus military games occurred in the East Coast. A Halifax Football Club was formed in 1870, which subsequently played rugby games against sides organized by the military garrison officers and members of visiting warships. In fact, "the garrison troops contributed in no small way to the popularity of rugby football."[138] Again, it was Merchiston School in Scotland where one Scottish maritime rugby player, "Lieutenant Fraser," learned the game.[139] Of course, the Maritimes was an area of strong Scottish settlement (which was reflected in subsequent rugby developments), as indeed was Merchiston School.

The first sports to be played in New Glasgow were cricket, football (soccer), and shinty. Rugby football was introduced in 1884, when George G. Patterson, who had played rugby at Dalhousie University, and was appointed principal of New Glasgow High School, formed a boys' team there. A senior side soon followed, and one at Pictou as well:

> Some of the New Glasgow players in these early years were: R. McColl, J. Fraser, W. Rice, E. McLeod, W. S. Thompson, H. Townsend, A. D. McRae, D. H. McKenzie, Fraser, H. Graham, J. Smith Williams, Gillian, Stewart and E. McKay. Pictou was represented by: Mellish, Johnston, G. G. Paterson, W. K. Fraser, F. Carroll, Creighton, Pyke, Stewart, F. Fraser, Davis, Logan, Gammell, J. C. McMillan, Primrose and Fulton.

A New Glasgow Amateur Athletic Association was formed in 1888, when its first president was Hector R. Sutherland and the secretary was A. P. Douglas. Two years later it was shown that there was a Scottish substance behind this plethora of Scottish names, when a Maritime Provinces Rugby Football Union was formed by representatives from Dalhousie, King's College, Acadia College, New Glasgow, the Wanderers, and the West Riding Regiment (for whom Lieutenant Fraser played). This new body adopted the constitution and playing rules of the *Scottish* Rugby Union. The link was emphasized a year later when a dispute arose regarding a match between Dalhousie and the Wanderers, in which the latter had used sixteen players, and a cablegram was sent to Scotland for a ruling.

The cable was sent by a Halifax barrister, W. A. Henry, Jr., and outstanding all-round athlete and member of the Wanderers, "the most prominent of the sporting clubs in Halifax." Henry had also received some education at Merchiston School in Scotland, to which institution the cable was actually sent:

Halifax, Nov. 18.

Rogerson, Merchiston Castle, Edinburgh:

Game of football was two to one; next day, winners discovered their team numbered sixteen. They immediately notify losers, offering to replay match, but the losers decline, claiming match. Get prompt opinion of Scottish Football Union and wire answer.

Henry.

The reply from Rogerson was brief and to the point: "Cannot claim match; simply null," and after subsequent meetings both clubs decided the disputed game should be held over until next year. Scots were active in rugby throughout the Maritimes area for the remainder of the nineteenth century, and in the next, as demonstrated by a newly formed team in Cape Breton in 1906. This was the Caledonia Rugby Football Club of Glace Bay, which consisted of the following members: "Red" Jack Wilson, Dan Willis Ferguson, Jim Wadden, Ewen Hillier, Neil Patterson, Wilson McLean, Pius McNeil, Thomas Meeking, John Hector Nolan, "Dabbie" McVicar, Hugh McIntyre, Angus McMillan, Alex McKay, Joseph McNeil, Alex McEachern and William McKenzie.[140] As usual, and as already stated, such names appeared frequently and with monotonous regularity wherever rugby football, or soccer was played in Canada.

At this point, the names of educational institutions mentioned in this chapter can be recalled: Dalhousie, King's College, McGill, Queen's, Toronto, Trinity, and Upper Canada College.

Each of these was founded by Scotsmen, three of them by Bishop John Strachan. As Campbell has noted:

> In all grades of our educational development from the University to the common school, the personality and influence of the Scotsmen have been prominent. It is a significant fact in our intellectual history, and one remarkable in the history of any young country, that all our leading universities, with scarcely one exception, and our other higher institutions of learning, have been from the first established and controlled by Scotsmen. This fact, more than any other, shows to how great an extent Canada has been a New Scotland in character and ideal."[141]

To the list of Scottish educational endowments can also be included McMaster University, St. Francis Xavier College, Pictou Academy, Toronto Grammar School, and several others.[142] Obviously these institutions were all a reflection of the traditional Scottish respect for learning and were established for educational purposes. But the later sporting activities of the students and staff from these institutions also became a paramount feature in the development of sport in nineteenth-century Canada.[143] Roxborough has noted this fact in a special chapter entitled "From Halls of Learning," stating particularly that "the major contributions to the national sports scene came from the Big Three—McGill University, The University of Toronto and Queen's University."[144]

By directly catering to educational instincts through their provision of the largest number of the most important educational institutions in Canada in the nineteenth century, the Scots indirectly also provided for the sporting instincts of students and others in years to come. This Scottish academic base became the foundation of Canadian intercollegiate sport. The cult of nineteenth-century athleticism in the British Isles emerged in the English public schools and universities, from where it spread to other parts of the world.[145] It may fairly be said that "muscular Christianity" was able to thrive in Canada, largely because the Scots had earlier provided the widespread institutions necessary to receive and preach its gospel. However, many of the disciples who preached it here in the schools and universities, of course, were "Englishmen steeped in the traditional English love of sports."[146] This academic aspect is an area of Canadian sports history which needs more research; and one would not wish to exaggerate or underestimate either English or Scottish influence (or indeed any other) in this regard. But given the acknowledged preponderance of Scottish influence in Canadian educational history, perhaps it is forgivable to recall the words of this Loretto song, and to easily imagine it being lustily sung by exiled alumni, when considering the import of muscular Christian sentiments into the Dominion:

> On cricket or on football fields,
> Begins our schoolboy life,
> We fill our years with health and strength,
> For life's long earnest strife.
> Oh time to teach—oh time to prove,
> Each lesson stern and true,
> And come down hard on the fastest ball,
> Time's changing hand shall bowl to you.[147]

Upper Canada College was the first educational institution in Canada where the sport of cricket was played, the development of which has been rightly attributed to English influence.[148] Too much should not therefore be claimed for the Scots in this regard, except to remember that cricket has been played in Scotland for over two hundred years (albeit imported from England), so it was natural that they should play the game in Canada as well. In addition to the brief historical information on cricket in Scotland given in chapter 2, Bull informs us that a double-wicket game, similar to cricket, was played in the counties of Angus and Lothian in Scotland, as early as 1700. Be that as it may, he described some English origins as well, and goes on to provide details of some early cricket in Canada with the usual liberal supply of Scottish names among the participants, including an Oakville eleven with four Chisholms.[149] There were many St. George's Cricket Clubs in Canada, but a few St. Andrew's Cricket Clubs, also.[150] Halifax had a Thistles Cricket Club by 1857, and Hamilton had a Caledonian Cricket Club in the early 1860s.[151] The Scarborough Cricket Club of Toronto was organized before 1860, with Scottish quoits champion Alexander Muir as its first secretary-treasurer, and other Scots were involved too.[152] It is likely that Governor Mactavish, president of the North West Cricket Club, formed in the Scottish settlement of Red River on 24 September 1864, was a Scot, as well as some team members.[153]

Merchiston School in Scotland has previously been mentioned in connection with rugby, yet cricket was obviously played there as well in the second half of the nineteenth century, as Lindsey provides the the following information:

> George W. Jones had just returned from Merchiston College in Scotland, where he had been captain of the eleven, and when he had been chosen captain of the St. John Club took the men in hand. A reference to the records of the Canadian eleven in England will show what a fine bat this gentleman is, and he at all times proved a tower of strength to his own eleven. Under his management for five years the club flourished, frequent visits being interchanged with Fredericton, Moncton and Halifax, when St. John always held its own. The men who developed, about this time, were Fred C. Jones, also trained at Merchiston, H. Harvey . . ., W. J. Starr . . ., J. Thomas . . ., A. McIntyre, Gordon McLeod, Hansard, S. Smith, and Claude S. Skinner.[154]

The other ex-Merchiston pupil, W. A. Henry, Jr., in Halifax, who sent the cablegram to the Scottish Football Union, was also an international cricketer of renown.[155]

As Lindsay has pointed out: "The impetus given by the military regiments to the game of cricket cannot be too strongly emphasized . . . [it] was most certainly *the* game of the period," i.e., from 1807 to 1867.[156] It was mainly the English officers who were responsible for promoting the game to this prominence, but some Scottish military men were involved, such as the men of the Scots Fusilier Guards who played against the Victoria Rifles (Volunteers) in 1863. This cricket match was played in heavy rain which caused the fielders to stand ankle deep in water.[157] Scottish names appear regularly in all types of cricket matches during the nineteenth century,[158] although not to the same extent as they do in soccer or rugby. But in the same way that some Englishmen took part in those sports attributable to Scottish influence, and so added their measure to the sports' popularity, so the Scots joined with Englishmen and others in the sport of cricket.

Naturally, *all* kinds of British names, Scots included, can be found in all sorts of other sports in nineteenth-century Canada. Thomas L. Grahame wrote a eulogy of sport of British Columbia nearly two years before the century ended, in which he stated:

> The people here are mainly of that robust stock which has made the name British synonymous with vigour of body and mind. They have all the well-known British proclivities towards the bold and manly games and pastimes which have always distinguished the race, and which in Canada find an even finer field for their exercise than the English meadows, the Scottish dales, the Irish moors, or the Welsh llans afforded. If there is any branch of manly sport that is not followed by the youth of British Columbia, I shall be much surprised to learn the fact.[159]

Of course, such stock was not confined to British Columbia, and the sports-loving British provided the dominant influence on sport throughout the country in the nineteenth century. As we have seen, within this British tradition, the Scots were significantly characterized by their love of sports—some their own, some generally British or specifically English, and others indigenous to North America. Therefore, it is difficult to find ''any branch of manly sport'' in which Scots did not take part.

It is not surprising to find them enthusiastically playing American baseball, along with other nationalities in Canada who took up the game.[160] They were among the exponents of tennis in the new Dominion, also.[161] Lawn bowling is a sport of great antiquity and debatable origin, which was played in Britain for centuries. Q. D. McCulloch, writing in *Athletic Life* in 1895, confidently asserted:

> It is probably well known that the game, like curling, is of

Scotch origin, and "There's mony a gude sport, mon, that comes fra the land o' lakes.''* Still it was played too in England at a very early date, and the people were passionately fond of the game.

The asterisk was inserted by the editor who felt obliged to add a footnote, stating: "We are told this is an error. Tradition says the game is of English origin—Ed."[162] Both England and Scotland had hundreds of bowling clubs, with thousands of members, by the time of McCulloch's article, but the codification of the present game is generally credited to Scotland.[163] In any case, Scots as well as English pioneered the game in Canada, and a Hamilton Thistle Lawn Bowling Club was formed in 1852. [164] Mention has been made of a St. Andrew's Curling and Bowling Association of Montreal; and the Toronto Lawn Bowling Club, reported in 1876, was an off shoot of the Toronto Curling Club.[165] (Kerr later noticed, in fact, that "in a great many cases a bowling green is attached" to a curling club's facilities during his tour.)[166] It seems that, besides quoits, lawn bowling was another popular summer game for curlers. Day informs us that "it took several score of years for Canadian curlers to transform the 'roarin' game' into a summer pastime, but by the late 1880s lawn bowling was popular in many Ontario regions."[167] Many clubs for the sport were formed in Ontario, including a Toronto Granite Club, and Ontario Lawn Bowling Association was formed in 1890.[168] McCulloch states that a past president of this Association brought out some bowls from Glasgow, Scotland, about 1885.[169] In 1892, a trophy for lawn bowling was presented by Hiram Walker and Sons for Annual Competition between clubs, and this became the main trophy in the sport.[170]

Another game which was popular in parts of nineteenth-century Canada, "but especially so in those areas where Scottish and English settlers predominated," was checkers (or draughts). However, the Scots seem to have been predominant:

The outstanding draughts player of his times was James Wylie, the Scottish "Herd Laddie," who decided that his playing was more interesting and profitable than his weaving. In

1844 he competed against Anderson of Carluke and in a series of games lasting eight days won 65. In 1873 he toured America and played eleven thousand games, winning all but fifty. In 1881 Wylie made another tour and reaped a monetary harvest when he played nearly twenty thousand games and charged his adversaries twenty-five cents a game.[171]

One of Wylie's defeated opponents later in 1883 was James Labadie of Chatham, who nevertheless "withstood all challenges for the Canadian title during the 1880's"[172] John Muir and his talented son, Alexander Muir, who excelled in so many sports, were "two of the better players of the 1860's" in Scarborough, along with many other Scots. In fact, Boyle maintains that "there is no field of amusement in which her sons have taken a higher place than in the realm of checkers." Scarborough enjoyed another keen rivalry here with Toronto. Adam Core, a native of Biggar in Scotland, was referred to as "the father of checker-playing" in Scarborough. William Fleming was born there of Scottish parents, and became the champion of Canada in 1868, until he retired undefeated twenty-two years later.[173]

By the beginning of the twentieth century, the inhabitants of Canada had a miscellany of sports available to them. In a chapter entitled "Hotbeds of Sport," Roxborough has indicated how different sports were pursued in small townships, similar to Scarborough, throughout the Dominion during the nineteenth century, as well as in the larger centers, such as Halifax, Montreal, and Toronto. The term "Canadian" could be applied more accurately and liberally as the years multiplied after Confederation in 1867. As the Dominion had been shaped by many forces, so Canadian sport when it emerged was an amalgam of American, British, French, Indian, and other influences.[174] Such diverse contributions ensured a rich sporting heritage of considerable merit. It may be symbolized, in fact, by the description of a new Canadian yacht, in 1892, named the *Zelma*. She was designed by William Fife, Jr., of Fairlie, Scotland; shipped in cases to Toronto; and assembled by one of the best yacht builders in America. Her frames were of English oak, and her canvas from Gosport in England. The main fittings and rigging were imported from

Scotland. Below the water line, the planking was of Georgia pine, but the spars were "of Canadian spruce, and very heavy." Because of her built-in quality, taken from so many sources, the yacht was expected to do well in future competition.[175] The same hope could be expressed for Canadian sport at the end of the nineteenth century, and for the same reasons.

The quality and quantity of the Scottish contribution within the British influence has been a significant ingredient in the development of sport in nineteenth-century Canada. Before leaving it, another final and unique individual Scottish contribution may be noted. It was made by one of the many Scottish giants in Canadian history, Sandford Fleming, a contemporary of Macdonald, Stephen, Strathcona, and others. He was born in Kirkcaldy, Fife, Scotland, in 1827, and came to Canada in 1845. He later became chief engineer of the government-owned Intercolonial Railway, and from 1871 to 1880 he was Engineer-in-Chief of the CPR. In 1880 he was elected chancellor of Queen's University; in 1888 he was made president of the Royal Society of Canada; and in 1897, he was promoted from Companion to be Knight Commander of the Order of St. Michael and St. George. Many other honors were also bestowed on Fleming, but he is probably best remembered as the man who devised a workable system of standard time.[176]

The highest mountain in the British Isles is Ben Nevis in the Scottish Highlands, which is 4,406 feet above sea level. One can therefore imagine the thoughts of the Scottish explorers, fur traders, missionaries, and CPR men who first viewed the towering mountains of the Canadian Rockies, with peaks several thousand feet higher than any in the Scottish Highlands. Fleming was certainly affected in 1883 when he was surveying there for the CPR in the company of his son Frank, George Grant, and Albert Rogers, stating: "I do not think that I can ever forget the sight as I then gazed upon it." At a summit of about 4,300 feet, surrounded by higher peaks, Fleming "proposed that a Canadian alpine club be organized on the spot." He also proposed a game of leapfrog, "an act of Olympic worship to the deities in the heart of the Selkirks!"[177] This spontaneous club actually survived, and the first issue of the *Canadian Alpine Journal*, in 1907, honored Fleming as the founder of the sport in Canada. Again, among the authors of this first issue were Scottish names in plenty, i.e., John D. Patterson, Rev. S. H. Gray, P. D. McTavish, Rev. A. M. Gordon, Rev. Alex. Dunn, A. O. Macrae, and the well-known Rev. C. W. Gordon, alias "Ralph Connor." In it, too, Fleming recollected the founding of the Canadian Alpine Club in his own words:

> As we view the landscape we feel as if some memorial should be preserved of our visit here, and we organize a Canadian Alpine Club. The writer, as a grandfather, is appointed interim president, Dr. Grant, Secretary, and my son, S. H. Fleming, treasurer. A meeting is held, and we turn to one of the springs rippling down to the Illecillewaet and drink success to the organization.

Berton has noted that almost every member of the original CPR syndicate was a Scot, and as Fleming had also been so closely involved with this great enterprise, it is not surprising that he referred to it at the conclusion of his article:

> The passage of the first railway train from Ocean to Ocean must, I think, be recognised as an important epoch in Canadian mountaineering. Before the existence of the railway, the Rockies could only be approached by toilsome journeys occupying months or more than months. Now all is changed, and our mountain region, a rich heritage, is made accessible to the world, and many persons may now enjoy the privilege of participating in the healthful and noble sport of the Alpine Club of Canada.[178]

Of course, mountaineering was only one sport affected by the CPR. As Jobling has noted:

> The Canadian Pacific Railway did much to promote many sports. . . . the advancements made in transportation facilitated sporting activity between individuals and teams on a village, town, city, regional, provincial, national and international basis.[179]

Partly because of Fleming himself, and other Scots who lived in Canada before he wrote, many people were able to ''enjoy the privilege of participating'' in numerous sports during the nineteenth century. Whether they were tossing quoits, pulling ropes, skating in a hockey game or running in a lacrosse match, kicking a football, using a cricket bat, playing checkers or lawn bowls, snowshoeing, or leapfrogging in the mountains, the Scots and their descendants were usually notably involved.

Notes

1. David Webster, *Scottish Highland Games* (Glasgow: William Collins Sons and Co., 1959), p. 84.

2. Henry Roxborough, *One Hundred—Not Out: The Story of Nineteenth-Century Canadian Sport* (Toronto: Ryerson Press, 1966), pp. 48–57; 99–111.

3. Ibid., p. 108.

4. *Montreal Gazette*, 4 September 1856. Quoits was also scheduled in the program for the Beauharnois Games a few days later, but did not take place because of inclement weather (Ibid., 16 September 1856).

5. *Ottawa Citizen*, 21 June 1867.

6. *Montreal Gazette*, 3 July 1871.

7. *Canadian Illustrated News*, 28 August 1875.

8. Wm. Perkins Bull, *From Rattlesnake Hunt to Hockey: The History of Sports in Canada and of the Sportsmen of Peel, 1798 to 1934* (Toronto: George J. McLeod, 1934), p. 248.

9. David Boyle, ed., *The Township of Scarboro, 1796–1896* (Toronto: William Briggs, 1896), p. 250.

10. *Kingston Chronicle and Gazette*, 21 August 1839.

11. Boyle, *Township of Scarboro*, p. 251.

12. Peter Leslie Lindsay, ''A History of Sport in Canada, 1807–1867'' (Ph.D. diss., University of Alberta, 1969), p. 133; *Montreal Gazette*, 1 October 1841.

13. Boyle, *Township of Scarboro*, p. 251.

14. Globe, 9 September 1859; Roxborough, *One Hundred—Not Out*, p. 175.

15. *Montreal Gazette*, 14 September 1841.

16. Ibid., 30 August 1844.

17. Lindsay, ''Sport in Canada, 1807–1867,'' p. 134; *Montreal Gazette*, 10 September 1846.

18. Boyle, *Township of Scarboro*, pp. 248–50.

19. Lindsay, ''Sport in Canada, 1807–1867,'' p. 135.

20. Ibid., p. 134.

21. *Montreal Gazette*, 19 August 1852.

22. Ibid., 25 July 1853.

23. Ibid., 15 November 1848; Roxborough, *One Hundred—Not Out*, p. 108.

24. *Montreal Gazette*, 19 June 1856.

25. Boyle, *Township of Scarboro*, p. 250.

26. Phylis R. Blakeley, *Glimpses of Halifax, 1867–1900* (Halifax, N.S.: The Public Archives of Nova Scotia, 1949), p. 150; Lindsay, "Sport in Canada, 1807–1867," p. 136; John Quinpool, *First Things in Acadia* (Halifax: First Things Publishers, 1936), p. 72; *Times* (Hamilton), 27 June 1859, 5 July 1859.

27. *Globe*, 25 August 1859.

28. *Montreal Gazette*, 11 August 1862.

29. *Morning Chronicle* (Quebec), 27 October 1863, 30 October, 1863.

30. Blakeley, *Glimpses of Halifax*, p. 150.

31. *Daily Colonist* (Victoria), 14 June 1860.

32. Ibid., 8 May 1865.

33. Roxborough, *One Hundred—Not Out*, p. 108.

34. Boyle, *Township of Scarboro*, p. 251.

35. Robert Douglas Day, "Impulse to Addiction: A Narrative History of Sport in Chatham, Ontario: 1790–1895" (M.A. thesis, University of Western Ontario, 1977), p. 366. Lindsay, "Sport in Canada, 1807–1867," p. 135, states: "Therefore, although quoiting received very meagre press coverage, it is not presumptuous to assume that other curling centres has established quoit clubs as well."

36. Bull, *Sportsmen of Peel*, pp. 248–51.

37. Foster Rhea Dulles, *A History of Recreation: America Learns to Play* (New York: Appleton-Century-Crofts, 1965), p. 73.

38. Roxborough, *One Hundred—Not Out*, p. 108. See also the account of the "Toronto Sons of Scotland" tug-of-war team at the Guelph Highland Gathering, in the *Globe*, 19 August 1890.

39. Webster, *Highland Games*, pp. 84–85.

40. Henry Roxborough, *Great Days in Canadian Sport* (Toronto: Ryerson Press, 1957), p. 29; hereafter referred to as *Great Days*.

41. Roxborough, *One Hundred—Not Out*, p. 108. Those police meets were similar to the Caledonian Games, also, and the same author states: "weight throwers stood behind a caber that had been placed on the ground as a measuring line, and tossed the sixteen-pound hammer and hurled the heavy stone without any run-up or turns. Right from the inception of police games, the big event was the tug-of-war." (Ibid., pp. 171–72). See also the long account of a tug-of-war contest at the eighth annual games of the Police Amateur Athletic Association in Toronto, for a $60 prize, in the *Globe*, 28 August 1890.

42. Bull, *Sportsmen of Peel*, p. 155.

43. Roxborough, *Great Days*, pp. 27–36.

44. Bull, *Sportsmen of Peel*, p. 33.

45. Roxborough, *Great Days*, pp. 27–28.

46. *Globe*, 26 August 1890; Roxborough, *One Hundred—Not Out*, p. 187.

47. Roxborough, *Great Days*, p. 33.

48. *Globe*, 11 October 1890; Roxborough, *One Hundred—Not Out*, p. 188.

49. Roxborough, *One Hundred—Not Out*, p. 188.

50. Roxborough, *Great Days*, p. 35.

51. Roxborough, *One Hundred—Not Out*, p. 189.

52. This is the title of the nineteenth chapter in Roxborough, *One Hundred—Not Out*, pp. 183–92, in which four pages are devoted to the Zorra tug-of-war team.

53. Fred Eugene Leonard and George B. Affleck, *The History of Physical Education* (Philadelphia: Lea and Febiger, 1947), p. 400.

54. Lindsay, "Sport in Canada, 1807–1867," pp. 114–30. See also: George T. Vellathottam, "A History of Lacrosse in Canada" (M.A. thesis, University of Alberta, 1968).

55. Leonard and Affleck, *Physical Education*, p. 401.

56. *Montreal Gazette*, 29 August 1844.

57. Ibid., 30 August 1844.

58. Ibid., 16 September 1856.

59. Alexander M. Weyand and Milton R. Roberts, *The Lacrosse Story* (Baltimore, Md.: H. and A. Herman, 1965), p. 15.

60. Nancy Howell and Maxwell L. Howell, *Sports and Games in Canadian Life, 1700 to the Present* (Toronto: Macmillan of Canada, 1969), p. 55.

61. See Gerald Redmond, *Sport and Ethnic Groups in Canada* (Ottawa: CAHPER Sociology of Sport Monograph Series, 1978).

62. See chapter 8, entitled "Fighter to Preacher," in Roxborough, *Great Days*, pp. 67–75.

63. Allan Elton Cox, "A History of Sports in Canada, 1868 to 1900" (Ph.D. diss., University of Alberta, 1969), p. 138; Weyand and Roberts, *Lacrosse Story*, p. 30.

64. Cox, "Sports in Canada, 1868 to 1900," p. 138; Roxborough, *One Hundred—Not Out*, p. 7.

65. B. W. Collinson and J. K. Munro, "Lacrosse in Canada," *Canadian Magazine*, September 1902, p. 419.

66. H. H. Allingham, "Lacrosse in the Maritime Provinces," *Dominion Illustrated Monthly*, May 1892, p. 225. See the references to G. McLeod, C. H. McLean, A. B. Cameron, J. R. McFarlane, C. McNutt, R. Wallace, W. E. McLellan, W. McKay, H. W. Mackintosh, and D. Patterson, among others.

67. Collinson and Munro, "Lacrosse in Canada," pp. 410–26; W. Cruikshank, "The Game of La Crosse," *Illustrated London News*, 16 October 1875; Ross Mackenzie, "Lacrosse," *Outing*, October 1892, pp. 76–80.

68. Roxborough, *One Hundred—Not Out*, p. 46.

69. Weyand and Roberts, *Lacrosse Story*, pp. 378–79.

70. S. F. Wise and Douglas Fisher, *Canada's Sporting Heroes: Their Lives and Times* (Don Mills, Ontario: General Publishing Co., 1974), p. 16.

71. *Canadian Illustrated News*, 30 August 1879.

72. Weyand and Roberts, *Lacrosse Story*, p. 45.

73. Ibid., p. 23. See also Leonard and Affleck, *Physical Education*, p. 402.

74. See also Weyand and Roberts, *Lacrosse Story*, p. 24.

75. *Encyclopedia of Sports, Games and Pastimes* (London: Fleetway House, n.d.), pp. 378–82.

76. Hugh W. Becket, *The Montreal Snow Shoe Club* (Montreal: Becket Bros., 1882); John K. Munro, "The Newer Associations," *Canadian Magazine*, September 1902, p. 419. Other members of the team were: W. G. Beers, W. K. McNaught, Ross McKenzie, W. C. Bonnell, L. Dwight, F. W. Garvin, S. Struthers, J. R. Craven, N. J. Fraser, W. D. Aird, W. J. Cleghorn, E. Smith, D. Nicholson, and W. O. Griffin.

77. Roxborough, *One Hundred—Not Out*, pp. 2, 33–37.

78. Becket, *Montreal Snow Shoe Club*, passim.

79. As quoted in Roxborough, *One Hundred—Not Out*, p. 2.

80. Ibid., pp. 34–36.

81. Becket, *Montreal Snow Shoe Club*, p. 300.

82. Roxborough, *One Hundred—Not Out*, p. 36. Bull, *Sportsmen of Peel*, p. 256, also tells of a "Snowshoeing Club" in Brampton, whose officers included W. H. McFadden, J. Scott, Alex Murray, K. A. Chisholm, and James Fleming.

83. Wise and Fisher, *Sporting Heroes*, p. 17.

84. The Rev. John Kerr, *Curling in Canada and the United States* (Edinburgh: Geo. A. Morton, 1904), pp. 186–87.

85. R. Tait McKenzie, ''Hockey in Eastern Canada,'' *Dominion Illustrated Monthly*, February 1893, pp. 57–58.

86. The Rev. D. J. Rankin, *A History of the County of Antigonish, Nova Scotia* (Toronto: Macmillan Company of Canada, 1929), pp. 51–52.

87. *Kingston Chronicle and Gazette*, 2 January 1839, 11 January 1840, 15 January 1840, 25 January 1843, 28 January 1843.

88. Roxborough, *One Hundred—Not Out*, p. 138.

89. Day, ''Sport in Chatham,'' pp. 98–99.

90. Blakeley, *Glimpses of Halifax*, p. 143; George Gale, *Quebec, 'twixt Old and New* (Quebec: Telegraph Printing Co., 1915), p. 263; Foster Hewitt, *Hockey Night in Canada* (Toronto: Ryerson Press, 1968), p. 3; W. A. Hewitt, *Down the Stretch* (Toronto: Ryerson Press, 1958); p. 175; Frank Orr, *The Story of Hockey* (New York: Random House, 1971), pp. 2–6; T. H. Raddall, *Halifax, Warden of the North* (Toronto: McClelland and Stewart, 1948), p. 281; and Roxborough, *One Hundred—Not Out*, pp. 137–39.

91. Lindsay, ''Sport in Canada, 1807–1867,'' pp. 45–46.

92. E. M. Orlick, ''McGill Contributions to the Origin of Ice Hockey,' *McGill News*, Winter 1943, pp. 13–17.

93. Roxborough, *One Hundred—Not Out*, p. 164.

94. *Globe*, 14 January 1888, 16 January 1888, 17 February 1888.

95. Orr, *Story of Hockey*, p. 7.

96. Charles L. Coleman, *The Trail of the Stanley Cup*, vol. 1 (Sherbrooke: National Hockey League, 1966), p. 11.

97. W. A. H. Kerr, ''Hockey in Ontario,'' *Dominion Illustrated Monthly*, March 1838, p. 105.

98. *The Pioneers* (The Canadian Illustrated Library; Toronto: McClelland and Stewart, 1968), p. 104.

99. *Edmonton Bulletin*, 29 November 1894.

100. Kerr, ''Hockey in Ontario,'' p. 107.

101. *Edmonton Bulletin*, 12 December 1892.

102. Day, ''Sport in Chatham,'' pp. 461–63.

103. J. Hedley, ''Curling in Canada,'' *Dominion Illustrated Monthly*, 1 (1892):181.

104. *Globe*, 23 December 1863; Ian F. Jobling, ''Sport in Nineteenth-Century Canada: The Effects of Technological Changes on Its Development'' (Ph.D. diss., University of Alberta, 1970), pp. 311–15. Also, see *Montreal Gazette*, 4 March 1875 and 17 March 1875, for mention of hockey enthusiasts using skating and curling rinks in Montreal.

105. *Montreal Gazette*, 4 March 1875, 17 March 1875.

106. Cox, ''Sports in Canada, 1868 to 1900,'' p. 219.

107. *Globe*, 26 December 1876.

108. Kerr, *Curling in Canada*, pp. 238–39. See also p. 343 and p. 606, which makes reference to curling club facilities'' being used for skating (ibid.).

109. Gerald Eskenazi, *Hockey* (Toronto: Ryerson Press, 1969), pp. 28–29.

110. Roxborough, *One Hundred—Not Out*, pp. 48–57, 99–111. Soccer is included in chapter eight, entitled ''Early Field Games,'' and rugby in chapter sixteen, ''From Halls of Learning'' (ibid., pp. 68–76, 155–64.

111. As quoted in Lindsay, ''Sport in Canada, 1807–1867,'' pp. 108–13; Howell and Howell, *Sports in Canadian Life*, p. 39; and Roxborough, *One Hundred—Not Out*, pp. 72–74.

112. John McDougall, *Forest, Lake and Prairie* (Toronto: William Briggs, 1895), p. 84.

113. Ibid., p. 266. The same author mentions another game of football on New Year's Day, 1866, in John McDougall, *Path-finding on Plain and Prairie* (Toronto: William Briggs, 1898, p. 131.

114. *Daily Colonist* (Victoria), 29 June 1865. Soccer matches were featured at Caledonian Games long after Confederation, also; see, for example, the account of a game between the Toronto Scots and the Marlboros at the Guelph Highland Gathering in the *Globe*, 19 August 1890. See also: *MG 28 1 40 vol. 10, page 23, Public Archives of Canada, Ottawa.*

115. *Montreal Gazette*, 22 July 1865.

116. Cox, "Sports in Canada, 1868 to 1900," pp. 94–128; Howell and Howell, *Sports in Canadian Life*, pp. 80–82. See also Frank Cosentino, *Canadian Football* (Toronto: Musson Book Co., 1969).

117. Dennis Signy, *A Pictorial History of Soccer* (Toronto: Paul Hamlyn, 1968), p. 30.

118. Roxborough, *One Hundred—Not Out*, p. 74.

119. W. Edward Laurendau, "Sport and Canadian Culture in the Border Cities, 1867 to 1929" (M.P.E. thesis, University of Windsor, 1971), p. 16.

120. T. A. Reed, *The Blue and White* (Toronto: University of Toronto Press, 1944), pp. 128–39.

121. Fred C. Lucas, *An Historical Souvenir: Diary of the City of Winnipeg Canada* (Winnipeg: Cartwright and Lucas, 1923), p. 124; *Manitoba Free Press* (Winnipeg), 10 October 1908; Gerald Redmond, "Born Again Soccer," *Edmonton Magazine*, May 1979, pp. 36–38; John E. Reid, "Sports and Games in Alberta before 1900" (M.A. thesis, University of Alberta, 1969), pp. 45–48.

122. *Daily Colonist* (Victoria), 17 November 1889 and 20 July 1890; *Globe*, (Toronto), 5 January 1892.

123. *Daily Colonist*, 17 November 1889.

124. Bull, *Sportsmen of Peel*, pp. 279–300.

125. *Globe*, 30 October 1888; Reed, *Blue and White*, p. 130. Three years before this, Canada had defeated the United States, 2–0, in an international soccer match played at Galt, Ontario (Roxborough, *One Hundred—Not Out*, p. 74).

126. *Globe*, 20 July 1890, 5 December 1891, 14 February 1892, 23 January 1892.

127. For example, Douglas Norman Sturrock, "A History of Rugby Football in Canada" (M.A. thesis, University of Alberta, 1971), p. 58, states that soccer and rugby matches were played in the 1880's at Winnipeg between "footballers, cricketers, Ireland and Scotland, England and Canada, and old countrymen, and Canadians." Thirty years later, an "international" soccer match took place at Banff between English and Scottish men drawn from teams in Banff, Bankhead, and Canmore, which the English won 3–2. See *Crag and Canyon* (Banff), 17 June 1910.

128. Wise and Fisher, *Sporting Heroes*, pp. 80–81, 288.

129. *Globe*, 17 November 1875.

130. Guy M. Lewis, "Canadian Influence on American Collegiate Sports," *Canadian Journal of History of Sport and Physical Education*, December 1970, p. 11; Sturrock, "Rugby Football," p. 128.

131. Reed, *Blue and White*, pp. 86–87.

132. Howell and Howell, *Sports in Canadian Life*, p. 79.

133. Bull, *Sportsmen of Peel*, pp. 300–305; Sturrock, "Rugby Football," pp. 122–41.

134. *Manitoba Free Press*, 10 October 1908.

135. Sturrock, "Rugby Football," p. 60.

136. *Manitoba Free Press*, 24 October 1890.

137. Sturrock, "Rugby Football," p. 19.

138. Ibid., p. 90.

139. *Dominion Illustrated*, 21 February 1891, p. 186.

140. Sturrock, "Rugby Football," pp. 90–105. A "Montreal Scottish" Rugby Club was formed in 1910 (p. 141).

141. Wilfred Campbell, *The Scotsman in Canada*, vol. 1 (Toronto: Musson Book Co., n.d.), pp. 269–70.

142. Ibid., pp. 269–70; D. C. Masters, "The Scottish Tradition in Higher Education," in W. Stanford Reid, ed., *The Scottish Tradition in Canada* (Toronto: McClelland and Stewart, 1976), pp. 250–51.

143. See chapter ten in Lindsay, "Sport in Canada, 1807–1867," pp. 335–50, entitled "Sport in School and Colleges"; and chapter eight in Cox, "Sports in Canada, 1868 to 1900," pp. 391–406, entitled "The Influence of Schools and Universities."

144. Roxborough, *One Hundred—Not Out*, pp. 155–64.

145. Peter C. McIntosh, *Sport in Society* (London: C. A. Watts and Co., 1963), pp. 57–79; and *Physical Education in England since 1800* (London: G. Bell and Sons, 1968), pp. 15–76.

146. Cox, "Sports in Canada, 1868 to 1900," pp. 391–406. See also G. G. Watson, "Sports and Games in Ontario Private Schools" (M.A. thesis, Universtiy of Alberta, 1970).

147. As quoted in J. A. Mangan, "Play up and Play the Game: Victorian and Edwardian Public School Vocabularies of Motive" *British Journal of Educational Studies* 23, no. 3 (October 1975): 329.

148. George Dickson and Adam G. Mercer, eds., *A History of Upper Canada College, 1829–1892* (Toronto: Rowsell and Hutchinson, 1893); G. G. S. Lindsey, "Cricket in Canada—Part IV," *Dominion Illustrated Monthly*, April 1893, pp. 160–67.

149. Bull, *Sportsmen of Peel*, pp. 269–77.

150. For example, a St. Andrew's Cricket Club was formed in Montreal in 1855 (as quoted in Lindsay, "Sport in Canada, 1807–1867," p. 100); and in the Legislative Library, Legislative Buildings, in Winnipeg, are the cricket score-books of the St. Andrew's Society in Winnipeg, up to 1922. It is likely that other St. Andrew's Societies in Canada played cricket during the summer, also.

151. Lindsay, "Sport in Canada, 1807–1867," p. 104. The same author, on page 102, states: "Junion bandsmen, Hibernian, and Caledonian Societies also succumbed to the cricketing urge" in the 1860s. G. G. S. Lindsey, "Cricket in Canada—Part III," *Dominion Illustrated Monthly*, November 1892, p. 609; *Novascotian*, 20 July 1857.

152. Boyle, *Township of Scarboro*, pp. 251–52.

153. *Nor' Wester*, 1 October 1864.

154. Lindsey, "Cricket in Canada—Part III," p. 615. G. W. Jones had an average of 18.36 on the tour of Britain in 1887; see G. G. S. Lindsey, "Cricket in Canada—Part 2," *Dominion Illustrated Monthly*, September 1892, pp. 496–97.

155. Ibid., Part III, p. 611; Part 2, p. 497. W. A. Henry was top of the touring team's average with 25.85.

156. Lindsay, "Sport in Canada, 1807–1867," p. 90.

157. *Montreal Gazette*, 6 August 1863.

158. For example, see the article in four parts by G. G. S. Lindsey, entitled "Cricket in Canada," in the *Dominion Illustrated Monthly* for August 1892, pp. 432–41; September 1892, pp. 493–508; November 1892, pp. 609–19; and April 1893, pp. 160–67.

159. Thomas L. Grahame, "National Sport, Pastimes in British Columbia," *Canadian Magazine*, March 1898, p. 464.

160. Bull, *Sportsmen of Peel*, pp. 323–42.

161. H. G. Mackenzie, "History of Lawn Tennis in Canada," *Athletic Life*, January 1895, pp. 16–21; Boyle, *Township of Scarboro*, pp. 260–61.

162. Q. D. McCulloch, "Bowling," *Athletic Life*, January 1895, pp. 21, 260–61.

163. George Elliott, "Bowling on the Green," *Canadian Magazine*, September 1902, p. 516; *Encyclopedia of Sports*, p. 94.

164. Lindsay, "Sport in Canada, 1807–1867," p. 133.

165. *Globe*, 8 September 1876; Roxborough, *One Hundred—Not Out*, p. 176.

166. Kerr, *Curling in Canada*, p. 606.

167. Day, "Sport in Chatham," p. 464.

168. *Globe*, 16 July 1888, 23 August 1890.

169. McCulloch, "Bowling," p. 21.

170. Cox, "Sports in Canada, 1868 to 1900," p. 162; *Globe*, 19 June 1893.

171. Roxborough, *One Hundred—Not Out*, p. 91.

172. Day, "Sport in Chatham," pp. 351–52.

173. Boyle, *Township of Scarboro*, pp. 252–57.

174. Roxborough, *One Hundred—Not Out*, pp. 228–38.

175. T. V. Hutchinson, "Evolution in Yacht Building," *Dominion Illustrated Monthly*, October 1892, p. 528.

176. *M.G. 28 1 40 vol. 10, page 71. Public Archives of Canada, Ottawa*. See also the chapter on Sanford Fleming in *Great Canadians* (Toronto: Canadian Centennial Publishing Co., 1965), pp. 59–62.

177. As quoted in Pierre Berton, *The Last Spike: The Great Railway, 1881–1885* (Toronto: McClelland and Stewart, 1971), pp. 177–78.

178. (Sir) Sanford Fleming, "Memories of the Mountains," *Canadian Alpine Journal* 1 (1907):29–33.

179. Jobling, "Technological Changes," pp. 51, 70.

8

Summary and Conclusions

O Caledonia! stern and wild,
Meet nurse for a poetic child!
Land of brown heath and shaggy wood,
Land of the mountain and the flood,
Land of my sires! What mortal hand
Can e'er untie the filial band
That knits me to thy rugged strand!

Sir Walter Scott (1771–1832)

THE panorama of sports in Canada today inevitably reflects the influences of the people who contributed to its creation. The majority of the most popular major sports, such as baseball, curling, Canadian football, golf, ice hockey, and lacrosse, emerged in organized form during the nineteenth century. Americans, Britons, and Canadians (including the native Indians), were mainly responsible for the blend. Remembering that it was British North America which became the Dominion of Canada in 1867, it is not surprising to find the British contribution to Canadian sport as the largest ingredient. And within the total sporting influence from Britain, the special contribution of the Scots was unsurpassed, and corresponded with their general status in Canadian life during the nineteenth century.

Sport has been an essential element in the culture of Scotland for centuries, as it has been in other parts of the British Isles. Some sports of dubious origin, however, which later attained worldwide popularity were first developed and codified entirely in Scotland. These sports have been acknowledged as Scottish throughout the world, because they were introduced and pio-

294

neered abroad by emigrant Scotsmen. Other British sports were also promoted overseas by Britons, including Scots. Nowhere else outside Scotland have her sports-loving people so successfully followed their sporting instincts than in the Dominion of Canada, in the nineteenth century.

The most ancient records of Scottish sport begin in the Highlands. Clansmen are said to have participated in shinty as early as the fifth century A.D., a game which has survived to the present day. Highlanders were early noted for their athletic prowess, in fact, a necessary ability during inter-Clan warfare. From at least the eleventh century onwards their exploits in running, jumping and throwing contests have been recorded, and a Highland Gathering included such events, together with Highland dancing and bagpipe music. Putting the stone and throwing the hammer, in particular, became organized events at Highland Games Meetings. The Disarming Acts of the eighteenth century suspended Highland activities for a time, but in the nineteenth century Highland Games experienced a great national revival in all parts of Scotland. They have retained their popular appeal to date.

Two other sports which are also popular in many countries today, curling and golf, were developed in the Lowlands of Scotland. Crude curling stones have been discovered in Scotland dating from the sixteenth century. From about the beginning of the nineteenth century a polished circular stone was used, as the sport became more sophisticated. More than forty curling clubs had existed in Scotland in the previous century, and by 1850 there were nearly two hundred in operation. Edinburgh alone had eighteen curling clubs before 1839. A year earlier the Grand Caledonian Curling Club had been formed there, later the Royal Caledonian Curling Club, and this became the governing body of the sport. The first reference to golf in recorded form was contained in a Scottish Act of Parliament of 1457, and it is clear that the game was common in the fifteenth and sixteenth centuries in Scotland. Like curling, it increased in popularity, and was a particular favorite of royalty and the nobility. Edinburgh, the capital city, was the main center of early golfing activity and club formation, but the Royal and Ancient Golf Club of St. Andrews, so named in 1834, eventually became the arbiter of this sport.

Perhaps the most popular sport of all throughout the British Isles, however, especially among the poorer classes, was football. This was unsuccessfully discouraged, under penalties of fines, even earlier than golf by the Scottish Parliament of 1424. Other edicts against the violent folk-football then in vogue followed, but the sport survived them all. It was particularly popular in the Border counties of Scotland. When the two forms of modern football, association and rugby, were codified in England during the nineteenth century, both soon became very popular in Scotland as well.

Cricket is acknowledged to be an English sport, but it had spread northward early in the eighteenth century and become fairly widespread in Scotland, too, although never as popular as other sports already mentioned. Nevertheless, many local and county cricket clubs were formed there in the nineteenth century, where it is still played today. It is possible that the famous Edinburgh Skating Club was also in existence in the eighteenth century. Other sports, too, have been popular in Scotland for a considerable time, from lawn bowls and pedestrianism to horse racing and quoits. In short, a notable characteristic of Scotland and her people has been a long and distinct tradition in sport. This fact has been noted by many authors, one of whom was moved to produce a special work entitled *Sports and Pastimes of Scotland*, in 1891.

Another feature of Scottish history has been the spectacular outward movement of people from Scotland to all parts of the world. The vitality which stimulated this vast expansion was caused by changing economic, political, religious, and social conditions within Scotland itself. During many centuries there has not been a decade when some Scots did not emigrate somewhere; a state of affairs which led Professor Gordon Donaldson, in *The Scots Overseas* (1966), to entitle his concluding chapter: ''Scotland's Greatest Export—Men.'' Canada is one of the many countries which has received a large and consistent infusion of Scottish stock since early in the eighteenth century.

The name ''Nova Scotia'' (New Scotland) appeared on the

East Coast in 1621, and early in the nineteenth century a Scottish explorer named "New Caledonia" on the West Coast of British North America. In the meantime, Scots had also distinguished themselves as fur traders, governors, missionaries, and soldiers, elsewhere on the continent. Consistent emigration from Scotland led to an increasing number of Scottish settlements being established, many of them in Upper Canada, later Ontario. Scots were also among the United Empire Loyalists who came up from the United States after the Revolutionary War. But it was in the nineteenth century that the Scots in Canada came into their own. Although they formed approximately only one-fifteenth of the population, Scots controlled the fur trade, the main banking and financial houses, and the major educational institutions. They were also most prominent in politics, and almost every member of the original CPR Syndicate was a self-made Scot. In fact, their widespread settlement and concomitant achievements meant that Canada was, to a considerable degree, truly a "New Scotland," as many authors have noted.

Scottish sports certainly found a new home in Canada from an early date. Scots were reported to be taking part in curling and golf here in the eighteenth century, and they established both sports on a nationwide basis in the next century, although circumstances favored the earlier development of curling. The Montreal Curling Club, formed by Scots in 1807, was the first organized sports club in British North America. Curling was more suited to the climate and geography of Canada than Scotland itself, and the widespread Scots enthusiastically pioneered and promoted their game in practically ideal conditions. The formation of curling clubs led to local, provincial, national, and international competition, aided by improved transportation facilities and the new indoor curling rinks. Its democratic character was no hindrance to those who took up the sport, and it was also well patronized by public figures, and well reported in the press. Scottish governors-general exhibited a particular interest in sponsoring curling. Soon after the Royal Caledonian Curling Club had been formed in Scotland in 1838, clubs and associations in Canada affiliated to it, and this link was maintained across the Dominion throughout the nineteenth century. After many attempts to arrange it, since 1858, a curling team from Scotland eventually toured Canada in 1902–3. Its members confirmed that the game had a most glorious future before it in the Dominion. The ultimate success of this Scottish sport in Canada, in fact, ranks as probably the most spectacular and fortunate sports transplant of all time. Nowhere else in the world today, Scotland included, is curling as widespread and popular as it is in Canada, a country which has also tended to dominate international competition in the sport.

Of course, golf is a universally popular Scottish sport, also. Rather than being particularly transplanted from Scotland to special adoption elsewhere, golf became ''Scotland's gift'' to the entire world, although its most spectacular development occurred in the United States. But the Montreal Golf Club, formed in 1873, was the first permanent golf club in the Western Hemisphere. Despite its comparatively late arrival as a formally organized sport, golf was introduced and developed here mainly by enthusiastic and knowledgeable Scots. Within the last quarter of the nineteenth century in Canada, golf clubs multiplied and all levels of competition quickly materialized, laying a secure base for the tremendous progress in Canadian golf in the twentieth century. As they had done in curling as well, women gained part of their sporting emancipation by playing golf.

A unique and special contribution of the Scots, in fact, has been their invention and export of two sports—curling and golf—which can be played by both sexes, of a wide age range, and at many levels of skill. Both sports require a high degree of accuracy rather than strength, and afford high pleasure and deep frustration in equal measure to their participants, while always holding out the challenge of a never-attainable score. Golf in particular has been well described by a Scot as ''an awfu' humblin' game.'' Both sports also allow for leisurely social intercourse while an earnest game is in progress, a quality which endows them with peculiar social advantages and civilizing tendencies. Each has a tranquil etiquette undisturbed by any physical contact with an opponent, except for a handshake, or any likelihood of bodily injury. The appeal of this unique combination has held the devotees of curling and golf for centuries, and continues to do so. It may well be that the canny side of the Scottish character was reflected and rewarded in their devotion to curling and golf. If so, it must be admitted that both sports have obviously appealed to other people's natures as well; and that the Scots themselves have notably participated in many other more vigorous sports with similar enthusiasm.

For example, much vigorous activity was exhibited at Highland Games, from running, jumping, and throwing events, to tug-of-war, games of shinty, and Highland Dancing. These were usually referred to as "Caledonian Games" in North America, being sponsored mainly by Caledonian Clubs, although other Scottish Societies held Games as well. These Scottish Games enjoyed their greatest popularity in Canada and the United States in the nineteenth century. Beginning early in the century, they expanded at a tremendous rate shortly after the Civil War and Confederation, becoming a favorite occurrence, attended by thousands, in towns and cities across the continent. So extensive and rich was the North American Caledonian Games circuit, in fact, that famous athletes from Scotland frequently came over to undertake profitable tours of the centers. International Caledonian Games were first held at New York in 1867, and in 1870 the North American United Caledonian Association was formed between Caledonian Clubs in Canada and the United States. For the remainder of the nineteenth century, this Association was the ruling body for Caledonian Games in both countries. Its title was an indication of Scottish ethnic pride, and this was the first such international organization for sport to be formed. The Caledonian Games were a significant influence on the subsequent development of amateur track and field athletics, which featured many Caledonian events. The rise of track and field clubs and appearance of national associations in the sport, together with the emergence of other sports in the public favor, represented counterattractions to Caledonian Games, which then declined in popularity in the late nineteenth century. However, they have existed to the present in North America, although it is in Canada, because of the strong Scottish heritage here, that Caledonian Games have survived best. In fact, nowhere else outside Scotland are so many Highland Games meetings enthusiastically held, as throughout the Dominion of Canada.

Caledonian Games, curling, and golf, were traditional Scottish sports which Scots introduced, pioneered, and established in Canada. There were other sports, too, common to Britain, in which the Scots played a significant part in nineteenth-century Canada. Tug-of-war was a popular event at Scottish Highland or Caledonian Games, and a favorite sport in Canada during the last twenty years of the nineteenth century, particularly in Ontario. Scots excelled in the sport and dominated the competitions. One tug-of-war team of Scottish farmers from Zorra, in Ontario, won a world championship at the Chicago World Fair of 1893. Quoits was another favorite sport at Caledonian Games at which the Scots naturally did well. They were also the protagonists of the many quoit clubs that were formed, and again dominated competition in this sport during the nineteenth century. Quoits was a summer game participated in by many curlers; lawn bowling was another, and many greens were attached to curling clubs. Not surprisingly, Scots were skillful enthusiasts at this sport, also. They even excelled at the common indoor pastime of draughts, or checkers, which enjoyed an amazing popularity in Scottish settlements during the nineteenth century. Scots were greatly involved in the introduction and progress of cricket, rugby football, and soccer in nineteenth century Canada. Together with other Britons, mostly English, they were frequently among the early organizers of sports wherever they were played, and many individual Scots and Scottish teams attained distinctions. Many rugby football and soccer clubs in nineteenth-century Canada were actually affiliated to Scottish governing bodies.

In common with other nationalities, the Scots were also involved in the promotion of indigenous Canadian sports. Lacrosse matches were featured at early Caledonian Games and athletic meetings, and Scots were among the players in various lacrosse teams, including Canadian teams which toured Britain. A Scottish governor-general, Lord Minto, presented a cup for competition between lacrosse clubs. Scots were also lively members of the famous Montreal Snow Shoe Club, formally organized in 1843, as well as later clubs, several of which had Scottish names. Many curling clubs allowed their indoor facilities to be used for skating, and for ice hockey later on. The Scottish game of shinty, which was popular throughout the nineteenth century in Canada, was one of the forerunners of ice hockey. Scots were also keen participants in this sport. The first two ice-hockey teams in Toronto were the Caledonians and the Granites. Ice-hockey teams named "the Thistles" were also in vogue. In fact, it is difficult to find a sport at all in nineteenth-century Canada in which many of the sports-loving Scots did not take part with enthusiasm and success.

All kinds of Scotsmen had been involved in this wide range of sporting endeavor, from the humblest to the most exalted rank. The soldiers and officers of Scottish Regiments were always prominent sportsmen in their off-duty hours. Ministers and their congregations also took part, although not usually on a Sunday. Rural Scottish farmers as well as urban Scottish workers were all involved in a variety of sports. In the major colleges and universities of nineteenth-century Canada, which they founded, Scottish staff and students were active with others in the development of collegiate and intercollegiate sport. Scottish bankers, businessmen, fur traders, and politicians, all found time for sport. Even the Scottish giants of nineteenth century Canadian history relaxed in a sporting manner. George Brown was president of the Toronto Caledonian Society and attended its Games. (Sir) John A. Macdonald was a member of a curling club, and donated prizes for the annual Games of the St. Andrew's Society of Ottawa. So did (Sir) Sanford Fleming, who also founded the Canadian Alpine Club in 1883. Donald A. Smith (later Lord Strathcona) donated a small fortune to *many* sports, especially curling, and attended sports meetings on occasion.

Berton has used the hard upbringing and subsequent personal philosophy of another impressive Scottish figure, George Stephen (later Lord Mountstephen) to explain the dominance of the Scot in pioneer Canada. In his perspicacious analysis, Berton has stated: "For the Scots it was work, save and study; study, save and work." But this was not entirely so. For it is clear that the Scots in nineteenth-century Canada also consistently set aside time for play, (and even Stephen himself occasionally indulged in salmon fishing). And characteristically, when the Scots played, at their own sports or others, they were as calculating and commanding as they were in any other aspect of Canadian life. In short, their sporting contributions were also significant and successful, adding another dimension to their already considerable enrichment of Canadian history.

Bibliography

Newspapers and Periodicals

Canada

Athletic Life, 1895–96.
Calgary Herald, 1883–1900.
Canadian Alpine Journal, The, vol. 1, no. 1 (1907).
Canadian Illustrated News, 1871–80.
Canadian Journal of History of Sport and Physical Education, 1970–79.
Canadian Magazine, The, 1896–1905.
Canadian Magazine, 6 March 1971.
Canadian Sport Monthly, June 1949.
Canadian Weekend Magazine, 31 October 1964.
Crag and Canyon (Banff), 1910–35.
Daily Colonist (Victoria), 1858–90.
Dominion Illustrated Monthly, The, 1888–93.
Edmonton Bulletin, 1880–1900.
Edmonton Magazine, May 1979.
Globe (Toronto), 1844–1904.
Hamilton Times, 1858–68.
Inland Sentinel, 26 July 1895.
Kingston Chronicle and Gazette, 1833–45.
Lethbridge News, 9 January 1895.
Maclean's, February 1974.
McGill News, Winter 1943.
Medicine Hat Times, 26 November 1896.
Merit News, July 1965.
Montreal Gazette, 1800–1877.
Montreal Herald, 1811–26; 1863–73.
Montreal Star, 13 January 1934.
Morning Chronicle (Quebec), 1847–68.
Nor'wester (Winnipeg), 1859–65.
Novascotian, 1824–70.
Ottawa Citizen, 1846–92.
Reporter and Fredericton Advertiser, 1844–1902.

303

Saskatchewan History, Spring 1965.
Society and Leisure, April 1979.
Winnipeg Free Press, 1874–1900.

United Kingdom

Baily's Magazine of Sports and Pastimes, 1861–79.
Belgravia, vol. 8 (1869).
Blackwood's Edinburgh Magazine, 1843–62.
Chambers' Edinburgh Journal, vol. 3 (1844).
Edinburgh Review, 1810–90.
Gaelic Society of Inverness, vol. 30 (1924).
History Today, December 1963.
Illustrated London News, The, 1847–75.
Observer, The, 1970–71.
Sport and Recreation, July 1966.
World Sports, September 1970.

United States of America

Amherst Student, October 1874.
Boston Daily Globe, 1878–84.
British American Magazine, The, December 1863.
Century Magazine, 1877–85.
College Argus, The, 18 December 1875.
Cornell Era, The, 12 September 1873.
Emigrant and Old Countryman, 19 October 1836.
Frank Leslie's Illustrated Newspaper, 18 September 1869.
Harper's Weekly, 1867–95.
Mississippi Valley Historical Review, vol. 40 (1953).
New York Times, 1868–85; and 25 February 1920.
Outing, 1891–1915.
Princeton Alumni Weekly, 23 May 1952.
Scottish-American Journal, 1868–1907.
Scribner's, 1872–95.
Spirit of the Times (New York), 1858–75.
Sporting Goods Dealer, The, May 1969.

Articles, Books, Minutes, Papers, and Theses

Acts of the Parliament of Scotland (1424–1567), 11 (1814), 48
a and b (M).

Allingham, H. H. "Lacrosse in the Maritime Provinces." *Dominion
Illustrated Monthly*, May 1892, pp. 225–33.

Altham, H. S. *A History of Cricket: From the Beginnings to the First World War*, 5th ed. London: George Allen and Unwin, 1962.

Annual of the Ontario Curling Association for 1968–1969, vol. 94. Toronto: Maclean-Hunter, n.d.

Antigonish Highland Society, The. *Programme for 1966.*

Arlott, John, and Daley, Arthur. *Pageantry of Sport: From the Age of Chivalry to the Age of Victoria.* New York: Hawthorn Books, 1968.

Becket, Hugh W. *The Montreal Snow Shoe Club.* Montreal: Becket Bros., 1882.

Beers, George W. *The Game of Lacrosse.* Montreal: M. Longmore and Co., 1860.

———. *Lacrosse, the National Game of Canada.* Montreal: Dawson Bros., 1869.

———. "Canada in Winter." *British American Magazine*, December 1863, pp. 166–71.

Berthoff, Rowland Tappan. "Goldie and the Caledonian Games." *Princeton Alumni Weekly*, 23 May 1952, p. 6.

———. *British Immigrants in Industrial America.* Cambridge, Mass.: Harvard University Press, 1953.

Berton, Pierre. *The National Dream: The Great Railway, 1871–1881.* Toronto: McClelland and Stewart, 1970.

———. *The Last Spike: The Great Railway, 1881–1885.* Toronto: McClelland and Stewart, 1971.

Betts, John R. "The Technological Revolution and Rise of Sport, 1850–1900." *Mississippi Valley Historical Review* 40 (1953): 231–56.

Black, George Fraser. *Scotland's Mark on America.* New York: The Scottish Section of "America's Making," 1921.

Blakeley, Phyllis R. *Glimpses of Halifax, 1867–1900.* Halifax, N.S.: The Public Archives of Nova Scotia, 1949.

Blancke, Charles. "Cricket in America." *Harper's Weekly*, 26 September 1891, pp. 725–26, 732.

Bland, Ernest A. *Fifty Years of Sport.* London: The Daily Mail, 1946.

Bowen, Rowland. *Cricket: A History of Its Growth and Development Throughout the World.* London: Eyre and Spottiswoode, 1970.

Bowie, Gerald William. "The History and Trends of Curling." (M.S. thesis, Washington State University, 1962).

Boyle, David, ed. *The Township of Scarboro', 1796–1896.* Toronto: William Briggs, 1896.

Bradley, A. G. *The United Empire Loyalists*. London: Thornton Butterworth, 1932.

Brailsford, Dennis. *Sport and Society: Elizabeth to Anne*. London: Routledge and Kegan Paul, 1969.

Brebner, J. B. *The Explorers of North America*. London: A. and C. Black, 1933.

Brown, Nigel. *Ice-Skating: A History*. New York: A. S. Barnes and Co., 1959.

Browne, James. *The History of Scotland: Its Highlands, Regiments and Clans*. 8 vols. Edinburgh: Francis A. Niccolls and Co., 1909.

Bryce, George. *The Scotsman in Canada*. Vol. 2. Toronto: Musson Book Co., n.d.

———. *The Life of Lord Selkirk*. Toronto: Musson Book Co., n.d.

———. *The Remarkable History of the Hudson's Bay Company*. Toronto: William Briggs, 1900.

Buckingham, W., and Ross, G. *The Honourable Alexander Mackenzie*. Toronto: Rose, 1892.

Bull, Wm. Perkins. *From Rattlesnake Hunt to Hockey: The History of Sports in Canada and of the Sportsmen of Peel, 1798 to 1934*. Toronto: George J. McLeod, 1934.

Caledonian Society of Montreal, The Programme for 1964–65.

Calvin, D.D. *Queen's University at Kingston: The First Century of a Scottish-Canadian Foundation, 1841–1941*. Kingston, Ontario: The Trustees of the University, 1941.

Campbell, D., and MacLean, R. A. *Beyond the Atlantic Roar: A Study of the Nova Scotia Scots*. Toronto: McClelland and Stewart, 1974.

Campbell, Majorie Wilkins. *The North West Company*. Toronto: Macmillan Co. of Canada, 1957.

Campbell, Majorie F. *A Mountain and a City: The Story of Hamilton*. Toronto: McClelland and Stewart, 1966.

Canada, 1867–1967: The Founders and the Guardians. Ottawa: Queen's Printers, 1968.

Canadian Who's Who, 1967–1969, The. Vol. 11. Toronto: Who's Who Canadian Publications, 1969.

Careless, J. M. S. *Brown of the Globe*. 2 vols. Toronto: Macmillan Co. of Canada, 1959–63.

———. *Canada, A Story of Challenge*. Toronto: Macmillan Co. of Canada, 1963.

Carnochan, Janet. *History of Niagara*. Toronto: William Briggs, 1941.

Clark, Joseph T. "Golf in Canada." *Canadian Magazine*, November 1905, pp. 39–47.

Clark, S. D. *The Social Development of Canada*. Toronto: University of Toronto Press, 1942.

———. *The Developing Canadian Community*. Toronto: University of Toronto Press, 1941.

Cochrane, J.; Hoffman, A.; and Kincaid, P. *Women in Canadian Life: Sports*. Toronto: Fitzhenry and Whiteside, 1977.

Coleman, Charles L. *The Trail of the Stanley Cup*. Vol. 1. Sherbrooke National Hockey League, 1966.

Collard, Edgar. *Montreal Yesterdays*. Toronto: Longmans Canada, 1963.

Collison, B. W., and Munro, J. K. "Lacrosse in Canada." *Canadian Magazine*, September 1902, pp. 410–26.

Colguhoun, Sir Iain, and Machell, Hugh. *Highland Gatherings*. London: Heath Cranton, 1927.

Concise History of Golf in Canada, A. Toronto: Royal Canadian Golf Association, n.d.

Connor, Ralph [pseud.]. *The Man from Glengarry*. Toronto: McClelland and Stewart, 1967.

Constitution of the St. Andrew's Society of the City of Winnipeg. Winnipeg: Walker and May, 1886.

Cosentino, Frank. *Canadian Football: The Grey Cup Years*. Toronto: Musson Book Co., 1969.

Cosentino, Frank, and Leyshon, Glynn. *Olympic Gold: Canadian Winners of the Summer Games*. Toronto: Holt, Rinehart and Winston of Canada, 1975.

Cowan, Helen I. *British Immigration to British North America*. Toronto: University of Toronto Press, 1961.

Cowan, John. *Canada's Governors-General: Lord Monck to General Vanier*. Toronto: York Publishing Co., 1965.

Coward, Elizabeth Ruggles. *Bridgetown, Nova Scotia: Its History to 1900*. Kentville Publishing Co., 1955.

Cox, Allan Elton. "A History of Sports in Canada, 1868–1900." Ph.D. dissertation, University of Alberta, 1969.

Craig, G. M. *Upper Canada: The Formative Years*. Toronto: McClelland and Stewart, 1963.

Creelman, W. A. *Curling, Past and Present*. Toronto: McClelland and Stewart, 1950.

Creighton, D. G. *John A. Macdonald: The Young Politician*. Toronto: Macmillan Co. of Canada, 1952.

———. *John A. Macdonald: The Old Chieftain*. Toronto: Macmillan Co. of Canada, 1955.

Cruickshank, F. D., and Nason, J. *History of Weston*, Weston, Ontario: Times and Guide, 1937.

Cruickshank, W. "The Game of La Crosse." *Illustrated London News*, 16 October 1875.

"Curlers' Annual, The." *Chambers' Edinburgh Journal* 3 (1844): 120–22.

Davidson, Stewart Alexander. "A History of Sports and Games in Eastern Canada prior to World War I." Doctoral dissertation, Teachers College, Columbia University, 1951.

Davin, Nicholas F. *The Irishman in Canada*. Toronto: Maclean and Co., 1877.

Day, Robert Douglas. "Impulse to Addiction: A Narrative History of Sport in Chatham, Ontario: 1790–1895." M.A. thesis, University of Western Ontario, 1977.

Delisle, Alexander M. *Railroad between Quebec, Montreal, Bytown and Georgian Bay*. Montreal: W. Salter and Co., 1853.

Dickson, George, and Mercer, Adam G., eds. *A History of Upper Canada College*. Toronto: Rowsell and Hutchinson, 1893.

Diem, Carl. *Weltgeschichte des Sports und der Leibeserziehung*. Stuttgart: J. G. Cotta'shen Buchhandlung Nachf., 1960.

Donaldson, Charles. *Men of Muscle and the Highland Games of Scotland, with Brief Biographies of the Leading Athletes of the Last Fifty Years, with Portraits*. Glasglow: Carter and Pratt, 1901.

Donaldson, Gordon. *The Scots Overseas*. London: Robert Hale, 1966.

Dorian, Charles. *The First 75 Years: A Headline History of Sudbury, Canada*. Ilfracombe, Devon: Arthur H. Stockwell, 1959.

Douglas, Ronald Macdonald. *The Scots Book*. New York: E. P. Dutton & Co., n.d.

Drake, Earl G. *Regina, The Queen City*. Toronto: McClelland and Stewart, 1955.

Dufferin, Marchioness of. *My Canadian Journal, 1872–1878*. London: John Murray, 1891.

Dulles, Foster Rhea. *A History of Recreation: America Learns to Play*. New York: Appleton-Century-Crofts, 1965.

Dunbar, Nancy J. *Images of Sport in Early Canada*. Montreal: McGill Queen's University Press, 1976.

Dunn, Charles W. *Highland Settler: A Portrait of the Scottish Gael in Nova Scotia.* Toronto: University of Toronto Press, 1968.

Dunning, E. F. "Football in its Early Stages." *History Today,* December 1963, pp. 838–47.

Eckert, Helen Margaret. "The Development of Organized Recreation and Physical Education in Alberta." M.Ed. thesis, University of Alberta, Edmonton, 1953.

Edwards, Duncan. "Life at the Athletic Clubs." *Scribner's,* July–December 1895, pp. 4–23.

Elliott, George. "Bowling on the Green." *Canadian Magazine,* September 1902, pp. 513–23.

Encyclopaedia Britannica. London: William Benton, 1968.

Encyclopedia Canadiana. 10 vols. Toronto: Grolier of Canada, 1968.

Encyclopedia of Sports, Games and Pastimes. London: Fleetway House, n.d.

Ermatinger, C. O. *The Talbot Regime.* St. Thomas: Municipal World, 1904.

Eskenazi, Gerald. *Hockey.* Toronto: Ryerson Press, 1969.

Felker, Cart T. "Golf: From First Feather Ball to Modern Solids." *Sporting Goods Dealer,* May 1969, pp. 99–104.

Fenton, Wyness. *Royal Valley: The Story of the Aberdeenshire Dee.* Aberdeen: Alex. P. Reid & Sons, 1969.

Firth, Edith G. *The Town of York, 1815–1834.* Toronto: University of Toronto Press, 1966.

Fittis, Robert Scott. *Sports and Pastimes of Scotland.* Paisley: Alexander Gardner, 1891.

Fleming, Sir Sandford. "Memories of the Mountains." *The Canadian Alpine Journal* (1907): pp. 10–33.

Flint, David. *William Lyon Mackenzie: Rebel against Authority.* Toronto: Oxford University Press, 1971.

Forbes, R. Bruce. "Golf, The Royal and Ancient Game." *IAC Merit News* (July 1965): pp 1–4.

Ford, Henry Jones. *The Scotch-Irish in America.* New York: Peter Smith, 1941.

Ford, Malcolm W. "Hammer-Throwing." *Outing,* September 1892, pp. 448–54.

Fraser, Alexander. *The Last Laird of MacNab.* Toronto: Imrie, Graham I Co., 1899.

Frayne, Trent, and Gzowski, Peter. *Great Canadian Sports Stories.* Toronto: Canadian Centennial Publishing Co., 1965.

Gabriel, Ralph Henry. *The Course of American Democratic Thought*. New York: Ronald Press Co., 1940.

Galbraith, John Kenneth. *The Non-Potable Scotch*. Harmondsworth, Middlesex: Penguin Books, 1967.

Gale, George. *Quebec, 'twixt Old and New*. Quebec: Telegraph Printing Co., 1915.

Gardiner, E. Norman. *Athletics of the Ancient World*. London: Oxford University Press, 1967.

Gibb, Andrew Dewar. *Scottish Empire*. London: Alexander Maclehose & Co., 1937.

Gibbon, John Murray. *Scots in Canada*. Toronto: Musson Book Co., 1911.

———. *Steel of Empire*. Toronto: McClelland and Stewart, 1935.

———. *Canadian Mosaic: The Makings of a Northern Nation*. Toronto: McClelland and Stewart, 1938.

———. *Our Old Montreal*. Toronto: McClelland and Stewart, 1947.

Glazebrook, G. P. de T. *A History of Transportation in Canada*. 2 vols. Toronto: McClelland and Stewart, 1964.

Glover, T. R., and Calvin, D. D., *A Corner of Empire: The Old Ontario Strand*. Cambridge University Press, 1937.

Goff, The: An Heroi-Comical Poem in Three Cantos. Edinburgh: J. Cochran and Co., 1743.

Gourlay, Reginald. ''The Canadian Girl.'' *Canadian Magazine*, October 1896.

Graham, Gerald S. *A Concise History of Canada*. New York: Viking Press, 1968.

Graham, Henry Grey. *The Social Life of Scotland in the Eighteenth Century*. London: Adam & Charles Black, 1969.

Grahame, Thomas L. ''National Sport: Pastimes in British Columbia.'' *Canadian Magazine*, March 1898, pp. 464–66.

Grant, George M. ''The Canada Pacific Railway.'' *Century Magazine*, October 1885, pp. 882–89.

Gray, John M. *Lord Selkirk of Red River*. Toronto: Macmillan Co. of Canada, 1963.

Great Canadians. Toronto: Canadian Centennial Publishing Co., 1965.

Gresco, Paul. ''Any Game Played by 750,000 People Can't Be All Dull.'' *Canadian Magazine*, 6 March 1971, pp. 7–9.

Grimsley, Will. *Golf: Its History, People & Events*. Englewood Cliffs, N.J.: Prentice-Hall, 1966.

Gruneau, Richard S., and Albinson, John G. *Canadian Sport: Sociological Perspectives*. Don Mills, Ontario: Addison-Wesley (Canada), 1976.

Guillet, Edwin C. *Early Life in Upper Canada*. Toronto: Ontario Publishing Co., 1933.

————. *Toronto: From Trading Post to Great City*. Toronto: Ontario Publishing Co., 1934.

————. *Pioneer Days in Upper Canada*. Toronto: University of Toronto Press, 1970.

Hackensmith, C. W. *History of Physical Education*. New York: Harper & Row, 1966.

Hall, J., and McCulloch, R. *Sixty Years of Canadian Cricket*. Toronto: Bryant Publishing Co., 1895.

Hall, Margaret Ann. "A History of Women's Sport in Canada prior to World War I." Master's thesis, University of Alberta 1968.

Haniel, Fred Coyne. *Lake Erie Baron*. Toronto: Macmillan Co. of Canada, 1955.

Harkness, John Graham. *Stormont, Dundas and Glengarry: A History, 1784–1945*. Oshawa, Ontario: Mundy-Goodfellow Printing Co., 1946.

Harris, H. A. *Sport in Britain: Its Origins and Development*. London: Stanley Paul, 1975.

Hedley, J. "Curling in Canada." *Dominion Illustrated Monthly* 1 (1892):116–23.

————. "Curling in Canada, Part II." *Dominion Illustrated Monthly* 1 (1892):173–82.

Herrington, Walter S. *History of the County of Lennox and Addington*. Toronto: Macmillan Co. of Canada, 1913.

Hewitt, Foster. *Hockey Night in Canada*. Toronto: Ryerson Press, 1968.

Hewitt, W. A. *Down The Stretch*. Toronto: Ryerson Press, 1958.

Higginson, Thomas Wentworth. "A Day of Scottish Games." *Scribner's*, January 1872, pp. 329–36.

Hill, Christopher. *The Pelican Economic History of Britain*. Vol. 2, *1530–1780, Reformation to Industrial Revolution*. Harmondsworth, Middlesex: Penguin Books, 1969.

Hill, Douglas. *The Scots to Canada*. London: Gentry Books, 1972.

History of the Ottawa Collegiate Institute, A. Ottawa: Mortimer Co. 1904.

Hole, Christina. *English Sports and Pastimes*. London: B. T. Batsford, 1949.

Hounsom, Eric Wilfrid. *Toronto in 1810*. Toronto: Ryerson Press, 1970.

Howell, Nancy, and Howell, Maxwell L. *Sports and Games in Canadian Life: 1700 to the Present*. Toronto: Macmillan of Canada, 1969.

Hubbard, R. H. *Rideau Hall: An Illustrated History of Government House Ottawa*. Ottawa: Queen's Printer, n.d.

Hunter, Charles. "Golf in Canada." *Athletic Life*, February 1895, pp. 61–65.

Hutchinson, Horace G. *Golf*. London: Longmans, Green and Co., 1898.

Hutchinson, T. V. "Evolution in Yacht Building." *Dominion Illustrated Monthly*, October 1892, pp. 523–28.

Inglis, W. L. *A History of the Cowal Gathering*. Dunoon: Dunoon Observer, 1957.

Innis, H. A. *The Fur Trade in Canada*. Toronto: University of Toronto Press, 1956.

———. *A History of the Canadian Pacific Railway*. Toronto: University of Toronto Press, 1971.

Jamieson, D. A. *Powderhall and Pedestrianism*. Edinburgh: W. and A. K. Johnston, 1943.

Janssen, Frederick William. *A History of American Athletics and Aquatics, 1829–1888*. New York: Outing Co. 1888.

Jobling, Ian F. "Sport in Nineteenth-Century Canada: The Effects of Technological Changes on its Development." Ph.D. dissertation, University of Alberta, 1970.

Johnston, William. *History of the County of Perth from 1825 to 1902*. Stratford, Ontario: W. M. O'Beirne, 1903.

Jones, George Hilton. *The Main Stream of Jacobitism*. Cambridge, Mass.: Harvard University Press, 1954.

Jones, Kevin G. "Sport in Canada, 1900–1920." Ph.D. dissertation, University of Alberta, 1970.

Kavanagh, L. V. *History of Golf in Canada*. Toronto: Fitzhenry and Whiteside, 1973.

Kay, Marguerite. *Breugel*. London: Hamlyn Publishing Group, 1969.

Kerr, John. *History of Curling*. Edinburgh: David Douglas, 1890.

———. *Curling in Canada and the United States*. Edinburgh: F. A. Morton, 1904.

Kerr, W. A. R. "Hockey in Ontario." *Dominion Illustrated Monthly,* March 1893, pp. 99–108.

———. "Golf in Canada." *Canadian Magazine* 17 (1901):340–49.

Kilb, Brad L. "Sport in Banff before 1914." term paper, Faculty of Physical Education, University of Alberta, 1967.

Korsgaard, Robert. "A History of the Amateur Athletic Union of the United States." Ph.D. dissertation, Teachers' College, Columbia University, 1952.

Krout, John Allen. *Annals of American Sport, 15, The Pageant of America Series.* 15 vols. New York: United States Publishers Association, 1929.

Lamb, W. Kaye, ed. *The Journals and Letters of Sir Alexander Mackenzie.* Toronto: Macmillan of Canada, 1970.

Laurendau, W. Edward "Sport and Canadian Culture in the Border Cities, 1867–1929." M.P.E. thesis, University of Windsor, 1971.

Lavender, David. *Winner Take All: The Trans-Canada Canoe Trail.* Toronto: McGraw-Hill Book Company, 1977.

Lehmann, William C. *Scottish and Scotch-Irish Contributions to Early American Life and Culture.* Port Washington, N.Y.: Kennikat Press, 1978.

Leitch, Adelaide. *The Visible Past: The Pictorial History of Simcoe County.* Ontario: County of Simcoe, 1967.

Le Moine, J. M. *The Scot in New France: An Ethnological Study.* Montreal: Dawson Brothers, 1881.

Leonard, Fred Eugene, and Affleck, George B. *The History of Physical Education.* London: Henry Kimpton, 1947.

Lewis, Guy M. "Canadian Influence on American Collegiate Sports." *Canadian Journal of History of Sport and Physical Education,* December 1970, pp. 7–15.

Lindsay, Peter Leslie. "A History of Sport in Canada, 1807–1867." Ph.D. dissertation, University of Alberta, 1969.

———. "Woman's Place in Nineteenth Century Canadian Sport." *Journal of the Canadian Association for Health, Physical Education and Recreation,* September–October 1970, pp. 25–28.

Lindsey, Charles. *William Lyon MacKenzie.* Toronto: Morang & Co. 1910.

Lindsey, G. G. S. "Cricket in Canada—Part I." *Dominion Illustrated Monthly,* August 1892, pp. 432–41.

———. "Cricket in Canada—Part II." *Dominion Illustrated Monthly,* September 1892, pp. 493–508.

———. ''Cricket in Canada—Part III.'' *Dominion Illustrated Monthly,* November 1892, pp. 609–10.

———. ''Cricket in Canada—Part IV.'' *Dominion Illustrated Monthly,* April 1893, pp. 160–67.

Logan, James. *The Scotish [sic] Gael.* 5th American ed. Hartford: S. Andrews and Son, 1851.

Lower, Arthur R. M. *Canadians in the Making: A Social History of Canada* Toronto: Longmans, Green and Co. 1958.

———. *Colony to Nation: A History of Canada.* Toronto: Longmans, Green and Co. 1959.

Lovesey, Peter. *The Kings of Distance.* London: Eyre & Spottiswoode, 1968.

Lovesey, Peter, and McNab, Tom. *The Guide to British Track and Field Literature, 1275–1968.* London: Athletics Arena, 1969.

Lucas, Fred C. *An Historical Souvenir Diary of the City of Winnipeg Canada.* Winnipeg: Cartwright and Lucas, 1923.

Ludwig, Jack. ''Rocks of All Ages.'' *Maclean's,* February 1974, pp. 26–29.

Macdonald, Alexander. ''Shinty: Historical and Traditional.'' *Gaelic Society of Inverness* (1924):27–56.

Macdonald, James S. *Annals of the North British Society of Halifax, Nova Scotia.* Halifax, N.S.: ''Citizen'' Steam Book, Job and General Printing Office, 1868.

Macdonald, Norman. *Canada: Immigration and Colonization, 1841–1903.* Toronto: Macmillan of Canada, 1968.

MacEwan, Grant. *Between the Red and the Rockies.* Toronto: University of Toronto Press, 1952.

MacGregor, J. G., *Edmonton: A History.* Edmonton, Alta: M. G. Hurtig Publishers, 1967.

Machum, Lloyd A. *A History of Moncton Town and City, 1855–1965.* New Brunswick: The City of Moncton, 1965.

MacKay, Douglas. *The Honourable Company: A History of the Hudson's Bay Company.* London: Cassell and Co., 1937.

MacKay, Rev. W. A. *Pioneer Life in Zorra.* Toronto: William Briggs, 1899.

MacKenzie, M. G. ''History of Lawn Tennis in Canada.'' *Athletic Life,* January 1895, pp. 16–21.

Mackenzie, Ross. ''Lacrosse.'' *Outing,* October 1892, pp. 76–80.

Mackie, Albert. *Scottish Pageantry.* London: Hutchinson & Co., 1967.

Mackie, J. D. *A History of Scotland*. Harmondsworth, Middlesex: Penguin Books, 1969.

Macmillan Dictionary of Canadian Biography, The. Toronto: Macmillan, 1963.

MacNutt, W. S. *New Brunswick, A History: 1784–1867.* Toronto: Macmillan of Canada, 1963.

MacRae, Archibald Oswald. *A History of Alberta*. Vol. 1. Edmonton: Western Canada History Co., 1912.

Mactaggart, John. *Three Years in Canada, 1826–1828*. London: Henry Colburn, 1829.

Maier, Augustus. ''Physical Training in Athletic Clubs.'' Thesis, Springfield College, 1904.

Manchester, Herbert. *Four Centuries of Sport in America, 1490–1890*. New York: Derrydale Press, 1931.

Mangan, J. A. ''Play Up and Play the Game: Victorian and Edwardian Public School Vocabularies of Motive.'' *British Journal of Educational Studies* 23 (1975):329.

Manning, J. L. ''Who Took the Ball in His Arms?'' *The Observer*, 12 April 1970.

Marples, Morris. *A History of Football*. London: Secker & Warburg, 1954

Marshall, Rev., ed. *Football: The Rugby Union Game*. London: Cassell and Co., 1895.

Marshall, Major M. H. *The Scottish Curlers in Canada and the USA: A Record of Their Tour in 1922–23*. Edinburgh: T & A. Constable, 1924.

Martin, H. B. *Fifty Years of American Golf.* New York: Dodd, Mead and Co., 1936.

Martin, John Stuart. *The Curious History of the Golf Ball: Mankind's Most Fascinating Sphere*. New York: Horizon Press, 1968.

Masters, Donald C. *Rise of Toronto, 1850–1890*. Toronto: University of Toronto Press, 1947.

Menke, Frank G. *The Encyclopedia of Sports*. New York: A. S. Barnes and Co., 1953.

Meyer, Duane Gilbert. *The Highland Scots of North Carolina, 1732–1776*. Chapel Hill, N.D.: University of North Carolina Press, 1961.

Meyer, Robert Jr. *Festivals, U.S.A. and Canada*. New York: Ives Washburn, 1967.

MG 28 1 50, vol. 10. Public Archives of Canada, Ottawa, Ontario.

Michaud, William. *Pioneer Railways of Central Ontario*. Toronto: Canadian National Railways, 1964.

Middleton, Jesse Edgar. *Toronto's 100 Years*. Toronto: The Centennial Committee, 1934.

Minute Book of the St. Andrew's Society of London, 1860–1875.

Minutes of the London Curling Club, Ontario, 1849–1940. 3 vol.

Minutes of the New York Caledonian Club, November 5, 1862 to December 18, 1866.

Moncton, O. Paul. *Pastimes in Times Past*. London: West Strand Publishing Co. 1913.

Morgan, E. C. "Pioneer Recreation and Social Life." *Saskatchewan History*, Spring 1965, pp. 41–55.

Morley, Alan. *Vancouver—From Milltown to Metropolis*. Vancouver: Mitchell Press, 1961.

Morley, F. V., ed. *James Boswell: The Life of Samuel Johnson & The Journal of a Tour to the Hebrides with Samuel Johnson, LL.D.* New York: Harper & Row, 1966.

Morrison, E. C., and Morrison, D. N. R. *Calgary 1875–1950*. Calgary: Calgary Publishing Co., 1950.

Morton, Arthur S. *Sir George Simpson*. Toronto: J. M. Dent & Sons, 1944.

Morton, W. L. *Manitoba, A History*. Toronto: University of Toronto Press, 1957.

———. *The Kingdom of Canada*. Toronto: McClelland and Stewart 1963.

———. *The Canadian Identity*. Madison, Wis.: University of Wisconsin Press, 1968.

Mulvany, C. Pelham. *Toronto: Past and Present*. Toronto: W. E. Caiger, 1884.

Munro, John K. "Curling in Canada." *Canadian Magazine* 18 (1902):527–34.

———. "The Newer Associations." *Canadian Magazine* 18 (1902): 419–26.

Murdoch, Joseph S. F. *The Library of Golf, 1973–1966*. Detroit: Gale Research Co., 1968.

Mutimer, Brian T. P. "Arnold and Organised Games in the English Public Schools of the Nineteenth Century." Ph.D. dissertation, University of Alberta, Edmonton, 1971.

McCulloch, Q. D. "Bowling" *Athletic Life*, January 1895, pp. 21–23.

McDougall, John. *Forest, Lake and Prairie*. Toronto: William Briggs, 1895.

———. *Saddle, Sled and Snowshoe: Pioneering on the Saskatchewan in the Sixties*. Toronto: William Briggs, 1896.

McFarlane, Brian. *50 Years of Hockey*. Toronto: Pagurian Press 1969.

McInnis, Edgar. *Canada: A Political and Social History*. New York: Rinehart and Co., 1947.

McIntosh, Peter C. *Sport in Society*. London: C. A. Watts & Co. 1963.

———. *Physical Education in England since 1800*. London: G. Bell & Sons, 1968.

McKenzie, R. Tait. "Rugby Football in Canada." *Dominion Illustrated Monthly*, February 1892, pp. 11–19.

———. "Hockey in Eastern Canada." *Dominion Illustrated Monthly*, February 1893, pp. 57–64.

McKenzie, Ruth. *Leeds and Grenville: Their First Two Hundred Years*. Toronto: McClelland and Stewart, 1967.

McLennan, William. "Hockey in Canada." *Harper's Weekly*, January 1895, pp. 45–46.

McNab, Tom. "The Life and Sudden Death of Pedestrianism." *Sport and Recreation*. July 1966, pp. 26–28.

McNair, David. "Suggestions on sources of diffusion of physical education, sport and physical recreation from and into Great Britain." In *The History, The Evolution and Diffusion of Sports and Games in Different Cultures*. Proceedings of the 4th International HISPA Seminar, Leuven, Belgium 1–5 April 1975, Dept. Lichamelijke Opvoeding, K. U. Leuven. Brussels: B.L.O.S.O., 1976, pp. 227–235.

McNaught, Kenneth. *The Pelican History of Canada*. Harmondsworth, Middlesex: Penguin Books, 1970.

McWhirter, Ross. "A Century of Rugby." *World Sports*, September 1970, pp. 11–16.

McWilliams, Margaret. *Manitoba Milestones*. Toronto: J. M. Dent and Sons, 1928.

Notestein, Wallace. *The Scot in History*. London: Jonathan Cape, 1946.

O'Neil, Alfred. *Annals of Brechin Cricket, 1849–1927.* Brechin, Scotland: Black and Johnston, 1927.

Orlick, E. M. "McGill Contributions to the Origin of Ice Hockey." *McGill News*, Winter 1943, pp. 13–17.

Ormsby, Margaret A. *British Columbia: A History*. Vancouver: Macmillan Co. of Canada, 1968.

Orr, Frank. *The Story of Hockey*. New York: Random House, 1971.

Oxford Dictionary of Quotations, The. London: Oxford University Press, 1966.

Parker, Eric. *The History of Cricket*. London: Seeley Service & Co., n.d.

Pearson, W. H. *Recollections and Records of Toronto of Old, with References to Brantford, Kingston and other Canadian Towns*. Toronto: William Briggs, 1914.

Pethick, Derek. *James Douglas: Servant of Two Empires*. Vancouver: Mitchell Press, 1969.

Petrie, Sir Charles. *The Jacobite Movement: The Last Phase, 1716–1807*. London: Eyre & Spottiswoode, 1950.

Piers, Sir Charles P. *Sport and Life in British Columbia*. London: Heath Cranton, 1923.

Pioneers, The. The Canadian Illustrated Library; Toronto: McClelland and Stewart Ltd., 1968.

Prebble, John. *Culloden*. Harmondsworth, Middlesex: Penguin Books, 1967.

———. *The Highland Clearances*. Harmondsworth, Middlesex: Penguin Books, 1969.

———. *The Darien Disaster*. Harmondsworth, Middlesex: Penguin Books, 1970.

———. *Glencoe*. Harmondsworth, Middlesex: Penguin Books, 1971.

———. *Mutiny: Highland Regiments in Revolt, 1743–1804*. London: Martin Secker and Warburg, 1975.

Presbrey, Frank. *Athletics at Princeton: A History*. New York: Frank Presbrey Co., 1901.

Preston, William Thomas Rochester. *The Life and Times of Lord Strathcona*. London: E. Nash, 1914.

Punchard, Frank N. *Survivals of Folk Football*. Birmingham: n.p., 1928.

Quercetani, Roberto L. *A World History of Track and Field Athletics, 1864–1964*. London: Oxford University Press, 1964.

Quinpool, John. *First Things in Acadia*. Halifax: First Things Publishers, 1936.

Raddall, T. H. *Halifax, Warden of the North*. Toronto: McClelland and Steward, 1948.

Rankin, Rev. D. U. *A History of the County of Antigonish, Nova Scotia*. Toronto: Macmillan Co. of Canada, 1929.

Rattray, W. J. *The Scot in British North America*. 4 vols. Toronto: Maclear and Co., 1880.

Redmond, Gerald. "Apart from the Trust Fund: Some Other Contributions of Lord Strathcona to Canadian Recreation and Sport."*Canadian Journal of History of Sport and Physical Education*, December 1973, pp. 59–69.

———. "Born Again Soccer." *Edmonton Magazine*, May 1979, pp. 36–38.

———. *Caledonian Games in Nineteenth-Century America, The*. Rutherford, N.J.: Fairleigh Dickinson University Press, 1971.

———. "Ethnicity and Sport: The Social Scots in North America." Paper presented at the Sixty-Ninth Annual Meeting of the American Historical Association, University of California, San Diego, 17–19 August 1976.

———. "Some Aspects of Organized Sport and Leisure in Nineteenth-Century Canada." *Society and Leisure* 2 (1979):73–100.

———. *Sport and Ethnic Groups in Canada*. Ottawa: CAHPER Sociology of Sport Monograph Series, 1978.

Reed, T. A. *The Blue and White: A Record of Fifty Years of Athletic Endeavour at the University of Toronto*. Toronto: University of Toronto Press, 1944.

———, ed. *A History of the University of Trinity College, Toronto, 1852–1952*. Toronto: University of Toronto Press, 1952.

Reeve, Harold. *The History of the Township of Hope*. Cobourg: Cobourg Sentinel-Star, 1967.

Reid, John E. "Sports and Games in Alberta before 1900." M.A. thesis, University of Alberta, Edmonton 1969.

Reid, W. Stanford, ed. *The Scottish Tradition in Canada*. Toronto: McClelland and Stewart, 1976.

Rice, Emmett A.; Hutchinson, John L.; and Lee, Mabel. *A Brief History of Physical Education*. New York: Ronald Press Co., 1969.

Rich, E. E. *History of the Hudson's Bay Company, 1670–1870*. 2 vols. London: Hudson's Bay Record Society, 1958–1959.

———. *The Fur Trade and the Northwest, to 1857*. Toronto: McClelland and Stewart, 1967.

Robertson, R. W. W., ed. *Sir John A. Builds a Nation*. Burns and MacEachern, 1970.

Roche, John P. "Canadian Golf." *Outing*, June 1898, pp. 260–66.

Ross, A. H. D. *Ottawa, Past and Present*. Ottawa: Thorburn and Abbott, 1927.

Ross, Peter. *The Scot in America*. New York: Raeburn Book Co. 1896.

Routledge, Penelope Dawn. "The North-West Mounted Police and Their Influence on the Sporting and Social Life of the North-West Territories: 1870–1904." M.A. Thesis, University of Alberta, 1978.

Rowan, John J. *The Emigrant and Sportsman in Canada*. London: Edward Stanford, 1876.

Roxborough, Henry. *Great Days in Canadian Sport*. Toronto: Ryerson Press, 1957.

———. *Canada at the Olympics*. Toronto: Ryerson Press, 1963.

———. *The Stanley Cup Story*. Toronto: Ryerson Press, 1966.

———. *One Hundred—Not Out: The Story of Nineteenth-Century Canadian Sport*. Toronto: Ryerson Press, 1966.

Roy, James A., *The Scot and Canada*. Toronto: McClelland & Stewart, 1947.

Royal Canadian Golf Association: Report of the President and Board of Governors, 1971.

Ruhl, J. K. *Die "Olympischen Spiele" Robert Dovers*. Heidelberg: Carl Winter Universitätsverlag, 1978.

Sage, Walter Noble. *Sir James Douglas and British Columbia*. Toronto: University of Toronto Press, 1930.

Salmond, J. B. *Wade in Scotland*. Edinburgh: Moray Press, 1934.

———. *The Story of the R. & A.* London: Macmillan & Co. 1956.

Sawula, Lorne W. "Ancient Irish Pastimes and Assemblies." Unpublished paper, University of Alberta, Edmonton, December 1971.

Schooling, Sir William. *The Hudson's Bay Company, 1670–1920*. London: Hudson's Bay Company, 1920.

Schrodt, Barbara; Redmond, Gerald; and Baka, Richard. *Sport Canadiana: A Chronology of Canadian Sport to 1978*. Edmonton: Executive Sports Publications, 1980.

Schroeder. "History of the A.A.U. of the U.S." Thesis, Springfield College, 1912.

Scottish Athletic Association of Manitoba. *Programme for 1906*.

Scottish Tartans, The. Edinburgh: W. & A. K. Johnston, n.d.

Serra, Johnny. *The History of Armstrong, British Columbia*. Armstrong, B.C.: Branch of the Okanagan Historical Society, n.d.

Shearman, Montague. *Athletics and Football*. London: Longmans
Green & Co. 1894.

Sheridan, Peter Benedict, Jr. "The Immigrant in Philadelphia, 1827
1860." Ph.D. dissertation, Georgetown University 1957.

Signy, Dennis. *A Pictoral History of Soccer*. London: Paul Hamlyn
1969.

Sinclair-Stevenson, Christopher. *Inglorious Rebellion: The Jacobi
Risings of 1708, 1715 and 1719*. London: Hamish Hamilton, 197

Skilling, Brian. "The Remarkable Voyage of John MacGregor." *Spo
and Recreation*, July 1966, pp. 52–54.

Smith, D. A. *At The Forks of the Grand*. Paris, Ontario: Wall
Press, n.d.

Smith, Horatio. *Festivals, Games and Amusements*. New York: J. a
J. Harper. 1831.

Stacey, C. P. *Canada and the British Army, 1846–1871*. Toron
University of Toronto Press, 1963.

Stanley, George F. G. *Canada's Soldiers, 1604–1954: The Milit
History of an Unmilitary People*. Toronto Macmillan Co. of Can
1954.

Stevenson, John A. *Curling in Ontario, 1846–1946*. Toronto: Ont
Curling Association, 1950.

Stone, Lilly C. *English Sports and Recreations*. Washington, D
Folger Shakespeare Library, 1960.

Stonehenge [pseud.]. *British Rural Sports*. London: Frederick W
& Co., 1872.

Strathcona Papers, M.G.29, D.14, vol. 19, D.52. Public Arc
of Canada Ottawa, Ontario.

Strutt, Joseph. *The Sports and Pastimes of the People of Eng
London: Thomas Tegg, 1838.

———. *The Sports and Pastimes of the People of England*. Lo
Chatto and Windus, 1898.

Sturrock, Doublas Norman. "A History of Rugby Football in Can
M. A. thesis, University of Alberta, 1971.

Templin, Hugh. *Fergus: The Story of a Little Town*. The I
News-Record, 1933.

Thomson, D. C. *Alexander Mackenzie: Clear Grit*. Toronto:
millan Co. of Canada, 1960.

Trevelyan, G. M. *English Social History*. London: Longmans,
and Co. 1955.

Trout, J. M. and Trout, Edward. *The Railways of Canada.* Toronto: Office of the Monetary Times, 1871.

Tulloch, W. W. "A New Game for Ladies." *Belgravia* 8 (1869).

Uttley, W. V. *A History of Kitchener, Ontario.* Waterloo, Ontario: Chronicle Press, 1937.

Vellathottam, George T. "A History of Lacrosse in Canada." M.A. thesis, University of Alberta, 1968.

Vernon, C. W. *Cape Breton, Canada, at the Beginning of the Twentieth Century.* Toronto: Nation Publishing Co., 1903.

Walker, Donald. *Games and Sports.* London: Thomas Hurst, 1837.

Watman, Melvyn. *History of British Athletics.* London: Robert Hale, 1968.

Watson, John. *The Scot of the Eighteenth Century: His Religion and His Life.* London: Hodder and Stoughton, 1907.

Webster, David. *Scottish Highland Games.* Glasgow: William Collins Sons and Co., 1959.

———. *Scottish Highland Games.* Edinburgh: Reprographia, 1973.

Webster, Lt.-Col. F. A. M. *Olympic Cavalcade.* London: Hutchinson & Co., 1948.

Wegener, Albert B. *Track and Field Athletics.* New York: A. S. Barnes and Co., 1924.

Welsh, Robin. *Beginner's Guide to Curling.* London: Pelham Books, 1969.

Weyand, Alexander M., and Roberts, Milton R. *The Lacrosse Story.* Baltimore, Md.: H. & A. Herman, 1965.

Whalen, Mack. "Winter Sport in Canadian Colleges." *Outing*, January 1915, pp. 407–15.

Whiting, Colin F. *Cricket in Eastern Canada.* Montreal: Colmur Co., 1963.

Whitney, Casper W. *A Sporting Pilgrimage.* New York: Harper and Brothers, 1894.

Whittet, R. C. "The Game of Curling" *Outing* 19 (1891):364–68.

Wilson, Beckles. *The Life of Lord Strathcona and Mount Royal, 1820–1914.* London: Cassell and Company, 1915.

Wilson, Clifford. *Campbell of the Yukon.* Toronto: Macmillan of Canada, 1970.

Wilson, John L. "The Foreign Element in New York City, IV, The Scotch," *Harper's Weekly*, 5 July 1890, pp. 514–16.

Wise, S. F., and Fisher, Douglas. *Canada's Sporting Heroes: Their Lives and Times*. Don Mills, Ontario: General Publishing Co. 1974.

"The Woman's Pages." *Athletic Life*, April 1896.

Woodside, Henry J. "Curling in the Northwest—Part I." *Outing*, February 1895, pp. 422–26.

———. "Curling in the Northwest—Part II." *Outing*, March 1895, pp. 497–503.

———. "Hockey in the Canadian North-West." *Canadian Magazine*, January 1896, pp. 242–47.

Wright, J. F. C. *Saskatchewan: The History of a Province*. Toronto: McClelland and Steward, 1955.

Wymer, Norman. *Sport in England: A History of Two Thousand Years of Games and Pastimes*. London: George G. Harrap & Co. 1949.

Young, James. *Reminiscences of the Early History of Galt and the Settlement of Dumfries in the Province of Ontario*. Toronto: Hunter, Rose and Co. 1880.

Zeigler, Earle F. ed. *History of Physical Education and Sport*. Englewood Cliffs, N.J.: Prentice-Hall, 1979.

Zeigler, Earle F.; Howell, Maxwell; and Trekell, Marianna. *Research in the History, Philosophy, and International Aspects of Physical Education and Sport: Bibliographies and Techniques*. Champaign, Ill.: Stipes Publishing Co. 1971.

Zorra Caledonian Society. *Programme for 1956*.

Appendix A
Curling in Canada, 1892

"Why don't you make a trial of curling, doctor? You would grow fond of it," said a Canadian one day to an Englishman, newly arrived, who was looking on at an Ontario match.

"Oh dear no," was the reply, "I can't see anything in it. In fact it seems to me so very absurd, don't you know—sweeping, sweeping, where there is really nothing to sweep."

"But there is some virtue in the sweeping, and then there is fun in it too," persisted the Canadian, who was imbued with the spirit of sport and had experience of the grand old game. "And there is really something besides the sweeping."

"Now look here, my dear sir," went on the doctor. "See that fellow with the broom, sweeping and shouting and sweeping again in front of that curling stone, when any ass could see with half an eye that the ice is as smooth and clean as glass already. Why, he acts like a lunatic."

"Ah! but you don't understand—"

"No, and I don't want to understand. By Jove! rather than work as hard as those fellows do, I should hire a flunkey to do the sweeping. Besides, I can't see much room for skill in the game, sliding those funny things along the ice; a kind of shuffle-board business."

His companion, nettled at such determined obtuseness, as he deemed it, made a vigorous protest at this prejudging, and ex-

From James Hedley, "Curling in Canada," *Dominion Illustrated Monthly* (1892):116–17.

pended some eloquence in describing the qualities of the model curler, the intricacies and the proverbially slippery chances of the game. To which the other answered only:

"Can't say that I care for it. But I say, old man, there is a Scottish game, I don't recollect what you call it, but a man takes a small white ball and hits it a whack across country with a sort of hammer. Then he walks a quarter of a mile and hits it again. I could like that sort of thing, don't you know, because you get so much walking. But in this curling game I know I should take cold."

Doubtless there are those amongst ourselves who share the prejudices of our friend the doctor, and are thereby prevented from taking part in this invigorating and spirit-stirring recreation. A like class of critics would call cricket "slow," football, "brutal," tennis, "namby-pamby," lacrosse, "dangerous." But a little honest experience would convince any one that curling well deserves the name of the king of winter sports. It is simple, cheerful, healthful and not costly. Within a dozen years the discovery has been made by some thousands of people, in some scores of places in Canada and the States, that curling is a game not for elderly men alone, or for Scotchmen alone, but for young and old, for Saxon and Celt, for American and Canadian, for anyone indeed, who enjoys a simple and bracing sport, free from the professional as well as the gambling element. An American curler describes curling well in saying, "One of the first and strictest rules of the game is good humour and kindly feeling under all circumstances and provocations; and a training which results in the combination of this quality of self-control with manly strength and cool judgment cannot fail to make good men." There is another feature about curling which should commend it to the Americans; it is a democratic game. As in the old country, according to Norman McLeod's delightful curling song, we find "the master and servants, the tenant and laird" coming together o'er the brown heather to the curler's gathering, so on this side of the Atlantic we may see the millionaire and the artisan, the banker and his clerk, the university professor and his pupil, the dominie and the clergyman, all met in fine frosty weather and, if not as loving as Norman would have them, still all civil, all gleeful, all equally free.

Appendix B

The Montreal Caledonian Games, 1871

Caledonian Games at Decker Park

The sixteenth grand annual gathering of the Caledonian Society took place in Decker Park, Mile End. At an early hour in the morning the St. Lawrence Main Street cars began to fill up, and from the broad Highland brogue of many of the passengers, and the irrepressible Glasgow and Edinburgh twangs of others, it was not difficult to divine that all had the common object of reaching the scene of the gathering in view. The grounds had been carefully provided with swings for the young people; and a platform for the more elderly youngsters, who preferred to keep time to merry music with pattering feet and palpitating hearts, had been erected, and was a favourite resort. Shaded spots were also in great demand, for the sun by noonday had come out, as he usually does at this season of the year, very strong. As usual at picnics, there were old people and young people, people with baskets prepared with a forethought, and variety of contents, in the first instance highly creditable, and in the next highly gratifying and satisfactory when the inner man began to assert his wants. There was a fair sprinkling of bonnie lasses, guarded by blooming and

From *Canadian Illustrated News*, 8 July, 1871, and *Montreal Gazette*, 3 July 1871.

matronly dames, who were not slow to see by the tell-tale deepening of the colour of the cheek who was the favoured one who came to demand the hand for the next dance, and who had long ago secured the heart. The gathering by two o'clock in the afternoon had increased to a large number, and, as usual, was composed of the most respectable classes of the community. The games were the chief object of attraction, and although there were not as many contestants as on previous occasions, they were the more keenly contested by those present. Robert Fraser, from Glengarry, famous as the man who took fourteen prizes in New York in one day, was invincible, and carried off the first prize for everything he entered for. One of the most interesting features of the games was the struggles of the boys, divided into classes of fifteen years and under, and twelve years and under, for honours. The little fellows ran, leaped, and jumped with desperate determination and energy, and as three prizes were awarded for most of the prizes contended for, a fair share of their number succeeded in obtaining a reward for something or another. The clever performances of Master John McRobie, son of guardian McRobie, of No. 2 Fire Station, were particularly noticed; in almost all the games he entered for in the juvenile class, under twelve, he succeeded in carrying off the first prize. His hop, step, and jump of 24 feet, for a youngster of eleven years of age, is a capital performance. The games of quoits began at ten, and the others at eleven o'clock. The following gentlemen acted as judges: Lieut.-Col. Fletcher, C.M.G., Lieut.-Col. Isaacson, Messrs. Alexander McGibbon and Stanley C. Bagg. The President and officers of the society were indefatigable in their exertions to make everybody comfortable, and to add to the success of the occasion. About sunset the games came to a conclusion, and soon after the assembly dispersed, much pleased at the manner in which they had spent the day. The following is a list of the prizes and successful competitors:

List of Prizes

Quoits, 8 entries.—Mr. W. McRobie, 1st prize, silver quoit medal; D. Wright, 2nd do., cash, $3.

Grand Dam Brod Match, 4 entries.—Mr. Andrew White, gold medal.

Throwing Hammers, 22 lbs., and 16 lbs., 2 entries.—Mr. Peter Fraser, heavy, 28 ft.; light, 82–3 ft., 1st prize, $4; Geo. Anderson, heavy, 18 ft. 4 in.; light, 73 ft. 6 in., 2nd prize, $3.

Putting Heavy Stone, 22 lbs., 2 entries.—P. Fraser, 33 ft. 8 in., 1st prize, $4; Geo. Anderson, 30 ft. 1 in., 2nd prize,$3.

Putting Light Stone, 16 lbs., 2 entries.—P. Fraser, 38 ft. 1 in., 1st prize, $4; Geo. Anderson, 35 ft. 5 in., 2nd prize, $3.

Running Hop, Step and Leap, 8 entries.—P.Fraser, 39 ft. 4 in., 1st prize, $3; McDonald, 37 ft. 3 in., 2nd prize, $2.

Running Hop, Step and Leap, Juvenile Class, under 15 years of age, 11 entries.—Robert McGillis, 32 ft., 1st prize, Scott's Poems; Adam Allan, 29 ft. 5 in., 2nd prize, Kilt; W. Taylor, 28 ft. 8 in., 3rd prize Bonnet.

Running Hop, Step and Leap, class under 12 years of age, 7 entries.—John McRobie, 24 ft. 4 in., 1st prize, Kilt; George Baillie, 23 ft. 4 ins., 2nd prize, Sporran; Thos. Watson, 22 ft. 2 in., 3rd prize, Hose.

Tossing the Caber, 4 entries.—Peter Fraser, 39 ft. 8 in., 1st prize, $4; Inglis, 32 ft., 2nd prize, $3.

Running High Leap, 4 entries.—P. Fraser, 6 ft., 1st prize, $3; McDonald, 5 ft. 2 in., 2nd prize, $2.

Running High Leap, Juvenile Class, under 15 years of age, 13 entries.—W. Martin, 3 ft. 8 in., 1st prize, Burns' Poems; W. Taylor, 3 ft. 6 in., 2nd prize, Plaid; D. Neilson, 3 ft. 5 in., 3rd prize, Hose.

Running Long Leap, 5 entries.—P. Fraser, 17 ft. 2 in., 1st prize, $3; M. Newell, 17 ft. 1 in., 2nd prize, $2.

Do., Juvenile Class, under 12 years, 8 entries.—John McRobie, 10 ft. 6 in., 1st prize, Sporran; George Baillie, 10 ft. 4 in., 2nd prize, Bonnet; James McRobie, 9 ft. 2 in., 3rd prize, Hose.

Pole Leap, 4 entries.—Peter Fraser, 9 ft., 1st prize, $4; J. Fletcher, 8 ft., 2nd prize, $3.

Pole Leap, Juvenile Class, under 15 years, 13 entries.—C. Howler, 5 ft. 6 in., 1st prize, Tartan Bible; C. Harvey, 5 ft., 2nd prize, Bonnet and Thistle; W. Martin, 4 ft. 10 in., 3rd prize, Hose.

Do., Class under 12 years, 6 entries.—G. Martin, 4 ft. 6 in., 1st prize, Kilt; G. Gaillie, 4 ft. 4 in., 2nd prize, Sporran; J. McRobie, 4 ft. 3 in., 3 prize, Hose.

Highland Fling in Costume, 2 entries—D. McIntyre, Silver Medal.

Ghillie Callum in Costume,—W. Connell, Silver Medal.

Shetland Pony Race, qr.-mile, 3 entries.—R. D. McGibbon, Riding Whip.

Hurdle Sack Race, 4 entries.—G. Rose, 1st prize, $3; J. Huneman, 2nd prize.

Best Dressed Boys in Highland Costume, 6 entries, President's prize.—J. Fraser, 1st prize, Box Collars; 1st Vice-President, James A. Murray, 2nd do., Scott's Poems; 2nd Vice-President, David Allan, 3rd do., Pair Rabbits.

Appendix C
Canadian Golf (1898)

The delineation of preposterous little Dutchmen on preposterous Dutch pottery, wielding hugely disproportionate clubs,
may, in the very long ago, have given rise to the idea that
the royal and ancient game of golf is of Hollandish origin, but the
generally accepted idea is that golf is as Scotch as curling; and
there is never a loyal Scot, and Canada is full of them, but will lay
claim to a first mortgage on these two finest pastimes the ingenuity of many ever invented.

But that is not the question for discussion here. Golf in Canada
is the subject. It is no wise strange, seeing how deeply tinctured
with Scotch, who are still actuated and moved to a greater or less
extent by the traditions of the British Isles, Canada is, that golf
should have found an early home there; and it is a fact of which
latterday golfers are justly proud that the Royal Montreal Golf
Club was twice as old as the patriarch of clubs in the United
States, St. Andrew's of Yonkers, is now, when the first course in
the States was laid out.

As far as reliable information is available, golf was played in
Montreal between thirty and forty years ago by a few enthusiasts
who happily brought with them to the new world the healthy
ideas of sport imbibed in the land of their fathers. In those days
there was a common called Logan's Farm, that would have
delighted the heart of any golfer. Logan's Farm has been
transformed into the picturesque Logan's Park, but there are still

From John P. Roche, ''Canadian Golf,'' *Outing* 32, no. 3 (June 1898):260–66.

with us a few gentlemen who speak with feeling of those good old days in the sixties. If Mr. W. M. Ramsay or Mr. R. R. Grindlay could be prevailed upon to write his reminiscences, they would supply the golfing world with some very interesting reading matter anent them.

The golfer is gregarious, and golf naturally led to organized clubs, the first of which, the Royal Montreal Golf Club, will celebrate its twenty-fifth anniversary on the 4th of November next, a glorious fourth. In an old book of rules belonging to the club, the following entry fills the first page:

"A meeting convened to arrange the preliminaries of a golf club, for playing the royal and ancient game of golf on Mount Royal Park, was held on the fourth day of November, 1873, when it was resolved that the club be called 'The Montreal Golf Club.' The officers for the years were appointed: Alex. Dennistoun, president; W. M. Ramsay, Vice-president; D. D. Sidey, treasurer; Jos. Collins, secretary. The rules of St. Andrew's Club (Scotland) were adopted. According to the club minute-book there were also present at this initial meeting Hon. M. Aylmer, J. G. Sidey, H. McDougall, and T. Holland."

The gentleman, however, who is recognized as the father of golf in Canada, that is, who fostered and encouraged the game, and was the means of starting the Royal Montreal Golf Club, was the Mr. Alexander Dennistoun who was elected the club's first president. He recently died in Edinburgh, but for many years was a resident of Canada. Mr. Dennistoun had played in his early days over the famous links of St. Andrew's and Musselburgh and was a member of several other leading clubs in Scotland and England. He was not only an enthusiastic player, but an excellent exponent of all the intricacies of the game. Among other early players were such men as Hon. Geo. Drummond, J. K. Oswald, F. Braidwood, Eric Maim, Jno. Taylor, Homer Taylor, Rev. Dr. Campbell, Rev. Canon Ellegood, C. C. Foster, and R. M. Esdaile. Among the younger generation may be mentioned Mr. W. Wallace Watson, the present captain; Rev. Dr. Barclay, F. Stancliff, W. J. S. Gordon, J. R. Meeker, K. R. Macpherson, J. Hutton Balfour, G. W. MacDougall, J. L. Morris, Q. C., A. H. Harris, W. A. Fleming, Alex. Macpherson, Rev. W. W. McCuaig, A. A. Wilson, Rev. Mr. Dobson, Jno. Dunlop, Fayette Brown, Dr. Macdonald, Dr. Andrew Macphail, and A. Piddington.

Until the autumn of 1896 the club played over that part of Mount Royal Park known as Fletcher's Field. Owing to the increase in the number of people visting the park and consequent danger to them from flying golf-balls, it was then decided to acquire the property now occupied by the club at Dixie. This step necessitated, for proprietary reasons, the conversion of the club into a company. This marked a new phase in the club's career. The new grounds, which are laid out as a nine-hole course, are rapidly getting into shape; indeed, they were sufficiently improved last season to admit of the Royal Canadian Golf Association meeting, including the contest for the amateur championship of Canada, taking place there in September last.

The disused links over Fletcher's Field were eagerly snapped up by the Metropolitan Golf Club, a young but enthusiastic organization.

In 1892 the Montreal Ladies' Golf Club was formed, with nearly a hundred members, among the founders and first officers being Mrs. George H. Drummond, President; Mrs. H. Vincent Meredith, Secretary; Mrs. W. W. Watson, Mrs. Halton, Misses P. Young, A. Lamb, and A. Peterson. Since this club was formed the membership has largely increased, and the ladies are even more enthusiastic than the gentlemen.

The next year after the formal launching of the Montreal club the Quebec club was founded, and it was two years later (1876) these two pioneer organizations met. This is the first golf-club match on record in America, and according to Mr. Morris ''it was played in May or June, 1876, Quebec winning with twelve holes to their credit.'' A second match seems to have been played in the following September, of which we have a record of the teams. As it is the first recorded golfing event of the continent, it is worthy of a republication to a wider circle than its first issue reached:

Quebec		vs.	Montreal	
Mr. Scott	0	vs.	Dr. Argyle Robertson (Edinburgh)	4
Mr. Thomas Scott . . .	0	vs.	Mr. Dennistoun	13
Mr. McNaughton . . .	4	vs.	Mr. D. D. Sidey	0
Mr. A. Nicoll	3	vs.	Mr. J. G. Sidey	0
Mr. C. F. Smith	0	vs.	Mr. J. K. Oswald	2
	7			19

Montreal thus won by 12 holes. The draw was played off in Montreal, the home team winning by 13 holes, and so the Royal Montreal Golf Club won its first club victory.

Individual and match play was then of course, as it is indeed now, the backbone of the pastime; and some few years ago Mr. John L. Morris wrote a very interesting sketch, from which the following extract is made as illustrating what was considered good play in those early days: ''A match was played on November 26th, 1876, between Messrs. Taylor and J. K. Oswald. The play was about the best ever seen on the Montreal links. Mr. Taylor made the 18 holes in 115, Mr. Oswald 105 strokes.''

It may surprise some of our readers, whose ideas of Canada and its climate may have been gathered from the perusal of ''Our Lady of the Snows,'' to note the date of this match, November 26th. It will, perhaps, surprise them more to learn that, the next year, play was continued until New Year's Day.

But to turn from the lesser-chronicled individual play to club play, annual matches between the Montreal and Quebec clubs have, ever since 1877, been fixtures eagerly looked forward to.

Several valuable prizes are competed for every year, among them being the Drummond Silver Cup, the Sidey Medal, and the Burnett Cup. The Dennistoun Scratch Medal is a much-coveted trophy. Last year it was won by Mr. T. R. Henderson, the acknowledged champion of the Province of Quebec, and the year previous was captured by Mr. Wallace Watson, one of the keenest golfers in the country.

Quebec's golf links form part of the historic battle-ground, the Plains of Abraham. Scarlet coats are still numerous there, where Wolfe and Montcalm led, but the contest now is a bloodless one. As has before been pointed out, the Quebec Club was founded in 1874, but there is no doubt in the minds of old curlers that the game was played many years previously by a relative of old Tom Morris, one Mr. Hunter, who with several companions negotiated the somewhat difficult links on the Plains.

Index

GLASSBORO STATE COLLEGE